BOLLINGEN SERIES LXIV

ZEN
AND JAPANESE CULTURE

Daisetz T. Suzuki

BOLLINGEN SERIES LXIV · PRINCETON UNIVERSITY PRESS

First Princeton / Bollingen Paperback printing, 1970

Third printing, 1973

ISBN 0-691-01770-0 (paperback edn.)
ISBN 0-691-09849-2 (hardcover edn.)

Library of Congress Catalogue Card No. 58-12174
Manufactured in the United States of America
DESIGNED BY ANDOR BRAUN

THIS book was first published in Japan in 1938, with the title *Zen Buddhism and Its Influence on Japanese Culture*, by the Eastern Buddhist Society of Otani Buddhist University, at Kyoto.

Since then, I have come to be better informed on the subjects it treats; and naturally, I have desired to rewrite the whole book. But to do so would involve a great deal of time and labor that I can ill afford in the present circumstances. What I have done, however, is to revise the original material only in so far as necessary, and add independently written chapters on such subjects as have happened to arouse my new concern, such as Swordsmanship (*kendō*), the Art of Tea (*cha-no-yu*), and the Haiku. As a result, repetitions have become unavoidable in some cases. Since the present work is not meant to be a textbook or a scholarly presentation, the author begs the reader's indulgence, hoping that he will not find the shortcomings too obtrusive or too prone to interfere with the coherence of thought.

Much of the contents originated as lectures given on various occasions in England and America in 1936. A section of the study on Love of Nature was given in Japan to a group of Western people in 1935, and was published in *The Eastern Buddhist* (Kyoto), VII: 1 (1936).

As the Japanese pronunciation of Chinese characters is different from the Chinese and often causes irritating confusion, I have tried to give in the index the original Chinese characters. Since my chief interest is not philological, I have perhaps not been entirely consistent, by present-day scholarly standards, in romanizing Japanese words and names. I have mainly used the forms I learned in my younger days (e.g., Kwannon, Yedo), but sometimes it has seemed preferable to use one of the newer spellings. Again I beg indulgence, particularly of more academic readers, to this aspect of my book.

Besides adding the index and the bibliography, which may be of assistance to students, I have taken the opportunity to increase the number of illustrations. I acknowledge my gratitude to those who have made photographs available as well as data about the pictures. I have given what information I could obtain about each picture, but in some cases the complete data proved to be inaccessible. The references to the plates are given in the margin.

Japanese personal names are given throughout this book in the way they are used in Japan, that is, with the family name first, except in the author's case.

For permission to use quotations, I gratefully acknowledge as follows: to the *Atlantic Monthly*, for passages from Juan Belmonte's essay on bullfighting; to Harcourt, Brace and Co. and Faber and Faber, for a quotation from T. S. Eliot's *The Waste Land*; to Harper and Brothers, for poetic quotations from *Masterpieces of Religious Verse*, edited by J. D. Morrison; to The Macmillan Co., for a poem by Ralph Hodgson in the same work; to the New American Library, for a quotation from the Isherwood/Prabhavananda translation of the *Bhagavad Gita*, copyright by the Vedanta Society of Southern California; to Dodd, Mead and Co., for quotations from Okakura Kakuzo's *The Book of Tea*; and to John Murray, London, for a passage from the Lionel Giles translation of Lieh Tzŭ.

It is with deep gratitude that I acknowledge here the debt I owe to the editorial staff of Bollingen Series, especially to Mr. and Mrs. William McGuire, who have done everything to improve my borrowed plumage and to advise me in the technique of editing a book.

New York, 1958   *D. T. Suzuki*

CONTENTS

EDITORIAL NOTE

For the name "Yama-uba," which occurs in Appendix III, research indicates that the reading "Yamamba" is preferable and should be substituted.

16. Liang K'ai (Ryōkai). A drunken man
Early 13th century. Ink on silk. 21 × 18.8 cm. Private
collection. (*See p. 29.*)

17. Liang K'ai (Ryōkai). Snow scene
Early 13th century. Color on silk. 111 × 50 cm. National Museum, Tokyo. (*See p. 29.*)

18. Yin-t'o-lo (Indara, Indra). Han-shan (Kanzan)
Middle 14th century. 68 × 53 cm. Private collection,
Tokyo. (*See p. 25 n.*)

19. Yin-t'o-lo (Indara, Indra). Shih-tê (Jittoku)
Middle 14th century. 68 × 53 cm. Private collection,
Tokyo. (*See p. 25 n.*)

20. Shuai-wêng (Sotsu-ō). Hui-nêng (Enō) listening to the Diamond Sūtra
13th–14th centuries. 92 × 36 cm. Private collection,
Tokyo. (*See p. 126 n.*)
Inscription, by Enkei Kōmon (Yen-ch'i Kuang-wên,
1189–1263):

The heavy load is carried on his shoulders,
He makes no mistake in wending his homeward steps:
When he knows the mind that moves on, abiding no-
wher,
He knows at whose house to deliver his kindlings.

21. Calligraphy of Hsü-t'ang Chih-yü (Kidō Chigu, 1185–1269)
Early 13th century. (*See p. 30.*)

A letter from Hsü-t'ang Chih-yü to his friend
Wu-wêng (Goō), the Zen master, who had been the
first to send a message of sympathy when Hsü-t'ang's
temple was plundered by a band of robbers. Hsü-t'ang
expresses his deep gratitude for his friend's words of
consolation, saying that he can never forget the kindness. In the preceding year he had been informed
that Wu-wêng was sick; but later, learning that the
friend was recovering, he is relieved and congratulates him, saying "with a man of virtue and merit,
things are sure to take a smooth and harmonious
turn in every way." He goes on: "Now I am told

that one of my head monks, Ming, is about to
visit your place, and I hasten to write this letter of
inquiry and friendship, and pray that everything
continue well with you. Most respectfully yours . . ."

A poem probably on his monastery life. Abstract:
"I enjoy its remoteness from worldly affairs; I share
my life with creatures and objects of nature,
and also with my Brotherhood—though the latter may
not be one of the best desirable, just as I cannot be
said to equal an ancient master such as Huang-po. But
who can say there is no one able to discover a
genius among us?"

25a. Calligraphy of Ikkyū (1396–1481)

Late 15th century. (*See p. 30.*)

*Last night's rain scattered the flowers all over the
     ground,
And the scented streams are flooding the whole village.*

25b. Calligraphy of Hakuin

Middle 18th century. 31.1 × 81.5 cm. Private collection.
(*See p. 30.*)

A vertical combination of two Sanskrit characters in
the *siddham* (*shittan*) style: *hāṃ* and *maṃ*. They
symbolize Acala-vidyā-rāja, "the immovable one."

26. Calligraphy of Kokwan Shiren (1278–1346)

Late 13th century. (*See p. 30.*)
A passage from a sūtra:

> *The world-honored one, when he was about to enter
> nirvāṇa, stroking his golden-colored body, said:
> You all see me now, but if you would say, "He is
> passing into a state of nonexistence," you are
> not my disciples. Nor are they my disciples who
> would say, "He is not passing into a state of non-
> existence."*

27. Kao Jan-hui (Kō Zenki). Sunrise in the mountains

14th century. Painting on silk. 50.8 × 52.6 cm. Konji-in
Temple, Kyoto. (*See p. 30.*)

28. Artist unknown. Musō Kokushi

Late 13th century. Painting on silk. 120 × 54 cm.
Obai-in Temple, Kamakura. (*See p. 31.*)

The writing is a kind of public announcement which
the writer (also called Mugaku Sogen [Wu-hsüeh
Tsŭ-yüan]) made on behalf of Ichi-ō of Chōrakuji,
whose attainment in Zen is here testified to be in full
accordance with the writer's. Ichi-ō while in China
studied Zen under Busshun Shihan, who was
also the teacher of the writer. But they did not
know each other until Sogen came to Kamakura at the
invitation of Hōjō Tokimune, who was at the time
virtually ruler of the island empire. Signed: "Kofuku,
1279. Mugaku Sogen."

37a. Shi K'o (Sekkaku). A Zen master and a tiger
   10th century. 35 × 64 cm. Shōhōji Collection, Kyoto.
   (See p. 105 n.)

37b. Calligraphy of Takuan
   Late 16th century. Tōkaiji Temple, Tokyo. (See p. 30.)

	the angry face with a broadly
	relaxing air of tenderness
BITTER SEVERITY	*the compassionate heart with*
	the frosty wintriness of an
	unbending spirit
	1644, Takuan

38. Artist unknown. Miyamoto Musashi (Niten). Possibly a
   self-portrait
   Early 17th century. Toryūji Temple, Fukuoka. (Photo-
   graphed under the direction of Taniguchi Tetsuo,
   Kyūshū University.) (See p. 143 n.)
   The inscription says, in essence, that Miyamoto
   Musashi is the originator of the Nitōryu school of "two
   swords." The writer eulogizes Musashi's wonderful attainment in the art and describes with what
   briskness and freedom, agility and efficiency, the
   swordsman handles his swords, giving the opponent no
   chance whatever for defense once Musashi makes up his
   mind to attack.

39. Detail of 38

40. Hakuin's portrait, by one of his disciples, with an inscription
by Hakuin
> Early 18th century. (*See p. 203.*)
> Hakuin's "self-eulogy":

In the assembly of one thousand Buddhas, the one dis-
liked by one thousand Buddhas;
In the company of a multitude of demonic spirits, the
one hated by all the demonic spirits;
The one who would crush all the false devotees of
"silent illumination" of the present day;
The one who would slaughter all the blind monks ad-
vocating the doctrine of "annihilation"—
Such an ugly, shabby, dim-sighted, bald-headed one
[that he is]!
[As he is portrayed here], his ugliness is all the more
aggravated, indeed!

> Hakuin was one of the greatest Zen masters and the
> most inspiring pedagogue of modern times. The survival
> of Zen in Japan today can probably be attributed
> to him.

41. Miyamoto Musashi (Niten). Bodhidharma (Daruma)
> Early 17th century. (*See p. 143 n.*)

42. Hakuin. Bodhidharma (Daruma)
> Early 18th century. (*See p. 203.*)

> *To attain Buddahood*
> *By seeing into the Nature.*

43. Sengai. A traveling monk with a *kyōku* ("crazy poem")
> Late 18th century. Private collection, Tokyo. (*See*
> *p. 244.*)

> *The pilgrim's progress is beset*
> *With one frontier gate after another:*
> *Fifty-three in all,*
> *Equal to the number of winds*
> *The horse breaks out.*

44. Miyamoto Musashi (Niten). A shrike on a dead branch
> Early 17th century. 125.6 × 54.3 cm. National Museum,
> Tokyo. (*See p. 22.*)

> *The voice of the bagworms;*
> *O come to my hut,*
> *And hear them cry.*
>   (Tr. Blyth.)

> *It rains over all the earth;*
> *Still more upon the dwelling-place*
> *Of Sōgi.*
>   (Tr. Blyth.)

> *Bending, bending,*
> *The way the bamboos keep on waiting*
> *For the snow ever steadily falling!*
>
> *How yieldingly the bamboos bend,*
> *They are waiting for more snow—*
> *Oh, the bamboos!*

Kesō's descendants know nothing of Zen;
Who dares talk about Zen in front of Kyōun?
For thirty years my shoulders have borne the heavy
*   load—*
It is I, a lone person, who is upholding Shōgen's Zen.

Ikkyū, who sometimes called himself "Kyōun" (a cloud
gone mad), was a strange personality. He strongly
protested against the Zen of his contemporaries. He
thought he was the only one who could teach Zen as
it ought to be taught, hence this diatribe and "self-
eulogy."

58. Sengai. The three laughing sages at Hu-ch'i (Kokei), with a
thirty-one-syllable poem
Late 18th century. Private collection, Tokyo. (*See p.
244.*)

> *What are they laughing at?*
> *The clouds making no vows,*
> *In the morning, in the evening,*
> *How easily they pass over*
> *The stone bridge spanning the valley.*

59. Artist unknown. Toyotomi Hideyoshi (1536–98), with inscription by Hideyoshi's young son Hideyori
Early 17th century. (*See p. 301.*)

Hideyori has written his father's posthumous name:
Toyokuni Daimyōjin, "The Great Illuminating God of
the Prosperous Land." The two poems in Japanese
refer to the "dream" and "dewdrop" mentioned in
Hideyoshi's farewell poem. (*See p. 303 n.*)

60. Hakuin. The three sages tasting vinegar
Early 18th century. (*See p. 203.*)

> *The three teachings agree in one point,*
> *In one point the three teachings agree.*
> *What is it after all?*
> *The limit is absolute good.*

61. Enkai. Prince Shōtoku
1069. Wood. H. c. 109 cm.
Yumedono, Hōryūji Temple, Nara. (*See p. 410.*)

Japan

Prehistoric Period

JŌMON NEOLITHIC CULTURE: 2nd millennium B.C.–3rd century B.C.
YAYOI BRONZE CULTURE: 3rd century B.C.–3rd century A.D.
PERIOD OF THE GREAT TOMBS: 3rd–6th centuries A.D.

Asuka Period: 538–671

Introduction of Buddhism. Formation of Yamato state

Nara Period: 672–780

EARLY NARA OR HAKUHŌ: 672–710. LATE NARA OR TEMPYŌ: 710–780
Capital established at Heijōkyō (Nara) in 710

Heian Period: 781–1184

EARLY HEIAN OR JŌGAN: 781–897. LATE HEIAN OR FUJIWARA: 898–1184
Capital established at Heiankyō (Kyoto) in 794

Kamakura Period: 1185–1338

Rule of Minamoto and Hōjō Shōguns at Kamakura 1274 and 1281:
attempted invasion of Japan by the Mongols

Ashikaga Period: 1338–1568

Rule of Ashikaga Shōguns at Kyoto. 1543, arrival of Portuguese

Momoyama Period: 1568–1614

Dictators: Oda Nobunaga, Toyotomi Hideyoshi, and Tokugawa Iyeyasu

Tokugawa Period: 1615–1867

Rule of Tokugawa Shōguns at Tokyo
1637–1638: Shimabara rebellion. Expulsion of the Portuguese
Ports closed to foreign ships. Japanese forbidden to go abroad

1640: Dutch confined in Deshima. Other Europeans excluded
1867–1868: Feudalism abolished and monarchy restored

Meiji and Taishō Periods: 1868–1911; 1912–1926
Imperial rule from Tokyo

China

Japanese forms in parentheses

Shang or Yin (In) Dynasty:	*c.* 1766–1027 B.C.
Chou (Shū) Dynasty:	1122–255 B.C.
Ch'in (Shin) Dynasty:	221–206 B.C.
Han (Kan) Dynasty:	206 B.C.–A.D. 23
Later Han (Gokan) Dynasty:	25–220
The Three Kingdoms (San-goku):	220–277
Western Chin (Sei-shin) }*Dynasties:* *Eastern Chin (Tō-shin)*	265–419
Northern and Southern Dynasties (Namboku-cho):	420–581
Sui (Zui) Dynasty:	589–618
T'ang (Tō) Dynasty:	618–906
Five Dynasties (Godai):	907–959
Northern Sung (Sō) Dynasty:	960–1126
Southern Sung (Nansō) Dynasty:	1127–1279
Chin (Kin) Dynasty:	1115–1234
Yüan (Gen) Dynasty:	1280–1368
Ming (Min) Dynasty:	1368–1644
Ch'ing (Shin) Dynasty:	1644–1912
Republic (Minkoku):	1912–

I

What Is Zen?

1

B EFORE I proceed to write about the influence of Zen on
Japanese culture, I must explain what Zen is, for it is
possible that my present readers may not know anything about
it. As I have already written some books on Zen, however, I
will not go into a detailed presentation here.

Briefly, Zen is one of the products of the Chinese mind after
its contact with Indian thought, which was introduced into China
in the first century A.D. through the medium of Buddhist teachings. There were some aspects of Buddhism in the form in which
it came to China that the people of the Middle Kingdom did not
quite kindly cherish: for instance, its advocacy of a homeless
life, its transcendentalism or world-fleeing and life-denying tendency, and so on. At the same time, its profound philosophy, its
subtle dialectics and penetrating analyses and speculations,
stirred Chinese thinkers, especially the Taoists.

Compared with Indians, the Chinese people are not so very
philosophically-minded. They are rather practical and devoted
to worldly affairs; they are attached to the earth, they are not
stargazers. While the Chinese mind was profoundly stimulated
by the Indian way of thinking, it never lost its touch with the
plurality of things, it never neglected the practical side of our
daily life. This national or racial psychological idiosyncrasy
brought about the transformation of Indian Buddhism into Zen
Buddhism.

One of the first things Zen accomplished in China, as soon
as it had gathered its forces and was strong enough to stand

by itself, was to establish a special form of monasticism quite distinct from the older kind of monkish living. The Zen monastery became a self-governing body divided into so many departments, each of which had its own office to serve the community. A noteworthy feature of this institution was the principle of complete democracy. While the elders were naturally respected, all members were equally to engage in manual labor, such as gathering fuel, cultivating the land, and picking tea leaves. In this even the master himself joined, and while working with his brotherhood he guided them to the proper understanding of Zen.

This way of living significantly distinguished the Zen monastery from the *sangha* brotherhood of the earlier Buddhists of India. The Zen monks were not only democratic; they were willing to employ themselves in all the practical ways of life. They were thus economically-minded as well as politically-minded.

In metaphysics Zen absorbed much of Taoist teachings modified by Buddhist speculations. But in its practical conduct of life, it completely ignored both the Taoist transcendentalism and the Indian aloofness from productive life. When a Zen master was asked what his future life would be, he unhesitatingly answered, "Let me be a donkey or a horse and work for the villagers."

Another departure from the older pattern of monkish brotherhood, whether Christian or Buddhist or anything else, was that the Zen monks were not always engaged in offering prayers, practicing penance, or performing other so-called deeds of piety, nor in reading or reciting the canonical books, discussing their contents, or studying them under the master, individually or collectively. What the Zen monks did, besides attending to various practical affairs, both manual and menial, was to listen to the master's occasional sermons, which were short and cryptic, and to ask questions and get answers. The answers, however, were bizarre and full of incomprehensibles, and they were quite frequently accompanied by direct actions.

I will cite one of such examples—perhaps an extreme one. Though it did not take place between master and monk but between monks themselves, it will illustrate the spirit of Zen which prevailed in its earlier days, towards the end of the T'ang dynasty. A monk, coming out of the monastery that was under the leadership of Rinzai (Lin-chi, d. 867), met a party of three traveling monks belonging to another Buddhist school, and one of the three ventured to question the Zen monk: "How deep is the river of Zen?" The reference to the river arose from their encounter taking place on a bridge. The Zen monk, fresh from his own interview with Rinzai, who was noted for his direct actions, lost no time in replying. "Find out for yourself," he said, and offered to throw the questioner from the bridge. But fortunately his two friends interceded and pleaded for mercy, which saved the situation.

Zen is not necessarily against words, but it is well aware of the fact that they are always liable to detach themselves from realities and turn into conceptions. And this conceptualization is what Zen is against. The Zen monk just cited may be an extreme case, but the spirit is there. Zen insists on handling the thing itself and not an empty abstraction. It is for this reason that Zen neglects reading or reciting the sūtras [1] or engaging in discourse on abstract subjects. And this is a cause of Zen's appeal to men of action in the broadest sense of the term. Through their practical-mindedness, the Chinese people and also to a certain extent the Japanese have taken greatly to Zen.

2

ZEN is discipline in enlightenment. Enlightenment means emancipation. And emancipation is no less than freedom. We talk very much these days about all kinds of freedom, political, economic, and otherwise, but these freedoms are not at all real.

[1] Collections of sermons given by the Buddha.

As long as they are on the plane of relativity, the freedoms or liberties we glibly talk about are far from being such. The real freedom is the outcome of enlightenment. When a man realizes this, in whatever situation he may find himself he is always free in his inner life, for that pursues its own line of action. Zen is the religion of *jiyū* (*tzŭ-yu*), "self-reliance," and *jizai* (*tzŭ-tsai*), "self-being."

Enlightenment occupies the central point of teaching in all schools of Buddhism, Hīnayāna and Mahāyāna, "self-power" and "other-power," the Holy Path and the Pure Land, because the Buddha's teachings all start from his enlightenment experience, about 2,500 years ago in the northern part of India. Every Buddhist is, therefore, expected to receive enlightenment either in this world or in one of his future lives. Without enlightenment, either already realized or to be realized somehow and sometime and somewhere, there will be no Buddhism. Zen is no exception. In fact, it is Zen that makes most of enlightenment, or *satori* (*wu* in Chinese).

To realize *satori*, Zen opens for us two ways in general: verbal and actional.

First, Zen verbalism is quite characteristic of Zen, though it is so completely differentiated from the philosophy of linguistics or dialectics that it may not be correct to apply the term "verbalism" to Zen at all. But, as we all know, we human beings cannot live without language, for we are so made that we can sustain our existence only in group life. Love is the essence of humanity, love needs something to bestow itself upon; human beings must live together in order to lead a life of mutual love. Love to be articulate requires a means of communication, which is language. Inasmuch as Zen is one of the most significant human experiences, one must resort to language to express it to others as well as to oneself. But Zen verbalism has its own features, which violate all the rules of the science of linguistics. In Zen, experience and expression are one. Zen verbalism expresses the most concrete experience.

To give examples: A Zen master produces his staff before his congregation and declares: "You do not call it a staff. What would you call it?" Someone comes out of the audience, takes the master's staff away from him, breaks it into two, and throws it down. All this is the outcome of the master's illogical announcement.

Another master, holding up his staff, says: "If you have one, I give you mine; if you have none, I will take it away from you." There is no rationalism in this.

Still another master once gave this sermon: "When you know what this staff is, you know all, you have finished the study of Zen." Without further remark he left the hall.

This is what I call Zen verbalism. The philosophy of Zen comes out of it. The philosophy, however, is not concerned to elucidate all these verbal "riddles" but to reach the mind itself, which, as it were, exudes or secretes them as naturally, as inevitably, as the clouds rise from the mountain peaks. What concerns us here is not the substance thus exuded or secreted, that is, words or language, but a "something" hovering around there, though we cannot exactly locate it and say "Here!" To call it the mind is far from the fact of experience; it is an unnamable "X." It is no abstraction; it is concrete enough, and direct, as the eye sees that the sun is, but it is not to be subsumed in the categories of linguistics. As soon as we try to do this, it disappears. The Buddhists, therefore, call it the "unattainable," the "ungraspable."

It is for this reason that a staff is a staff and at the same time not a staff, or that a staff is a staff just because it is not a staff. The word is not to be detached from the thing or the fact or the experience.

The Zen masters have the saying, "Examine the living words and not the dead ones." The dead ones are those that no longer pass directly and concretely and intimately on to the experience. They are conceptualized, they are cut off from the living roots. They have ceased, then, to stir up my being from within, from itself. They are no more what the masters would call "the one word" which when understood leads immediately to the understanding of hundreds of thousands of other words or statements given by the Zen masters. Zen verbalism deals with these "living words."

3

THE SECOND disciplinary approach to the experience of enlightenment is actional. In a sense, verbalism is also actional as long as it is concrete and personal. But in the actional what we call "the body," according to our sense testimony, is involved. When Rinzai was asked what the essence of Buddhist teaching was, he came right down from his seat and, taking hold of the questioner by the front of his robe, slapped his face, and let him go. The questioner stood there, stupefied. The bystanders remarked, "Why don't you bow?" This woke him from his reverie; and when he was about to make a bow to the master, he had his *satori*.[2]

When Baso (Ma-tsu, d. 788) took a walk with Hyakujō (Pai-chang), one of his attendant monks, he noticed the wild geese flying. He asked, "Where are they flying?" Hyakujō answered, "They are already flown away." Baso turned around and, taking hold of Hyakujō's nose, gave it a twist. Hyakujō cried, "It hurts, O Master!" "Who says they are flown away?" was the master's retort.[3] This made Hyakujō realize that the master was not talking at all about the conceptualized geese disappearing far away in the clouds. The master's purpose was to call Hyakujō's attention to the living goose that moves along with Hyakujō himself, not outside but within his person.

This person is Rinzai's "true man in all nakedness going

[2] *The Sayings of Rinzai.*
[3] The *Hekigan-shū* ("Blue Rock Collection"), case 53. For a fuller explanation of this book, see p. 399 n.

in and out through your senses." I wonder if this is symbolized in that "third man" who is often referred to by some modern writers as walking "beside you" or "on the other side of you" or "behind you." [4]

We may say this is a practical lesson, teaching by action, learning by doing. There is something like it in the actional approach to enlightenment. But a direct action in Zen has another meaning. There is a deeper purpose which consists in awakening in the disciple's mind a certain consciousness that is attuned to the pulsation of Reality. The following story is in a somewhat different vein; it simply illustrates how important it is to grasp a trick by going through a practical situation oneself without any outside aid. It exemplifies the pedagogic methodology of Zen's spirit of "self-reliance." This is in perfect accord with the teaching of the Buddha and other masters: "Do not rely on others, nor on the reading of the sūtras and śāstras.[5] Be your own lamp."

Goso Hōyen (Wu-tsu Fa-yen, d. 1104), of the Sung dynasty, tells us the following to illustrate the Zen spirit that goes beyond intellect, logic, and verbalism:

"If people ask me what Zen is like, I will say that it is like

[4] In *The Waste Land* (V, 359-65), T. S. Eliot gives this description of the anguish of the apostles after Calvary:

> *Who is the third who walks always beside you?*
> *When I count, there are only you and I together*
> *But when I look ahead up the white road*
> *There is always another one walking beside you*
> *Gliding wrapt in a brown mantle, hooded*
> *I do not know whether a man or a woman*
> *—But who is that on the other side of you?*

Eliot remarks in his notes that these lines were suggested by the account of an Antarctic expedition: "The explorers, at the extremity of their strength, had the constant delusion that there was *one more member* than could actually be counted." (*Complete Poems and Plays*, pp. 48, 54.)

The idea of a third person is significant. Can we take it for the hallucinatory projection of Rinzai's "true man," which assumes an objective form when one's physical strength reaches the point of exhaustion? This, however, seems to be a somewhat wild suggestion.

[5] The philosophical discourses.

learning the art of burglary. The son of a burglar saw his father growing older and thought, 'If he is unable to carry on his profession, who will be the breadwinner of the family, except myself? I must learn the trade.' He intimated the idea to his father, who approved of it.

"One night the father took the son to a big house, broke through the fence, entered the house, and, opening one of the large chests, told the son to go in and pick out the clothing. As soon as the son got into it, the father dropped the lid and securely applied the lock. The father now came out to the courtyard and loudly knocked at the door, waking up the whole family; then he quietly slipped away by the hole in the fence. The residents got excited and lighted candles, but they found that the burglar had already gone.

"The son, who had remained all the time securely confined in the chest, thought of his cruel father. He was greatly mortified, then a fine idea flashed upon him. He made a noise like the gnawing of a rat. The family told the maid to take a candle and examine the chest. When the lid was unlocked, out came the prisoner, who blew out the light, pushed away the maid, and fled. The people ran after him. Noticing a well by the road, he picked up a large stone and threw it into the water. The pursuers all gathered around the well trying to find the burglar drowning himself in the dark hole.

"In the meantime he went safely back to his father's house. He blamed his father deeply for his narrow escape. Said the father, 'Be not offended, my son. Just tell me how you got out of it.' When the son told him all about his adventures, the father remarked, 'There you are, you have learned the art.' " [6]

The idea of the story is to demonstrate the futility of verbal instruction and conceptual presentation as far as the experience of enlightenment is concerned. *Satori* must be the outgrowth of one's inner life and not a verbal implantation brought from the outside.

[6] *The Sayings of Goso Hōyen.*

4

THERE is a famous saying given by one of the earlier masters of
the T'ang dynasty, which declares that the Tao is no more than
one's everyday-life experience. When the master was asked
what he meant by this, he replied, "When you are hungry you
eat, when you are thirsty you drink, when you meet a friend
you greet him."

This, some may think, is no more than animal instinct or
social usage, and there is nothing that may be called moral,
much less spiritual, in it. If we call it the Tao, some may think,
what a cheap thing the Tao is after all!

Those who have not penetrated into the depths of our consciousness, including both the conscious and the unconscious, are
liable to hold such a mistaken notion as the one just cited. But
we must remember that, if the Tao is something highly abstract
transcending our daily experiences, it will have nothing to do
with the actualities of life. Life as we live it is not concerned with
generalization. If it were, the intellect would be everything, and
the philosopher would be the wisest man. But, as Kierkegaard
points out, the philosopher builds a fine palace, but he is doomed
not to live in it—he has a shed for himself next door to what
he constructed for others, including himself, to look at.

Mencius says, "The Tao is near and people seek it far away."
This means that the Tao is our everyday life itself. And, indeed,
it is due to this fact that the Tao is so hard to grasp, so elusive to
point out. How elusive! How ungraspable! "The Tao that
can at all be predicated is not the Tao of always-so-ness
(*Ch'ang tao*)."

The Tao is really very much more than mere animal instinct
and social usage, though those elements are also included in it.
It is something deeply imbedded in every one of us, indeed in
all beings sentient and nonsentient, and it requires something
altogether different from the so-called scientific analysis. It

defies our intellectual pursuit because of being too concrete, too familiar, hence beyond definability. It is there confronting us, no doubt, but not obtrusively and threateningly, like Mount Everest to the mountain-climbers.

"What is Zen?" (This is tantamount to asking, "What is Tao?")

"I do not understand," was one master's answer.

"What is Zen?"

"The silk fan gives me enough of a cooling breeze," was another master's answer.

"What is Zen?"

"Zen," was still another's response.

Perhaps Lao-tzŭ's description may be more approachable for most of us than those of the Zen masters:

> *The Tao is something vague and undefinable;*
> *How undefinable! How vague!*
> *Yet in it there is a form.*
> *How vague! How undefinable!*
> *Yet in it there is a thing.*
> *How obscure! How deep!*
> *Yet in it there is a substance.*
> *The substance is genuine*
> *And in it sincerity.*
> *From of old until now*
> *Its name never departs,*
> *Whereby it inspects all things.*[7]
> *How do I know all things in their suchness?*
> *It is because of this.*[8]

[7] When the name does not depart, as we usually make it do, from the substance to which it is undetachably fixed, the name is the substance and the substance the name. There is a perfect identity. And thereby as soon as the "name" is pronounced, the substance, that is, the All, is "inspected," not in its abstraction, but in its "sincerity" and concreteness.

[8] *Tao Tê Ching*, Ch. XXI. (When no translator's name is specified, the translations from the Chinese or the Japanese texts throughout this book are the author's.)

The object of Zen training consists in making us realize that Zen is our daily experience and that it is not something put in from the outside. Tennō Dōgo (T'ien-huang Tao-wu, 748–807) illustrates the point most eloquently in his treatment of a novice monk, while an unknown Japanese swordmaster demonstrates it in the more threatening manner characteristic of his profession. Tennō Dōgo's story runs as follows:

Dōgo had a disciple called Sōshin (Ch'ung-hsin). When Sōshin was taken in as a novice, it was perhaps natural of him to expect lessons in Zen from his teacher the way a schoolboy is taught at school. But Dōgo gave him no special lessons on the subject, and this bewildered and disappointed Sōshin. One day he said to the master, "It is some time since I came here, but not a word has been given me regarding the essence of the Zen teaching." Dōgo replied, "Since your arrival I have ever been giving you lessons on the matter of Zen discipline."

"What kind of lesson could it have been?"

"When you bring me a cup of tea in the morning, I take it; when you serve me a meal, I accept it; when you bow to me, I return it with a nod. How else do you expect to be taught in the mental discipline of Zen?"

Sōshin hung his head for a while, pondering the puzzling words of the master. The master said, "If you want to see, see right at once. When you begin to think, you miss the point."

The swordsman's story is this:

When a disciple came to a master [9] to be disciplined in the art of swordplay, the master, who was in retirement in his mountain hut, agreed to undertake the task. The pupil was made to help him gather kindling, draw water from the nearby spring, split wood, make fires, cook rice, sweep the rooms and the

[9] Was he Tsukahara Bokuden (1490–1572), who flourished during the Ashikaga era? I do not remember where I read the story, and at present I have no means of confirming it.

garden, and generally look after his household. There was no
regular or technical teaching in the art. After some time the
young man became dissatisfied, for he had not come to work as
servant to the old gentleman, but to learn the art of swordsmanship. So one day he approached the master and asked him to
teach him. The master agreed.

The result was that the young man could not do any piece
of work with any feeling of safety. For when he began to cook
rice early in the morning, the master would appear and strike
him from behind with a stick. When he was in the midst of his
sweeping, he would be feeling the same sort of blow from somewhere, some unknown direction. He had no peace of mind, he
had to be always on the *qui vive*. Some years passed before he
could successfully dodge the blow from wherever it might come.
But the master was not quite satisfied with him yet.

One day the master was found cooking his own vegetables
over an open fire. The pupil took it into his head to avail himself of this opportunity. Taking up his big stick, he let it fall
over the head of the master, who was then stooping over the
cooking pan to stir its contents. But the pupil's stick was
caught by the master with the cover of the pan. This opened the
pupil's mind to the secrets of the art, which had hitherto been
kept from him and to which he had so far been a stranger. He
then, for the first time, appreciated the unparalleled kindness of
the master.

The secrets of perfect swordsmanship consist in creating a
certain frame or structure of mentality which is made always
ready to respond instantly, that is, im-mediately, to what comes
from the outside. While technical training is of great importance, it is after all something artificially, consciously, calculat-
ingly added and acquired. Unless the mind that avails itself of
the technical skill somehow attunes itself to a state of the utmost
fluidity or mobility, anything acquired or superimposed lacks
spontaneity of natural growth. This state prevails when the mind
is awakened to a *satori*. What the swordsman aimed at was to

make the disciple attain to this realization. It cannot be taught by any system specifically designed for the purpose, it must simply grow from within. The master's system was really no system in the proper sense. But there was a "natural" method in his apparent craziness, and he succeeded in awakening in his young disciple's mind something that touched off the mechanism needed for the mastery of swordsmanship.

Dōgo the Zen master did not have to be attacking his disciple all the time with a stick. The swordsman's object was more definite and limited to the area of the sword, whereas Dōgo wanted to teach by getting to the source of being from which everything making up our daily experience ensues. Therefore, when Sōshin began to reflect on the remark Dōgo made to him, Dōgo told him: "No reflecting whatever. When you want to see, see im-mediately. As soon as you tarry [that is, as soon as an intellectual interpretation or mediation takes place], the whole thing goes awry." This means that, in the study of Zen, conceptualization must go, for as long as we tarry at this level we can never reach the area where Zen has its life. The door of enlightenment-experience opens by itself as one finally faces the deadlock of intellectualization.

The slipperiness or elusiveness of the truth or reality or, shall I say, God, when one tries to get hold of it or him by means of concepts or intellection, is like trying to catch a catfish with a gourd. This is aptly illustrated by Josetsu, a Japanese painter of the fifteenth century. The picture of his which is reproduced among our illustrations is a well-known one; as we notice, the [2 upper part of it is filled with poems composed by renowned Zen masters of the day.

5

W E N O W can state a few things about Zen in a more or less summary way:

(1) Zen discipline consists in attaining enlightenment (or *satori*, in Japanese).

(2) *Satori* finds a meaning hitherto hidden in our daily concrete particular experiences, such as eating, drinking, or business of all kinds.

(3) The meaning thus revealed is not something added from the outside. It is in being itself, in becoming itself, in living itself. This is called, in Japanese, a life of *kono-mama* or *sono-mama.*[10] *Kono-* or *sono-mama* means the "isness" of a thing, Reality in its isness.

(4) Some may say, "There cannot be any meaning in mere isness." But this is not the view held by Zen, for according to it, isness is the meaning. When I see into it I see it as clearly as I see myself reflected in a mirror.

(5) This is what made Hō Koji (P'ang Chü-shih), a lay disciple of the eighth century, declare:

> *How wondrous this, how mysterious!*
> *I carry fuel, I draw water.*

The fuel-carrying or the water-drawing itself, apart from its utilitarianism, is full of meaning; hence its "wonder," its "mystery."

(6) Zen does not, therefore, indulge in abstraction or in conceptualization. In its verbalism it may sometimes appear that Zen does this a great deal. But this is an error most commonly entertained by those who do not at all know Zen.

(7) *Satori* is emancipation, moral, spiritual, as well as intel-

---

[10] *Kono* is "this," *sono* "that," and *mama* means "as-it-is-ness." *Kono-mama* or *sono-mama* thus corresponds to the Sanskrit *tathatā*, "suchness," and to the Chinese *chih-mo* or *shih-mo.*

lectual. When I am in my isness, thoroughly purged of all intellectual sediments, I have my freedom in its primary sense.

(8) When the mind, now abiding in its isness—which, to use Zen verbalism, is not isness—and thus free from intellectual complexities and moralistic attachments of every description, surveys the world of the senses in all its multiplicities, it discovers in it all sorts of values hitherto hidden from sight. Here opens to the artist a world full of wonders and miracles.

(9) The artist's world is one of free creation, and this can come only from intuitions directly and im-mediately rising from the isness of things, unhampered by senses and intellect. He creates forms and sounds out of formlessness and soundlessness. To this extent, the artist's world coincides with that of Zen.

(10) What differentiates Zen from the arts is this: While the artists have to resort to the canvas and brush or mechanical instruments or some other mediums to express themselves, Zen has no need of things external, except "the body" in which the Zen-man is so to speak embodied. From the absolute point of view this is not quite correct; I say it only in concession to the worldly way of saying things. What Zen does is to delineate itself on the infinite canvas of time and space the way the flying wild geese cast their shadow on the water below without any idea of doing so, while the water reflects the geese just as naturally and unintentionally.

(11) The Zen-man is an artist to the extent that, as the sculptor chisels out a great figure deeply buried in a mass of inert matter, the Zen-man transforms his own life into a work of creation, which exists, as Christians might say, in the mind of God.[11]

---

[11] After writing the above I feel somewhat uneasy lest my readers may not be able to comprehend what Zen means to us of modern time. Everything of life nowadays shows the tendency to turn into a complete routine of mechanization, leaving nothing that will demonstrate the dignity and destiny of human existence. Hence the two extracts from the *Hekigan-shū* ("Blue Rock Collection") and an abstract of the *Yuima Kyō* ("Vimalakīrti Sūtra"), which make up the first part of the appendices. Those who wish to pursue the study of Zen Buddhism further are advised to consult the works of the present author on the subject. See the bibliography.

With this preliminary, I wish to treat in the following pages the part Zen Buddhism has played in the molding of Japanese culture and character, especially as exhibited in the arts generally, and particularly in the development of Bushido ("the way of the warrior"), in the study and propagation of Confucianism and general education, in the rise of the art of tea, and also in the composition of a form of poetry known as *haiku;* while incidentally some other points will be touched upon.

II

General Remarks
on Japanese Art Culture

1

H AVING noted the foregoing specifications of the atmosphere emanating from Zen, we may now proceed to see
what contributions Zen has made to the building up of Japanese
culture. It is a significant fact that the other schools of Buddhism
have limited their sphere of influence almost entirely to the
spiritual life of the Japanese people; Zen has gone beyond it.
Zen has entered internally into every phase of the cultural life
of the people.

In China this was not necessarily the case. Zen united itself
to a great extent with Taoist beliefs and practices and with the
Confucian teaching of morality, but it did not affect the cultural
life of the people so much as it did in Japan. (Is it due to the
racial psychology of the Japanese people that they have taken up
Zen so intensely and deeply that it has entered intimately into
their life?) In China, however, I ought not omit to mention the
noteworthy fact that Zen gave great impetus to the development
of Chinese philosophy in the Sung dynasty and also to the growth
of a certain school of painting. A large number of examples of
this school were brought over to Japan beginning with the Kamakura era in the thirteenth century, when Zen monks were constantly traveling between the two neighboring countries. The
paintings of Southern Sung thus came to find their ardent
admirers on our side of the sea and are now national treasures
of Japan, while in China no specimens of this class of painting
are to be found.

Before proceeding further, we may make a few general remarks about one of the peculiar features of Japanese art, which
is closely related to and finally deducible from the world conception of Zen.

Among things which strongly characterize Japanese artistic
talents we may mention the so-called "one-corner" style, which
originated with Bayen (Ma Yüan, fl. 1175–1225), one of the
greatest Southern Sung artists. The "one-corner" style is
psychologically associated with the Japanese painters' "thrifty
brush" tradition of retaining the least possible number of lines or
strokes which go to represent forms on silk or paper. Both are
very much in accord with the spirit of Zen. A simple fishing
boat in the midst of the rippling waters is enough to awaken in
the mind of the beholder a sense of the vastness of the sea and
at the same time of peace and contentment—the Zen sense of the
Alone. Apparently the boat floats helplessly. It is a primitive
structure with no mechanical device for stability and for
audacious steering over the turbulent waves, with no scientific
apparatus for braving all kinds of weather—quite a contrast to
the modern ocean liner. But this very helplessness is the virtue
of the fishing canoe, in contrast with which we feel the incom-
prehensibility of the Absolute encompassing the boat and all
the world. Again, a solitary bird on a dead branch, in which
not a line, not a shade, is wasted, is enough to show us the
loneliness of autumn, when days become shorter and nature
begins to roll up once more its gorgeous display of luxurious
summer vegetation.[1] It makes one feel somewhat pensive, but
it gives one opportunity to withdraw the attention towards the
inner life, which, given attention enough, spreads out its rich
treasures ungrudgingly before the eyes.

Here we have an appreciation of transcendental aloofness in
the midst of multiplicities—which is known as *wabi* in the

---

[1] For a picture of a similar nature, see my *Zen Essays*, III, facing p. 310. (See
bibliography for full references.) Here the fishing boat as one of the most
representative specimens is reproduced.

dictionary of Japanese cultural terms. *Wabi* really means "poverty," or, negatively, "not to be in the fashionable society of the time." To be poor, that is, not to be dependent on things worldly—wealth, power, and reputation—and yet to feel inwardly the presence of something of the highest value, above time and social position: this is what essentially constitutes *wabi*. Stated in terms of practical everyday life, *wabi* is to be satisfied with a little hut, a room of two or three *tatami* (mats), like the log cabin of Thoreau, and with a dish of vegetables picked in the neighboring fields, and perhaps to be listening to the pattering of a gentle spring rainfall. While later I will say something more about *wabi,* let me state here that the cult of *wabi* has entered deeply into the cultural life of the Japanese people. It is in truth the worshiping of poverty— probably a most appropriate cult in a poor country like ours. Despite the modern Western luxuries and comforts of life which have invaded us, there is still an ineradicable longing in us for the cult of *wabi*. Even in the intellectual life, not richness of ideas, not brilliancy or solemnity in marshaling thoughts and building up a philosophical system, is sought; but just to stay quietly content with the mystical contemplation of Nature and to feel at home with the world is more inspiring to us, at least to some of us.

However "civilized," however much brought up in an artificially contrived environment, we all seem to have an innate longing for primitive simplicity, close to the natural state of living. Hence the city people's pleasure in summer camping in the woods or traveling in the desert or opening up an unbeaten track. We wish to go back once in a while to the bosom of Nature and feel her pulsation directly. Zen's habit of mind, to break through all forms of human artificiality and take firm hold of what lies behind them, has helped the Japanese not to forget the soil but to be always friendly with Nature and appreciate her unaffected simplicity. Zen has no taste for complexities that lie on the surface of life. Life itself is simple enough, but when it is surveyed by the analyzing intellect it presents unparalleled in‑ tricacies. With all the apparatus of science we have not yet fathomed the mysteries of life. But, once in its current, we seem to be able to understand it, with its apparently endless pluralities and entanglements. Very likely, the most characteristic thing in the temperament of the Eastern people is the ability to grasp life from within and not from without. And Zen has just struck it.

In painting especially, disregard of form results when too much attention or emphasis is given to the all-importance of the spirit. The "one-corner" style and the economy of brush strokes also help to effect aloofness from conventional rules. Where you would ordinarily expect a line or a mass or a bal‑ ancing element, you miss it, and yet this very thing awakens in you an unexpected feeling of pleasure. In spite of shortcomings or deficiencies that no doubt are apparent, you do not feel them so; indeed, this imperfection itself becomes a form of perfection. Evidently, beauty does not necessarily spell perfection of form. This has been one of the favorite tricks of Japanese artists— to embody beauty in a form of imperfection or even of ugli‑ ness.

When this beauty of imperfection is accompanied by anti‑ quity or primitive uncouthness, we have a glimpse of *sabi*, so prized by Japanese connoisseurs. Antiquity and primitiveness may not be an actuality. If an object of art suggests even superficially the feeling of a historical period, there is *sabi* in it. *Sabi* consists in rustic unpretentiousness or archaic imperfec‑ tion, apparent simplicity or effortlessness in execution, and rich‑ ness in historical associations (which, however, may not always be present); and, lastly, it contains inexplicable elements that raise the object in question to the rank of an artistic production. These elements are generally regarded as derived from the ap‑ preciation of Zen. The utensils used in the tearoom are mostly of this nature.

The artistic element that goes into the constitution of *sabi*, which literally means "loneliness" or "solitude," is poetically defined by a teamaster thus:

As I come out
To this fishing village,
Late in the autumn day,
No flowers in bloom I see,
Nor any tinted maple leaves.[2]

Aloneness indeed appeals to contemplation and does not lend itself to spectacular demonstration. It may look most miserable, insignificant, and pitiable, especially when it is put up against the Western or modern setting. To be left alone, with no streamers flying, no fireworks crackling, and this amidst a gorgeous display of infinitely varied forms and endlessly changing colors, is indeed no sight at all. Take one of those *sumiye* sketches, perhaps portraying Kanzan and Jittoku (Han-shan and Shih-tê),[3] hang it in a European or an American art gallery, and see what effect it will produce in the minds of the visitors. The idea of aloneness belongs to the East and is at home in the environment of its birth.

It is not only to the fishing village on the autumnal eve that aloneness gives form but also to a patch of green in the early spring—which is in all likelihood even more expressive of the idea of *sabi* or *wabi*. For in the green patch, as we read in the following thirty-one-syllable verse, there is an indication of life impulse amidst the wintry desolation:

To those who only pray for the cherries to bloom,
How I wish to show the spring
That gleams from a patch of green
In the midst of the snow-covered mountain-village! [4]

---

[2] Fujiwara Sadaiye (1162–1241).

[3] Zen poet-recluses of the T'ang dynasty. A collection of their poems known as the *Kanzan Shi* (*Han-shan Shih*) or *Sanrai Shi* (*San-lai Shih*) or *Sanin Shi* (*San-yin shih*) is still in existence. The pair together, Kanzan and Jittoku, has been a favorite subject for Far Eastern painters. There is something in their transcendental air of freedom which attracts us even in these modern days. We give two sets of representative pictures of the T'ang poet-recluses. [6, 18, 19

[4] Fujiwara Iyetaka (1158–1237).

This is given by one of the old teamasters as thoroughly expressive of *sabi,* which is one of the four principles governing the cult of tea, *cha-no-yu.* Here is just a feeble inception of life power as asserted in the form of a little green patch, but in it he who has an eye can readily discern the spring shooting out from underneath the forbidding snow. It may be said to be a mere suggestion that stirs his mind, but just the same it is life itself and not its feeble indication. To the artist, life is as much here as when the whole field is overlaid with verdure and flowers. One may call this the mystic sense of the artist.

Asymmetry is another feature that distinguishes Japanese art. The idea is doubtlessly derived from the "one-corner" style of Bayen. The plainest and boldest example is the plan of Buddhist architecture. The principal structures, such as the Tower Gate, the Dharma Hall, the Buddha Hall, and others, may be laid along one straight line; but structures of secondary or supplementary importance, sometimes even those of major importance, are not arranged symmetrically as wings along either side of the main line. They may be found irregularly scattered over the grounds in accordance with the topographical peculiarities. You will readily be convinced of this fact if you visit some of the Buddhist temples in the mountains, for example, the Iyeyasu shrine at Nikko. We can say that asymmetry is quite characteristic of Japanese architecture of this class.

7]   This can be demonstrated *par excellence* in the construction of the tearoom and in the tools used in connection with it. Look at the ceiling, which may be constructed in at least three different styles, and at some of the utensils for serving tea, and
8, 9, 54]   again at the grouping and laying of the steppingstones or flagstones in the garden. We find so many illustrations of asymmetry, or, in a way, of imperfection, or of the "one-corner" style.

Some Japanese moralists try to explain this liking of the Japanese artists for things asymmetrically formed and counter to the conventional, or rather geometrical, rules of art by the theory that the people have been morally trained not to be obtrusive but always to efface themselves, and that this mental habit of self-annihilation manifests itself accordingly in art— for example, when the artist leaves the important central space unoccupied. But, to my mind, this theory is not quite correct. Would it not be a more plausible explanation to say that the artistic genius of the Japanese people has been inspired by the Zen way of looking at individual things as perfect in themselves and at the same time as embodying the nature of totality which belongs to the One?

The doctrine of ascetic aestheticism is not so fundamental as that of Zen aestheticism. Art impulses are more primitive or more innate than those of morality. The appeal of art goes more directly into human nature. Morality is regulative, art is creative. One is an imposition from without, the other is an irrepressible expression from within. Zen finds its inevitable association with art but not with morality. Zen may remain unmoral but not without art. When the Japanese artists create objects imperfect from the point of view of form, they may even be willing to ascribe their art motive to the current notion of moral asceticism; but we need not give too much significance to their own interpretation or to that of the critics. Our consciousness is not, after all, a very reliable standard of judgment.

However this may be, asymmetry is certainly characteristic of Japanese art, which is one of the reasons informality or approachability also marks to a certain degree Japanese objects of art. Symmetry inspires a notion of grace, solemnity, and impressiveness, which is again the case with logical formalism or the piling up of abstract ideas. The Japanese are often thought not to be intellectual and philosophical, because their general culture is not thoroughly impregnated with intellectuality. This criticism, I think, results somewhat from the Japanese love of asymmetry. The intellectual primarily aspires to balance, while the Japanese are apt to ignore it and incline strongly towards imbalance.

Imbalance, asymmetry, the "one-corner," poverty, *sabi* or

wabi, simplification, aloneness, and cognate ideas make up the most conspicuous and characteristic features of Japanese art and culture. All these emanate from one central perception of the truth of Zen, which is "the One in the Many and the Many in the One," or better, "the One remaining as one in the Many individually and collectively."

2

T H A T Zen has helped to stimulate the artistic impulses of the Japanese people and to color their works with ideas characteristic of Zen is due to the following facts: the Zen monasteries were almost exclusively the repositories of learning and art, at least during the Kamakura and the Muromachi eras; the Zen monks had constant opportunities to come in contact with foreign cultures; the monks themselves were artists, scholars, and mystics; they were even encouraged by the political powers of the time to engage in commercial enterprises to bring foreign objects of art and industry to Japan; the aristocrats and the politically influential classes of Japan were patrons of Zen institutions and were willing to submit themselves to the discipline of Zen. Zen thus worked not only directly on the religious life of the Japanese but also most strongly on their general culture.

The Tendai, the Shingon, and the Jōdō [5] contributed greatly to imbue the Japanese with the spirit of Buddhism, and through their iconography to develop their artistic instincts for sculpture, color painting, architecture, textile fabrics, and metalwork. But the philosophy of Tendai is too abstract and abstruse to be understood by the masses; the ritualism of Shingon is too elaborate and complicated and consequently too expensive for popularity. On the other hand, Shingon and Tendai and Jōdō pro-

---

[5] These, with the Shin and the Nichiren, are the principal schools of Buddhism in Japan, other than Zen.

duced fine sculpture and pictures and artistic utensils to be used in their daily worship. The most highly prized "national treasures" belong to the Tempyō, the Nara, and the Heian periods, [10, 11 when those two schools of Buddhism were in the ascendency and intimately involved with the cultured classes of the people. The Jōdō teaches the Pure Land in all its magnificence, where the Buddha of Infinite Light is attended by his retinue of Bodhisattvas, and this inspired the artists to paint those splendid pictures of Amida preserved in the various Buddhist temples of Japan. [13 The Nichiren and the Shin are the creation of the Japanese religious mind. The Nichiren gave no specifically artistic and cultural impetus to us; the Shin tended to be somewhat iconoclastic and produced nothing worth mentioning in the arts and literature except the hymns known as *wasan* and the "honorable letters" (*gobunsho* or *ofumi*) chiefly written by Rennyo (1415–99).

Zen came to Japan after Shingon and Tendai and was at once embraced by the military classes. It was more or less by an historical accident that Zen was set against the aristocratic priesthood. The nobility, too, in the beginning felt a certain dislike for it and made use of their political advantage to stir up opposition to Zen. In the beginning of the Japanese history of Zen, therefore, Zen avoided Kyoto and established itself under the patronage of the Hōjō family in Kamakura. This place, as the seat of the feudal government in those days, became the headquarters of Zen discipline. Many Zen monks from China settled in Kamakura and found strong support in the Hōjō family— Tokiyori, Tokimune, and their successors and retainers.

The Chinese masters brought many artists and objects of art along with them, and the Japanese who came back from China [front., 14–17 were also bearers of art and literature. Pictures of Kakei (Hsia Kuei, fl. 1190–1220), Mokkei (Mu-ch'i, fl. c. 1240), Ryōkai (Liang K'ai, fl. c. 1210), Bayen (Ma Yüan, fl. 1175–1225), and others thus found their way to Japan. Manuscripts of the noted Zen masters of China were also given shelter in the

21–26] monasteries here. Calligraphy in the Far East is an art just as much as *sumiye* painting, and it was cultivated almost universally among the intellectual classes in olden times. The spirit pervading Zen pictures and calligraphy made a strong impression on them, and Zen was readily taken up and followed. In it there is something virile and unbending. A mild, gentle, and graceful air—almost feminine, one might call it—which prevailed in the periods preceding the Kamakura, is now superseded by an air of masculinity, expressing itself mostly in the sculpture and calligraphy of the period. The rugged virility of the warriors of the Kwanto districts is proverbial, in contrast to the grace and refinement of the courtiers in Kyoto. The soldierly quality, with its mysticism and aloofness from worldly affairs, appeals to the willpower. Zen in this respect walks hand in hand with the spirit of Bushido ("Warriors' Way").

Another factor in the discipline of Zen, or rather in the monastic life in which Zen carries out its scheme of teaching, is this: as the monastery is usually situated in the mountains, its inmates are in the most intimate touch with nature, they are close and sympathetic students of it. They observe plants, birds, animals, rocks, rivers which people of the town would leave unnoticed. And their observation deeply reflects their philosophy, or better, their intuition. It is not that of a mere naturalist. It penetrates into the life itself of the objects that come under the monks' observation. Whatever they may paint of nature will in- 27] evitably be expressive of this intuition; the "spirit of the mountains" will be felt softly breathing in their works.

The fundamental intuition the Zen masters gain through their discipline seems to stir up their artistic instincts if they are at all susceptible to art. The intuition that impels the masters to create beautiful things, that is, to express the sense of perfection through things ugly and imperfect, is apparently closely related to the feeling for art. The Zen masters may not make good philosophers, but they are very frequently fine artists. Even

their technique is often of the first order, and besides they know
how to tell us something unique and original. One such is Musō
the National Teacher (1275–1351). He was a fine calligrapher   [28
and a great landscape gardener; wherever he resided, at quite a
number of places in Japan, he designed splendid gardens, some
of which are still in existence and well preserved after so many
years of changing times. Among the noted painters of Zen in the
fourteenth and fifteenth centuries we may mention Chō Densu   [30–33, A
(d. 1431), Kei Shoki (fl. 1490), Josetsu (fl. 1375–1420),
Shūbun (fl. 1420–50), Sesshū (1421–1506), and others.

Georges Duthuit, the author of *Chinese Mysticism and Modern Painting*, seems to understand the spirit of Zen mysticism.
From him we have this: "When the Chinese artist paints, what
matters is the concentration of thought and the prompt and
vigorous response of the hand to the directing will. Tradition
ordains him to see, or rather to feel, as a whole the work to be
executed, before embarking on anything. 'If the ideas of a man
are confused, he will become the slave of exterior conditions.'
. . . He who deliberates and moves his brush intent on making
a picture, misses to a still greater extent the art of painting. [This
seems like a kind of automatic writing.] Draw bamboos for ten
years, become a bamboo, then forget all about bamboos when
you are drawing. In possession of an infallible technique, the
individual places himself at the mercy of inspiration."

To become a bamboo and to forget that you are one with it
while drawing it—this is the Zen of the bamboo, this is the moving with the "rhythmic movement of the spirit" which resides in
the bamboo as well as in the artist himself. What is now required
of him is to have a firm hold on the spirit and yet not to be conscious of the fact. This is a very difficult task achieved only
after long spiritual training.[6] The Eastern people have been
taught since the earliest times to subject themselves to this kind
of discipline if they want to achieve something in the world of

[6] Cf. Takuan on "Prajñā Immovable," pp. 95 ff.

art and religion. Zen, in fact, has given expression to it in the following phrase: "One in All and All in One." When this is thoroughly understood, there is creative genius.

It is of utmost importance here to interpret the phrase in its proper sense. People imagine that it means pantheism, and some students of Zen seem to agree. This is to be regretted, for pantheism is something foreign to Zen and also to the artist's understanding of his work. When the Zen masters declare the One to be in the All and the All in the One, they do not mean that there is a thing to be known as the One or as the All and that the one is the other and *vice versa*. As the One is in the All, some people suppose that Zen is a pantheistic teaching. Far from it; Zen would never hypostatize the One or the All as a thing to be grasped by the senses. The phrase "One in All and All in One" is to be understood as an expression of absolute *prajñā-intuition* and is not to be conceptually analyzed. When we see the moon, we know that it is the moon, and that is enough. Those who proceed to analyze the experience and try to establish a theory of knowledge are not students of Zen. They cease to be so, if they ever were, at the very moment of their procedure as analysts. Zen always upholds its experience as such and refuses to commit itself to any system of philosophy.

Even when Zen indulges in intellection, it never subscribes to a pantheistic interpretation of the world. For one thing, there is no One in Zen. If Zen ever speaks of the One as if it recognized it, this is a kind of condescension to common parlance. To Zen students, the One is the All and the All is the One; and yet the One remains the One and the All the All. "Not two!" may lead the logician to think, "It is One." But the master would go on, saying, "Not One either!" "What then?" we may ask. We here face a blind alley, as far as verbalism is concerned. Therefore, it is said that "If you wish to be in direct communion [with Reality], I tell you, 'Not two!' "

The following *mondo* [7] may help to illustrate the point I wish

[7] This and what follows are all from the *Hekigan-shū*, case 79.

Tê-shan (Tokusan), also of the 9th century

to make in regard to the Zen attitude towards the so-called pantheistic interpretation of nature.

A monk asked Tōsu (T'ou-tzŭ), a Zen master of the T'ang period: "I understand that all sounds are the voice of the Buddha. Is this right?" The master said, "That is right." The monk then proceeded: "Would not the master please stop making a noise which echoes the sound of a fermenting mass of filth?" The master thereupon struck the monk.

The monk further asked Tōsu: "Am I in the right when I understand the Buddha as asserting that all talk, however trivial or derogatory, belongs to ultimate truth?" The master said, "Yes, you are in the right." The monk went on, "May I then call you a donkey?" The master thereupon struck him.

It may be necessary to explain these *mondo* in plain language. To conceive every sound, every noise, every utterance one makes as issuing from the fountainhead of one Reality, that is, from one God, is pantheistic, I imagine. For "he giveth to all life, and breath, and all things" (Acts 17 : 25); and again, "For in him we live, and move, and have our being" (Acts 17 : 28). If this be the case, a Zen master's hoarse throat echoes the melodious resonance of the voice flowing from the Buddha's golden mouth, and even when a great teacher is decried as reminding one of an ass, the defamation must be regarded as reflecting something of ultimate truth. All forms of evil must be said somehow to be embodying what is true and good and beautiful, and to be a contribution to the perfection of Reality. To state it more concretely, bad is good, ugly is beautiful, false is true, imperfect is perfect, and also conversely. This is, indeed, the kind of reasoning in which those indulge who conceive the God-nature to be immanent in all things. Let us see how the Zen master treats this problem.

It is remarkable that Tōsu put his foot right down against such intellectualist interpretations and struck his monk. The latter in all probability expected to see the master nonplussed by his statements which logically follow from his first assertion.

The masterful Tōsu knew, as all Zen masters do, the uselessness of making any verbal demonstration against such a "logician." For verbalism leads from one complication to another;
there is no end to it. The only effective way, perhaps, to make
such a monk as this one realize the falsehood of his conceptual
understanding is to strike him and so let him experience within
himself the meaning of the statement, "One in All and All in
One." The monk was to be awakened from his logical somnam-
bulism. Hence Tōsu's drastic measure.

Secchō [8] here gives his comments in the following lines:

Pity that people without number try to play with the tide;
They are all ultimately swallowed up into it and die!
Let them suddenly awake [from the deadlock],
And see that all the rivers run backward, swelling and surging.

What is needed here is an abrupt turning or awakening, with
which one comes to the realization of the truth of Zen—which
is neither transcendentalism nor immanentism nor a combina-
tion of the two. The truth is as Tōsu declares in the following:
A monk asks, "What is the Buddha?"
Tōsu answers, "The Buddha."
Monk: "What is the Tao?"
Tōsu: "The Tao."
Monk: "What is Zen?"
Tōsu: "Zen."
The master answers like a parrot, he is echo itself. In fact,
there is no other way of illumining the monk's mind than af-
firming that what is is—which is the final fact of experience.

Another example [9] is given to illustrate the point. A monk
asked Jōshu (Chao-chou), of the T'ang dynasty: "It is stated

---

[8] Secchō (Hsüeh-tou, 980–1052) was one of the great Zen masters of the
Sung, noted for his literary accomplishment. The *Hekigan-shū* is based on
Secchō's "One Hundred Cases," which he selected out of the annals of Zen.
See p. 399 n. for further information.
[9] *Hekigan-shū,* case 57.

that the Perfect Way knows no difficulties, only that it abhors discrimination. What is meant by No-discrimination?"

Jōshu said, "Above the heavens and below the heavens, I alone am the Honored One."

The monk suggested, "Still a discrimination."

The master's retort was, "O this worthless fellow! Where is the discrimination?"

By discrimination the Zen masters mean what we have when we refuse to accept Reality as it is or in its suchness, for we then reflect on it and analyze it into concepts, going on with intellection and finally landing on a circulatory reasoning. Jōshu's affirmation is a final one and allows no equivocation, no argumentation. We have simply to take it as it stands and remain satisfied with it. In case we somehow fail to do this, we just leave it alone, and go somewhere else to seek our own enlightenment. The monk could not see where Jōshu was, and he went further on and remarked, "This is still a discrimination!" The discrimination in point of fact is on the monk's side and not on Jōshu's. Hence "the Honored One" now turns into "a worthless fellow."

As I said before, the phrase "All in One and One in All" is not to be analyzed first to the concepts "One" and "All," and the preposition is not then to be put between them; no discrimination is to be exercised here, but one is just to accept it and abide with it, which is really no-abiding at all. There is nothing further to do. Hence the master's striking or calling names. He is not indignant, nor is he short-tempered, but he wishes thereby to help his disciples out of the pit which they have dug themselves. No amount of argument avails here, no verbal persuasion. Only the master knows how to turn them away from a logical impasse and how to open a new way for them; let them, therefore, simply follow him. By following him they all come back to their Original Home.

When an intuitive or experiential understanding of Reality is verbally formulated as "All in One and One in All," we have there the fundamental statement as it is taught by all the various schools of Buddhism. In the terminology of the Prajñā school, this is: *śūnyatā* ("emptiness") is *tathatā* ("suchness"), and *tathatā* is *śūnyatā: śūnyatā* is the world of the Absolute, and *tathatā* is the world of particulars. One of the commonest sayings in Zen is "Willows are green and flowers red" or "bamboos are straight and pine trees are gnarled." Facts of experience are accepted as they are; Zen is not nihilistic, nor is it merely positivistic. Zen would say that just because the bamboo is straight it is of Emptiness, or that just because of Emptiness the bamboo cannot be anything else but a bamboo and not a pine tree. What makes the Zen statements different from mere sense experience, however, is that Zen's intuition grows out of *prajñā* and not out of *jñā*.[10] It is from this point of view that when asked "What is Zen?" the master sometimes answers "Zen" and sometimes "Not-Zen."

We can see now that the principle of *sumiye* painting is derived from this Zen experience, and that directness, simplicity, movement, spirituality, completeness, and other qualities we observe in the *sumiye* class of Oriental paintings have organic relationship to Zen. There is no pantheism in *sumiye* as there is none in Zen.

There is another thing I must not forget to mention in this connection, which is perhaps the most important factor in *sumiye* as well as in Zen. It is creativity. When it is said that *sumiye* depicts the spirit of an object, or that it gives a form to what has no form, this means that there must be a spirit of creativity moving over the picture. The painter's business thus is not just to copy or imitate nature, but to give to the object something living in its own right. It is the same with the Zen master. When he says that the willow is green and the flower is red, he is not just giving us a description of how nature looks, but something whereby green is green and red is red. This

[10] *Prajñā* may be translated "transcendental wisdom," while *jñā* or *vijñā* is "relative knowledge." For a detailed explanation, see my *Studies in Zen Buddhism*, pp. 85 ff.

something is what I call the spirit of creativity. *Śūnyatā* is formless, but it is the fountainhead of all possibilities. To turn what is possible into an actuality is an act of creativity. When Tōsu is asked, "What is Dharma?" he answers, "Dharma"; when asked, "What is Buddha?" he answers "Buddha." This is by no means a parrotlike response, a mere echoing; all the answers come out of his creative mind, without which there is no Zen in Tōsu. The understanding of Zen is to understand what kind of mind this is. Yakusan's meeting with Rikō will illustrate this.[11]

Yakusan (Yao-shan, 751–834) was a great master of the T'ang era. When Rikō (Li Ao), governor of the province, heard of his Zen mastership, he sent for him to come to the capital. Yakusan, however, refused to come. This happened several times. Rikō grew impatient and came in person to see the master in his own mountain retreat. Yakusan was reading the sūtras and paid no attention whatever to the arrival of the governor. The attendant monk reminded the master of the fact, but he still kept on reading. Rikō felt hurt and remarked, "Seeing the face is not at all like hearing the name." By this he meant that the person in actuality was not equal to his reputation. Yakusan called out, "O Governor!" Rikō echoed at once, "Yes, Master." The master then said, "Why do you evaluate the hearing over the seeing?" The governor apologized and asked, "What is Tao?" Yakusan pointed up with his hand and then down, and said, "Do you understand?" Rikō said, "No, Master." Thereupon Yakusan remarked, "The clouds are in the sky and water in the jar." It is said that this pleased the governor very much.

Did Rikō really understand what Yakusan meant? Yakusan's is no more than a plain statement of the facts as they are, and we may ask, "Where is Tao?" Rikō was a great scholar and philosopher. He must have had some abstract conception of Tao. Could he so readily reconcile his view with Yakusan's? Whatever we may say about this, Yakusan and Tōsu and other Zen masters are all walking the same track. The artists are also required to strike it.

[29

[11] *Dentōroku* ("Transmission of the Lamp"), fasc. 14.

III

Zen and
the Study of Confucianism

P ARADOXICAL and ironical though it may seem, Zen, whose teaching is against all learning, all literary reconstruction, was the agency in Japan for encouraging the study of Confucianism—and, furthermore, for promoting the art of printing, not only of Buddhist books but also of Confucian and Shinto literature. The Kamakura (1185–1338) and the Ashikaga (1338–1568) periods are generally considered the dark ages of Japanese history; the fact is, they are far otherwise. During those times, the Zen monks were active in bringing Chinese culture into Japan and preparing the way for its assimilation later on. Indeed, what we now regard as particularly Japanese was in the process of hatching during those periods. In them we may trace the beginnings of *haiku, nō-gaku,*[1] theater, landscape gardening, flower arrangement, and the art of tea. Here I wish to confine myself to the development of Confucian study in Japan, as it was influenced by the Zen monks. To do this, it is advisable to say a word about the "Sung philosophy" in China.

Politically, the Sung was a troubled age in the history of China. The Middle Kingdom was constantly menaced from the North, so that it had to retreat southward, crossing the Huai, and finally in 1126 to submit to the domination of the Northern "barbarian" tribes. This marks the end of the Northern Sung (960–1126). The Southern Sung started (1127) when the Emperor Kao Tsung was enthroned at Lin-an, south of the

[1] An abstract of a Nō play, "Yama-uba," is given in Appendix II.

Yangtze River. This lasted until (1279) the Yüan invaders succeeded in completely overturning the steadily declining dynasty,
which had first been established by the Chao family more than
three hundred years before. In spite of the succession of these
politically eventful days, the Sung, both Northern and especially
Southern, left brilliant records in the world of thought and general culture. There were poets, artists, Confucian philosophers, and Buddhist thinkers, including Zen masters.

Philosophy achieved a phenomenal development in the South.
It seemed as if the original speculative impulse pent up during
the Han and succeeding dynasties, and more or less suppressed
by the powerful thought of India, burst out and asserted itself
in this period, even under the pressure of an alien power. The
result was the rise of a philosophy we may properly call "Chinese," in which all the trends of thought imported from abroad,
as well as those primarily native to China, were syncretized and
formulated on the basis of the Chinese mentality, and therefore
made more readily acceptable to it. The Sung philosophy is the
flower of the Chinese mind.

One powerful factor, at least, that helped to give such a fruitful stimulus to Chinese speculation was the teaching of Zen. Zen
is always stimulating and thought-provoking, because it goes
directly to the root of things regardless of superstructures. When
Confucianism turned into the mere study of ritual and the
practice of earthly morals, all scarcely more than textual criticism by schools of commentators, we can say that it was on the
verge of collapse and final death as a source of creative speculation. It required a new force to resuscitate it. Taoism, the rival
school of Chinese thought, was deeply buried under its own more
popular and superstitious framework. There was in it nothing
of intellectual vigor that would instill fresh blood into Confucianism. If Zen had failed to stir the depths of Chinese
psychology during the T'ang, the people of the Sung would
probably never have newly taken up their own philosophy and
pursued its reconstruction and further unfolding. Almost all the

thinkers of the Sung, at least once in their lives, betook themselves to the Zen monasteries. With whatever insight or no-insight they carried out of these institutions, they re-examined their own philosophy born of their own soil. The Sung philosophy is the outcome of their spiritual adventures. While denouncing Buddhism and the Buddhist way of thinking, they drank deeply from the Indian fountain presented to them in Zen.

The Zen monks, on the other hand, were students of Confucianism as well. As Chinese, they could be nothing else. The difference between Confucian scholars and Zen masters was that the Confucians based their philosophy on the native system, while the Zen Buddhists adhered to their own although they adopted the Confucian vocabulary. Indeed, they quite frequently expressed themselves in terms of Confucianism. It may be said that the difference between the two classes of mind lay in the placing of emphasis. The Zen monks interpreted the Confucian texts in the Indian fashion, so to speak—that is, more or less idealistically—and they were not averse to commenting on Buddhist literature from the Confucian point of view.

When these monks came to Japan, they brought both Zen and Confucianism. The Japanese monks who went over to China to study Zen brought back the same; that is, together with their own Zen books they filled their traveling cases with books on Confucianism and Taoism. While in China, they sat at the feet of the Zen-Confucian masters and learned much of both disciplines. And there were many such Chinese masters in the Sung areas, especially in Southern Sung.

I will not enter into too much detail in regard to the interrelationship of Zen with Confucianism and Taoism in China. Suffice it to state here that Zen is, in fact, the Chinese way of responding to Indian thought as represented by Buddhism and that, this being so, Zen, as it developed in the T'ang and later flourished in the Sung, could be nothing else but a reflection of Chinese mentality—by which I mean it was eminently practical and ethical. In this respect, there was every probability of Zen's taking on Confucian coloring. But in the beginning of Zen's history its philosophy was Indian, that is, Buddhistic, for there was nothing corresponding to it in the traditional teaching of Confucianism. And this was the element the later Confucian thinkers consciously or unconsciously wished to incorporate into their own system. In other words, Zen acquired its practicalness from Confucianism, whereas Confucianism absorbed through the teaching of Zen (though in some respects indirectly) the Indian habit of abstract speculation and finally succeeded in giving a metaphysical foundation to the teaching of Confucius and his followers. To do this, the Sung philosophers emphasized the utmost importance of the "Four Books" [2] in the study of Confucianism. They found in them some statements which could be elaborated for the establishment of their system. This naturally paved the way to a *rapprochement* between Zen and Confucianism.

It was thus natural for the Zen monks to become propagators of Confucianism in addition to being Buddhists. Strictly speaking, Zen has no philosophy of its own. Its teaching is concentrated on an intuitive experience, and the intellectual content of this experience can be supplied by a system of thought not necessarily Buddhistic. If the masters find it more expedient for some reason, they may build up their own philosophical structure not always in accordance with the traditional interpretation. Zen Buddhists are sometimes Confucianists, sometimes Taoists, or

[2] The Four Books are: (1) *Daigaku* (*Ta Hsüeh*), Great Learning; (2) *Chūyō* (*Chung Yung*), Doctrine of the Mean; (3) *Rongo* (*Lun Yü*), Confucian Analects; and (4) *Mōshi* (*Mêng-tzŭ*), Works of Mencius. The Great Learning and the Doctrine of the Mean were originally incorporated in the Record of Rites (*Li Chi*), one of the Five Canons (see n. 3). They are ascribed to Tzŭ-ssŭ, grandson of Confucius. They contain the gist of Confucian teaching and were taken up as such for the first time by the Sung scholars, one of whom, Chu-tzŭ (1130–1200), wrote commentaries on them. Confucius' Analects, compiled by his disciples after his death, record the master's sayings, conduct, talks with his disciples, etc. Mencius (372–289 B.C.), one of the most prominent early advocates of Confucianism, was an eloquent and astute thinker of his day.

sometimes even Shintoists; Zen experience can also be explained by Western philosophy.

In the fourteenth and the fifteenth centuries, the "Five Mountains," that is, the five Zen monasteries in Kyoto, were the publishing headquarters of the Confucian texts, to say nothing about the Zen books. Some of these earlier texts, including those of the thirteenth century, both Buddhist and Confucian, are still obtainable and among the most highly prized woodcut prints in the Far East.

Not only did the Zen monks edit and print the textbooks of Buddhism and Confucianism, but they compiled books for popular education. These they used in their monasteries, where people crowded who were desirous of improving their knowledge and culture. The term *terakoya* thus came in vogue. (*Tera* means "Buddhist temple," *ko* "children," and *ya* "house.") The *Terakoya* system was the only institution of popular education during the feudal ages of Japan, until it was replaced by the modern system after the Restoration in 1868.

The activities of the Zen monks were not confined to the central parts of Japan; they were invited by the provincial lords to look after the education of their vassals and retainers. They were Buddhist-Confucianists. As one of the most notable examples we mention a Zen monk, Keian (1427–1508), who went to Satsuma, the southwestern province in Kyūshū. His special study was the "Four Books," which he explained according to the commentaries of Shūshi (Chu Hsi in Chinese). But, being a Zen monk, he did not forget to emphasize his own teaching in connection with the Confucian philosophy. The study of Mind was the guiding spirit of his discipline. He also lectured on the *Shu Ching,* one of the "Five Canons," [3] which contains the ethical

[3] The Five Canons are: (1) *Yekikyō* (*I Ching*), Book of Changes; (2) *Shikyō* (*Shih Ching*), Book of Odes; (3) *Shokyō* (*Shu Ching*), Book of Annals; (4) *Shunjū* (*Ch'un Ch'iu*), Spring and Autumn; (5) *Raiki* (*Li Chi*), Record of Rites. The Book of Changes is a very strange and enigmatic book. It may be regarded as containing the old Chinese way of thinking based

edicts of the ancient rulers of China. He left in Satsuma an en-
during spiritual influence. Among his distant disciples the name
of Shimadzu Nisshinsai (1492–1568) stands out most promi-
nently. Although he was not taught by Keian himself, his mother
and his teachers were personally acquainted with Keian, and all
their families were great admirers of the monk-scholar. Nisshinsai was born of the Shimadzu family, and his eldest son was
later adopted by the main family and came to rule the three
provinces of Satsuma, Ōsumi, and Hyūga, in the southwestern
part of Japan. Nisshinsai's moral influence spread, through his
son, all over the feudal estate under his jurisdiction. Until the
Restoration of 1868, he was rightly honored by the people as
one of the greatest figures among them.

Of the Zen masters of the "Five Mountains," mention may be
made of Musō the National Teacher (1275–1351), Genye
(1269–1352), Kokwan Shiren (1278–1346), Chūgan Yenge-
tsu (1300–75), Gidō Shūshin (1321–88), and others, all of
whom furthered the study of the Confucian classics in accordance
with the spirit of Zen Buddhism. The emperors and the
shōguns also followed the example of the Zen masters. They
were earnest students of Zen and at the same time attended
their lectures on Confucianism. The Emperor Hanazono (reigned
1308–17) was a sincere scholar of the Sung school of Chinese
philosophy and an earnest follower of Zen, in which he went far
beyond dilettantism. The admonition he left for his successor is
a remarkable document of royal wisdom. His statue, in the at-

on the dualistic principles of *yin* (female) and *yang* (male). It also contains
ten expository essays ascribed to Confucius. The Book of Odes is a collection
of popular songs as well as hymns on the state occasions prevailing from
about the fifteenth century B.C. down to the third B.C. The Book of Annals
is a kind of political history beginning with the eras of Yao (legendarily
reigning 2357–2255 B.C.) and Shun (2255–2205 B.C.) down to the Chou
dynasty (1122–255 B.C.). The Spring and Autumn is another political history,
first compiled by the historians of the state of Lu and revised by Confucius
and completed in 478 B.C. The Record of Rites contains rites in practice
from toward the end of the Chou dynasty down to 140 B.C. The Record in
current circulation has 47 sections, comprising the Great Learning, the Doctrine of the Mean, and others.

tire of a Zen monk sitting cross-legged in serene dignity, is still preserved in his own room at Myōshinji, where he used to sit in meditation. His "journal" is important historical source material. And his residence, which was given to his Zen teacher, Kwanzan (1277–1360), became the foundation of the present Myōshinji, the most powerful branch of Rinzai Zen, in the western part of Kyoto.

I may add here that even in the early days of the Tokugawa Shogunate, that is, at the beginning of the seventeenth century, the Confucian scholars used to shave their heads like Buddhist priests. From this fact we gather that the study of Confucianism was kept up among the Buddhists, especially the Zen monks, and even when the study came to be pursued independently among the intellectuals, its professors simply followed the old custom.

In connection with this essay, the writer wishes to add a few remarks about the part played by Zen in the cultivation of the nationalistic spirit during the Kamakura and the Ashikaga periods. Theoretically speaking, Zen has nothing to do with nationalism. As long as it is a religion, its mission has universal validity, and its field of applicability is not limited to any one nationality. But from the point of view of history it is subject to accidents and particularization. When Zen first came to Japan, it became identified with persons steeped in Confucianism and patriotic spirit, and Zen naturally took their color unto itself; that is to say, Zen was not received in Japan in its pure form, free of the effect of all accidents of place and time. Not only that, the Japanese followers themselves were willing to take Zen with everything that came along with it, until later the accidentals were separated from the body to which they were attached and came to establish themselves independently, even in defiance of their original association. A description of this process in the history of Japanese thought does not belong here, but I wish to refer to it more or less tentatively in tracing it back to the Chinese thought-movement.

As I said elsewhere, the culmination of Chinese intellectuality is found in the philosophy of Shūshi or Chu Hsi (1130–1200), who flourished mainly in the Southern Sung. He was probably the greatest among Chinese thinkers who tried to systematize Chinese thought along the lines of the psychology of the people. There were greater philosophers before him among his countrymen, but their thought moved along the Indian line of speculation, somewhat against their native trends. For this reason their philosophy did not influence the people so directly as did that of the Southern Sung. It is no doubt true that the Southern Sung school could not have had its existence without its Buddhist predecessors. We must now see how the so-called "Science of the Tao" developed in Sung, for this will help us to understand Zen's specific influence on the thought and feeling of the Japanese people.

There are two original currents of Chinese thought, Confucianism and pure Taoism, that is, the Taoism not colored by popular beliefs and superstitions. Confucianism represents the practicality or positivism of Chinese mentality, whereas Taoism represents its mystic and speculative trends. When Buddhism was brought to China in the early Latter Han Dynasty (A.D. 64), it found a real associate in the thought of Lao-tzŭ and Chuang-tzŭ. In the beginning, Buddhism was not much active in Chinese thought; its adherents occupied themselves mostly with translating its texts into Chinese, and the people did not know exactly how to take it into their system of thoughts and beliefs. But through the translations they must have realized that there was something very deep, very inspiring, in the philosophy of Buddhism. Since the second century, when the *Prajñāpāramitā Sūtras* [4] were first rendered into Chinese, thinkers were deeply impressed by them and took up their study in all seriousness. While they could not

---

[4] The first Chinese translation of parts of this important Mahāyāna text was completed in A.D. 179 by Lokarakṣa, from ancient Bactria (now northern Afghanistan), who came to Loyang, China, in 147.

clearly grasp the idea of *śūnyatā,* "emptiness," they found it somewhat akin to the Lao-tzuan idea of *wu,* "nothingness."

During the Six Dynasties (386–587), when the study of Taoism carried the day to the extent that the Confucian texts themselves were interpreted in the light of Taoism, Kumārajīva came from a western kingdom to China in 401 and translated a number of the Mahāyāna sūtras. He was not only a brilliant translator but a great original thinker who shed much light on the understanding of the Mahāyāna, and his Chinese disciples busied themselves in developing his ideas in the way most adapted to the mentality of their people. The San-lun (Sanron in Japanese) School of Buddhism thus came to be established in China by Chi-tsang [5] (549–623), who based his philosophy on the teaching of Nāgārjuna. It was a wonderful system of thought, rising for the first time in the land of Confucius and Lao-tzŭ. But we can say that the author of the school was still under the influence of Indian thought. He thought as Indians did and not necessarily in the Chinese fashion. He was no doubt a Chinese Buddhist, but a Buddhist scholar; if this were possible, he thought as a Buddhist and not as a Chinese.

The San-lun School was followed by the T'ien-t'ai (Tendai), Wei-shih (Yuishiki), and the Hua-yen (Kegon) in the Sui and the T'ang dynasties. [6] The T'ien-t'ai is based on the *Saddharmapuṇḍarīka,* the Wei-shih on the idealistic teaching of Asaṅga and Vasubandhu, and the Hua-yen on the philosophy of the infinite as expounded in the *Avataṃsaka.* The last was the culmination of Chinese Buddhist thought. It demonstrates the height of

---

[5] Kichizō in Japanese. He is also known as Chia-hsiang Ta-shih (Kajō Daishi).

[6] The T'ien-t'ai started with Hui-wên (Yemon, 550–77), Hui-ssŭ (Yeshi, 514–77), and Chih-i (Chigi, 538–97). The Wei-shih began its movement with Hsüan-chuang (Genjō, 600–64), when he translated Vasubandhu's treatise on the philosophy of "Mind-only" (*Vijñānamātra*); and its great exponent was his chief disciple, K'uei-chi (Kiki, 632–82). The systematizer of the Hua-yen school was Fa-tsang (Hōzō, 643–712), whose great predecessors were T'u-shun (Tojun, 557–640) and Chih-yen (Chigon, 602–68).

religious speculation reached by Chinese Buddhist minds. It is the most remarkable thought system ever elaborated by people of the East. The *Avataṃsaka Sūtra,* including the *Daśabhūmika* and the *Gaṇḍavyūha,* is no doubt the climax of Indian creative imagination, which is utterly foreign to Chinese thinking and feeling, and it is really an intellectual feat of the Chinese Buddhists that this so completely strange imagination of the Indians could be intelligently and systematically digested. The philosophy of the Hua-yen School proves the depths of the Chinese religious consciousness, which revealed itself after centuries of Buddhist education and reflection. And this was really what stirred up the Chinese mind from its long slumber and gave it the strongest possible stimulus to bloom forth as the Sung philosophy.

While the Hua-yen School represented the intellectuality, so to speak, of the Chinese Buddhists, there was another school rising to power along with it and taking a stronger hold of their minds— which was Zen (*Ch'an* in Chinese). Zen appealed partly to the empirical proclivity of Chinese mentality and partly to its craving for mysticism. Zen despised learning of letters and upheld the intuitive mode of understanding, for its followers were convinced that this was the most direct and effective instrument with which to grasp ultimate reality. In fact, empiricism and mysticism and positivism can walk hand in hand quite readily. They all look for the facts of experience and are shy of building up an intellectual framework around them.

But as a social being man cannot remain content with mere experience; he wants to communicate it to his fellow beings— which means that intuition is to have its contents, its ideas, its intellectual reconstruction. Zen did its best to remain on its intuitive plane of understanding, and made the best use of imagery, symbols, and poetic tricks (not a very dignified term). When, however, it had to have recourse to intellection, it was a good friend of the Hua-yen philosophy. The amalgamation of Zen and Hua-yen (Kegon) philosophy, though by no means deliberately carried out, became most noticeable with Ch'êng-

kuan (Chōkwan, 738–838) and Tsung-mi (Shūmitsu, 780–841),
both of whom were great scholars of the Hua-yen School and at
the same time followers of Zen. It was through this approach
that Zen came to influence the Confucian thought of the Sung
scholars.

The T'ang dynasty thus prepared the way for the rise of the
Sung "Science of the Tao" (*tao-hsüeh*), which I consider to be
the most precious native product from the Chinese mental
crucible into which the Hua-yen, Zen, Confucianism, and Lao-
tzuanism were thrown together.

Chu Hsi (Shūki or Shūshi) had his predecessors: Chou
Tun-i (Shū Ton-i, 1017–73), Chang Hêng-ch'ü (Chō Ō-kyo,
1077–1135), and the Ch'êng (Tei) brothers, Ming-tao (Meidō,
1085–1139), and I-ch'uan (Isen, 1107–82). They all tried to
establish philosophy on a purely Chinese basis, as they found
it chiefly in the "Four Books"—the *Lun Yü*, the *Mêng-tzǔ*, the
Ta Hsüeh, and the *Chung Yung*—and also in the *I Ching*.[7]
That they all studied Zen and were indebted to it in the formula-
tion of their doctrine is seen from the fact that they place so
much significance on the experience of a sudden illumination
that will come to them when they have duly applied themselves
to the study of the classics or meditated on their meaning. In
their cosmogony or ontology, they set up as primordial substance *Wu-chi*, or *T'ai-chi*, or *T'ai-hsü*, which has a Buddhist ring.
Translated in terms of ethics, this principle is sincerity (*ch'êng*),
and the ideal of man's life consists in cultivating the virtue of
sincerity. For it is by this that the world is what it is; it is
by this that the male principle and the female principle originating in the "great limit" interact and enable the orderly growth
of all things. Sincerity is also called *li* (Reason) or *t'ien-li*
(Heavenly Reason).

The Sung philosophers have *ch'i* (*ki*) opposed to *li* (*ri*),
and this antithesis is unified in *t'ai-chi*, which is *wu-chi*. *Li* is the
Reason running through all things, impartially possessed by

7 See above, n. 2.

every one of them; without *li* nothing is possible, existences lose their being and are reduced to nonentity. *Ch'i* is a differentiating agency, whereby one Reason multiplies itself and produces a world of pluralities. *Li* and *ch'i* are thus interpenetrating and complementary.

The relation of *t'ai-chi* to *li* and *ch'i* is not very clear, except that it is the synthesis of the two principles; the Sung philosophy did not apparently wish to remain dualistic, which is probably due to the influence of the Hua-yen School of Buddhism. As to *t'ai-chi* itself, it is an ambiguous idea—it appears to be primordial matter, which is *wu-chi*, the "limitless"; the one is something "above matter" and the other is something "below matter," and how can that which is above become that which is below and *vice versa?* The same dilemma may be encountered in the case of *li* and *ch'i;* but in this respect the Sung philosophers were decidedly Chinese and had no inclination to follow the Buddhists, who did not hesitate to deny the materiality of the world and declare it and all things in it to be equally "empty" (*śūnya*). The Chinese mind always upheld a world of particular realities. Even when it closely approaches the Hua-yen, it stops short at materiality.

What is significant in the Sung philosophy of Chu Hsi, and what made it wield a great influence in China and Japan in the most practical way, is its view of history. It is the development of the idea dominating the *Spring and Autumn* (*Ch'un Ch'iu*), one of the great classical works compiled by Confucius. The work was written by the Master with a view to weigh morally the claims of the different states of his day, in a period known as "Warring States." China was then divided into several kingdoms, each trying to gain the upper hand; usurpers claimed to be transmitting the orthodox line of kingship; politics drifted along with the fancy of the rulers, as if the compass was lost. Confucius's idea of compiling annals of his time was to establish a universal ethical standard for all the future statesmen of his country. The *Spring and Autumn*, therefore, embodies the practical codes of ethics as they were illustrated by the events of history.

Chu Hsi followed the example of Confucius by compiling a history of China abridged from Ssŭ-ma Kuang's larger work.[8] In this he enunciated the great principle of propriety known as "Names and Parts" (*ming-fên*), which he thought ought to be made the governing principle of politics for all ages. The universe is governed by the laws of Heaven, so are human affairs; and these laws require of each of us to observe what is proper to him. He has a "name," he performs a certain "part" as he occupies a definite position in society, he is assigned a place where he is asked to render his service to a member of the group he belongs to. This network of social relationships is not to be ignored if the peace and happiness of its components are to be preserved and enhanced. The ruler has his proper duties to perform and his subjects theirs, parents and children have their well-defined obligations to each other, and so on. There ought to be no disturbance or usurpation of names, titles, and parts.

Chu Hsi was quite emphatic about what he called "names and parts," for the northern invaders were beating hard against the suzerainty of the Sung, the government dignitaries were uncertain how to deal with these encroaching enemies, and some of the former were even negotiating with the latter to carry out a policy of compromise. All these scenes going on before his eyes stirred Chu Hsi's patriotic and nationalistic spirit, and he upheld his teaching strongly, even at the risk of his life, against some of the politicians who were trying to induce the government to yield to the pressure of the northerners. Although his

---

[8] This monumental political history of China was compiled by the order of the Emperor Ying-tsung, of the Sung dynasty. Ssŭ-ma Kuang (1019–86) and his collaborators spent nineteen years of most assiduous scholarly labor upon it. The Emperor Shên-tsung, who succeeded Ying-tsung, was greatly pleased with the work and himself chose its title: *Tzŭ-chih T'ung-chien* (*Shichi Tsugan*), which may be popularly translated as "An Imperial Guidebook for a Successful Government."

philosophy was not able to save the Southern Sung from the invasion of the overwhelming Mongolian armies, it has enjoyed popular support ever since, not only in China but particularly in Japan during her feudal days.

One of the principal reasons the philosophy of Chu Hsi appealed so forcibly to Chinese psychology and came to be an officially sanctioned system of thought under successive dynasties was that in its framework it comprehended, even to the fulfillment of all conditions required by the Chinese way of thinking and feeling, all the representative orthodox thoughts that had played any part in the advancement of Chinese culture. Another reason: it was the philosophy of order dear to the Chinese heart and earnestly sought by the people in general. The Chinese are, no doubt, just as patriotic and full of nationalistic pride as any other nation; but they are more practical than sentimental, I imagine, more given up to positivism than to idealism. Their feet are glued to the earth. They may occasionally gaze at the stars, for those are very beautiful to look at, but they never forget that they cannot live even for a day separated from mother earth. They are, therefore, attracted more to Chu Hsi's philosophy of social order and utility than to his idealism and emotionalism. In this respect, the Chinese differ from the Japanese.

The following statement by Ch'êng Ming-tao (Tei Meidō) fitly describes the Chinese mentality:

"The reason the Tao is not made more manifest is the harmful interference of heathenism. This harm was more obvious in ancient times and more easily detected, but in these days it goes deeper and is harder to discern. Of old they [the followers of heathenism] took advantage of our ignorance and put us into a state of intellectual perplexity; but nowadays, saying that they have fathomed the mysteries of existence and know the reason of transformation, they appeal to our intelligence. But their speculation falls short of exploring particular things and performing social duties. They claim the universal applicability of their teaching, but in reality they go against the moral order of our ordinary life. They state that there is nothing in their system whose depths and subtleties have not been thoroughly examined, but they are unable to follow the path of the wise men of ancient days such as Yao and Shun."

By "heathenism" here is no doubt meant Buddhist thought, whose soaring flight, however high, is not suitable (those Sung philosophers think) for the consumption of their practical and socially-minded countrymen. This practicalness of the Sung philosophy came over to Japan on the same boat with Zen and with its nationalism, instilled into it by the militaristic spirit of Chu Hsi.

In those latter days of the Southern Sung there were many patriotic soldiers and statesmen and even Zen monks who volunteered as fighters against the aggressors. The spirit of nationalism penetrated into all the intellectual layers of society, and the Japanese Zen monks who visited China at the time came back also saturated with the spirit and the philosophy formulated by Chu Hsi and his school. Not only Japanese travelers returning from China but also the Chinese monks who came mostly from the Southern Sung to settle in Japan, brought along with their Zen the message of the Sung philosophers. Their combined efforts to propagate the philosophy of nationalism in Japan met with success in various quarters. The most notable instance was the epoch-making decision on the part of the Emperor Godaigo (reigned 1318–1339) and his court to restore to their own hands the power of government that had hitherto been entrusted to the Kamakura Bakufu. This imperial movement is said to have started from the inspiration which the Emperor and his ministry received from the study of Chu Hsi's history of China, and this study was carried on under the guidance of the Zen monks. It is also stated by the historians that Kitabatake Chikafusa's monumental work on the "Succession of the Imperial Rulers in Japan" (*Jinnō Shōtō Ki*) was a result of his pursuit of Chu Hsi. Chikafusa (1292-1354) was one of

[53

the great literary men who surrounded the Emperor Godaigo, and like his august master he was also a student of Zen.

Unfortunately, the Emperor Godaigo and his court failed to restore the imperial government to their own power. The political abnormality that followed, however, did not mean the weakening of the Confucian learning among the intellectual elements of Japan; for, assisted by the Zen monks of the Five Mountains and also by those in the provinces, it went on as vigorously as ever. During the Ashikaga period, the position of the Chu Hsi philosophy in upholding the orthodox doctrine of Confucianism was generally recognized, and the Zen monks began to pursue its study with more than zeal for sheer learning. They knew where their Zen was most needed and· where the Sung philosophy was most practically useful. Thus they became its real official propagators, and their influence radiated from Kyoto out to the remoter parts of the country.

This tendency on the part of the Zen scholars to differentiate Zen from the Sung philosophy as systematized by Chu Hsi and his school helped to define sharply the division of labor or the sphere of influence between Buddhism and Confucianism in Japan under the regime of the Tokugawa Shogunate. The practical spirit animating the Chinese way of thinking and feeling, especially recognizable in Chu Hsi, strongly appealed to the founders of the Tokugawa; for they were now most anxious to see peace and order quickly restored all over the country after so many years of war. For this purpose they found the Chinese teaching most eminently suited. The first official exponents of the Sung philosophy to use Chu Hsi's commentaries were Fujiwara Seikwa (1561–1619) and his disciple Hayashi Razan (1583–1657). Seikwa was originally a Buddhist monk, but he took so much to the study of the Confucian texts that he finally cast off his Buddhist robe, although he retained his shaven head for some time. After him and Razan, the study of Confucianism found its own followers, and the Zen monks were quite satisfied to confine themselves, at least officially, to the exposition of their own doctrine. We must not, however, forget to notice that, as in China, in Japan ever since the introduction of the Sung philosophy there had been a constant attempt to syncretize the three teachings, Confucianism, Buddhism, and Shintoism. One remarkable fact deserving notice at this point in the history of Japanese thought is that Shintoism, which is regarded as the official embodiment of the national spirit of Japan, did not assert itself as doctrinally independent of either Confucianism or Buddhism. The most probable reason for this is that Shintoism has no philosophy of its own to stand on; it is awakened to its own consciousness and existence only when it comes in contact with one of the others, and thereby learns how to express itself. It is true that Motoori Norinaga (1730–1801) and his disciples started a vigorous attack on Confucianism and Buddhism as imported doctrines not quite congenial to the Japanese way of living and feeling. Their patriotic conservatism, however, was instigated more by political than by philosophical motives. They no doubt helped a great deal to usher in the new Meiji regime, known as the Restoration of 1868. But from the purely philosophical point of view, it is highly problematical whether their religio-nationalistic dialectic had much of the universal element.

IV

Zen and the Samurai

I T M A Y B E considered strange that Zen has in any way been affiliated with the spirit of the military classes of Japan. Whatever form Buddhism takes in the various countries where it flourishes, it is a religion of compassion, and in its varied history it has never been found engaged in warlike activities. How is it, then, that Zen has come to activate the fighting spirit of the Japanese warrior?

In Japan, Zen was intimately related from the beginning of its history to the life of the samurai. Although it has never actively incited them to carry on their violent profession, it has passively sustained them when they have for whatever reason once entered into it. Zen has sustained them in two ways, morally and philosophically. Morally, because Zen is a religion which teaches us not to look backward once the course is decided upon; philosophically, because it treats life and death indifferently. This not turning backward ultimately comes from the philosophical conviction; but, being a religion of the will, Zen appeals to the samurai spirit morally rather than philosophically. From the philosophical point of view, Zen upholds intuition against intellection, for intuition is the more direct way of reaching the Truth. Therefore, morally and philosophically, there is in Zen a great deal of attraction for the military classes. The military mind, being—and this is one of the essential qualities of the fighter—comparatively simple and not at all addicted to philosophizing finds a congenial spirit in Zen. This is probably one of the main reasons for the close relationship between Zen and the samurai.

Secondly, Zen discipline is simple, direct, self-reliant, self-denying; its ascetic tendency goes well with the fighting spirit. The fighter is to be always single-minded with one object in view: to fight, looking neither backward nor sidewise. To go straight forward in order to crush the enemy is all that is necessary for him. He is therefore not to be encumbered in any possible way, be it physical, emotional, or intellectual. Intellectual doubts, if they are cherished at all in the mind of the fighter, are great obstructions to his onward movement, while emotionalities and physical possessions are the heaviest of encumbrances if he wants to conduct himself most efficiently in his vocation. A good fighter is generally an ascetic or stoic, which means he has an iron will. This, when needed, Zen can supply.

Thirdly, there is an historical connection between Zen and the military classes of Japan. The Buddhist priest Eisai [1] (1141–1215) is generally regarded as the first to introduce Zen into Japan. But his activities were more or less restricted to Kyoto, which was at the time the headquarters of the older schools of Buddhism. The inauguration of any new faith here was almost impossible owing to the strong opposition they offered. Eisai had to compromise to some extent by assuming a reconciliatory attitude towards the Tendai and the Shingon. Whereas in Kamakura, which was the seat of the Hōjō government, there were no such historical difficulties. Besides, the Hōjō regime was militaristic, as it succeeded the Minamoto family, who had risen against the Taira family and the court nobles. The latter had lost their efficacy as a governing power because of their over-refinement and effeminacy and consequent degeneration. The Hōjō regime is noted for its severe frugality and moral discipline and also for its powerful administrative and militaristic equipments. The directing heads of such a strong governing machine

[1] "Yōsai" is the proper pronunciation, I am told.

embraced Zen as their spiritual guide, ignoring tradition in the matter of religion; Zen thus could not help but exercise its varied influence in the general cultural life of the Japanese ever since the thirteenth century and throughout the Ashikaga and even in the Tokugawa period.

Zen has no special doctrine or philosophy, no set of concepts or intellectual formulas, except that it tries to release one from the bondage of birth and death, by means of certain intuitive modes of understanding peculiar to itself. It is, therefore, extremely flexible in adapting itself to almost any philosophy and moral doctrine as long as its intuitive teaching is not interfered with. It may be found wedded to anarchism or fascism, communism or democracy, atheism or idealism, or any political or economic dogmatism. It is, however, generally animated with a certain revolutionary spirit, and when things come to a deadlock—as they do when we are overloaded with conventionalism, formalism, and other cognate isms—Zen asserts itself and proves to be a destructive force. The spirit of the Kamakura era was in this respect in harmony with the virile spirit of Zen.

We have the saying in Japan: "The Tendai is for the royal family, the Shingon for the nobility, the Zen for the warrior classes, and the Jōdō for the masses." This saying fitly characterizes each sect of Buddhism in Japan. The Tendai and the Shingon are rich in ritualism and their ceremonies are conducted in a most elaborate and pompous style appropriate to the taste of the refined classes. The Jōdō appeals naturally more to plebeian requirements because of the simpleness of its faith and teaching. Besides its direct method of reaching final faith, Zen is a religion of will-power, and will-power is what is urgently needed by the warriors, though it ought to be enlightened by intuition.

The first Zen follower of the Hōjō family was Tokiyori (1227–63), who succeeded his father Yasutoki in the Hōjō regency. He invited to Kamakura the Japanese Zen masters in Kyoto and also some Chinese masters directly from the Southern

Sung, under whom he earnestly devoted himself to the study of Zen. He finally succeeded in mastering it himself, and this fact must have greatly encouraged all his retainers to imitate the example of their master.

Wu-an (Gottan; 1197–1276), the Chinese Zen master, under whom Tokiyori had his final enlightenment after twenty-one years of constant application, composed the following verse for his illustrious disciple:

I have no Buddhism about which I can this moment talk to
*   you,*
Nor have you any mind with which you listen to me hoping
*   for an attainment:*
Where there is neither preaching nor attainment nor mind,
There Śākyamuni has a most intimate interview with Bud-
*   dha Dīpankara.*

After a very successful regency, Tokiyori died in 1263, when he was only thirty-seven years old. When he realized that the time for departure was approaching he put on his Buddhist robe and sat on a straw seat of meditation. After writing his farewell song, he passed away quietly. The song reads:

The karma mirror raised high,
These thirty-seven years!
'Tis broken now with one hammer blow.
The Great Way remains ever serene!

Hōjō Tokimune (1251–84) was his only son, and when his father's mantle fell on him in 1268 he was only eighteen years old. He proved to be one of the greatest personages whom Japan has produced. Without him, indeed, the history of the country would not be what it actually is. He it was who most effectively crushed the Mongolian invasions, lasting several years—in fact during the whole length of his regency, 1268–84. It seems that Tokimune was almost a heaven-sent agent to stave off the direst calamity that might have befallen the nation, for he passed away with the termination of the greatest event in the history of Japan. His short life was simply and wholly devoted to this affair. He was then the body and soul of the whole nation. His indomitable spirit controlled the whole situation, and his body in the form of a most strongly consolidated army stood like a solid rock against the tumultuously raging waves of the Western Sea.

A still more wonderful thing about this almost superhuman figure, however, is that he had time and energy and aspiration to devote himself to the study of Zen under the masters from China. He erected temples for them, especially one for Bukkō Kokushi (1226–86), the National Teacher, which was meant also to console the departed spirits both Japanese and Chinese at the time of the Mongolian invasions. Tokimune's grave is still in this last-mentioned temple known as Engakuji. Some letters are still preserved which were sent to him by his several spiritual masters, and from these we know how studiously and vigorously he applied himself to Zen. The following story, though not quite authenticated, gives support to our imaginative reconstruction of his attitude towards Zen. Tokimune is said to have once asked Bukkō, "The worst enemy of our life is cowardice, and how can I escape it?"

Bukkō answered, "Cut off the source whence cowardice comes."

Tokimune: "Where does it come from?"

Bukkō: "It comes from Tokimune himself."

Tokimune: "Above all things, cowardice is what I hate most, and how can it come out of myself?"

Bukkō: "See how you feel when you throw overboard your cherished self known as Tokimune. I will see you again when you have done that."

Tokimune: "How can this be done?"

Bukkō: "Shut out all your thoughts."

Tokimune: "How can my thoughts be shut out of consciousness?"

Bukkō: "Sit cross-legged in meditation and see into the source of all your thoughts which you imagine as belonging to Tokimune."

Tokimune: "I have so much of worldly affairs to look after and it is difficult to find spare moments for meditation."

Bukkō: "Whatever worldly affairs you are engaged in, take them up as occasions for your inner reflection, and some day you will find out who this beloved Tokimune of yours is."

Something like the above must have taken place sometime between Tokimune and Bukkō. When he received definite reports about the Mongolian invaders coming over the sea of Tsukushi, he appeared before Bukkō the National Teacher and said:

"The greatest event of my life is at last here."

Bukkō asked, "How would you face it?"

Tokimune uttered "*Katsu!*" [2] as if he were frightening away all his enemies actually before him.

Bukkō was pleased and said, "Truly, a lion's child roars like a lion."

This was the courage with which Tokimune faced the over-

---

[2] "*Katsu!*" is pronounced "*Ho!*" in modern Chinese. In Japan when it is actually uttered by the Zen people, it sounds like "*Kātz!*" or "*Kwātz!*"—*ā* somewhat like *a* in "ah!" and *tz* like *tz* in German "*Blitz*." It is primarily a meaningless ejaculation. Since its first use by Baso Dōichi (Ma-tsu Tao-i, d. 788), from whom it may be said that Zen made its real start in China, it came to be extensively used by the Zen masters. Rinzai distinguishes four kinds of "*Kātz!*" (1) Sometimes the "*Kātz!*" is like the sword of Vajrarāja; (2) sometimes it is like the lion crouching on the ground; (3) sometimes it is like the sounding pole or a bundle of shading grass; (4) sometimes it serves no purpose whatever. The third kind of "*Kātz!*" may require an explanation. According to a commentator, the sounding pole is used by the burglar to find out whether or not a house is vacant, whereas a bundle of grass is used by the fisherman in a way to entice the fish. In Zen, what is most significant among these four "*Kātz!*" is the fourth, when the cry ceases to serve any kind of purpose, good or bad, practical or impractical. Someone remarks that Rinzai with all his astuteness omits a fifth "*Kātz!*" and then he proceeds to challenge us: "Do you know what that is? If you do, let me have it." See below, p. 145, n. 6.

whelming enemies coming over from the continent and successfully drove them back.

Historically speaking, however, it was not courage alone with
which Tokimune accomplished the greatest deed in the history
of Japan. He planned everything that was needed for this task,
and his ideas were carried out by the armies engaged in the
different parts of the country to resist the powerful invaders.
He never moved out of Kamakura, but his armies far out in the
western parts of Japan executed his orders promptly and effectively. This was extraordinary in those remote days, when there
was no speedier method of communication than relay horses.
Unless he had the perfect confidence of all his subordinates, it
was impossible for him to achieve such a feat.

Bukkō's eulogy of Tokimune at his funeral ceremony sums up
his personality: "There were ten wonders in his life, which
was the actualization of a Bodhisattva's great *praṇidhāna*
(vows): he was a filial son to his mother; he was a loyal
subject to his Emperor; he sincerely looked after the welfare of
the people; studying Zen he grasped its ultimate truth; wielding
an actual power in the Empire for twenty years, he betrayed no
signs of joy or anger; sweeping away by virtue of a gale the
threatening clouds raised by the barbarians, he showed no
feeling of elation; establishing the Engakuji monastery, he
planned for the spiritual consolation of the dead [both Japanese
and Mongolian [3]]; paying homage to the teachers and fathers

---

[3] The idea that both friends and enemies when dead are to be equally
treated with respect originated with Buddhism; for it teaches that we are all
of the same Buddha-nature and, while living in this world of particulars,
may espouse a variety of causes and principles, but these controversies vanish
when we pass from these individual existences to the other shore of transcendental wisdom. From the samurai point of view, the idea of loyalty and
sincerity is emphasized more than anything else: enemies are as faithful to
their cause as we are to ours, and this sentiment when genuine is to be
revered wherever and however displayed. Hence one monument dedicated to
the spirits of friends and foes. The Shimadzu family erected a great stone
monument at Kōya for all those fallen in the Korean war of 1591–98. This
was no doubt due to the spiritual influence of Shimadzu Nisshinsai (1492–

[of Buddhism] he sought for enlightenment—all this proves that his coming among us was solely for the sake of the Dharma. And then when he was about to depart, he managed to rise from his bed, put the Buddhist robe I gave him over his enfeebled body, and write his death song in full possession of his spirit. Such a one as he must be said to be really an enlightened being, or a Bodhisattva incarnate. . . ."

Tokimune was born great, no doubt, but his study of Zen must have helped him a great deal in his dealing with state affairs and also in his private life. His wife was also a devout Zen follower, and after his death she founded a nunnery in the hills just opposite the Engakuji.

When we say that Zen is for the warrior, this statement has a particular significance for the Kamakura period. Tokimune was not merely a fighting general, but a great statesman whose object was peace. His prayer offered to the Buddha at the time of a great religious ceremony performed at the Kenchōji under the leadership of the abbot, when an intimation of the first Mongolian invasion was received, runs as follows:

"The only prayer Tokimune, a Buddhist disciple, cherishes is: that the Imperial House continue in prosperity; that for a long time to come he [the Emperor] may be the guardian of the Buddha's doctrine; that the four seas remain unruffled without an arrow being shot; that all evil spirits be kept under subjection without a spearhead being unsheathed; that the masses be benefited by means of a benevolent administration so that they could enjoy a long life in happiness more than ever; that the darkness of the human mind be illumined by the torch of transcendental wisdom which should be raised high;

1568), who was one of the greatest scholar-barons of the feudal days. It is interesting to observe that Shimadzu Yoshihiro, one of Nisshinsai's grandsons, instituted for his ill-behaved subjects a novel form of punishment known as *tera-iri*, "entering into the Buddhist monastery." The offenders, while in the monastery, were made to study the Confucian texts under the personal supervision of the presiding monk. When they made decided progress in their understanding of the classics, they were restored to their original status.

that the needy be properly ministered to and those in danger be saved by the heart of compassion being widely open. May all the gods come and protect us, all the sages extending their quiet help, and every hour of the day may there be a great gathering of auspicious signs! . . ."

Tokimune was a great Buddhist spirit and a sincere follower of Zen, and it was due to his encouragement that Zen came to be firmly established in Kamakura and then in Kyoto and began to spread its moral and spiritual influence among the warrior classes. The constant stream of intercourse thus started between the Japanese and the Chinese Zen monks went even beyond the boundaries of their common cause. Books, paintings, porcelains, potteries, textiles, and many other objects of art were brought from China; even carpenters, masons, architects, and cooks came along with their masters. Thus the trading with China that later developed in the Ashikaga period had its initiation in the Kamakura.

Led by such strong characters as Tokiyori and Tokimune, Zen was auspiciously introduced into the Japanese life, especially into the life of the samurai. As Zen gained more and more influence in Kamakura it spread over to Kyoto, where it was strongly supported by Japanese Zen masters. The latter soon found strong followers among members of the Imperial family, headed by the emperors Godaigo, Hanazono, and others. Large monasteries were built in Kyoto, and masters noted for their virtue, wisdom, and learning were asked to be founders and successive abbots of such institutions. Shoguns of the Ashikaga regime were also great advocates of Zen Buddhism, and most generals under them naturally followed suit. In those days we can say that the Japanese genius went either to priesthood or to soldiery. The spiritual co-operation of the two professions could not help but contribute to the creation of what is now generally known as Bushido, "the way of the warrior."

At this juncture, let me touch upon one of the inner relationships that exist between the samurai mode of feeling and Zen.

What finally has come to constitute Bushido, as we generally understand it now, is the act of being an unflinching guardian-god of the dignity of the samurai, and this dignity consists in loyalty, filial piety, and benevolence. But to fulfill these duties successfully two things are needed: to train oneself in moral asceticism, not only in its practical aspect but in its philosophical preparation; and to be always ready to face death, that is, to sacrifice oneself unhesitatingly when occasion arises. To do this, much mental and spiritual training is needed.

There is a document that was very much talked about in connection with the Japanese military operations in China in the 1930's. It is known as the *Hagakure*,[4] which literally means "Hidden under the Leaves," for it is one of the virtues of the samurai not to display himself, not to blow his horn, but to keep himself away from the public eye and be doing good for his fellow beings. To the compilation of this book, which consists of various notes, anecdotes, moral sayings, etc., a Zen monk had his part to contribute. The work started in the middle part of the seventeenth century under Nabeshima Naoshige, the feudal lord of Saga in the island of Kyūshū. The book emphasizes very much the samurai's readiness to give his life away at any moment, for it states that no great work has ever been accomplished without going mad—that is, when expressed in modern terms, without breaking through the ordinary level of consciousness and letting loose the hidden powers lying further below. These powers may be devilish sometimes, but there is no doubt that they are superhuman and work wonders. When the unconscious is tapped, it rises above individual limitations. Death now loses its sting altogether, and this is where the samurai training joins hands with Zen.

To quote one of the stories cited in the *Hagakure:* Yagyū Tajima no kami Munenori was a great swordsman and teacher in the art to the Shogun of the time, Tokugawa Iyemitsu. One of the personal guards of the Shogun one day came to Tajima

---

[4] The full text was published at Tokyo: Kyōzaisha, 1937. 2 vols.

no kami wishing to be trained in swordplay. The master said, "As I observe, you seem to be a master of the art yourself; pray tell me to what school you belong, before we enter into the relationship of teacher and pupil."

The guardsman said, "I am ashamed to confess that I have never learned the art."

"Are you going to fool me? I am teacher to the honorable Shogun himself, and I know my judging eye never fails."

"I am sorry to defy your honor, but I really know nothing."

This resolute denial on the part of the visitor made the swordsmaster think for a while, and he finally said, "If you say so, that must be so; but still I am sure of your being master of something, though I know not just what."

"Yes, if you insist, I will tell you this. There is one thing of which I can say I am complete master. When I was still a boy, the thought came upon me that as a samurai I ought in no circumstances to be afraid of death, and ever since I have grappled with the problem of death now for some years, and finally the problem has entirely ceased to worry me. May this be what you hint at?"

"Exactly!" exclaimed Tajima no kami. "That is what I mean. I am glad I made no mistake in my judgment. For the ultimate secrets of swordsmanship also lie in being released from the thought of death. I have trained ever so many hundreds of my pupils along this line, but so far none of them really deserve the final certificate for swordsmanship. You need no technical training, you are already a master." [5]

The problem of death is a great problem with every one of us; it is, however, more pressing for the samurai, for the soldier, whose life is exclusively devoted to fighting, and fighting means death to fighters of either side. In feudal days nobody could

[5] Cf. Sec. V, below, where the Zen master Takuan's letter to Yagyū Tajima no kami on "Prajñā Immovable" is epitomized, pp. 95 ff. This letter is a remarkable document, for it definitely establishes a relationship between Zen and swordsmanship.

predict when this deadly encounter might take place, and the samurai worth his name was always to be on the alert. A warrior-writer of the seventeenth century, Daidōji Yūsan, therefore, writes in the beginning of his book called a "Primer of Bushido" as follows:

"The idea most vital and essential to the samurai is that of death, which he ought to have before his mind day and night, night and day, from the dawn of the first day of the year till the last minute of the last day of it. When this notion takes firm hold of you, you are able to discharge your duties to their fullest extent: you are loyal to your master, filial to your parents, and naturally can avoid all kinds of disasters. Not only is your life itself thereby prolonged, but your personal dignity is enhanced. Think what a frail thing life is, especially that of a samurai. This being so, you will come to consider every day of your life your last and dedicate it to the fulfillment of your obligations. Never let the thought of a long life seize upon you, for then you are apt to indulge in all kinds of dissipation, and end your days in dire disgrace. This was the reason why Masashige is said to have told his son Masatsura to keep the idea of death all the time before his mind."

The writer of this "Primer" has rightly given expression to what has been unconsciously going on in the mind of the samurai generally. The notion of death, on the one hand, makes one's thought extend beyond the limitations of this finite life, and, on the other hand, screws it up so as to take daily life seriously. It was, therefore, natural for every sober-minded samurai to approach Zen with the idea of mastering death. Zen's claim to handle this problem without appealing either to learning or to moral training or to ritualism must have been a great attraction to the comparatively unsophisticated mind of the samurai. There was a kind of logical relationship between his psychological outlook and the direct practical teaching of Zen.

Further, we read the following in the *Hagakure:* "Bushido

means the determined will to die. When you are at the parting of the ways, do not hesitate to choose the way to death. No special reason for this except that your mind is thus made up and ready to see to the business. Some may say that if you die without attaining the object, it is a useless death, dying like a dog. But when you are at the parting of the ways, you need not plan for attaining the object. We all prefer life to death, and our planning and reasoning will be naturally for life. If then you miss the object and are alive, you are really a coward. This is an important consideration. In case you die without achieving the object, it may be a dog-death—the deed of madness, but there is no reflection here on your honor. In Bushido honor comes first. Therefore, every morning and every evening, have the idea of death vividly impressed in your mind. When your determination to die at any moment is thoroughly established, you attain to perfect mastery of Bushido, your life will be faultless, and your duties will be fully discharged."

A commentator adds a verse by Tsukahara Bokuden: [6]

> For the samurai to learn
> There's one thing only,
> One last thing—
> To face death unflinchingly.

According to Nagahama Inosuke, as told in the *Hagakure:* "The essence of swordsmanship consists in giving yourself up altogether to the business of striking down the opponent. [As long as you are concerned about your own safety you can never win in the fight.] If the enemy, too, is ready to give his life to it, you are then well matched. The final outcome will depend on faith and fate." The commentary note on this reads: "Araki Matayemon [a great swordsman of the early Tokugawa era] gave this instruction to his nephew, Watanabe Kazuma, when they were about to engage in the deadly fight with their enemy:

[6] One of the greatest swordsmen, 1490–1572. See below for further information about him.

'Let the enemy touch your skin and you cut into his flesh; let him cut into your flesh and you pierce into his bones; let him pierce into your bones and you take his life!' In another place, Araki advises: 'When you are to measure swords with your enemy, be ready at all times to lay down your life before him. As long as you are in the least concerned with your escaping safely you are doomed.' "

Further, the *Hagakure* states: "The samurai is good for nothing unless he can go beyond life and death. When it is said that all things are of one mind, you may think that there is such a thing as to be known as mind. But the fact is that a mind attached to life and death must be abandoned, when you can execute wonderful deeds." That is to say, all things are accomplished when one attains a mind of "no-mind-ness" according to the great Zen master, Takuan, as quoted below. It is a state of mind which is no more troubled with the questions of death or of immortality.

Inasmuch as Tsukahara Bokuden was mentioned just now as one of those swordsmen who really understood the mission of the sword, not as a weapon of murder but as an instrument of spiritual self-discipline, let me mention here the two best-known incidents in his life:

When Bokuden was crossing Lake Biwa in a rowboat with a number of passengers, there was among them a rough-looking samurai, stalwart and arrogant in every possible way. He boasted of his skill in swordsmanship, saying that he was the foremost man in the art. The fellow passengers were eagerly listening to his blatant talk, while Bokuden was dozing as if nothing were going on about him. This irritated the braggart very much. He approached Bokuden and shook him, saying, "You also carry a pair of swords, why not say a word?" Answered Bokuden quietly, "My art is different from yours; it consists not in defeating others, but in not being defeated." This incensed the fellow immensely.

"What is your school then?"

"Mine is known as the *mutekatsu* school" (which means to defeat the enemy "without hands," that is, without using a sword).

"Why, then, do you yourself carry a sword?"

"This is meant to do away with selfish motives, and not to kill others."

The man's anger now knew no bounds, and he exclaimed in a most impassioned manner, "Do you really mean to fight me with no swords?"

"Why not?" was Bokuden's answer.

The braggart samurai called out to the boatman to row toward the nearest land. But Bokuden suggested that it would be better to go to the island farther off because the mainland might attract people who were liable to get somehow hurt. The samurai agreed. The boat headed toward the solitary island at some distance. As soon as they were near enough, the man jumped off the boat and drawing his sword was all ready for a combat. Bokuden leisurely took off his own swords and handed them to the boatman. To all appearances he was about to follow the samurai onto the island, when Bokuden suddenly took the oar away from the boatman and, pushing it against the land, gave a hard backstroke to the boat. Thereupon the boat made a precipitous departure from the island and plunged into the deeper water safely away from the man. Bokuden smilingly remarked, "This is my 'no-sword' school."

Another interesting and instructive anecdote is told of how Bokuden's mastery of the art really went beyond merely acquiring proficiency in swordplay. He had three sons, who were all trained in swordsmanship. He wanted to test their attainments. He placed a little pillow over the curtain at the entrance to his room, and it was so arranged that a slight touch on the curtain, when it was raised upon entering, would make the pillow fall right on one's head.

Bokuden called in the eldest son first. When he approached he noticed the pillow on the curtain, so he took it down, and after entering he placed it back in the original position. The second son was now called in. He touched the curtain to raise it, and as soon as he saw the pillow coming down, he caught it in his hands, and then carefully put it back where it had been. It was the third son's turn to touch the curtain. He came in brusquely, and the pillow fell right on his neck. But he cut it in two with his sword even before it came down on the floor.

Bokuden passed his judgment: "Eldest son, you are well qualified for swordsmanship." So saying, he gave him a sword. To the second son he said, "Train yourself yet assiduously." But the youngest son Bokuden most severely reproved, for he was pronounced to be a disgrace to his family.

Takeda Shingen (1521–73) and Uyesugi Kenshin (1530–78) were two great generals of the sixteenth century, when Japan was in a state of war within its own boundaries. The two are generally mentioned together, for their provinces—the one in the north and the other in central Japan—lay close together, and they had on several occasions to fight for supremacy. They were well matched as able soldiers and good rulers, and they were also students of Zen. When Kenshin once learned that Shingen was suffering very much from lack of salt for his people, he supplied his enemy from his own province, which, facing the Japan Sea, produced enough salt.[7] In one of the pitched battles at Kawanaka-jima, Kenshin grew impatient, it is said, at the slow progress of his army, and, wishing to decide at once the fate of the day, he personally rode into the camp of Shingen. Seeing the general

[7] The salt famine was caused in Shingen's province of Kai in this way. Kai is surrounded by mountains, and its people had to get their supply of salt from the southern district facing the Pacific Ocean. But Shingen was not on friendly terms with the feudal lords governing that district, and they contrived to withdraw the supply of salt from Kai. Uyesugi Kenshin of Echigo, who was also at war with Shingen, heard of it and was very much incensed over the cowardly attitude of those war barons of the Pacific coast. He thought that any fighting between them ought to be carried on on a fair basis, that is, on the battlefield. He then wrote to Shingen and asked if the latter would accept the needed substance from Echigo. Shingen naturally appreciated the generosity of his big-hearted rival in the north.

of the opposing force quietly sitting on a camp chair with a few of his guards, Kenshin drew his sword and let it fall squarely over the head of Shingen, saying, "What would you say at this moment?"—a usual Zen question. Shingen was not disturbed at all; answering, "A snowflake on the blazing stove," he warded off the threatening weapon with an iron fan which was at the time in his hand. The *mondo* probably never took place, but the story well illustrates how the two intrepid head-shaven warriors were Zen-men.

The way Kenshin came to study Zen in full earnest under Yekiwo was thus: When Yekiwo once gave his sermon on Bodhidharma's "I know not," [8] Kenshin was among the audience. He knew something of Zen and wished to test this monk. He appeared in the dress of an ordinary samurai indistinguishable from the rest, and waited for the opportunity, but the monk suddenly turned toward Kenshin and demanded, "O Lord General! What is the meaning of Dharma's 'I know not'?" Kenshin was taken by surprise and did not know what to say. Thereupon Yekiwo continued, "O Lord General, why not give me an answer today, when you talk so glibly about Zen on all other occasions?" [9]

[8] *Zen Essays*, I, p. 187.

[9] Date Masamune's interview with his Zen monk took place in the following manner. Masamune, whose poems on Mount Fuji are quoted elsewhere (pp. 332 f.), was a great student of Zen. He wished to have a good abbot for the Zen temple where his ancestral spirits were enshrined, and a certain monk residing in an insignificant country temple was recommended to him. Wishing to test his attainment, he invited the monk to his castle in Sendai. The monk, whose name was Rin-an, accepted the invitation, and on the day agreed upon he came up to the city. He was at once ushered into Lord Masamune's residence. After walking through a long corridor, he was told that the Lord was waiting in one of the adjoining rooms. He opened the sliding door to enter the room, but nobody was there. So, passing through it, he went into another room at the back of it. Still nobody greeted him. Feeling this strange, he proceeded further on. When he opened the door, Lord Masamune unexpectedly welcomed him with a drawn sword, with which he seemed ready to strike the monk, saying, "What would you say at this moment of life and death?" Rin-an seemed not at all frightened at this most extraordinary way of greeting on the part of his Lord. He lost no time in stepping forward underneath the sword and, taking hold of Masamune's waist, gave him a severe shaking. The great war-god and the lord of the entire northeastern provinces

Kenshin's pride gave way. He now began to study Zen most seriously under the leadership of this monk, who used to tell him, "If you are really desirous of mastering Zen, it is necessary for you once to give up your life and to plunge right into the pit of death."

Kenshin later left the following admonition for his retainers: "Those who cling to life die, and those who defy death live. The essential thing is the mind. Look into this mind and firmly take hold of it, and you will understand that there is something in you which is above birth-and-death and which is neither drowned in water nor burned by fire. I have myself gained an insight into this *samādhi* and know what I am telling you. Those who are reluctant to give up their lives and embrace death are not true warriors."

Shingen also made reference to Zen and death in his "Constitution": "Pay proper reverence to the gods and the Buddha. When your thoughts are in accord with the Buddha's, you will gain more power. If your domination over others issues from your evil thoughts, you will be exposed, you are doomed. Next, devote yourselves to the study of Zen. Zen has no secrets other than seriously thinking about birth-and-death."

From these statements we can see unmistakably that there is an inner necessary relationship between Zen and the warrior's life. This is readily explained also from the behavior of the Zen masters themselves, who sometimes even seem to make sport of death. Shingen's Zen teacher was Kwaisen, abbot of Yerin-ji, in the province of Kai. After Shingen's death, the

of Japan then exclaimed, "What a dangerous trick you play!" Pushing him away, the monk retorted, "O this pretentious man!"

In olden times, many such encounters took place between Zen monks and feudal lords who wanted personally and in a realistic manner to test the monks with regard to their *dhyāna* practice and understanding of Zen. Being warriors who had to face death any moment, even in their supposedly peaceful home life, they were to be trained in this objectively and not scholastically. They did not want philosophy or religion so called, they wanted only some practical guide immediately effective in their professional life. Zen was the very thing they needed.

monastery was besieged by the soldiers of Oda Nobunaga on
the third of April, 1582, because the abbot refused to give up
Nobunaga's enemies, who had taken refuge in it. The soldiers
forced all the monks, including Kwaisen himself, to go up to
the top story of the monastery gate. The plan was to burn the
recalcitrants alive by setting the whole edifice on fire. The monks
headed by the abbot quietly gathered and sat cross-legged, taking
their seats in due order in front of the Buddha image. The
abbot gave his last sermon in his usual manner, saying, "We
are now encircled by the flames, and how would you revolve
your Wheel of the Dharma at this critical moment? Let each
one of you say a word." Thereupon, each expressed himself
according to his light of understanding. When all were finished,
the abbot gave his view and all entered into the fire-*samādhi*.
The abbot's words were these:

> *For a peaceful meditation, we need not to go to the mountains*
> *   and streams;*
> *When thoughts are quieted down, fire itself is cool and re-*
> *   freshing.*

The Japan of the sixteenth century, from a certain point of
view, produced many fine specimens of humanity. The country
was torn to pieces, as it were, politically and socially. All over
Japan the feudal lords were at war with one another. The
masses must have suffered very much, but this deadly compe-
tition for military and political supremacy among the soldier
classes helped to strain the mental and moral powers to the
utmost in every possible way. Virility asserted itself in various
departments of life. We can say that most of the virtues composing Bushido were formed in this period, and that Shingen
and Kenshin were typical representatives of the samurai-lords.
They both were personally brave and never flinched in the face
of death; they were wise and thoughtful and resourceful not only
in war but in governing the people under them; they were not
merely fighters, ignorant and callous, they were accomplished in

literature and highly religious. It is interesting that both Shingen and Kenshin were great Buddhists. Shingen's secular name is Harunobu and Kenshin's Terutora, but they are better known by their Buddhist titles. They were both educated in youth at Buddhist monasteries, and they had their heads shaven in their middle years, calling themselves "Nyūdo" [10] of Buddhism. Kenshin was a celibate and vegetarian like the Buddhist monks.

Like most Japanese of culture, they loved Nature and composed poems both in Japanese and in Chinese. One of the poems Kenshin wrote while engaged in a campaign in the neighboring provinces, reads in substance:

The bracing frosty autumnal air descends upon the soldiers in bivouac.
The night is advancing, the wild geese in orderly formation are seen flying in the moonlight.
The mountains of Ecchū are silhouetted over against the dreamy waves of Noto Bay—
What a splendid view this is, and how entranced I am!
Albeit that we are far away from the people at home, who may be thinking of our expedition [beneath the same moonlight].

Shingen's appreciation of Nature was by no means inferior to that of his rival in Echigo. When he once visited a Buddhist temple in the remoter part of his province, where Acala-vidyā-rāja (Fudō Myōō) was enshrined, the abbot of a monastery nearby requested him to pass by it on his way home. Shingen first declined the invitation, saying that he was busily preparing for a campaign taking place in a few days and would not have time to call on the abbot just now, and he added that when he came back from the engagement, he would surely visit the monastery. But the abbot (who by the way was the one who

[10] Literally, "entering the path," that is, the spiritual path or the Buddhist life.

later allowed himself to be burned alive in the hands of Oda Nobunaga's soldiers) insisted: "The cherries are just beginning to bloom, and I have already set up a fine seat for you where you can enjoy the glorious spring. I hope you will not fail to appreciate the flowers."

Shingen acquiesced: "It would not do to set my face against the cherries, and then I ought also to mind the pressing invitation of the abbot."

In appreciation of the fine opportunity to enjoy the flowers and an unworldly conversation with the abbot, Shingen composed the following verse in Japanese:

> *If I had not had this invitation from my friend,*
> *How greatly I should have missed this magnificent sight of*
>   *the cherry blossoms!*
> *The monastery might be found all swathed in snow next*
>   *spring*
> *When I proposed to visit it.*[11]

Such a disinterested enjoyment of Nature as shown by Shingen and Kenshin, even in the midst of warlike activities, is known as *fūryū*, and those without this feeling of *fūryū* are classed among the most uncultured in Japan. The feeling is not merely aesthetical, it has also a religious significance. It is perhaps the same mental attitude that has created the custom among cultured Japanese of writing a verse in either Japanese or Chinese at the moment of death. The verse is known as the "parting-with-life verse." The Japanese have been taught and

[11] The love of the cherry blossoms among the Japanese seems to be their second nature. There was once, in the Koishikawa dungeon in the days of the Tokugawa regime, a woman prisoner who was destined to be executed before the spring. She used to look out from her window, and, observing a cherry-tree, she wished to see it bloom. When the sentence was given, she expressed her intense desire to see the tree in bloom before she parted forever from this earth. The jailer was a kind-hearted man who understood *fūryū*, and he granted her last wish. It is said that the woman met her death in the happiest spirit. The cherry came to be known by her name, Asatsuma.

trained to be able to find a moment's leisure to detach themselves from the intensest excitements in which they may happen
to be placed. Death is the most serious affair absorbing all one's
attention, but the cultured Japanese think they ought to be able
to transcend it and view it objectively. The custom of leaving a
farewell song, though not necessarily observed universally by
the cultured even in feudal days, started in all likelihood in the
Kamakura period with the Zen monks and their followers. When
the Buddha passed into Nirvāna, he had his disciples about
him and gave them his farewell exhortation. This must have
been imitated by the Chinese Buddhists, especially by the Zen
Buddhists, who left instead of a farewell instruction for their
followers an expression of their own views of life.

Takeda Shingen's farewell words were a quotation from
Zen literature: "It is largely left to her own natural bodily perfection, and she has no special need to resort to artificial coloring
and powdering in order to look beautiful." This refers to the
absolute perfection of Reality, from which we all come and to
which we all return and in which we all are; a world of multitudes passes away and comes again, but what is at the back
of it always retains its perfect beauty unchangingly.

Uyesugi Kenshin composed his own verses, the one in
Chinese and the other in Japanese, thus:

Even a life-long prosperity is but one cup of sake;
A life of forty-nine years is passed in a dream;
I know not what life is, nor death.
Year in year out—all but a dream.

Both Heaven and Hell are left behind;
I stand in the moonlit dawn,
Free from clouds of attachment.

Following are accounts of the deaths of the Kamakura warriors as recorded in the *Taiheiki* (compiled late in the fourteenth century), which will clarify, side by side with those of

the Yerinji monks, the influence of Zen on Bushido, especially in regard to their attitude toward death.

Among the retainers of Hōjō Takatoki, who was the last of the Hōjō family, there was one Shiaku Shinsakon Nyūdo, not very high in the official rank of the samurai hierarchy of Kamakura. When he was about to commit suicide to follow his master, whose destiny was going to be sealed, he called in his eldest son, Saburozaemon, and said to him: "Kamakura is doomed, as it is surrounded by enemies on all sides, and I am going to share the fate of the master as his loyal follower. But you are still young and have not yet been in active service and are not so intimately related to the master as I have been. You manage to escape the approaching tragedy, and after saving your life you must become a monk and serve the Buddha and look after the spiritual welfare of us all. Nobody will blame you for doing this."

Saburozaemon, however, showed no inclination to follow his father's rational advice, for he said: "Even though I have not yet been actively and personally connected with our master, as your son I have been brought up under the benevolent protection of his grace. If I already followed the life of monkhood, it would be a different matter. Having been born into the family of a samurai, how can I leave you and our master and save myself to become a monk? No shame is greater than this. If you are to share the destiny of our master, let me be your guide to the next world." Even before he finished his last sentence, he disemboweled himself and gave up the ghost.

His brother Shiro, observing this, hastily prepared to follow his example. But the father Nyūdo stopped him and said, "Do not be so hasty. You must follow order and wait for me." Shiro put his dagger back into its scabbard and sat meekly before his father, waiting the latter's further command. The father now told him to bring him a chair. He sat in it cross-legged in the fashion of a Zen monk, and quietly making ink dipped his brush into it and wrote his song of death on a piece of paper:

Holding forth this sword,
I cut vacuity in twain;
In the midst of the great fire,
A stream of refreshing breeze!

When he finished writing, he committed suicide like the brave samurai that he was, and Shiro completed the deed by cutting off his father's head in accordance with the samurai code of honor. As to himself, using the same sword he pierced his own body with it up to the hilt and fell forward on the ground dead.

At the time of the Hōjō downfall, there was another Zen warrior called Nagasaki Jirō Takashige. He called on his Zen master, who also happened to be the teacher of Hōjō Takatoki, and asked, "How should a brave warrior behave at a moment like this?" The Zen teacher at once said, "Go straight forward wielding your sword!" The warrior at once perceived what it meant. He fought most gallantly until, exhausted, he fell before his master, Takatoki.

This was indeed the kind of spirit Zen cultivated among its warrior followers. Zen did not necessarily argue with them about immortality of the soul or righteousness or the divine way or ethical conduct, but it simply urged going ahead with whatever conclusion rational or irrational a man has arrived at. Philosophy may safely be left with intellectual minds; Zen wants to act, and the most effective act, once the mind is made up, is to go on without looking backward. In this respect, Zen is indeed the religion of the samurai warrior.

"To die *isagi-yoku*" is one of the thoughts very dear to the Japanese heart. In some deaths, if this characteristic is present, crimes committed by the offenders are judged even charitably. *Isagi-yoku* means "leaving no regrets," "with a clear conscience," "like a brave man," "with no reluctance," "in full possession of mind," and so on. The Japanese hate to see death met irresolutely and lingeringly; they desire to be blown away like the cherries before the wind, and no doubt this Japanese attitude toward death must have gone very well with the teaching of Zen. The Japanese may not have any specific philosophy of life, but they have decidedly one of death, which may sometimes appear to be that of recklessness. The spirit of the samurai deeply breathing Zen into itself propagated its philosophy even among the masses. The latter, even when they are not particularly trained in the way of the warrior, have imbibed his spirit and are ready to sacrifice their lives for any cause they think worthy. This has repeatedly been proved in the wars Japan has so far had to go through. A foreign writer [12] on Japanese Buddhism aptly remarks that Zen is the Japanese character.

---

[12] This is either from Sir George Sansom's book on Japan or from the late Sir Charles Eliot's book on Buddhism. It is possible, however, that I got it from one of the conversations I had with Dr. Eliot while he was still alive, when he frequently visited Kyoto. (Cf. below, pp. 345 f.)

V

Zen and Swordsmanship

I

1

"THE SWORD is the soul of the samurai": therefore, when the samurai is the subject, the sword inevitably comes with him. The samurai who wishes to be faithful to his vocation will have first of all to ask himself the question: How shall I transcend birth and death so that I can be ready at any moment to give up my life if necessary for my Lord? This means exposing himself before the enemy's swordstroke or directing his own sword toward himself. The sword thus becomes most intimately connected with the life of the samurai, and it has become the symbol of loyalty and self-sacrifice. The reverence universally paid to it in various ways proves this.

The sword has thus a double office to perform: to destroy anything that opposes the will of its owner and to sacrifice all the impulses that arise from the instinct of self-preservation. The one relates itself to the spirit of patriotism or sometimes militarism, while the other has a religious connotation of loyalty and self-sacrifice. In the case of the former, very frequently the sword may mean destruction pure and simple, and then it is the symbol of force, sometimes devilish force. It must, therefore, be controlled and consecrated by the second function. Its conscientious owner is always mindful of this truth. For then destruction is turned against the evil spirit. The sword comes to be identified with the annihilation of things that lie in the way of peace, justice, progress, and humanity. It stands for all that is desirable for the spiritual welfare of the world at large. It is now the embodiment of life and not of death.

Zen speaks of the sword of life and the sword of death, and it is the work of a great Zen master to know when and how to wield either of them. Mañjuśrī carries a sword in his right hand and a sūtra in his left. This may remind us of the prophet Mohammed, but the sacred sword of Mañjuśrī is not to kill any sentient beings, but our own greed, anger, and folly. It is directed toward ourselves, for when this is done the outside world, which is the reflection of what is within us, becomes also free from greed, anger, and folly. Acala (Fudō Myōō) also carries a sword, and he will destroy all the enemies who oppose the practice of the Buddhist virtues. Mañjuśrī is positive, Acala is negative. Acala's anger burns like a fire and will not be put down until it burns up the last camp of the enemy: he will then assume his original features as the Vairocana Buddha, whose servant and manifestation he is. The Vairocana holds no sword, he is the sword itself, sitting alone with all the worlds within himself. In the following *mondo,* "the one sword" signifies this sword:

Kusunoki Masashige (1294–1336) came to a Zen monastery at Hyōgo when he was about to meet the overwhelming army of Ashikaga Takauji (1305–1358) at the Minatogawa, and asked the master, "When a man is at the parting of the ways between life and death, how should he behave?" Answered the master, "Cut off your dualism, and let the one sword stand serenely by itself against the sky!" [1] This absolute "one sword" is neither the sword of life nor the sword of death, it is the sword from which this world of dualities issues and in which they all have their being, it is the Vairocana Buddha himself. You take hold of him, and you know how to behave where ways part.

The sword here represents the force of intuitive or instinctual directness, which unlike the intellect does not divide itself, blocking its own passageway. It marches onward without looking backward or sideways. It is like Chuang-tzŭ's dissecting knife that cuts along the joints as if they were waiting to be separated.

---

[1] Literally, "Cut off two heads, and let one sword stand cold against the sky!"

Chuang-tzǔ would say then: The joints separate by themselves, and then the knife, even after many years of use, is as sharp as when it first came from the hands of the grinder. The One Sword of Reality never wears out after cutting up ever so many victims of selfishness.

The sword is also connected with Shinto. But I do not think that it has attained in this connection so highly developed a spiritual significance as in Buddhism. It still betrays its naturalistic origin. It is not a symbol but an object endowed with some mysterious power. In the feudal days of Japan, the samurai class cherished this kind of idea toward the sword, although it is difficult to define exactly what was going on in their minds. At least they paid the utmost respect to it: at the samurai's death it was placed beside his bed, and when a child was born it found its place in the room. The idea was probably to prevent any evil spirits from entering the room that might interfere with the safety and happiness of the departed or the coming spirit. Here lingers an animistic way of thinking. The idea of a sacred sword, too, may be interpreted in this way.

It is noteworthy that, when making swords, the swordsmith [34 invokes the aid of the guardian god. To invite him to the workshop, the smith surrounds it with consecrated ropes, thus excluding evil spirits, while he goes through the ceremony of ablution and dons the ceremonial dress in which he works. While striking the iron bar and giving it baths of fire and water, the smith and his helper are in the most intensified state of mind. Confident the god's help will be given to their work, they exert themselves to the limit of their powers, mental, physical, and spiritual. The sword thus produced is a true work of art. The Japanese sword must reflect something deeply appealing to the soul of the people. They look at it, indeed, not as a weapon of destruction but as an object of inspiration. Hence the legend of Okazaki Masamune the swordsmith and his products.

Masamune flourished in the latter part of the Kamakura era, and his works are uniformly prized by all the sword

connoisseurs for their excellent qualities. As far as the edge of
the blade is concerned, Masamune may not exceed Muramasa,
one of his ablest disciples, but Masamune is said to have something morally inspiring that comes from his personality. The
legend goes thus: When someone was trying to test the sharp-
ness of a Muramasa, he placed it in a current of water and
watched how it acted against the dead leaves flowing down-
stream. He saw that every leaf that met the blade was cut in
twain. He then placed a Masamune, and he was surprised to
find that the leaves avoided the blade. The Masamune was not
bent on killing, it was more than a cutting implement, whereas
the Muramasa could not go beyond cutting, there was nothing
divinely inspiring in it. The Muramasa is terrible, the Masamune
is humane. One is despotic and imperialistic, the other is superhuman, if we may use this form of expression. Masamune almost
never engraved his name on the hilt, although this was customary
with swordsmiths.

The Nō play *Kokaji* gives us some idea about the moral
and religious significance of the sword among the Japanese.
The play was probably composed in the Ashikaga era. The
Emperor Ichijō (reigned 986–1011) once ordered a sword to
be made by Kokaji Munechika, who was one of the great swordsmiths of the day. Munechika felt greatly honored, but he could
not fill the order unless he had an able assistant equal in skill
to himself. He prayed to the god of Inari, who was his guardian
god, to send him someone fully competent for the work. In the
meantime he prepared his sacred platform in due accordance with
the traditional rites. When all the process of purification was
completed, he offered this prayer: "The work I am going to
undertake is not just for my selfish glorification; it is to obey
the august order of the Emperor who reigns over the entire
world. I pray to all the gods numbering as many as the sands
of Gaṅgā to come here and give their help to this humble Munechika, who is now going to do his utmost to produce a sword
worthy of the virtue of the august patron." Looking upward to

the sky and prostrating himself on the ground, he offers to the gods the *nusa* [2] symbolic of his most earnest desire to accomplish the work successfully. Would that the gods might have pity on his sincerity! A voice is now heard from somewhere: "Pray, pray, O Munechika, in all humbleness and in all earnestness. The time is come to strike the iron. Trust the gods and the work will be done." A mysterious figure appeared before him and helped him in hammering the heated iron, which came out of the forge in due time with every desirable mark of perfection and auspiciousness. The Emperor was pleased with the sword, which was worthy to be treasured as sacred and merit-producing.

As something of divinity enters into the making of the sword, its owner and user ought also to respond to the inspiration. He ought to be a spiritual man, not an agent of brutality. His mind ought to be at one with the soul which animates the cold steel. The great swordsmen have never been tired of instilling this feeling into the minds of their pupils. When the Japanese say that the sword is the soul of the samurai, we must remember all that goes with it, as I have tried to set forth above: loyalty, self-sacrifice, reverence, benevolence, and the cultivation of other higher feelings. Here is the true samurai.

2

IT WAS natural, therefore, for the samurai, who carried two swords—the longer one for attack and defense and the shorter one for self-destruction when necessary—to train himself with the utmost zeal in the art of swordsmanship. He could never be separated from the weapon that was the supreme symbol of his dignity and honor. Training in its use was, besides its practical purpose, conducive to his moral and spiritual enhancement. It was here that the swordsman joined hands with Zen. Although

---

[2] Or *go-hei*. It is a pendant of paper cuttings that is symbolically offered to the Shinto gods.

this fact has already been demonstrated to a certain extent, I wish to give here further quotations illuminative of the intimate relationship between Zen and the sword, in the form of Takuan's [3] letter to Yagyū Tajima no kami Munenori [4] (1571–1646) concerning the relationship between Zen and the art of swordsmanship.

As the letter is long and somewhat repetitive, I have condensed or paraphrased it here, trying to preserve the important thoughts of the original, and sometimes interpolating explanations and notes. It is an important document in more ways than one, as it touches upon the essential teaching of Zen as well as the secrets of art generally. In Japan, perhaps as in other countries too, mere technical knowledge of an art is not enough to make a man really its master; he ought to have delved deeply into the inner spirit of it. This spirit is grasped only when his mind is in complete harmony with the principle of life itself, that is, when he attains to a certain state of mind known as *mushin* (*wu-hsin* in Chinese), "no-mind." In Buddhist phraseology, it means going beyond the dualism of all forms of life and death, good and evil, being and non-being. This is where all arts merge into Zen. In this letter to the great master of swordsmanship, Takuan strongly emphasizes the significance of *mushin*, which may be regarded in a way as corresponding to the concept of the unconscious. Psychologically speaking, this state of mind gives itself up unreservedly to an unknown "power" that comes to one from nowhere and yet seems strong enough to possess the whole field of consciousness and make it work for the unknown. Hereby he becomes a kind of automaton, so to speak, as far as his own consciousness is concerned. But, as Takuan explains, it ought not to be confused with the helpless passivity

[3] Takuan (1573–1645) was the abbot of Daitokuji, in Kyoto. He was invited by the third Shōgun, Tokugawa Iyemitsu, to come to Tokyo, where Iyemitsu built a great Zen temple, called Tōkaiji, and made him its founder.

[4] Belonged to a great family of swordsmen flourishing in the early Tokugawa era. Tajima no kami was the teacher of Iyemitsu and studied Zen under Takuan.

of an inorganic thing, such as a piece of rock or a block of wood. He is "unconsciously conscious" or "consciously unconscious." With this preliminary remark, the following instruction of Takuan will become intelligible.

TAKUAN'S LETTER TO
YAGYŪ TAJIMA NO KAMI MUNENORI ON
THE MYSTERY OF PRAJÑĀ IMMOVABLE

Affects Attendant on the Abiding Stage of Ignorance [5]

"IGNORANCE" (*avidyā*) means the absence of enlightenment, that is, delusion. The "abiding stage" means "the point where the mind stops to abide." In Buddhist training we speak of fifty-two stages, of which one is a stage where the mind attaches itself to any object it encounters. This attaching is known as *tomaru*, "stopping" or "abiding." The mind stops with one object instead of flowing from one object to another [as the mind acts when it follows its own nature].

In the case of swordsmanship, for instance, when the opponent tries to strike you, your eyes at once catch the movement of his sword and you may strive to follow it. But as soon as this takes place. you cease to be master of yourself and you are sure to be beaten. This is called "stopping." [But there is another way of meeting the opponent's sword.]

No doubt you see the sword about to strike you, but do not let your mind "stop" there. Have no intention to counterattack him in response to his threatening move, cherish no calculating

---

[5] Mahāyāna Buddhism sometimes distinguishes fifty-two stages leading up to the supreme enlightenment (*sambodhi*). "Ignorance" (*avidyā*) may be regarded as the first of those stages and the "affects" (*kleśa*) are affective disturbances which accompany those who abide on this stage. In Japanese, "ignorance" is *mumyō* and "affects" is *bonnō*.

thoughts whatever. You simply perceive the opponent's move, you do not allow your mind to "stop" with it, you move on just as you are toward the opponent and make use of his attack by turning it on to himself. Then his sword meant to kill you will become your own and the weapon will fall on the opponent himself.

In Zen, this is known as "seizing the enemy's spear and using it as the weapon to kill him." The idea is that the opponent's sword being transferred into your hands becomes the instrument of his own destruction. This is "no-sword" in your terminology. As soon as the mind "stops" with an object of whatever nature— be it the opponent's sword or your own, the man himself bent on striking or the sword in his hands, the mode or the measure of the move—you cease to be master of yourself and are sure to fall a victim to the enemy's sword. When you set yourself against him, your mind will be carried away by him. Therefore, do not even think of yourself. [That is to say, the opposition of subject and object is to be transcended.]

For beginners, it is not a bad idea to keep the mind thoughtfully applied to their own disciplining. It is important not to get your attention arrested by the sword or by the measure of its movement. When your mind is concerned with the sword, you become your own captive. This is all due to your mind being arrested by something external and losing its mastership. This, I believe, is all very well known to you; I only call your attention to it from my Zen point of view. In Buddhism, this "stopping" mind is called delusion, hence "Affects Attendant on the Abiding-stage of Ignorance."

[The swordsman's "unconscious" and the psychoanalysts' "unconscious" are not to be confused, for the former is free from the notion of the self. The perfect swordsman takes no cognizance of the enemy's personality, no more than of his own. For he is an indifferent onlooker of the fatal drama of life and death in which he himself is the most active participant. In spite of all the concern he has or ought to have, he is above himself, he tran-

scends the dualistic comprehension of the situation, yet he is
not a contemplative mystic, he is in the thickest of the deadly
combat. This distinction is to be remembered when we compare
Eastern culture with Western. Even in such arts as that of
swordsmanship, in which the principle of opposition is most in
evidence, the one who is to be most intensely interested in it is
advised to be liberated from the idea.]

Prajñā Immovable

[PRAJÑĀ is possessed by all Buddhas and also by all sentient
beings. It is transcendental wisdom flowing through the relativity
of things] and it remains immovable, though this does not mean
the immovability or insensibility of such objects as a piece of
wood or rock. It is the mind itself endowed with infinite motili-
ties: it moves forward and backward, to the left and to the
right, to every one of the ten quarters, and knows no hindrances
in any direction. Prajñā Immovable is this mind capable of
infinite movements.

There is a Buddhist god called Fudō Myōō (Acala-vidyā-
rāja), the Immovable. He is represented holding a sword in his
right hand and a rope in his left. His teeth are bared and his
eyes glare angrily. He stands up threateningly in order to destroy
the devils who try to do harm to Buddha's teaching. Though
he is thus seen assuming a realistic form, he is not hiding anywhere on earth. He is the symbolic protector of Buddhism,
essentially incarnating Prajñā Immovable for us sentient beings.
When the ordinary people confront him, they are reminded of
what he stands for and will refrain from interfering with the
spread of Buddhist doctrine. The wise, on the other hand, who
are approaching a state of enlightenment, realize that Fudō
symbolizes Prajñā Immovable as the destroyer of delusion. He
who thus becomes enlightened and carries on his life as exemplified by Fudō Myōō will not be touched even by devilish

spirits. The Myōō is the symbol of immovability both of mind and body. Not to move means not to "stop" with an object that is seen. For as it is seen it passes on and the mind is not arrested. When the mind "stops" with each object as it is presented, the mind is disturbed with all kinds of thought and feeling. The "stopping" inevitably leads to the moving that is disturbance. Though the mind is thus subject to "stoppings," it in itself remains unmoved, however superficially it may seem so.

For instance, suppose ten men are opposing you, each in succession ready to strike you with a sword. As soon as one is disposed of, you will move on to another without permitting the mind to "stop" with any. However rapidly one blow may follow another, you leave no time to intervene between the two. Every one of the ten will thus be successively and successfully dealt with. This is possible only when the mind moves from one object to another without being "stopped" or arrested by anything. If the mind is unable to move on in this fashion, it is sure to lose the game somewhere between two encounters.

Kwannon Bosatsu (Avalokiteśvara) is sometimes represented with one thousand arms, each holding a different instrument. If his mind "stops" with the use, for instance, of a bow, all the other arms, 999 in number, will be of no use whatever. It is only because of his mind not "stopping" with the use of one arm but moving from one instrument to another that all his arms prove useful with the utmost degree of efficiency. Even Kwannon cannot be expected to equip himself with one thousand arms on one body. The figure is meant to demonstrate that, when Prajñā Immovable is realized, even as many as one thousand arms on one body may each and all be serviceable in one way or another.

I will give another illustration: When I look at a tree, I perceive one of the leaves is red, and my mind "stops" with this leaf. When this happens, I see just one leaf and fail to take cognizance of the innumerable other leaves of the tree. If instead of this I look at the tree without any preconceived ideas, I shall see all the leaves. One leaf effectively "stops" my mind from seeing all the rest. But when the mind moves on without "stopping," it takes up hundreds of thousands of leaves without fail. When this is understood we are Kwannons.

The simple-minded bow before Kwannon, taking him for an extraordinary being simply because his one body is seen as in possession of one thousand arms and one thousand eyes. Some, however, whose intelligence does not go very far, deny the reality of Kwannon, saying, "How can one person be provided with so many arms as one thousand?" Those who know the reason of things will neither blindly believe nor hastily negate. They will discover that it is the wisdom of Buddhism to demonstrate the rationality of things by means of one object. This is also the case with other schools of teaching, especially with Shintoism. Those symbolical figures are not to be taken naïvely as they appear, nor are they to be rejected as irrational. One must know that there is reason in them. Reasons may be varied, but they all point ultimately to one truth.

Beginners all start from the first stage of Ignorance and Affects, finally reaching that of Prajñā Immovable, and when they reach the final stage they find that it stands next to the first stage. There is reason for this.

To state it in terms of swordsmanship, the genuine beginner knows nothing about the way of holding and managing the sword, and much less of his concern for himself. When the opponent tries to strike him, he instinctively parries it. This is all he can do. But as soon as the training starts, he is taught how to handle the sword, where to keep the mind, and many other technical tricks—which makes his mind "stop" at various junctures. For this reason whenever he tries to strike the opponent he feels unusually hampered; [he has lost altogether the original sense of innocence and freedom]. But as days and years go by, as his training acquires fuller maturity, his bodily attitude and his way of managing the sword advance toward "no-mind-ness," which resembles the state of mind he had at the very beginning of training when he knew nothing, when he was altogether ignorant of the art. The beginning and the end thus turn into nextdoor neighbors. First we start counting one, two, three, and when finally ten is counted we return to one.

In musical scales, one may start with the lowest pitch and gradually ascend to the highest. When the highest is reached, one finds it located next to the lowest. In a similar way, when the highest stage is reached in the study of Buddhist teaching, a man turns into a kind of simpleton who knows nothing of Buddha, nothing of his teaching, and is devoid of all learning or scholarly acquisitions. The Ignorance and Affects character-izing the first stage are merged into Prajñā Immovable of the last stage of Buddhist discipline: intellectual calculations are lost sight of and a state of no-mind-ness (*mushin*) or of no-thought-ness (*munen*) prevails. When the ultimate perfection is attained, the body and limbs perform by themselves what is assigned to them to do with no interference from the mind. [The technical skill is so autonomized it is completely divorced from conscious efforts.]

Bukkoku Kokushi (1241–1316) of Kamakura has the poem:

> *Though not consciously trying to*
> *guard the rice fields from intruders,*
> *The scarecrow is not after all standing*
> *to no purpose.*

All is like this: The scarecrow in imitation of a human figure is erected in the middle of the rice paddies, it holds a bow and an arrow as if ready to shoot, and seeing this birds and animals are frightened away. This human figure is not endowed with a mind, but it scares away the deer. The perfect man who has attained the highest stage of training may be likened to it.[6] All is left to the [unconscious or reflexive] activities of the body

[6] Cf. "The Wooden Cock," from the *Chuang-tzŭ*, in Appendix V, p. 437, below.

and limbs, whereas the mind itself stops with no objects and at no points. Nor is it to be located at any definitely designable spot. Yet it here exists all by itself, with no thoughts, no affects, resembling a scarecrow in the rice fields. It is the case of a simple-minded man whose naïve intelligence does not go very far, holds to himself, and is not self-assertive. This nonassertiveness also applies to one who has attained the highest degree of intelligence. But there are some who know a great deal, and just because of this knowledge they put themselves very much forward. We come across many such these days among people of my profession, and I am really ashamed of them.

We have to distinguish between two ways of training: one is spiritual,[7] the other practical. As I said before, as far as spirituality is concerned, it is a very simple matter when it is realized to its full extent; it all depends on how one gives up one's own Ignorance and Affects and attains to no-mind-ness.[8] This has already been developed step by step. But training in detailed technique is also not to be neglected. The understanding of principle alone cannot lead one to the mastery of movements of the body and its limbs. By practical details I mean such as what you call the five ways of posing the body, designated each by one character. The principle of spirituality is to be grasped—this goes without saying—but at the same time one must be trained in the technique of swordplay. But training is never to be one-sided. *Ri* (*li*) and *ji* (*shih*) [9] are like two wheels of a cart. . . .

[7] I do not like this term in this connection, for it has a certain odium attached to it. The original Japanese is *ri* (*li* in Chinese). It ordinarily means "something transcendental," "something standing in contrast to detailed actualities," and is concerned with the innerliness or supersensuousness of things.

[8] In Japanese the whole sentence reads, "*Tada isshin no sute yō nite sōrō*," literally, "It all depends on how one gives up one's own mind." In this case "mind" is not "one absolute Mind," but "the mind one ordinarily has," that is, "the mind of ignorance and affects, which stops with an object or experience it may have and refuses to be restored to its native state of fluidity or emptiness or no-mind-ness."

[9] *Ri* (*li*) and *ji* (*shih*) are terms used very much in Kegon philosophy. *Ji* is a particular object or event, and *ri* is a universal principle. As long

Spark of the Flint Striking Steel

THIS IS another way of expressing the idea "not to leave a hairbreadth interval." When a flint strikes steel, no moment is lost before a spark issues from the contact. This is likened to the mind not "stopping" with any one object, and no time being left for deliberation, [for affects of any sort to assert themselves]. It does not mean just the instantaneity of events happening one after another. The point is not to let the mind "stop" with anything. Mere instantaneity is of no avail if the mind "stops" even for a moment. As soon as there is a moment's "stoppage," your mind is no longer your own, for it is then placed under another's control. When the mind calculates so as to be quick in movement, the very thought makes the mind captive. [You are no more master of yourself.]

In Saigyō's collection of poems (*Sankashū*) we have:

> *As I understand you to be a man*
> *who has grown weary of the world,*
> *I only think of you as not at all longing for* [10]
> *a temporary shelter.*

as these two are kept separate, life loses its freedom and spontaneity, and one fails to be master of oneself. Psychologically speaking, this is the unconscious breaking into the field of consciousness when consciousness loses itself, abandoning itself to the dictates of the unconscious. Religiously, it is dying to one's self and living in Christ or, as Bunan Zenji would say, "living as a dead man." In the case of a swordsman, he must free himself from all ideas involving life and death, gain and loss, right and wrong, giving himself up to a power which lives deeply in his inner being. *Ri* and *ji* are then in harmonious co-operation. Bunan's poem reads:

> *While living*
> *Be a dead man,*
> *Be thoroughly dead—*
> *And behave as you like,*
> *And all's well.*

[10] "Longing for" is Japanese *kokoro tomeru*, of which Takuan talks so much in this letter of his to Yagyū Tajima no kami. The second part of the poem may also be translated: "I only think that you would not have your mind 'stopped' with a temporary shelter."

This is said to have been composed by a courtesan of Yeguchi. The reference I wish to make is to the latter part of the poem containing the phrase *kokoro tomuna*, "not to have the mind 'stopped.'" For this applies most fittingly to the art of swordsmanship, which ultimately consists in not having one's mind "stopped" with any object.

In Zen Buddhism one asks, "What is Buddha?" and the master raises his fist. "What is the ultimate signification of Buddhist teaching?" and the master replies, even before the questioner fully finishes, "A spray of plum blossoms," or "The cypress tree in the courtyard." The point concerned here is not necessarily the appropriateness of the answer, but to see the mind not "stopping" with anything. Such a mind "stops" [11] neither with the color nor with the odor. This "nonstopping" mind in its suchness (*tai*) is blessed as a god or honored as a Buddha, which is no less than the Zen mind or the ultimate limit of an art. An answer given after deliberation to a question such as the above may be splendid and full of wisdom, but it is after all at the stage of Ignorance and Affects (*avidyā-kleśa*).

Zen is concerned with a movement of instantaneity in which the flint emits a spark when it strikes steel. It is the same as a flash of lightning. A voice calls out "O Uyemon!" and the man immediately responds to it, "Yes." Here is Prajñā Immovable. When the man is called, "O Uyemon," he "stops" and deliberates, wondering, "What business can it be?" Finally, the answer is given, "What is it?" This comes from a mind abiding in Ignorance and Affects. Whenever or wherever it "stops"—this is the sign of being moved by something external, which is a delusion, and such is said to be the mind of an ordinary being belonging to the stage of Ignorance and Affects.

On the other hand, that which gives an immediate answer to the call, "O Uyemon!" is the *prajñā* of all Buddhas. Buddhas

---

[11] Takuan has *utsuru* here for "stopping" or "stop." *Utsuru* is synonymous with *kokoro wo tomeru*. It literally means "drifting or shifting from one thing to another," or "one's attention being arrested by an object and being transferred onto it and staying there."

and all beings are not two, nor are gods and men. God or the Buddha is the name given to such a mind [identified with *prajñā*]. The Way of the Gods, the Way of Poetry, the Way of Confucius—there may be many Ways (*tao*), but they all are ways of illustrating the One Mind.

When they just follow the letters and have no true understanding of what the One Mind (Prajñā Immovable) is, they abuse it in every possible way throughout their life. They are day and night engaged in doing good things and evil things according to their karma. They would abandon the family, ruin the whole nation, or do anything contrary to the dictates of the One Mind. They are all confused and altogether fail to see what the One Mind looks like. Unfortunately, there are only a few people who have really penetrated into the depths of the One Mind. The rest of us are sadly going astray.

But we must know that it is not enough just to see what the Mind is, we must put into practice all that makes it up in our daily life. We may talk about it glibly, we may write books to explain it, but that is far from being enough. However much we may talk about water and describe it quite intelligently, that does not make it real water. So with fire. Mere talking of it will not make the mouth burn. To know what they are means to experience them in actual concreteness. A book on cooking will not cure our hunger. To feel satisfied we must have actual food. So long as we do not go beyond mere talking, we are not true knowers.

Confucianism as well as Buddhism strives to explain what the One Mind is, but unless life itself conforms to those explanations, Buddhist or Confucian, we cannot call ourselves knowers of the Mind even though every one of us is in possession of it. The reason why those who are devoting themselves to the study of Tao are yet unable to see into its ultimate significance is due to their relying on mere learning. If they really wish to see the One Mind, a deep *kufū* [12] is needed. . . .

___

[12] *Kufū* has been explained elsewhere. It is not just thinking with the head, but the state when the whole body is involved in and applied to the solving of a

Where to Locate the Mind

THE QUESTION is often asked: Where is the mind [or attention] to be directed? When it is directed to the movements of the opponent, it is taken up by them. When it is directed to his sword, it is taken up by the sword. When it is directed to striking down the opponent, it is taken up by the idea of striking. When it is directed to your sword, it is taken up by that. When it is directed to defending yourself, it is taken up by the idea of defense. When it is directed to the pose the opponent assumes, it is taken up by it. At all events, they say they do not know just where the mind is to be directed.

Some would say: Wherever the mind is directed, the whole person is liable to follow the direction and the enemy is sure to take full advantage of it, which means your defeat. It is after all better to keep the mind in the lower part of the abdomen just below the navel, and this will enable one to adjust oneself in accordance with the shifting of the situation from moment to moment.

This advice is reasonable enough, but from the ultimate point

problem. Rodin's *The Thinker* is typical. The Japanese often talk about "asking the abdomen," or "thinking with the abdomen," or "seeing or hearing with the abdomen." This is *kufū*. The head is detachable from the body, but the abdomen, which includes the whole system of the viscera, symbolizes the totality of one's personality.

It may not be uninstructive, I think, in this connection, to notice how Rodin's *The Thinker* is differentiated from Sekkaku's Zen master in meditation. [36a, 37a] Both are intently engaged in concentrating the mind on a subject of the utmost interest or significance. But Rodin's figure seems to me at least to be on the plane of relativity and intellection, while the Oriental one is somewhere beyond it. We also have to notice the difference in the posture assumed by each one of the two "thinkers." The one sits on a raised seat while the other squats on the ground. The one is less in contact with earth than the other. The Zen "thinker" is rooted in the foundation, as it were, of all things, and every thought he may cherish is directly connected with the source of being from which we of the earth come. To raise oneself from the ground even by one foot means a detachment, a separation, an abstraction, a going away to the realm of analysis and discrimination. The Oriental way of sitting is to strike the roots down to the center of earth and to be conscious of the Great Source where we have our "whence" and "whither."

of view which is held by Buddhists it is still limited, it is not the highest, it is not the supreme end of training. While being trained, the keeping of the mind in the lower region of the abdomen may not be a bad idea. But it is still the stage of reverence,[13] and it also corresponds to what Mencius advises— to get the runaway mind [14] back in its original seat. As to "the runaway mind" I have explained it in another letter for your inspection.

If you try to keep the mind imprisoned in the lower region of the abdomen, the very idea of keeping it in one specified locality will prevent the mind from operating anywhere else, and the result will be the contrary to what had been first intended. Then the question may arise: If keeping the mind shut up below the navel restricts its free movements, in what part of the body shall we keep it? I answer: "When you put it in the right hand, it will be kept captive in the right hand, and the rest of the body will be found inconvenienced. The result will be the same when you put it in the eye or in the right leg or in any other particular part of the body, because then the remaining parts of the body will feel its absence."

The second question is: Where is the mind to be kept after all?

---

[13] *Kei* in Japanese, *ching* in Chinese. The Confucian scholars, especially those of the Sung, consider that the feeling of reverence is of great importance in making progress in the study of Tao (the Way). But Zen-men think reverence is far from being the ultimate end of training. It is meant for beginners.

[14] *Hōshin* in Japanese, *fang-hsin* in Chinese. *Hō* (*fang*) means "free and unrestrained," "running wild," "gone loose," "lost," "letting go." Mencius (Book VI, "Kao-tzŭ") says that *jên* ("love") is human mind ("heart") and *i* ("justice") is human path. It is a pity that people leave the path and do not observe it, that people let go the mind and do not seek it. When they let loose chickens or dogs, they know they must search for them, but when they let go the mind they do not know that they must search for it. The way of learning is no more or less than searching for the heart they have let go. *Kokoro* means both mind and heart, intellect and affection, and is also often used in the philosophical sense as subject, substance, or soul. Wherever "mind" is mentioned in this letter of Takuan's, it is to be understood in its comprehensive sense.

I answer: "The thing is not to try to localize the mind anywhere but to let it fill up the whole body, let it flow throughout
the totality of your being. When this happens you use the hands
when they are needed, you use the legs or the eyes when they
are needed, and no time or no extra energy will be wasted. [The
localization of the mind means its freezing. When it ceases to
flow freely as it is needed, it is no more the mind in its suchness.]

[Localization is not restricted to the physical side of one's
being. The mind may be psychologically imprisoned. For instance,] one may deliberate when an immediate action is imperative, as in the case of swordsmanship. The deliberation
surely interferes and "stops" the course of the flowing mind.
Have no deliberation, no discrimination. Instead of localizing or
keeping in captivity or freezing the mind, let it go all by itself
freely and unhindered and uninhibited. It is only when this is
done that the mind is ready to move as it is needed all over the
body, with no "stoppage" anywhere.

Zen-men talk about the right or true (*shō*) and the partial
(*hen*) in their teaching. When the mind fills up the body entirely, it is said to be right; when it is located in any special
part of the body, it is partial or one-sided. The right mind is
equally distributed over the body and not at all partitive. The
partial mind on the other hand is divided and one-sided. Zen
dislikes partialization or localization. When the mind is kept
hardened at one place it fails to pervade or flow over every part
of the body. When it is not partialized after any schematized
plan, it naturally diffuses itself all over the body. It thus can
meet the opponent as he moves about trying to strike you down.
When your hands are needed they are there to respond to your
order. So with the legs—at any moment they are needed the
mind never fails to operate them according to the situation.
There is no need for the mind to maneuver itself out from any
localized quarters where it has been prearranged for it to station
itself.

The mind is not to be treated like a cat tied to a string. The mind must be left to itself, utterly free to move about according to its own nature. Not to localize or partialize it is the end of spiritual training. When it is nowhere it is everywhere. When it occupies one tenth, it is absent in the other nine tenths. Let the swordsman discipline himself to have the mind go on its own way, instead of trying deliberately to confine it somewhere.

———

[15] The main thesis of Takuan's letter to Yagyū Tajima no kami is almost exhausted in the passages translated more or less literally above. It consists in preserving the absolute fluidity of the mind (*kokoro*) by keeping it free from intellectual deliberations and affective disturbances of any kind at all that may arise from Ignorance and Delusion. The fluidity of mind and Prajñā Immovable may appear contradictory, but in actual life they are identical. When you have one, you have the other, for the Mind in its suchness is at once movable and immovable, it is constantly flowing, never "stopping" at any point, and yet there is in it a center never subject to any kind of movement, remaining forever one and the same. The difficulty is how to identify this center of immovability with its never-stopping movements themselves. Takuan advises the swordsman to solve the difficulty in his use of the sword as he actually stands against the opponent. The swordsman is thus made to be constantly facing a logical contradiction. As long as he notices it, that is, as long as he is logically minded, he finds his movements always hampered in one way or another—which is *suki*,[16] and the

---

[15] The following several paragraphs consist mainly of extracts from Takuan's letter paraphrased in modern terms so as to be more intelligible for readers. Takuan's original texts and our explanatory interpolations may cause some confusion in the minds of readers. But we crave their indulgent patience, for a careful perusal will be rewarding not only in understanding the swordsman's psychology in relation to what may be called Zen metaphysics but also in clarifying certain aspects of psychology which come up in the study of the Oriental arts generally.

[16] *Suki* literally means any space between two objects where something else can enter. A psychological or mental *suki* is created when a state of tension

enemy is sure to avail himself of it. Therefore, the swordsman cannot afford to indulge in an idle intellectual employment when the other side is always on the alert to detect the slightest *suki* produced on your part. You cannot relax and yet keep the state of tension deliberately for any length of time. For this is what makes the mind "stop" and lose its fluidity. How then can one have relaxation and tension simultaneously? Here is the same old contradiction, though presented in a different form.

When the situation is analyzed intellectually, we can never escape a contradiction in one form or another: moving and yet not moving, in tension and yet relaxed, seeing everything that is going on and yet not at all anxious about the way it may turn, with nothing purposely designed, nothing consciously cal- culated, no anticipation, no expectation—in short, standing in- nocently like a baby and yet with all the cunning and subterfuge of the keenest intelligence of a fully matured mind: how can this be achieved? No amount of intellection can ever be of any help in this paradoxical situation.

What is known as *kufū* is the only way to reach this result. The *kufū* is altogether personal and individualistic, it is to develop out of oneself, within one's own inner life. *Kufū* literally means "to strive," "to wrestle," "to try to find the way out," or, in Christian terms, "to pray incessantly for God's help." Psychologically speaking, it is to remove all the inhibitions there are, intellectual as well as affective or emotional, and to bring out what is stored in the unconscious and let it work itself out quite independently of any kind of interfering consciousness. The *kufū*, therefore, will be directed toward how to remove the inhibitions, though not analytically. If such an expression is permissible, let us say the *kufū* is to be conatively carried out— a process involving one's whole person; that is to say, it is to be totalistic, growing out of the depths of one's own being.

To make clear the immovability of the most mobile mind, Takuan distinguishes the original mind from the delusive mind,

is relaxed. More notes about this in "Zen and Swordsmanship," II, p. 143, n. 4.

which is an intellectually bifurcated state of consciousness. The original mind is a mind unconscious of itself, whereas the delusive mind is divided against itself, interfering with the free working of the original mind.

The original mind is *honshin* and the delusive mind is *mōshin*. *Hon* means "original," "primary," "real," "true," "native," or "natural," and *mō* means "not real," "deceiving" or "deceived," "deluded" or "delusive." *Shin* is *kokoro*, that is, "mind" in its broad sense.

The delusive mind may be defined as the mind intellectually and affectively burdened. It thus cannot move on from one topic to another without stopping and reflecting on itself, and this obstructs its native fluidity. The mind then coagulates before it makes a second move, because the first move still lingers there—which is a *suki* for the swordsman—the one thing that is to be avoided with the utmost scrupulosity. This corresponds to the mind conscious of itself (*ushin no shin* in Japanese). To be conscious is characteristic of the human mind as distinguished from the animal mind. But when the mind becomes conscious of its doings, it ceases to be instinctual and its commands are colored with calculations and deliberations—which means that the connection between itself and the limbs is no longer direct because the identity of the commander and his executive agents is lost. When dualism takes place, the whole personality never comes out as it is in itself. Takuan calls this situation "stopping," "halting," or "freezing." One cannot bathe in solid ice, he would warn us. Consciousness and its consequent dichotomy bring rigidity to the freely-flowing original mind, and the delusive mind begins functioning—which is fatal to the life of the swordsman.

The conscious mind is *ushin no shin* contrasting with *mushin no shin*, mind unconscious of itself. *Mushin* literally means "no-mind," it is the mind negating itself, letting go itself from itself, a solidly frozen mind allowing itself to relax into a state of perfect unguardedness. [We resume Takuan's own words—]

The Mind of No-Mind (*Mushin no Shin*)

A MIND unconscious of itself is a mind that is not at all disturbed by affects of any kind. It is the original mind and not the delusive one that is chock-full of affects. It is always flowing, it never halts, nor does it turn into a solid. As it has no discrimination to make, no affective preference to follow, it fills the whole body, pervading every part of the body, and nowhere standing still. It is never like a stone or a piece of wood. [It feels, it moves, it is never at rest.] If it should find a resting place anywhere, it is not a mind of no-mind. A no-mind keeps nothing in it. It is also called *munen*, "no-thought." *Mushin* and *munen* are synonymous.[17]

When *mushin* or *munen* is attained, the mind moves from one object to another, flowing like a stream of water, filling every possible corner. For this reason the mind fulfills every function required of it. But when the flowing is stopped at one point, all the other points will get nothing of it, and the result will be a general stiffness and obduracy. The wheel revolves when it is not too tightly attached to the axle. When it is too tight, it will never move on. If the mind has something in it, it stops functioning, it cannot hear, it cannot see, even when a sound enters the ears or a light flashes before the eyes. To have something in mind means that it is preoccupied and has no time for anything else. But to attempt to remove the thought already in it is to refill it with another something. The task is endless. It is best, therefore, not to harbor anything in the mind from the start. This may be difficult, but when you go on

[17] *Mushin* (*wu-hsin*) or *munen* (*wu-nien*) is one of the most important ideas in Zen. It corresponds to the state of innocence enjoyed by the first inhabitants of the Garden of Eden, or even to the mind of God when he was about to utter his fiat, "Let there be light." Enō (Hui-nêng), the sixth patriarch of Zen, emphasizes *munen* (or *mushin*) as most essential in the study of Zen. When it is attained, a man becomes a Zen-man, and, as Takuan would have it, he is also a perfect swordsman.

exercising *kufū* toward the subject, you will after some time
come to find this state of mind actualized without noticing each
step of progress. Nothing, however, can be accomplished hurriedly.

[We paraphrase again. Takuan here notes an ancient poem,
on some phase of romantic love:

> *To think that I am not going*
> *To think* [18] *of you any more*
> *Is still thinking of you.*
> *Let me then try not to think*
> *That I am not going to think of you.*

[Before we part with Takuan, I wish to touch upon what may
be regarded as an eternal paradox, which may run like this: How
can one keep the mind in this state of no-thinking when its function is to think? How can the mind be at once a mind and a not-
mind? How can "A" be simultaneously both "A" and "not-A"?
The problem is not only logical and psychological, it is also metaphysical. The swordsman may have it solved in the most concrete and practical way, for it is for him a matter of life and
death, whereas most of us can assume a more or less intellectual
attitude and remain indifferent, as it were. But, philosophically,
it concerns us in various ways, and it also constitutes the crucial
point in the study of Oriental thought and culture. The question
has never been presented to the Western mind, I believe, in the
way the East faces it.

[Tradition has it that Yagyū Tajima no kami Munenori left a
poem to one of his sons expressive of the secret of his school of
swordsmanship. The poem is a poor one from the literary

---

[18] "To think" is *omou* in Japanese. *Omou* means not only "to think" but
"to recollect," "to long for," "to love," etc. It has an affective as well as an
intellectual value. The word is almost a general term for anything that goes
on in one's mind. Therefore, not to think (*omowanu*) is to keep the mind
utterly empty of all contents—a blank state of emptiness which is *mushin* or
munen.

point of view, as poems of this nature known as *dōka,* "poems of Tao," generally are. It runs thus:

> *Behind the technique, know that there*
> *   is the spirit (ri):*
> *It is dawning now;*
> *Open the screen,*
> *And lo, the moonlight is shining in!*

We may say this is highly mystical. The strangest thing, however, is: What has the art of swordplay—which, bluntly speaking, consists in mutual killing—to do with such content as is communicated in the poem on the moon at the break of day? In Japan, the dawn-moonlight has rich poetical associations. Yagyū's allusion to it is understandable from this angle, but what has the sword to do with poetry about the moon? What inspirations is the swordsman expected to get from viewing the moon as the day dawns? What secret is here? After going through many a tragic scene, which the man must no doubt have witnessed, with what poetic enlightenment is he expected to crown all his past experience? The author is here telling us, naturally, to have an inner light on the psychology of swordsmanship. Yagyū the master knows that technique alone will never make a man the perfect swordplayer. He knows that the spirit (*ri*) or inner experience (*satori*) must back the art, which is gained only by deeply looking into the inmost recesses of the mind (*kokoro*). That is why his teacher Takuan is never tired of dilating on the doctrine of emptiness (*śūnyatā*), which is the metaphysics of *mushin no shin* ("mind of no-mind"). Emptiness or no-mind-ness may appear to some to be something most remote from our daily experience, but we now realize how intimately it is related to the problem of life and death with which most of us nowadays remain unconcerned.]

[End of Takuan's Letter]

The gist of Takuan's advice to Yagyū Tajima no kami can be summed up by quoting his reference to Bukkō Kokushi's encounter with the soldiers of the Yüan invading army, which Takuan mentions toward the end of his long epistle. The incident is told in the section following this. Takuan comments on the sword cleaving the spring breeze in a flash of lightning:

"The uplifted sword has no will of its own, it is all of emptiness. It is like a flash of lightning. The man who is about to be struck down is also of emptiness, and so is the one who wields the sword. None of them are possessed of a mind which has any substantiality. As each of them is of emptiness and has no 'mind' (kokoro), the striking man is not a man, the sword in his hands is not a sword, and the 'I' who is about to be struck down is like the splitting of the spring breeze in a flash of lightning. When the mind does not 'stop,' the sword swinging cannot be anything less than the blowing of the wind. The wind is not conscious of itself as blowing over the trees and working havoc among them. So with the sword. Hence Bukkō's stanza of four lines.

"This 'empty-minded-ness' applies to all activities we may perform, such as dancing, as it does to swordplay. The dancer takes up the fan and begins to stamp his feet. If he has any idea at all of displaying his art well, he ceases to be a good dancer, for his mind 'stops' with every movement he goes through. In all things, it is important to forget your 'mind' and become one with the work at hand.

"When we tie a cat, being afraid of its catching a bird, it keeps on struggling for freedom. But train the cat so that it would not mind the presence of a bird. The animal is now free and can go anywhere it likes. In a similar way, when the mind is tied up, it feels inhibited in every move it makes, and nothing will be accomplished with any sense of spontaneity. Not only that, the work itself will be of a poor quality, or it may not be finished at all.

"Therefore, do not get your mind 'stopped' with the sword you raise; forget what you are doing, and strike the enemy. Do not keep your mind on the person who stands before you. They are all of emptiness, but beware of your mind being caught up with emptiness itself."

To supplement Takuan, the following story is given to illustrate the mind of "no-mind-ness":

A woodcutter was busily engaged in cutting down trees in the remote mountains. An animal called "satori" appeared. It was a very strange-looking creature, not usually found in the villages. The woodcutter wanted to catch it alive. The animal read his mind: "You want to catch me alive, do you not?" Completely taken aback, the woodcutter did not know what to say, whereupon the animal remarked, "You are evidently astonished at my telepathic faculty." Even more surprised, the woodcutter then conceived the idea of striking it with one blow of his ax, when the satori exclaimed, "Now you want to kill me." The woodcutter felt entirely disconcerted, and fully realizing his impotence to do anything with this mysterious animal, he thought of resuming his business. The satori was not charitably disposed, for he pursued him, saying, "So at last you have abandoned me."

The woodcutter did not know what to do with this animal or with himself. Altogether resigned, he took up his ax and, paying no attention whatever to the presence of the animal, vigorously and singlemindedly resumed cutting trees. While so engaged, the head of the ax flew off its handle, and struck the animal dead. The satori, with all its mind-reading sagacity, had failed to read the mind of "no-mind-ness."

At the last stage of swordsmanship there is a secret teaching which is not given to any but a fully qualified disciple. Mere technical training is not enough, proficiency in this does not go beyond apprenticeship. The secret teaching is known among the masters of a certain school as "The Moon in Water." According to one writer, it is explained as follows, which is in truth no more than the teaching of Zen—the doctrine of *mushin:*

"What is meant by 'the moon in water'?

"This is explained variously in the various schools of swordsmanship, but the main idea is to grasp the way the moon reflects itself wherever there is a body of water, which is done in a state of *mushin* ('no-mind-ness'). One of the imperial poems composed at the Pond of Hirosawa reads:

> *"The moon has no intent to cast its shadow anywhere,*
> *Nor does the pond design to lodge the moon:*
> *How serene the water of Hirosawa!*

"From this poem one must get an insight into the secrets of *mushin,* where there are no traces of artificial contrivance, everything being left to Nature itself.

"Again, it is like one moon reflecting itself in hundreds of streams: the moonlight is not divided into so many shadows, but the water is there to reflect them; the moonlight remains ever the same even where there are no waters to hold its reflections. Again, it is all the same to the moonlight whether there are so many bodies of water, or there is just one little puddle. By this analogy the mysteries of mind are made easier to understand. But the moon and water are tangible matter, while mind has no form and its working is difficult to trace. The symbols are thus not the whole truth, only suggestive."

From all these quotations we can see that the Oriental thought and culture lays great emphasis on the realization of a psychical state of no-mind-ness (*mushin* or *munen*). When this is not realized, the mind is always conscious of its own doings—which Takuan calls "mind-stopping." For, instead of flowing, as he says, from one object to another, the mind halts and reflects on what it is going to do or what it has already done. Recollection and anticipation are fine qualities of consciousness which distinguish the human mind from that of the lower animals. They are useful and serve certain purposes, but when actions are directly related to the problem of life and death, they must be given up so that they will not interfere with the fluidity of mentation and the lightning rapidity of action. The man must turn himself into a puppet in the hands of the unconscious. The unconscious must supersede the conscious. Metaphysically speaking, this is the philosophy of *śūnyatā* ("emptiness"). The technique of swordsmanship is based on its psychology, and the psychology is a localized application of the metaphysics.

3

THE *Atlantic Monthly*, February, 1937, contains an article by a Spanish bullfighter, Juan Belmonte, telling of his own experience in the art.[19] Bullfighting is evidently very much like the Japanese art of swordplay. His story is full of informative suggestions, and I quote part of the translator's note and Juan Belmonte's own account of the fight for which he earned a great reputation as the foremost fighter of the day. In this fighting he realized the state of mind referred to in Takuan's letter to Yagyū Tajima no kami; if the Spanish hero had had Buddhist training, he would have an insight into Prajñā Immovable.

The translator's note runs, in part:

"Bullfighting is not a sport, and you can't compare it with one. Bullfighting, whether you like it or not, whether you approve of it or not, is an art, like painting or music, and you can only judge it as an art: its emotion is spiritual, and it touches depths which

---

[19] "The Making of a Bullfighter," tr. Leslie Charteris.

can only be compared with the depths that are touched in a man who knows and understands and loves music by a symphony orchestra under a great conductor."

Juan Belmonte describes his psychology at the intensest moment of his fight in the following terms:

"As soon as my bull came out I went up to it, and at the third pass I heard the howl of the multitude rising to their feet. What had I done? All at once I forgot the public, the other bull-fighters, myself, and even the bull; I began to fight as I had fought so often by myself at night in the corrals and pastures, as precisely as if I had been drawing a design on a blackboard.

"They say that my passes with the cape and my work with the muleta that afternoon were a revelation of the art of bull-fighting. I don't know, and I'm not competent to judge. I simply fought as I believe one ought to fight, without a thought outside my own *faith* [20] in what I was doing. With the last bull I succeeded for the first time in my life in delivering myself body and soul to the pure joy of fighting without being consciously aware of an audience. When I was playing bulls alone in the country I used to talk to them; and that afternoon I held a long conversation with the bull, all the time that my muleta was tracing the arabesques of the faena. When I didn't know what else to do with the bull I knelt down under its horns and brought my face close to its muzzle.

" 'Come on, little bull,' I whispered. 'Catch me!'

"I stood up again, spread the muleta under its nose, and went on with my monologue, encouraging it to keep on charging:—

" 'This way, little bull. Charge me nicely. Nothing's going to happen to you. . . . Here you are. Here you are. . . . Do

---

[20] The italics are mine. The faith here is an absolute one, corresponding to what I call the Unconscious.

(The word *faena*, a few lines further on, means "the last stage of the fight terminating with the kill.")

you see me, little bull? . . . What? You're getting tired? . . .
Come on! Catch me! Don't be a coward. . . . Catch me!'

"I was executing the ideal faena, the faena that I had seen so
often and in so much detail in my dreams that every line of it
was drawn in my brain with mathematical exactness. The faena
of my dreams always ended disastrously, because when I went
in for the kill the bull invariably caught me in the 'leg. It must
have been some subconscious acknowledgment of my lack of
skill in killing that always dictated this tragic conclusion.
Nevertheless, I went on realizing my ideal faena, placing myself
right between the horns of the bull and hearing the acclamation
of the crowd only as a distant murmur; until at last, exactly
as I had dreamed it, the bull did catch me and wounded me in
the thigh. I was so intoxicated, so outside myself, that I scarcely
noticed it. I went in for the kill, and the bull fell at my feet."

I may add that before Belmonte had his final encounter with
the bull his mind was in a most distracted condition: rivalry,
desire for success, sense of inferiority, feeling for the public
ready to make fun of him. So he confessed: "I was overcome
with despair. Where had I got the idea that I was a bullfighter?
'You've been fooling yourself,' I thought. 'Because you had
some luck in a couple of novilladas without picadors, you can do
anything.' " Out of this feeling of despair, however, Belmonte
discovered something else in him lying hitherto altogether un-
suspected, when he saw his bull coming out and confronting him.
This something sometimes came out of his dreams—that is, it
was sleeping deeply in his Unconscious, but it never came out
in the broad daylight. The feeling of despair pushed him to the
very edge of his mental precipice, from which he finally leaped;
and the result was: "I was so intoxicated, so outside myself,
that I scarcely noticed it"—not only that he was wounded but
in fact everything. Prajñā Immovable was his guide, he left
himself entirely to its guidance. Sings Bukkoku Kokushi, a noted
Zen master of the Kamakura era:

The bow is broken,
Arrows are all gone—
This critical moment:
No fainting heart cherish,
Shoot with no delay.[21]

When a shaftless arrow is shot from a stringless bow, it will surely penetrate the rock, as once happened in the history of the Far Eastern people.

In all departments of art as well as in Zen Buddhism, this passing of the crisis is considered very important in order to reach the source of all creative works. I wish to discuss this more specifically from the religio-psychological point of view in a separate work on Zen.

4

THE SHINKAGE-RYŪ used to be one of the most popular schools of swordsmanship in the feudal days in Japan. It started in the Ashikaga era, with Kami-idzumi Ise no kami Hidetsuna (d. 1577) as its founder. He claimed that he learned the secrets of his art directly from the god of Kashima. It no doubt has gone through stages of development since then, and the so-called secrets must have increased in volume, for we have at the present day a variety of documents given by the masters to their most proficient pupils who were considered worthy of them.

---

[21] Here is another by the same author on the same subject:

No target's erected,
No bow's drawn,
And the arrow leaves the string:
It may not hit,
But it does not miss!

This was what the late Professor Eugen Herrigel, the author of *Zen in the Art of Archery*, tried to learn from his master.

Among such documents we find phrases and epigrams in verse
highly flavored with Zen, which have superficially no connection
whatever with the use of the sword.

The final certificate, for instance, which is given to one qualified to be a master of the school, contains nothing but a circle.
This is supposed to represent a mirror bright and altogether free
from film and dust, and its meaning is no doubt the allusion to
the Buddhist epistemology of the "great-perfect-mirror-wis-
dom," [22] which is no other than the Prajñā Immovable of Takuan
already mentioned. The swordsman's mind must be kept entirely
free from selfish affects and intellectual calculations so that "original intuition" is ready to work at its best—which is a state of no-
mind-ness. Mere technical skill in the use of the sword does not
necessarily give one full qualification as a swordsmaster. He must
once realize the final stage of spiritual discipline, which is to attain no-mind-ness, symbolized as a circle empty of contents—a
circle with no circumference.

There is a phrase, among other highly technical terms, in the
secret documents of the Shinkage-ryū school of swordsmanship,
which has apparently no connection with the art as far as its
literal meaning is concerned. As all these secrets are orally
transmitted and as I am a stranger to them, it is beyond my
conjecture to find out how this particular phrase obtains its
organic signification in the actual wielding of the sword. But,
so far as I can judge, the phrase is derived from Zen literature,
outside which it cannot mean anything. It reads: "Waters of the
West River." A commentator who evidently does not know the
real purport of it interprets it as indicating a bold venturesome
daredevil attitude of mind that does not recoil from swallowing
up the whole river. This is ridiculous, to say the least. It refers
to a Zen *mondo* that took place between Baso (Ma-tsu, d. 788),

---

[22] *Ādarśana jñānam*, in Sanskrit, which is one of four knowledges (*jñānam*)
given by the Yogācāra or Vijñāptimātra School of Buddhism. It is the fundamental poetic quality of consciousness in general, which is here compared to
the illuminating quality of the mirror.

of the T'ang dynasty, and his lay disciple Hō Koji (P'ang Chü-shih). Hō asked:

"What kind of man is he who does not keep company with anything [or anybody]?"

"I will tell you," said Baso, "when you have swallowed up in one gulp all the waters of the West River."

This is said to have opened the mind of Hō to a state of enlightenment.

When we have this incident in mind, we can understand why the phrase "Waters of the West River" has found its way into the secret documents of the school of Shinkage-ryū. Hō's question is a very important one, and so is Baso's answer. In Zen discipline this *mondo* [23] is frequently referred to, and there is no doubt that among the swordsmen of the feudal days there were many who gave their lives to the study of Zen in order to attain a state of absolute no-mind-ness in connection with their art. As has been mentioned elsewhere, the thought of death proves to be the greatest stumblingblock in the outcome of a life-and-death combat. To transcend the thought that is a great inhibitory factor in the free and spontaneous exercise of the technique acquired, the best way for the swordsman is to discipline himself in Zen. No amount of swinging the sword will ever qualify the man to swallow up the whole West River. It is Zen that performs this miracle, and until its successful performance takes place no one is expected to do away with the ever-haunting consciousness of the ghost called death. Zen is not a mere philosophical contemplation on the evanescence of life but a most practical entrance into the realm of nonrelativity, where a cupful of tea in my hand, when spilt, fills in no time the vast expanse of the Pacific Ocean, to say nothing of small rivers in some remote corners of the planet.

The secret documents also contain a number of *waka*, versified epigrams, in regard to the mastery of swordsmanship, some of which decidedly reflect the spirit of Zen:

[23] "Question and answer."

Into a soul (kokoro) absolutely free from
  thoughts and emotions,
Even the tiger finds no room to insert
  its fierce claws.

One and the same breeze passes
Over the pines on the mountain and the oak
  trees in the valley;
And why do they give different notes?

Some think that striking is to strike:
But striking is not to strike, nor is killing to kill.
He who strikes and he who is struck—
They are both no more than a dream that
  has no reality.[24]

No thinking, no reflecting,—
Perfect emptiness:
Yet therein something moves,
Following its own course.

The eye sees it,
But no hands can take hold of it—
The moon in the stream:
This is the secret of my school.

Clouds and mists—
They are midair transformations:
Above them eternally shine the sun and the moon.

Victory is for the one,
Even before the combat,
Who has no thought of himself,
Abiding in the no-mind-ness of Great Origin.

[24] As to this and the preceding *waka*, cf. Emerson's "Brahma," which is quoted in full at p. 207.

These statements are all in correspondence with the principle of "emptiness" as taught by Miyamoto Musashi (d. 1645), Yagyū Tajima no kami Munenori, and other great masters, as the ultimate secret of swordsmanship, which is attainable only after a long arduous training in the art. This insistence on the spiritual discipline entitles the art to be called creative. Musashi was great not only as a swordsman but as a *sumiye* painter.

Some more poems are given below showing how the spirit and even to a certain extent the philosophy of Zen has influenced the masters of swordsmanship. They are, of course, not philosophers; they never try to discuss the philosophy in connection with their discipline, for what they aim at has nothing to do with the conceptual understanding of the doctrine of emptiness or suchness but its personal experiential grasp as they face the problem of life and death in the form of the threatening sword in the hands of an opponent. The philosopher may take this "opponent" or "enemy," so called, not concretely as the swordsman does but more in the form of concepts such as "an objective world," or "ultimate reality," or *"Dasein,"* or "the given," or "the brute fact," or *"l'en-soi,"* or what not. The thinkers grapple with these unknown quantities, making use of every available source of learning and thinking, but the swordsman's problem is far more urgent and ominous and allows him no time for reflection and erudition. He has to "decide" with no delay, his "courage" is not something he can muster after much deliberation. The question is at the door, over the head, "sizzling the eyebrows." If the answer is not forthcoming, all is ruined. The situation here is more critical than the philosopher's. No wonder that Zen has come to rescue the swordsman, or the swordsman has run to Zen for immediate help. The poems, given as secrets of swordplay, all reflect the spirit of Zen, which inevitably involves the philosophy of Zen. All the following poems [25] become intelligible when the "West River Waters" of

[25] I refer here to the thirty-one-syllabic form of expression called the *waka* or *uta* poem.

Baso, or Daitō Kokushi's *uta* on the raindrops, as paradoxical as Baso's dictum, is thoroughly comprehended. The *uta* is given first and then the rest: [26]

If your ears see,
And eyes hear,
Not a doubt you'll cherish—
How naturally the rain drips
From the eaves!

The spring is come, softly blows the wind,
The peaches and apricots are in full bloom.
The dews are thick in the autumnal nights,
The leaves fall from the paulownia tree.

The flowers, the maple leaves in autumn,
And the wintry snows covering the field all white—
How beautiful they are each in its way!
I fear my attachments still did not go beyond
  the sensuous, [for I know now what Reality is].

Inside the sacred fence before which I bow
There must be a pond filled with clear water;
As my mind-moon becomes bright
I see its shadow reflected in the water.

Wherever and whenever the mind is found
  attached [27] *to anything,*
Make haste to detach yourself from it.
When you tarry for any length of time
It will turn again into your old home town. [28]

---

[26] These verses are taken from a book entitled (in translation) "Collected Works on Swordsmanship": *Bujutsu Sōsho* (Tokyo, 1925).

[27] That is, "stopped."

[28] That is, a man's old egoistic self.

Abandon all the arts
You have learned
In swordsmanship,
And in one gulp
Drink up all the waters of the West River.

I thought all the time
I was learning how to win;
But I realize now:
To win is no more,
No less, than to lose.

In the well not dug,
In the water not filling it,
A shadow is reflected;
And a man with no form, no shadow,
Is drawing water from the well.

A man with no form, no shadow,
Turns into a rice pounder
When he pounds rice.[29]

5

A RECENT WRITER on "the Way of the Sword" and its history [30] remarks to the following effect in regard to the principle of the art: In the *Kendō* ("the Way of the Sword"), what is most essential to attain besides its technique is the spiritual element controlling the art throughout. It is a state of mind known as *munen* or *musō*, "no-thought" or "no-reflection." This

[29] Hui-nêng (Enō), the sixth patriarch of Zen in China, is recorded to have been engaged in manual work like this (rice-pounding) when he was under his teacher Hung-jên (Gunin).

[30] Takano Hiromasa.

does not mean just to be without thoughts, ideas, feelings, etc., when you stand with the sword before the opponent. It means letting your natural faculties act in a consciousness free from thoughts, reflections, or affections of any kind. This state of mind is also known as egolessness (*muga* or non-*ātman*), in which you cherish no egoistic thoughts, no consciousness of your own attainments. The so-called spirit of *sabi-shiori* ("solitariness"), running through Saigyō or Bashō, must also have come from the psychic state of egolessness. This is often likened to the lunar reflection in water. Neither the moon nor water has any preconceived idea of producing the incident designated by us as "the moon in water." Water is in a state of "no-mind-ness" as much as the moon. But when there is a sheet of water, the moon is seen in it. The moon is but one, but its reflections are seen wherever there is water. When this is understood, your art is perfect. Finally, Zen and the Sword's Way are one in this, that both ultimately aim at transcending the duality of life and death. From of old, this has been recognized by masters of the sword, and the great ones have invariably knocked at the gate of Zen—as is instanced in the cases of Yagyū Tajima no kami and Takuan and of Miyamoto Musashi and Shunzan.

The writer of the aforementioned book gives an interesting piece of information: that in the feudal days of Japan a master of the sword or the spear was often called an "Oshō" ("master" or "teacher," *upādhyāna* in Sanskrit), which is the title commonly given to a Buddhist priest. The origin of this custom is traceable to the fact that there was once a great monk in the Kōfukuji Temple of Nara. He belonged to one of the minor temples, called Jizōin, under the jurisdiction of the Kōfukuji. He was an expert of the spear, and all the Jizōin monks learned the art from him. He was naturally an Oshō to all his disciples, and the title came to be transferred to all the masters both of the spear and the sword, irrespective of their Buddhist qualifications.

The hall in which swordsmanship is practiced is called a

Dōjō. Dōjō is the name of a place devoted to religious exercises, and its original Sanskrit meaning, *bodhimandala,* is the place of enlightenment. There is no doubt the name was borrowed from Zen Buddhism.

There is another thing the swordsmen learned from Zen. In olden days they used to travel all over Japan in order to perfect themselves in the art by experiencing every form of hardship which might befall them and by undergoing training in the various schools of swordsmanship. The example was furnished by the Zen monks, who did the same thing before they attained final enlightenment. This practice is known among the monks as *angya,* "traveling on foot," whereas the swordsmen call it *musha-shugyō,* "training in warriorship."

I do not know how early this practice started among the swordsmen, but we read about the founder of the Shinkage-ryū traveling all over the country. One incident connects him with a Zen monk, both of whom were engaged in a similar form of training: One day when Kami-idzumi Ise no kami was passing through a small village in a remote mountain district, he found the people in extreme excitement; for a desperate outlaw had taken refuge in a deserted house, snatching away a little village boy with him, and threatened to kill the victim if the villagers attempted to arrest or do harm to the criminal himself. Ise no kami realized the grave situation. Seeing a monk pass by, who was no doubt a wandering Zen monk, the swordsman asked him to lend him his monkish robe for a while. He had his head shaved so as to appear a genuine monk. He approached the deserted house with two lunch boxes, and told the outlaw that the child's parents did not wish to see it die of starvation and commissioned him to give it something to eat. So saying he threw out one of the boxes before the man. Ise no kami then continued: "As you yourself may be hungry, I had another box prepared for you." When the desperado stretched his arm to receive it, the monk-swordsman lost no time in seizing him by the arm and, forcibly throwing him down on the ground, made him a complete prisoner. The monkish robe was returned to its original owner, who praised him highly, saying, "You are truly a 'man of the sword,' " and gave him a *kara* (or *rakusu*), a symbol of monk-hood, which is generally carried by a Zen monk over his chest hanging from the neck—a kind of abridged *kesa* (*kāśāya* in Sanskrit). It is said that Ise no kami never parted with it. The wandering Zen monk could not have been a mere novice in Zen, he must have been one of some understanding. "A man of the sword" is a phrase much used in Zen to denote a seasoned Zen monk who has really gone beyond the bounds of life and death. Ise no kami must have indeed had good reason for treasuring the *kara* as a gift from the monk "traveling on foot."

It was probably sometime in the seventeenth century that the following story was circulated among the swordsmen, showing that the relationship between swordplay and Zen was one of the topics they were most interested in. The story is, as the author suggests, probably a fiction, but the fact that such a story came to be told proves that the swordsmen were very much concerned with Zen and also that Zen was regarded as something highly mystifying and able to achieve some wonders even against an expert swordsman.

The story is quoted from a book called *Gekken Sōdan*, in five fascicles, compiled by Minamoto Tokushū in 1844. It is a collec-tion of stories of swordsmanship, giving histories of the various schools, their founders, and some anecdotes. There was a school known as Tesshin-ryū, which flourished in certain localities west of Kyoto toward the end of the seventeenth century and extend-ing into the eighteenth. The originator of this school was known as Otsuka Tesshin. He had a great liking for swordplay and while still young became quite an expert. He was ambitious and wished to try his skill with men of the same profession out-side his own province so as to make his name better known in wider circles. He was well acquainted with a Zen abbot residing at a nearby monastery, and he visited him to say goodbye. The abbot's name was Ryūkō; he belonged to the Sōtō sect of Zen and was a renowned master of the day. When Tesshin spoke to him regarding his enterprise, the abbot advised him against it, saying: "We are living in a much wider world than you may think, and there must be many men of your profession who are far more skillful, and the outcome of your adventure will be disastrous." The young man, however, was obdurate against taking the advice kindly.

Ryūkō continued: "Look at myself. I also wanted to be better known in the world. I have been practicing meditation here for the last few decades, and how many disciples have I now? As to yourself, you have hardly anyone calling himself your pupil. We each have to know where we are and be content with the situation."

This incensed Tesshin very much, so that he excitedly exclaimed: "Do you think my sword is of no worth? Swordsmanship is not like your discipline. If I go out of my home town and challenge someone well known in his district and beat him, the event will naturally be talked about among his friends or pupils. If I meet another in another district and defeat him, my reputation will gradually be spread throughout the neighborhood. Besides, I am firmly convinced of my attainment in swordsmanship. I am not afraid of any encounter which may turn up in my tour."

Ryūkō could not help smiling at his self-conceit. "You had better start with the one who is right in front of you. If you come out victorious, you may undertake the grand tour throughout the whole country. In case, however, you lose, you must promise to become a monk and be my disciple."

At this Tesshin, laughing heartily, said, "You may be great in your Zen, but surely you are no swordsman. If you wish to try your luck, however, I am ready."

Ryūkō gave him a bamboo stick that had been found nearby

and then provided himself with a *hossu*.[31] Tesshin, full of confidence, tried to knock the Zen master down with one blow of his stick. But the stick completely missed the opponent, who was no longer within its reach. Tesshin was exasperated and tried again and again to reach him, but all to no purpose. Instead, he frequently felt the *hossu* gently sweeping over his face.

Ryūkō finally remarked, "What would you say now?"

Tesshin's braggart air was utterly crushed. He humbly acknowledged his defeat. Ryūkō lost no time in calling to his attendants to bring all the needed instruments to cut off Tesshin's hair and turn him into a regular monk with a shaven head.

Now Minamoto the author comments: This is most likely a story fabricated by Zen-men. If Ryūkō besides being a Zen master were not somehow acquainted with the art of swordsmanship, he could never beat Tesshin, as is told in the story. Otherwise, Tesshin knew nothing of the art as he claimed. It is true that there are many points where Zen and swordplay go hand in hand. For instance, when they refer to "no room being left even for a hair to be inserted between," or of "a spark of the flint striking steel," the dictum applies not only to Zen but also generally to the art of swordplay, for no school can ignore going through this momentous training. However excellently qualified in every way as a Zen master, if he had no training at all in the technique of the sword he could never expect to win a contest with a full-fledged swordsman. The fact is that the perfect art of swordsmanship consists in mastery of both technique and principle. While there is no doubt about the all-importance of spiritual training, one is also to be fully familiar with the practical details of swordplay.

From the professional point of view, Minamoto's idea is correct, I think: a parallel training in technique and principle. But there is at least one other school that emphasizes the spiritual side

[31] This is generally carried by a Zen priest. It was originally for shooing away mosquitoes; it consists of a short stick and a tuft of horsetail.

of the art though not necessarily neglecting the technique. Its chief exponent, Hori Kintayū (1688–1755), desired to utilize swordsmanship as the means to help one in his spiritual attainment and character building. His reasoning deserves consideration in more ways than one, as it sheds light not only on swordsmanship but on samuraiship generally. There has been much misunderstanding in the West as regards the spirit, function, and discipline of the samurai, who were the ruling class of Japan during her feudal days, especially in the Tokugawa regime. Kimura's point of view, as developed in the *Kenjutsu Fushiki Hen* [32] in regard to Hori the swordsman's discourse, may be summed up as follows:

The perfect swordsman avoids quarreling or fighting. Fighting means killing. How can one human being bring himself to kill a fellow being? We are all meant to love one another and not to kill. It is abhorrent that one should be thinking all the time of fighting and coming out victorious. We are moral beings, we are not to lower ourselves to the status of animality. What is the use of becoming a fine swordsman if he loses his human dignity? The best thing is to be a victor without fighting.

The sword is an inauspicious instrument to kill in some unavoidable circumstances. When it is to be used, therefore, it ought to be the sword that gives life and not the sword that kills. But when a man is born into the samurai family, he is not to shun learning the art of swordplay, for it is his profession to be trained in it. The point is, however, to utilize the art as a means to advance in the study of the Way (*tao*). When it is properly handled, it helps us in an efficient way to contribute to the cultivation of the mind and spirit.

One great advantage the sword has over mere book-reading is that once you make a false move you are sure to give the op-

[32] The *Kenjutsu Fushiki Hen* ("The Unknown in the Art of Swordsmanship") is a short treatise on swordplay compiled by Kimura Kyūho in 1768. Kimura was a disciple of Hori, and he records in this book his master's dialogue with a visitor. The manuscript was printed in 1925.

ponent a chance to beat you. You have to be on the alert all the time. While to be on the alert is not the ultimate of swordsmanship, it keeps you true to yourself: that is to say, you are not allowed to indulge in idle thinking. Thinking is useful in many ways, but there are some occasions when thinking interferes with the work, and you have to leave it behind and let the unconscious come forward. In such cases, you cease to be your own conscious master but become an instrument in the hands of the unknown. The unknown has no ego-consciousness and consequently no thought of winning the contest, because it moves at the level of nonduality, where there is neither subject nor object. It is for this reason that the sword moves where it ought to move and makes the contest end victoriously. This is the practical application of the Lao-tzuan doctrine of "doing by not doing." Sun-tzŭ, a great authority on warfare, says: "It is not the best thing to win every battle one is engaged in; the best thing is to win without planning to win. This is perfect victory."

To be on the alert means to be deadly serious, to be deadly serious means to be sincere to oneself, and it is sincerity that finally leads one to discover the Heavenly Way. The Heavenly Way is above the self, which is *mushin*, "no-mind," or *munen*, "no-thought." When *mushin* is realized, the mind knows no obstructions, no inhibitions, and is emancipated from the thoughts of life and death, gain and loss, victory and defeat. As long as a man is possessed of the thought of defeating the enemy, his mind will be kept fully occupied with all kinds of scheming to attain this end. If, however, the enemy happens to be more proficient in technical tactics—which is very likely the case—the defeat will not be on the side of the enemy. If both are equally matched, the outcome will be mutual killing. When a scheme meets a scheme, this is the inevitable fate. Therefore, the perfect swordsman goes beyond all manner of dichotomy, and it is in this way that he is more than a mere wielder of the sword.

The samurai carries two swords, a long and a short, and it is his profession to be trained in their use. But he ought not to be thinking of exercising power and making an appeal to the sword that kills. For the sense of power is always liable to be abused. The sword, therefore, is to be an instrument to kill the ego, which is the root of all quarrels and fightings. The Yagyū school makes "the drinking in one gulp of the waters of the West River" the culmination of training in swordsmanship, so far as its principle is concerned. The technical details are to be subordinated to the principle which really constitutes the spiritual personality of the swordsman. The school represented by Hori Kintayū primarily belongs to the original school of Yagyū Tajima no kami, and it was Yagyū himself who traced every stage of sword training to Zen Buddhism, as advocated by Takuan his teacher. "The waters of the West River," as I have already stated, comes from Baso's answer to Hō the Layman, whose question was: "Who is he that stands all alone with no company in the midst of the ten thousand objects?" I do not know if those swordsmen, who somewhat glibly refer to this Zen dictum, all understood what it really meant. Judging from the way they write about it, I am afraid they had no personal experience of it. While this might have been true, what is most remarkable is that they somehow connected "the waters of the West River" with the ultimate principle that controls the unconscious proceedings of swordsmanship. Even when they had all mastered the detailed intricacies of technique, they could not be termed perfect swordsmen unless they dived deeply into the West River and interviewed "the one who has no companion in the midst of the ten thousand objects." Probably the motive that prompted Kimura Kyūho, the disciple of Hori Kintayū, to write this short treatise on swordsmanship and call it "The Unknown in the Art of Swordplay" was that, in his day, there were probably very few swordplayers who really understood Baso.

Let me finish with the quotation making up the conclusion of Kimura's, or rather Hori's, dialogue:

Q. All that you say is fine. I am in complete agreement with you. But how difficult it is to apply it to practical details of the art!

A. The point is to realize that all that is expressible by symbols or letters is secondary, that they are no more than mere tracks. So Zen masters refuse to acknowledge that letters or words are final. What is important is to reach the ultimate substance by means of those tracks or letters or symbols. The ultimate reality itself is not a symbol, it leaves no tracks, it cannot be communicated by letters or words, but we come to it by tracing them to the source where they come forth. As long as we stop at symbolization or mere speculation, we cannot realize the principle.

Q. When we give up symbolization or speculation, are we not left in the utter nothingness of things?

A. Yes, it is of the utmost difficulty to come to a realization. Therefore, the masterly trainer is always careful to train the beginners along the parallel lines of technical exercises and the understanding of the principle. The latter may not come to a man, even throughout his life. The main business is to seek it not in things external but within oneself.

Q. In this case, there is no "secret transmission" in swordsmanship either?

A. The last thing can never be transmitted from one person to another. It comes from within oneself. All the technical discipline is meant to make swordsmen finally see this. It is also the case with learning generally. There is not much use in mere scholarship. You may read all the books there are on the subject of spiritual training and attainment, but the culmination is to realize the mystery of being, and the realization is from within yourself, for it cannot come from anywhere else. If it does, it is not yours but somebody else's.

Q. Can you tell me something about this mystery?

A. All that I can say is that I do not know or that it is not intelligible.

Q. If so, are we meant to remain utter simpletons?

A. No, not that. It is to know and yet not to know.

Q. Why?

A. No why. It is to know as though not knowing. The last word I can say is: it is beyond knowledge (*fushiki* or *fuchi*).[33]

---

[33] When Bodhidharma saw the Emperor Wu of the Liang dynasty, the Emperor asked, "What is the holy ultimate truth?" Dharma answered, "It is Emptiness itself and there is nothing holy." "Who then is the one who at present stands confronting me?" "I do not know (*fushiki, pu-shih*)!" *Heki-gan-shū* ("Blue Rock Collection"; *Pi-yen Chi*), fasc. 1, case 1.

VI

Zen and Swordsmanship

II

1

A MONK asked Daishu Ekai (Ta-chu Hui-hai),[1] one of the
T'ang masters, when Zen was in its heyday:
"What is great *nirvāṇa?*"
The master answered, "Not to commit oneself to the karma
of birth-and-death is great *nirvāṇa.*"
"What, then, is the karma of birth-and-death?"
"To desire great *nirvāṇa* is the karma of birth-and-death."

In Buddhism, *nirvāṇa* and *saṁsāra* (birth-and-death) are con-
trasted, and we are told that, in order to attain *nirvāṇa, saṁsāra*
is to be transcended. Daishu's first answer, therefore, is quite
correct, but his second answer will puzzle us, because if we did
not desire *nirvāṇa* how could we have it come to us all by itself?
This does not seem logical. Inasmuch as *nirvāṇa* is something
desirable and all Buddhists are advised to strive after it so as
to escape this bondage of *saṁsāra* that causes us to suffer all
kinds of tribulation, is it not the rational thing for us to desire
nirvāṇa and to strive after its attainment by all means? How
could the desire for *nirvāṇa* be the karma of birth-and-death?
Daishu's answer must be regarded as something utterly irrational. But the Zen masters are most irrational teachers, and

---

[1] Ekai was one of the disciples of Baso Dōichi (Ma-tsu Tao-i, d. 788). The
following *mondo* is taken from his work, *Tongo Nyūmon Ron*, "Treatise on
Attaining Sudden Enlightenment."

they would request us to carry out this irrationality in our daily life. It is a great mistake to adjust everything to the Procrustean bed of logic and a greater mistake to make logic the supreme test in the evaluation of human behavior. What is known as *myō* or *myōyū* [2] in Japanese arts comes out when the rationality of things ceases to be valued. In fact, all works of original creativity are the products of the unconscious that go beyond rationalistic schematization. It is not only the Mahāyāna Buddhists but all the Taoist philosophers who are set against intellectualization in the matter of spiritual training. For this reason, the Zen master declares that *nirvāna* is attained only when it is not desired. To desire is to make a choice, and the choosing is intellection, while *nirvāna* is on the other side of intellection.

In this connection, a passage from St. Paul's Epistle to the Corinthians might be quoted: "And they that weep, as though they wept not; and they that rejoice, as though they rejoiced not; and they that buy, as though they possessed not; and they that use this world, as not abusing it" (I Cor. 7 : 30). So let us desire *nirvāna* as though we desired not. When this paradox is understood we are in possession of *nirvāna*, which is to be as if not possessing it. To be consciously unconscious, or to be unconsciously conscious, is the secret of *nirvāna*, out of which issues the *myōyū* of creativity. *Myō* or *myōyū* is a Japanese word signifying "something defying the challenge of man's thinking powers." In other words, it is a mode of activity which comes directly out of one's inmost self without being intercepted by the dichotomous intellect. The act is so direct and immediate that intellection finds no room here to insert itself and cut it to pieces.

According to another Zen master, "As long as a student of Zen entertains any kind of thought in regard to birth-and-death, he falls into the path of the devil. As soon as he lets himself cherish any view, he joins the group of sophistic philosophers." This

---

[2] *Myō* (*miao* in Chinese) is "something beyond an analytical understanding"; *yū* (*yung*) is its "movement" or "operation." A fuller explanation is given in the next paragraph.

means that it is only when we are out of an intellectual grip of any kind that we transcend birth-and-death and can work freely in the mysterious realm of the Unborn, where the artists can display *myō* in all its varieties. A "view" or "thought" is the outcome of intellection, and wherever this is found this creativity of the Unborn or the Unconscious meets all sorts of obstacles. This is the reason why the Zen master advises us not to cherish even one "thought" or "view," negative or affirmative, concerning birth-and death as well as *nirvāṇa*. The intellect is meant for utilitarianism, and whatever creativity it may have operates within this limit and never beyond it.

2

THERE is something like this in the art of swordsmanship. I call it an art, and it is a deadly art, for when a man makes one false move he is sure to lose his life. It is a game of life and death. The sword is right before you, ready at any moment to strike you down. While in Buddhism we can say that the struggle is between the ideas of *nirvāṇa* and *saṁsāra,* in swordsmanship the struggle is between life and death. The Buddhist struggle is more on the plane of conceptualism, but the swordsman's is most realistic and therefore psychologically more poignantly felt. But as long as both are expressed in terms of struggle and dichotomy, the best way and the only way to get out of it, according to the ordinary way of thinking, is to choose either horn of the dilemma and go ahead, not thinking of the consequences it may bring upon the one who has made the decision. This may, in the case of the swordsman, mean certain death. But as long as the thought of death is in the consciousness, it will unconsciously but inevitably lead the swordsman in the direction he is most anxious to avoid. The other way then left for him to choose is to give up the idea of surviving the combat. For it often happens that he who loves life loses it and he who hates life finds it, as the Christians would say. But the truth is: You may "love" or "hate" anything, but as long as either of the feelings skulks anywhere in your brain, it will somehow color your behavior, and your sword will be affected to that extent. The true swordsman must also be "a perfect man" in the Taoist sense: he must be above life and death, as the Buddhist philosopher is above *nirvāṇa* and *saṁsāra*. A struggle of any nature can never be settled satisfactorily until the point is touched where neither side can affect the other. Not neutrality, not indifference, but transcendence is the thing needed. And this is exactly what the swordsman aims at. It may sound strange that he wishes to be a philosopher, but in Japan and also in China the arts are not a matter of technology but of spiritual insight and training. Swordsmanship is no exception.

He who transcends the dualistic idea of life and death goes on living, in the genuine sense of the term. When there is the thought either of life or of death, negatively or positively, this will surely prove to be a stumbling block in the way of life. As the thought of *saṁsāra* as well as of *nirvāṇa* is to be transcended in the Buddhist struggle, so with the swordsman, he must think of neither life nor death. When he attains to this he will be a great genius or a "perfect man" in the art of swordsmanship.

The swordsman may not have any desire for an "eternal life" or "immortality," but he must plan for his sword to be fully alive in order that it may exhibit all the secret *myōyū* [3] en-

---

[3] *Myōyū* (*miao-yung* in Chinese) or *daiyū* (*ta-yung*), or simply *myō*, is quite a difficult word for English-speaking people to grasp. It is a certain artistic quality perceivable not only in works of art but in anything in Nature or life. The sword in the hands of the swordsman attains this quality when it is not a mere display of technical skill patiently learned under the tutorship of a good master, for *myō* is something original and creative growing out of one's own unconscious. The hands may move according to the technique given out to every student, but there is a certain spontaneity and personal creativity when the technique, conceptualized and universalized, is handled by the master hand. *Myō* may also be applied to the intelligence and the instinctive activities of various animals, for example, the beaver

trusted to it, for his life entirely depends on it, as though not de-
pending on it. As long as the man resorts to his acquired technique in order to put the opponent to defeat, he will have to
watch the latter's every sword movement and follow it up to the
minutest point. This will, however, make his mind "stop" temporarily, however short this moment of stoppage may be. Instead of keeping his mind in a state of perfect fluidity, so that
he can strike the enemy the moment the latter shows a *suki*,[4] he
will have to have his attention glued to the enemy's sword. This
gluing is "stoppage," and every stoppage means giving an advantage to the enemy, which is a *suki*. *Suki* literally means "an
interval of relaxation." When one is engaged in a struggle of
life and death, one's psychology will experience the highest

building its nest, the spider spinning its web, the wasp or ant constructing
its castles under the eaves or beneath the ground. They are wonders of Nature. In fact, the whole universe is a miraculous exhibition of a master mind,
and we humans who are one of its wonderful achievements have been strain-
ing our intellectual efforts ever since the awakening of consciousness, and
are daily being overwhelmed by Nature's demonstrations of its unfathomable
and inexhaustive *myōyū*. The awakening of consciousness has been the greatest cosmological event in the course of evolution. We have been able by its
pragmatic applications to probe into the secrets of Nature and to make use
of them to serve our way of living, but at the same time we seem to be losing the many things we have otherwise been enjoying which Nature was liberal enough to grant us. The function of human consciousness, as I see it,
is to dive deeper and deeper into its source, the unconscious. And the unconscious has its strata of variable depths: biological, psychological, and
metaphysical. One thread runs through them, and Zen discipline consists in
taking hold of it in its entirety, whereas other arts, such as swordsmanship
or tea, lead us to the comprehension of respectively particularized aspects of
the string.

4 *Suki*, as has already been stated, means "a space between two objects,"
or "a slit or split or crack in one solid object." When continuity is broken
up and a crack begins to show, there is a *suki*. When tension slackens, certain signs of laxity appear—which is *suki*. In Takuan's terminology, *suki*
corresponds to "stopping." In swordsmanship, this is taken advantage of by
the enemy, who is always too ready not to let the opportunity slip away
vainly. In one of the self-portraits of Miyamoto Musashi, a great swordsman
and painter of the seventeenth century, his pose would indicate him to be
full of *suki*, but he keeps his eyes wide open so as not to allow the opponent
to make use of the *suki* that is really only apparent. A great deal of spiritual
training is needed for a swordsman to reach this stage, properly called "open
on all sides" (*happō biraki*).

[38, 39, 41

degree of keenness, and whenever and wherever the least interval
of relaxation is caught, the deadly blow will instantly follow from
the other side.

What might be called a "psychical stoppage" comes out of a
very much deeper source. When there is the slightest feeling of
fear of death or of attachment to life, the mind loses its "fluidity." The fluidity is nonhindrance. Have the mind devoid of all
fear, free from all forms of attachment, and it is master of itself,
it knows no hindrances, no inhibitions, no stoppages, no clog-
gings. It then follows its own course like water. It is like the
wind that bloweth where it listeth. It can further be likened to
a circle whose center is everywhere as it has no circumference.
Ontologically, the Buddhist philosophers call it a state of emptiness (*śūnyatā*). The artists might not attain to this metaphysical height of consciousness, which is really no consciousness in the ordinary sense. But they must have experienced
something akin to it, without becoming clearly conscious of it.
When the swordsman compares his art, as the Zen master does,
to the moon's reflection in the water, he must be said to have
experienced a state of the unconscious in which he holds his
sword as if not holding it and uses it as if not using it.

Morally or rather spiritually speaking, this is a state of egolessness. It is the ego that stands rigidly against things coming from
the outside, and it is this ego rigidity that makes it impossible
for us to accept everything that confronts us. We are now no
more like the babes and sucklings whom God prefers to wise
men, because those babes have not yet "developed" to the stage
of intellectual maturity. The intellect divides and discriminates,
resists and rejects, chooses and decides, and it is by these qualities that we are prevented from "letting thy will be done."
Without the sense of an ego, there is no moral responsibility,
but the divine transcends morality. So does art. Art lives where
absolute freedom is, because where it is not, there can be no creativity. Freedom and creativity and *myōyū* are synonymous. The

art of swordsmanship belongs in this category. Unless the swordsman reaches this stage of freedom where he has no ego rigidity,
he cannot expect to wield the sword that gives life instead of
taking it.

The sword is generally associated with killing, and most of us
wonder how it can come into connection with Zen, which is a
school of Buddhism teaching the gospel of love and mercy. The
fact is that the art of swordsmanship distinguishes between the
sword that kills and the sword that gives life. The one that is
used by a technician cannot go any further than killing, for he
never appeals to the sword unless he intends to kill. The case is
altogether different with the one who is compelled to lift the
sword. For it is really not he but the sword itself that does the
killing. He has no desire to do harm to anybody, but the enemy
appears and makes himself a victim. It is as though the sword
performs automatically its function of justice, which is the function of mercy. This is the kind of sword that Christ is said to
have brought among us. It is not meant just for bringing the
peace mawkishly cherished by sentimentalists; it is the sword
used by Rikyū [5] the teaman for self-immolation; it is the sword
of Vajrarāja recommended by Rinzai (Lin-chi) [6] for the use of
Zen-men; it is the sword Banzan Hōjaku (P'an-shan) [7] would
swing regardless of its lack of utilitarianism. When the sword
is expected to play this sort of role in human life, it is no more
a weapon of self-defense or an instrument of killing, and the
swordsman turns into an artist of the first grade, engaged in
producing a work of genuine originality.

[5] Rikyū, or Sen no Rikyū, was a great teaman. See "Zen and the Art of
Tea" and "Rikyū and Other Teamen."

[6] Rinzai Gigen (Lin-chi I-hsüan, d. 867) distinguishes four kinds of
"Katsu!" (ho in Chinese), and one of them is likened to the sacred sword
of Vajrarāja, which cuts and puts to death anything dualistic appearing before it. See above, p. 66, n. 2.

[7] Banzan (8th century), in one of his sermons, compares Zen's purposeless
activity to the swinging of the sword in the air. Dentōroku ("Transmission of
the Lamp"), fasc. 7.

3

S O M E may ask: How can the sword which implements the will to kill work out its function by itself without the willer's directive behind it? What originality, what creative work, can an inanimate mechanical tool be made to carry out all by itself? When a tool performs whatever function it is made to perform, can we say it has achieved something original?

The point is: When the sword is in the hands of a technician-swordsman skilled in its use, it is no more than an instrument with no mind of its own. What it does is done mechanically, and there is no *myōyū* discernible in it. But when the sword is held by the swordsman whose spiritual attainment is such that he holds it as though not holding it, it is identified with the man himself, it acquires a soul, it moves with all the subtleties which have been imbedded in him as a swordsman. The man emptied of all thoughts, all emotions originating from fear, all sense of insecurity, all desire to win, is not conscious of using the sword; both man and sword turn into instruments in the hands, as it were, of the unconscious, and it is this unconscious that achieves wonders of creativity. It is here that swordplay becomes an art.

As the sword is not separated from the man, it is an extension of his arms and accordingly a part of his body. Furthermore, the body and the mind are not separated, as they are in the case of intellectualization. The mind and the body move in perfect unison, with no interference from intellect or emotion. Even the distinction of subject and object is annihilated. The opponent's movements are not perceived as such and therefore the subject, so called, acts instinctually in response to what is presented to him. There is no deliberation on his part as to how to react. His unconscious automatically takes care of the whole situation.

The swordsman calls this unconscious "the mind that is no-mind" (*mushin no shin*), or "the mind that knows no stopping" (*tomaranu kokoro*), or "the mind abandoned and yet not abandoned" (*sutete sutenu kokoro*), or "the everyday mind" (*heijō-shin*). The secret of swordsmanship consists in attaining to this state of mentality—or, we may call it, spirituality, because it is beyond the realm of psychological phenomenalism. Yagyū Tajima no kami Munenori (1571–1646), one of the greatest swordsmen in the history of the art, taught Tokugawa Iyemitsu (1604–1651), the third Shōgun of the Tokugawa regime. This Tajima no kami studied Zen under Takuan (1573–1645) and incorporated much of the Zen teaching into his treatise on swordsmanship. He says that the mind that is no mind is the last stage in the art of swordplay. "To be of no-mind" (*mushin*) means the "everyday mind" (*heijō-shin*), and when this is attained, everything goes on well. In the beginning, one naturally endeavors to do his best in handling the sword, as in learning any other art. The technique has to be mastered. But as soon as his mind is fixed on anything, for instance if he desires to do well, or to display his skill, or to excel others, or if he is too anxiously bent on mastering his art, he is sure to commit more mistakes than are actually necessary. Why? Because his self-consciousness or ego-consciousness is too conspicuously present over the entire range of his attention—which fact interferes with a free display of whatever proficiency he has so far acquired or is going to acquire. He must get rid of this obtruding self- or ego-consciousness and apply himself to the work to be done as if nothing particular were taking place at the moment. When things are performed in a state of "no-mind" (*mushin*) or "no-thought" (*munen*), which means the absence of all modes of self- or ego-consciousness, the actor is perfectly free from inhibitions and feels nothing thwarting his line of behavior. If he is shooting, he just takes out his bow, puts an arrow to it, stretches the string, fixes his eyes on the target, and when he judges the adjustment to be right he lets the arrow go. He has no feeling of doing anything specifically good or bad, important or trivial; it is as if he hears a sound, turns around, and finds a bird in the court. This is one's "everyday mind" (*heijō-shin*).

The swordsman is thus advised to retain this state of mentality even when he is engaged in a deadly combat. He forgets the seriousness of his situation. He has no thought of life and death. His is an "immovable mind" (*fudō-shin*). The *fudō-shin* is like the moon reflected in the stream. The waters are in motion all the time, but the moon retains its serenity. The mind moves in response to the ten thousand situations but remains ever the same. The art culminates here. All the scheming of the intellect has been quieted, and no artifice finds room for its demonstration.

Yagyū Tajima no kami quotes in this connection words of Hō Koji (P'ang the Lay Disciple): "It is like the wooden horse facing the flowers or birds." [8] This is the state of *mushin* (no-mind). The wooden horse has no mind, no sentiency. Even when it confronts the flowers, or hears a bird singing, it is utterly unmoved. Man is altogether different from the wooden horse. He has sentiency and is subject to all kinds of stimulation. But when he finds himself moved in one way or another, he is committed. Even though engaged in the struggle for life, the swordsman must not be disturbed, he must remain master of himself, must be like the wooden horse, insensible to all the environmental vicissitudes.

The wooden horse's or wooden cock's insensibility may lead some readers to imagine that Yagyū Tajima no kami wishes us to be reduced to a stage of mental atrophy or imbecility. [9] But the fact is far from this, for what he really intends here is to free the mind from every possible psychic obstruction or inhibition and to restore it to its pristine purity in order to display its native activities to the utmost limit. In the case of swordsmanship, this is to sharpen the psychic power of seeing in order to act immediately in accordance with what it sees. Tajima no kami thinks that the seeing must first take place in the mind, and then it is transmitted to the eyes, and finally to the body and limbs. The latter mode of seeing means acting. As it is not the eyes but the inner mind itself that first catches up the movements of the

[8] See below, pp. 165, 439.   [9] See below, pp. 164, 436 ff.

enemy, the body loses no time in adjusting itself to the situation. If it is the physical organ of sight that first perceives the outside world, as our psychologists would tell us, the act that is needed to follow up the first perception will have to go through the anatomical process of transmission as we have it in our medical textbooks. This will, however, be too tortuous a procedure for the swordsman in the thick of combat involving life. He cannot afford such a luxury or refinement. He must act without intellectual jugglery or, as some would call it, tomfoolery. Hence Tajima no kami's most penetrating observation.

This reminds us of Chuang-tzŭ's advice regarding the practice of "mind-fasting" (shin-sai). He first refers to a highly unified state of consciousness and goes on to say: For instance, in hearing do not use the ear, but the mind (kokoro, hsin); do not use the mind but ch'i (spirit). When you use the ear, the hearing stops there, and the mind cannot go further than the symbol; ch'i is something empty and waiting. Tao abides in the emptiness, and the emptiness is mind-fasting.[10]

Ch'i is a difficult term to translate into English. It is something imperceptible, impalpable, that pervades the entire universe. In one sense, it corresponds to spirit (pneuma), it is the breath of heaven and earth. Where Chuang-tzŭ defines "mind-fasting" as seeing and hearing with ch'i, the idea is to transcend the centripetence of the ego-consciousness, for as long as there is "one thought" (ichi-nen, i-nien) of it in the mind, this will surely and efficiently block up the fluidity of movement and produce a suki for the enemy to take advantage of. Chuang-tzŭ's "mind-fasting" naturally goes much deeper than the art of swordsmanship. For Chuang-tzŭ is aware, though not in the ordinary sense of cognition, of the emptiness (kyo, hsü) [11] in which infinite possibilities are harbored, whereas the

[10] An abstract. Chuang Tzŭ, IV. Cf. Giles' translation, p. 43.
[11] This corresponds to the Buddhist idea of śūnyatā, emptiness (k'ung), but hsü as conceived by Lao-tzŭ, Chuang-tzŭ, and other Taoists still contains a residue of relativity and fails to reach the depths of the śūnyatā of Mahāyāna Buddhist metaphysics.

swordsman may be said to have not yet experienced the metaphysical source of all things. It is, however, possible for one who has seen deeply into the secrets of his art to have also touched the ground of reality. The difference between the swordsman and the Zen master as regards their insight is this: The swordsman's is restricted to his specialized art, while the master's covers the entirety of existence because of his background and equipment and special training.

4

IT MAY BE interesting in this connection to quote largely from Yagyū Tajima no kami's treatise on swordsmanship,[12] which gives so much insight into the psychology and philosophy of the art. The author goes profoundly into the inner experience of his profession and shows how essential it is to search thoroughly into the spirituality of the art, which is not after all a mere system of technology. The wielding of the sword does not mean just striking down the opponent, but it is concerned with the working of Tao and the harmonious cooperation of *yin* and *yang* in their cosmological movements. Metaphysics enters deeply into swordsmanship.

Yagyū Tajima no kami was a good student of Zen under Takuan, who instructed him well in the spirituality of swordplay. According to the Zen master, the art can never be understood unless one goes through a system of training in the philosophy of Buddhism. Yagyū's writing thus echoes a great deal of Takuan's point of view, which was quoted previously. This fact

---

[12] This was written in 1632 for the benefit of the author's sons. It was handed down in manuscript form as a secret document not to be perused by outsiders. In 1937, Dr. Fukui Kyūzō made a number of such manuscripts accessible to the general public. They were written mostly by feudal lords and other eminent personages during the Tokugawa regime, and were circulated among limited circles. The Yagyū manuscript on swordsmanship naturally shows the influence of Takuan, his Zen teacher.

can also be gleaned from the way Yagyū divides his treatise into three parts, adopting the terms currently used in the Zen texts, notably in the "Blue Rock Collection": (1) "The sword that kills," (2) "The sword that gives life," and (3) "The sword of no-sword." The first part treats mainly of the technique of swordplay; the second touches upon the "mystical" Zen aspect leading to the final stage; and this, making up the third part, gives the author's understanding of the Zen experience as applied to the art or the way of the sword.

YAGYŪ TAJIMA NO KAMI
ON THE 'MYSTICAL SWORD'[13]

ALL WEAPONS meant to kill are inauspicious, and must never be used except on occasions of extreme urgency. If any at all is to be used, however, let it be known that it is only for the purpose of punishing evils and not for depriving one of life. To understand this, learning is the first requisite. But mere learning will never do. It is an entrance gate through which one is to proceed to the residence proper to interview the master himself. The master is Tao (truth). Tao is above mere learning, but without learning one cannot expect to reach the ultimate Tao. Tao is reached when one's mind is entirely emptied of delusive thoughts and intriguing feelings. And when Tao is thus finally realized, you have the knowledge of all things, but this knowledge

---

[13] In the following pages I have freely culled passages from Yagyū's text disregarding the divisions, in order to present Yagyū's philosophy of swordplay as I understand it. The original is too long, too full of difficult terminology remote from modern thought, to be rendered into any of the Indo-European languages. Any translation of this sort of literature is inevitably an interpretation largely admixed with the translator's ideas and background. It is chiefly for this reason that I have not attempted to mark off Yagyū's words from mine. They are hopelessly mixed up. I hope that, some day, someone will strive to write specifically about what may be designated as the psychology of Zen applied to various fields of art in its development in the Far East.

is not to obstruct your living in Tao. For learning and knowledge are after all meant to be "forgotten," and it is only when this is realized that you feel perfectly comfortable in your transaction of business of any kind. As long as you have the sense of something still missing or, on the other hand, clinging on to you, you will be haunted by the feeling either of insufficiency or of "being bound" by something, and there will be no freedom for you.

When a man in the beginning of his life is ignorant of everything, he has no scruples, finds no obstacles, no inhibitions. But after a while he starts to learn, and becomes timid, cautious, and begins to feel something choking in his mind, which prevents him from going ahead as he used to before he had any learning. Learning is needed, but the point is not to become its slave. You must be its master so that you can use it when you want it. You have to apply this psychology to swordplay. The swordsman must not harbor anything external and superfluous in his mind, his mind must be perfectly purged of all egocentric emotions. When this is carried out and the mind itself is "lost" so that even devils cannot trace its whereabouts, he can for the first time make full use of the technique he has acquired. No, he goes even further than this, because he now forgets all that he has learned, because he is the learning itself and there is no separation of learner and learning. Indeed, this is the ultimate goal of discipline in all arts where learning gained is learning lost.

However well a man may be trained in the art, the swordsman can never be the master of his technical knowledge unless all his psychic hindrances are removed and he can keep the mind in the state of emptiness, even purged of whatever technique he has obtained. The entire body together with the four limbs will then be capable of displaying for the first time and to its full extent all the art acquired by the training of several years. They will move as if automatically, with no conscious efforts on the part of the swordsman himself. His activities will be a perfect model of swordplay. All the training is there, but the mind is utterly unconscious of it. The mind, it may be said, does not know where it is. When this is realized, with all the training thrown to the wind, with a mind perfectly unaware of its own workings, with the self vanishing nowhere anybody knows, the art of swordsmanship attains its perfection, and one who has it is called a *meijin* ("genius").

Yagyū Tajima no kami then proceeds to tell us how certain "diseases" are to be avoided in order to be a perfect master of swordsmanship. In what has been cited above, we can readily see how closely the training in the art approaches that in Zen. Learning of the technique corresponds to an intellectual apprehension in Zen of its philosophy, and in both Zen and swordplay a proficiency in this does not cover the whole ground of the discipline. Both require us to come to the attainment of ultimate reality, which is the Emptiness or the Absolute. The latter transcends all modes of relativity. In swordplay, all the technique is to be forgotten and the Unconscious is to be left alone to handle the situation, when the technique will assert its wonders automatically or spontaneously. So in Zen conceptualization, whatever form it may take is to be thrown out of the mind when the Emptiness reveals itself, illumining a world of multiplicities. For this reason we assert that the principle of Zen discipline pervades all the arts as they are studied in Japan. The personal experience of an inner meaning in any art which a man may take up is all in all; the technique is not to be neglected, of course, but after all it is secondary. The "diseases" the philosopher of swordplay enumerates are discernible in any branch of art, and their knowledge will also help us greatly in the understanding of the Japanese culture generally.

An idea, however worthy and desirable in itself, becomes a disease when the mind is obsessed with it. The diseases or obsessions the swordsman has to get rid of are: (*1*) the desire for victory, (2) the desire to resort to technical cunning, (3) the desire to display all that he has learned, (4) the desire to overawe the enemy, (5) the desire to play a passive role, and lastly, (6) the desire to get rid of whatever disease he is likely to be infected with. When any one of these obsesses him, he becomes its slave, as it makes him lose all the freedom he is entitled to as a swordsman.

How are we to be free from all these diseases or obsessions? If any kind of desire that is present in the mind—even the desire to be free from a desire—interferes with the spontaneous activities of an inner harmony, what shall we have to do? The desire must be cherished somewhere and somehow, for otherwise nothing will be attained; even desirelessness must be desired sometime. How can this dilemma be solved? A second wedge is needed to get the first one out, but how do we get rid of the second one unless a third is inserted? This process will have to go on infinitely if we are desirous of driving the last one out. So with "the disease" Yagyū wants the swordsman to be free from, there will be no time for him to be diseaseless when the desire to be free from the disease is also a disease. It is again like pursuing one's shadow; however hard one may run after it, he can never succeed as long as his own existence persists.

In Zen we have the same problem. It is desired to be free from attachment, but we can never do away with attachment if this is desired in any manner. In terms of logic, a desire can be expressed in a form of statement, either positive or negative. For instance, we can say, "I desire this" or "I do not desire this." "To desire" is an attachment, "to desire not to desire" is also an attachment. To be unattached then means to be free at once from both statements, positive and negative. In other words, this is to be simultaneously both "yes" and "no," which is intellectually absurd. The Zen master holds up a stick and demands, "I do not call it a stick, and what would you call it?"

Or he would declare, "I hold a spade and yet I am empty-handed, for it is the way I accomplish turning the soil." Disciples of Zen are required to achieve this impossibility.

Toward the solution of this eternal dilemma, Yagyū quotes an old Japanese poem:

> *It is mind that deludes Mind,*
> *For there is no other mind.*
> *O Mind, do not let yourself*
> *Be misled by mind.*[14]

The swordsman-philosopher undertakes to explain what these lines mean in connection with the solution of the enigma. He first distinguishes two kinds of mind, true or absolute and false or relative. The one is the subject of psychological studies, while the other is Reality, which constitutes the basis of all realities. In the poem quoted, mind is the false one and Mind is the true one. The true one is to be protected from the false one in order to preserve its purity and freedom unspoiled. But somehow a desire arises from the false relative mind and contaminates the true absolute Mind. Therefore, the former is to be carefully watched over. But who does this watching? It cannot be any other than the false one which is both the spoiler and the cleaner. For Mind, the true one, always remains pure and undefiled. This is indeed the strange experience we all have. Perhaps it is better to say that this is something inevitable to intellectualization, something unavoidable in language, and that, constructed as it is, the intellect cannot do any otherwise, for it is the very nature of the intellect that it involves itself in the contradiction and helplessly bemoans its destiny. As long as we

[14] *Kokoro koso*
Kokoro mayowasu
Kokoro nare;
Kokoro ni,
Kokoro,
Kokoro yurusu na.

have to use language in one way or another, we cannot help feeling a certain split taking place within ourselves, which is contradiction.

"Why" is a word useful only in a world of relativity where a chain of causes and effects has some meaning for human intellection. When we desire to transcend it the question ceases to have sense. A solitary mass of cloud somehow—nobody knows how—appears in the blue sky and, immediately spreading, covers its entirety, and we are unable to see beyond the veil. But somehow, again, we come to cherish a desire to penetrate it, we cannot help longing for the blue sky. We are thus again somehow urged to think that the clouds and the blue sky must be interrelated, though there is apparently no causal connection between the two. We are somehow to recognize the presence of the clouds along with the blue sky: we see somehow the presence of the blue sky in and with the darkness of the clouds. The clouds themselves then cease to be clouds—yes, they are there, and yet they cease to trouble us as such, as something veiling the blue. We then rest content with all things as they are, and feel free, emancipated from the bondage unnecessarily put upon us by our own ignorance. The "why" loses its meaning, the contradiction is no more here, and we are happy in the enjoyment of freedom and inner harmony under the blue sky, which is to all our knowledge the storehouse of infinite possibilities, that is, the source of creativity. The blue sky, it goes without saying, is here metaphysically used for the Mind.

The old question, however, still remains: How do we get to the blue sky? Is there any "definable" way to approach it? We have used the term "somehow" throughout the preceding statements, but we all know that this is far from giving satisfaction to our intellect. But what we have to remember here is that the intellect cannot supersede itself. It is the intellect that raises the question, but it is not the intellect that answers it. It is life itself that solves all the questions, that is to say, it is *prajñā*-intuition which sees directly into life. All the communication, therefore, that comes from this source can never be "definitely" described. So it is with Yagyū Tajima no kami in his treatise. As far as the novices, who are always intellectually possessed, are concerned, what he says is altogether unintelligible. He simply says that one has to go on disciplining oneself when one wishes to see the diseases disappear, and that when enough discipline is "accumulated" they will be removed by themselves without one's being conscious of it. Zen in this case generally uses the term *kufū* (*kung-fu* in Chinese) which is synonymous with "discipline" or "training" (*shugyō; hsiu-hsing*). *Kufū*, as defined before, means "employing oneself assiduously to discover the way to the objective." One may say, this is literally groping in the dark, there is nothing definite indicated, we are entirely lost in the maze. I am afraid, however, that this is as far as any master of Zen or swordsmanship can go with his disciples. He leads them until no more leading is possible, and the rest is left to their own devices. If it is a matter of intellection, the way to the goal may be "definitely" prescribed. But in things concerning one's personal experience, all that the master can do is to make the disciples realize that they are now at last in the dark or in the labyrinth and that they must resort to something very much deeper than mere intellection—something which they cannot obtain from another. The way to the objective, if there is such a thing in this training, is no other than the object which they thought was somewhere else than "the way" itself. The "seeking" or desiring is of course a preliminary step, but this step does not lead anywhere outside but within the seeker or desirer himself. The seeking and the seeker, the desire and the desirer, are identical. Thus naturally, there cannot be any intellectual guiding post. When the way and the wayfarer are one, what can the outsider do for him? An intellectual or logical pointer can never be more than a pointer or an onlooker. Personal experience and *Prajñā*-intuition [15] are the same thing.

[15] My *Studies in Zen*, pp. 85 ff.

Yagyū Tajima no kami sometimes calls the Mind the "Sword of Mystery," *Shimmyō-ken*. Being a swordsman, he inevitably emphasizes the activity aspect of the sword instead of its substantiality. That is to say, he wants to see the sword moving functionally. When the sword is held in his hands, it is at an undifferentiated center of a circle that has no circumference. It is ready either to assert itself or to negate itself. The negating is nonbeing and the asserting is being. The sword can be either, according to the situation it meets. Ordinary people are always one-sided. When they see a negation (nonbeing), they fail to see an assertion (being); when they see an assertion, they fail to see a negation. But the expert swordsman sees both negation and assertion at the same time. He perceives that a negation is not just the negation but implies an affirmation. So with the affirmation. This is the Mystery.

Yagyū the philosopher now turns to Lao-tzŭ and gives his interpretation: "Where what is eternal is in the state of non-being we may see the mystery [of being]; where what is eternal is in the state of being we may see the limits [of nonbeing]." By this, says Yagyū, Lao-tzŭ wants to make us see into the interfusion of being and nonbeing. Being does not remain as such, nor does nonbeing. They are always ready to change from one state to the other. This is the "fluidity" of things, and the swordsman must always be on the alert to meet this inter-changeability of the opposites. But as soon as his mind "stops" with either of them, it loses its own fluidity. The swordsman, therefore, is warned to keep his mind always in the state of emptiness so that his freedom in action will never be obstructed. Fluidity [16] and emptiness are convertible terms.

[16] "Fluidity" is an important idea in Oriental thought structure. Enō (Hui-nêng), the sixth patriarch of Chinese Zen, states that Tao is to flow unob-structedly, and the swordsman urges us to keep the mind from "stopping" at one point, to have it in a state of constant mobility, so that the sword loses no time in hitting the opponent as soon as he betrays the least sign of re-laxation (*suki*). This is a *tomaranu kokoro* ("nonstopping mind"), that is, "fluidity." In Kegon philosophy it is known as "Reality in its aspect of *jiji muge*" (cf. my *The Essence of Buddhism*, pp. 48 ff.). The *jiji muge* may

When there is no obstruction of whatever kind, the swords-man's movements are like flashes of lightning or like the mirror reflecting images. There is not a hairbreadth interval between one movement and another. When in his mind there is any shadow of doubt, any sense of fear or insecurity, this indecisive-ness at once reveals itself in his sword's movements, which means a defeat on his part. When the Sword of Mystery is off its original "seat," no *myō* (*miao*) can ever be expected to manifest itself.

This sword stands as symbol of the invisible spirit keeping the mind, body, and limbs in full activity. But we can never locate it in any part of the body. It is like the spirit of a tree. If it had no spirit, there would be no splitting buds, no bloom-ing flowers. Or it is like the spirit or energy (*ki, ch'i*) of heaven and earth. If there were no spirit, there would be no thunder, no lightning, no showers, no sweeping winds. But as to its whereabouts we can never tell. The spirit is no doubt the controlling agent of our existence, though altogether beyond the realm of corporeality. The Sword of Mystery must be made to occupy this invisible "seat" of spirit and control every movement in whatever external situation it may happen to find itself. It is thus to be extremely mobile, no "stopping" in any place at any moment. As soon as the moon is revealed from behind the clouds, it loses no time in casting its shadow wherever there is a body of water, no matter how large or how scanty it may be. An immense distance between heaven and earth is no hindrance to the moonlight to traverse. The swordsman's spirit must be like this. He may find it very difficult to act like this in every intricate situation he may encounter in life. Except for the Zen master who has gone through every stage of training and finds himself free from every psychic hindrance or attach-ment, it is no easy task to mix oneself in all social situations and human complexities and not get caught in them in one way

be interpreted as the metaphysical counterpart of the psychological *tomaranu kokoro.*

or another. However this may be, it is up to the swordsman to preserve this state of spiritual freedom and nonattachment as soon as he stands up holding the sword in his hands. He may not be able to extend this experience in swordsmanship to any other branches of art, but within the limits of his special field he must be master of himself. Those who can apply experience attained in one field to another with perfect readiness are called men of "all-around fluidity." Such are rare; most of us are specialized. In all events, what is most important is to grasp the original mind of truth and integrity that knows no falsehood, and the rest will follow by itself.

From these lengthy paraphrastic statements of Yagyū's philosophy of the sword, we can see how much of Zen metaphysics has entered into the body of swordsmanship. People of the West, particularly, may wonder how Zen came to be so intimately related to the art of killing. Inasmuch as Zen is a form of Buddhism and Buddhism is professedly a religion of compassion, how can Zen endorse the profession of the swordsman? This is the criticism we frequently hear from the Western readers of my books. But I hope they have now come to understand what lies underneath swordsmanship and how this is related to the training of Zen. For, as most students of Oriental culture may understand by this time, whatever field of art the Japanese may study they always emphasize the importance of the "subjective" side of it, giving to its technique a secondary, almost a negligible, consideration. While art is art and has its own significance, the Japanese make use of it by turning it into an opportunity for their spiritual enhancement. And this consists in advancing toward the realization of Tao, or Heavenly Reason of the universe, or Heavenly Nature in man, or the emptiness or suchness of things. Thus the sword is no longer the weapon to kill indiscriminately, but it is one of the avenues

through which life opens up its secrets to us. Hence Yagyū
Tajima no kami and other masters of the profession are in fact
great teachers of life.

5

FOR A further elucidation of Yagyū's position in regard to the
relation between Zen and swordsmanship, I will give here
a résumé of his philosophy, to which Takuan's tract on the
"Sword of Taia" is added. Takuan, as we have already seen,
helped his swordsman-disciple to understand the significance of
Zen in opening up the deepest recesses of the human soul.
Though I do not think he was a swordsman himself, he had profound knowledge of its principle, and there is no doubt that
Yagyū was in this respect a great pupil of the master.

There are five key points, as I see it, in Yagyū's philosophy,
which when understood will acquaint us with the secrets of his
swordsmanship.

(1) The first Yagyū calls *Shuji-shuri-ken.* "*Ken*" means the
sword, but the rest is cryptic, and he purposely refuses to dis-
close it. This forms the center of his art. Although it is impossible, as far as his verbalism is concerned, to find out what
kind of sword, symbolically or literally, the *Shuji-shuri-ken* is,
can it be identified with Takuan's "Sword of Taia"? [17]

Yagyū seems to be speaking psychologically when he makes
his sword see what is not visible as well as what is visible—
and this simultaneously. For the visible is the invisible and
conversely. In terms of logic, "A" is "not-A" and "not-A" is
"A." The sword is, as it were, held at the identification point of
opposites. It is never one-sided, it never stands immobile, it is
becoming itself. The first requisite for the swordsman is to dis-

[17] A full translation of Takuan's "The Sword of Taia" is appended to this
section, below.

cover this sword within himself. One may be the master of ever so many technical tactics, but if he lacks the eye to see the sword they are of no avail whatever.

(2) The second topic is concerned with the "base" or "seat" which the swordsman is to occupy. It is entitled "the moon and water." It is taken from one of the Buddhist similes that are used to illustrate the quickness or immediacy with which the mind perceives an object appearing before it. When the moon reveals itself behind a mass of clouds, as they are dispersed, it is reflected immediately on the water. It is the same with the mirror that reflects the flower as soon as the latter presents itself before it. So with the swordsman's position or base when he stands before his opponent, it must be such that he can readily invade the latter's field at his own pleasure and with the immediacy of the moon reflecting itself on the water.

(The present writer, not being himself a swordsman, finds it difficult to determine here exactly what Yagyū means. When he refers to a "base," does he mean a physical one or a spiritual one?)

(3) "The Sword of Mystery" (*Shimmyō-ken*) is next. The sword here is not just a physical one, but I do not know how definitely to distinguish it from the first secret sword which Yagyū refuses to clarify. He writes: "The divine [or the Unconscious] is within and the mysteries manifest themselves outwardly." That is to say, when the divine occupies the seat of the Sword of Mystery, the body and limbs are ready to exhibit all the "floweriness" that belongs to the Unthinkable. From this statement it is evident that this sword, like Takuan's Sword of Taia, is not at all material. It is the Unconscious which works behind the field of consciousness. Ordinarily it is the consciousness that creates all sorts of inhibitions and obstructs the free movements of the man. Because of ideologically or emotionally created inhibitions, he fails to see or detect the movements of the enemy's sword with the immediacy of the moon casting its reflection on the water. The seeing is the all-important factor in

the art of swordsmanship. When this is done, the acting of the body and limbs instantly follows. The Unconscious, therefore, must be brought out and made to occupy the entire field of mentation, so that what is primarily there as a force of instinctual irresistibility makes free use of the consciously accumulated knowledge. This is the wielding of Yagyū's Sword of Mystery.

By thus applying the modern psychology of the Unconscious to the art of swordplay we may be able to interpret not only Yagyū's methodology but also that of other schools, for instance, the school of *Mujūshin-ken* ("Sword of No-abiding Mind"), which will follow in the next section.

But how should we understand the secret "Sword of *Shuji-shuri*" in relation to this "Sword of Mystery"? Perhaps the secret sword belongs in the spiritual or metaphysical domain which must be postulated as lying beyond the psychological unconscious.

(*4*) To get rid of the diseases or obsessions is the fourth item of concern with Yagyū the philosopher. But as this was treated in the earlier part of the present section, let us be satisfied with the following remark: According to Yagyū, to be rid of the diseases is to see the *Shuri-ken*, "the Secret Sword." As long as we are obsessed with certain preconceived ideas, they are sure to hinder our seeing "the master of the house," and when he is not seen, all our doings are disintegrated. When this takes place in front of the enemy ready at any moment to strike you down, it is the most dangerous thing that could ever happen to the swordsman. The mind chock-full of ideas, therefore, is to be thrown aside, it is to be thoroughly cleared of all obstructing thoughts and feelings, it must be in the state of perfect "emptiness." When this is realized, the *Shuji-shuri-ken* will be an absolute commander, and may have everything according to his free will. The Unconscious dormant at the root of all existence is awakened, it now directs instinctually all the movements not only of the conscious mind but of the physical body. The movements, being instinctual, are as immediate and instantaneous as the moon, which is infinitely far away from us, yet loses no time as soon as the clouds are dispersed to impress its reflection on the water.

(5) Finally, the body and limbs. The seeing may be done with the mind, but the acting needs more substantiality, and seeing and acting must be one, must take place simultaneously. In the case of the perfect swordsman, this becomes possible because he has realized that all movements come out of emptiness and that the mind is the name given to this dynamic aspect of emptiness, and further that here is no crookedness, no ego-centered motivation, as the emptiness is sincerity, genuineness, and straightforwardness allowing nothing between itself and its movements. It is *veni, vidi, vici.* As soon as there appears a speck of cloud tinged with egotistic deviousness, the moonlight of emptiness is befouled and the swordsman is doomed to defeat, for the mind and body will no more obey the dictates of an absentee master.

These five key points, I hope, afford us some material for understanding the inner relation between Zen and swordsmanship. What is noteworthy here is that, while the Buddhist theory of emptiness seems such an abstract and negativistic idea, as some critics would interpret it, it enters deeply and inextricably into the fabric of swordplay, which is after all not child's play but the most dangerous business of life and death. When a stroke is missed all is lost eternally, no idle thinking could enter here. The philosophy of emptiness is in a most decided way and most intimately connected with swordsmanship. Here are a few short quotations from Yagyū's triple treatise on the sword:

The mind unmoved is emptiness; when moved it works the mysterious.

Emptiness is one-mind-ness, one-mind-ness is no-mind-ness, and it is no-mind-ness that achieves wonders.

There are free uninhibited activities besides merely mastering the technique, which constitute the marvels of the *ki* (*ch'i* in Chinese).[18]

Give up thinking as though not giving it up. Observe the technique as though not observing.

Have nothing left in your mind, keep it thoroughly cleansed of its contents, and then the mirror will reflect the images in their isness.

See first with the mind, then with the eyes, and finally with the body and limbs.

Don't be afraid of blinking when the eye unexpectedly confronts an object. It is a natural thing.

I am moving all day and not moving at all. I am like the moon underneath the waves that ever go on rolling and rocking.

Let yourself go with the disease, be with it, keep company with it: this is the way to get rid of it.

You are said to have mastered the art when the technique works through your body and limbs as if independent of your conscious mind.

Turn yourself into a doll made of wood:[19] it has no ego, it thinks nothing; and let the body and limbs work themselves out in accordance with the discipline they have undergone. This is the way to win.

[18] This corresponds to the modern conception of the "cosmic unconscious," which may be taken as reflecting something of the *ālayavijñāna* (*arayashiki* in Japanese) after it has been transformed into *ādarśana jñāna*, "mirror wisdom" (*daienkyōchi* in Japanese).

[19] This simile may be misconstrued by some readers who have never thought of transforming themselves into dolls of wood or clay or of any material. The idea is that our consciousness, which is generally too filled with thoughts and feelings and the like, stands in the way of successfully carrying out the momentous business of life and death, and that the best way to cope with the situation is to clear the field of all useless rubbish and to turn the consciousness into an automaton in the hands of the unconscious. See also *Chuang-tzŭ*, in Appendix V, sec. 3.

6

T A K U A N ' S short treatise on "the Sword of Taia," [20] here translated in full, will help us understand what may be called the
"metaphysics of the sword" of Yagyū Tajima no kami.

THE SWORD OF TAIA

T H E   A R T of the sword, as I see it, consists in not vying for
victory, not testing strength, not moving one step forward or
backward; it consists in your not seeing me and my not seeing
you.[21] When one penetrates as far as where heaven and earth
have not yet been separated, where the *yin* and the *yang* have
not yet differentiated themselves, one is then said to have attained proficiency [in the art].

A man who has thoroughly mastered the art does not use the
sword, and the opponent kills himself; when a man uses the
sword, he makes it serve to give life to others. When killing
is the order, it kills; when giving life is the order, it gives
life. While killing there is no thought of killing, while giving
life there is no thought of giving life; for in the killing or in the
giving life, no Self is asserted. The man does not see "this" or
"that" and yet sees well what is "this" or "that"; he makes no
discrimination and yet knows well what is what. He walks on

---

[20] The Taia is one of the three swords wrought by Fukoshi (Fêng Hu-tzŭ)
by the order of the king of Ch'u in ancient China. It is noted for its fine
qualities and is synonymous with the idealized sword as such.

[21] "You" and "I" not seeing each other, according to the commentator,
means that so long as one stands in the realm of Reality one sees no opposites of any kind, because there is yet no differentiation of heaven and earth,
of the *yin* (female) and the *yang* (male). Takuan's idea is that the combatant is not to cherish any thought of self and no-self, for when this
thought is present in his mind, his moves invite opposition and obstruction
everywhere and the combat will surely end in his own ruination.

water as if it were the earth; he walks on the earth as if it were water. One who has attained this freedom cannot be interfered with by anybody on earth. He stands absolutely by himself.

Do you wish to get "this"?

While walking or resting, sitting or lying, while talking or remaining quiet, while eating rice or drinking tea, do not allow yourself to be indolent, but be most arduous in search of "this." As months and years pass by, it will be like seeing a light in the dark when you come without knowing how upon the knowledge, which is not transmissible from the teacher, and discover the source of mysteries where action or non-action arises. When this is attained you will realize a state transcending the relativity of things as we have it in our everyday life and yet not going out of it. This I call the Sword of Taia.

This sharp Sword of Taia, possessed by every one of us, is perfect in itself. When it is brightened even the *devas* (celestial beings) are afraid of it, but when it is unpolished, the evil ones will play tricks on you. When a superior hand meets another and their swords are crossed, neither side will claim victory. So it is when the World-honored One raises a bunch of flowers and Mahākāśyapa smiles. To know the other three corners of a vessel when only one corner is lifted, or to detect a minute difference in weight by merely looking at a piece of gold or silver—these are no more than ordinary examples of intelligence. As regards one who has attained perfection in the art, he will cut you into three even before you have referred to one or cleared up three; [22] much more so when you stand face to face before him!

---

[22] The reference to "one" or "three" has no special meaning as far as the numbers are concerned. It is an allusion to the quickness with which the Zen master or swordsman detects the slightest movement made on the part of one who stands before him, whether a monk or another swordsman. The master makes the announcement: "If you utter a word, thirty blows of my stick for you. If you utter no words, just the same—thirty blows of my stick. Speak, speak!" A monk comes forward, and when he is about to bow before

Such a one will never expose his blade. He uses it as quickly as a flash of lightning, as the passing of a gale. Those, however, who have no such training are sure to get attached somewhere and to lose freedom of movement. They will not only injure the blade but will also hurt themselves. They are far from being called skilled. Do not entertain delusive thoughts, do not make vain calculations. "This" is beyond verbalizing, nor is there any stylization wherein you can be trained. It is something you have to experience by yourself outside the doctrinal teaching.

When "this" is realized, it moves with utmost freedom, disregarding all usage and conventionalism. Sometimes it asserts itself, sometimes it negates itself, and even the *devas* are at a loss what to make of it. What is the meaning of all this? Says one ancient wise man: "When you have no picture of the *hakutaku* [23] in your house, you then have no fear of the evil ones." When you come to this wisdom after much self-disciplining, the lifting of the single sword will keep the whole world in peace. No frivolities about it!

[End of Takuan's Treatise]

7

A L M O S T contemporaneous, I think, with Yagyū Tajima no kami Munenori was another swordsman in Yedo (now Tokyo),

the master, he is struck. The monk protests, "I have not even uttered a word. Why this striking?" Retorts the master, "If I wait for your speech, it is too late."

[23] The *hakutaku* (*pai-tsê* in Chinese) is a mythical creature whose body resembles a hand and whose head is human. It was anciently believed that the creature ate our bad dreams and evil experiences, and for this reason people, wishing it to eat up all the ills which we are likely to suffer, used to hang its picture on the entrance gate or inside the house. What Takuan means here is that the *hakutaku* for all we know may eat up everything bad in human life, but at the same time it is most likely that we actually invite bad things because of the presence of the mythical creature in the home. It is best not to have anything around that is connected with evils, for the very thought of them leads us to evils. "Even good things are better not to happen." Good and bad are complementary, and when we invite one the other is sure to follow.

1. Liang K'ai (Ryōkai). Hui-nêng (Enō) cutting the
bamboo. Early 13th century

2. Josetsu. Trying to catch a catfish with a gourd (detail). 1386

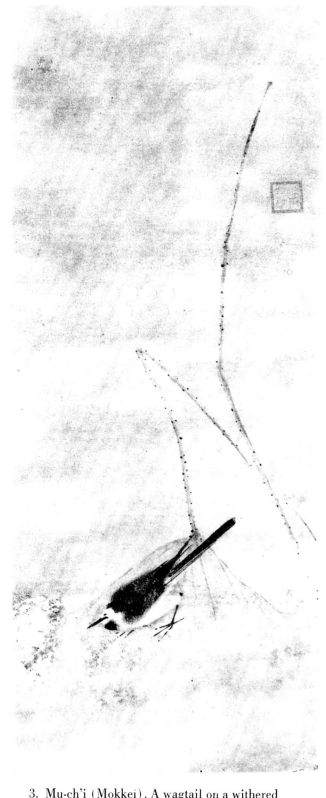

3. Mu-ch'i (Mokkei). A wagtail on a withered
lotus leaf. Late 13th century

4. Ascribed to Li Lung-mien (Ri Ryūmin). Yuima (Vimalakīrti), the
   Buddhist philosopher. 11th century

5. Ascribed to Ma Yüan (Bayen). A solitary angler. Late 12th century

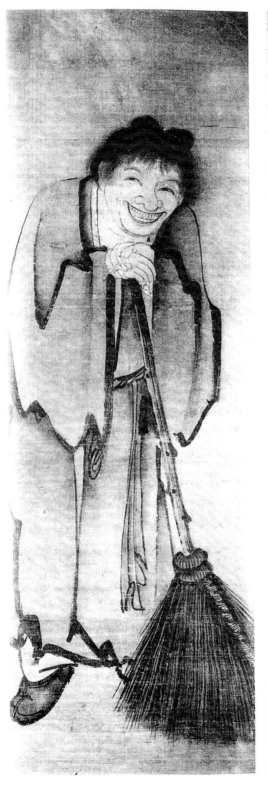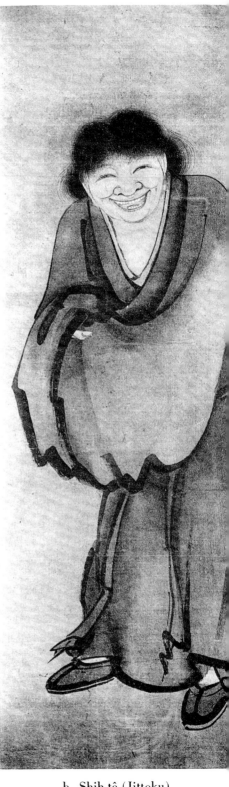

a. Han-shan (Kanzan)   b. Shih-tê (Jittoku)

6. Yen Hui (Ganki). Diptych. Late 12th century

7. The Myōki-an Tearoom (interior), Kyoto

8. Arrangement of flagstones at one of the garden corners in the Katsura Palace grounds, Kyoto

9. Entrance to the Shōkin-tei, one of the teahouses in the Katsura Palace grounds, Kyoto

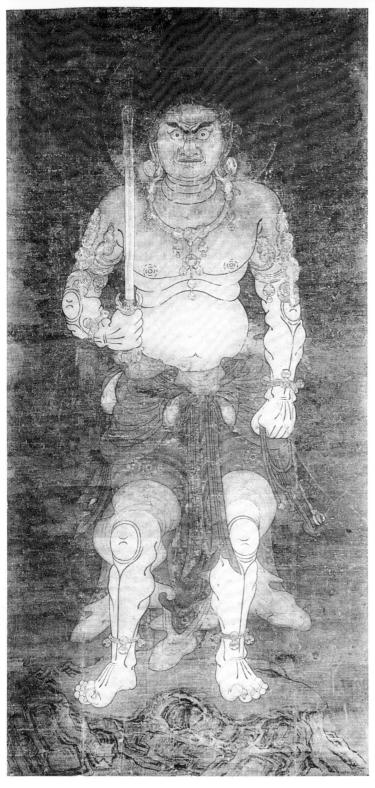

10. Chishō Daishi. Fudō Myōō (Acala-vidyā-rāja), popularly
known as the "Yellow Fudō." A.D. 838

11. Fugen (Samantabhadra) Bosatsu
12th century

12. Liang K'ai (Ryōkai). Sākya (Shaka) leaving his
mountain retreat. Early 13th century

13. Genshin Sōdzu. Amida with two attendant Bodhisattvas. Late 12th century

14. Mu-ch'i (Mokkei). Tiger. Late 13th century

15. Mu-ch'i (Mokkei). Dragon. Late 13th century

16. Liang K'ai (Ryōkai). A drunken man. Early 13th century

17. Liang K'ai (Ryōkai). Snow scene. Early 13th century

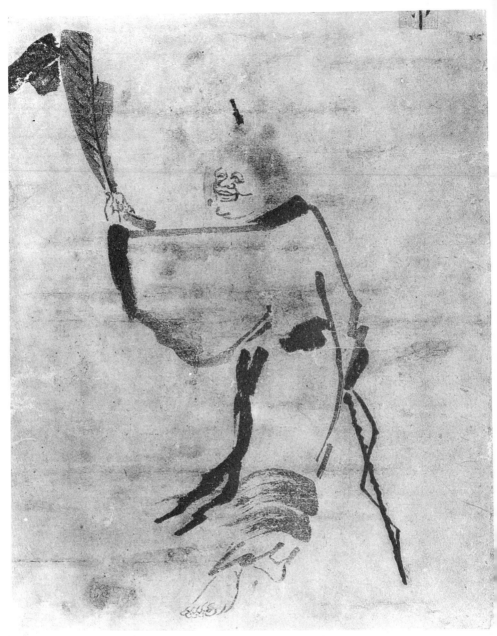

18. Yin-t'o-lo (Indara, Indra). Han-shan (Kanzan). Middle 14th century

19. Yin-t'o-lo (Indara, Indra). Shih-tê (Jittoku). Middle 14th century

住在泠泉　為間贊

知紫落吉誰家

心知應言所住

目前歸路無羞

捧手全身荷負

20. Shuai-wêng (Sotsu-ō). Hui-nêng
(Enō) listening to the Diamond
Sūtra. 13th–14th century

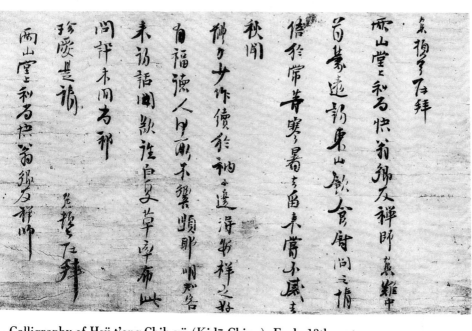

21. Calligraphy of Hsü-t'ang Chih-yü (Kidō Chigu). Early 13th century

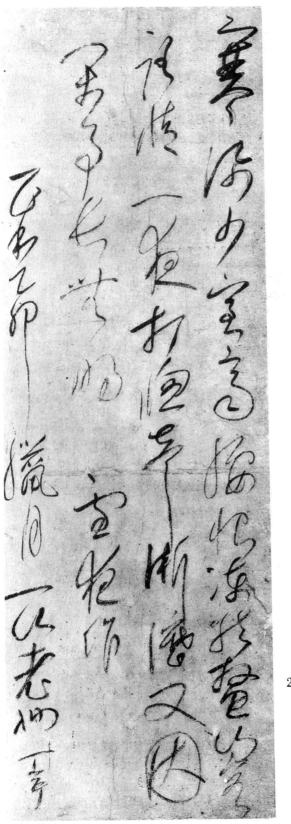

22. Calligraphy of Ning I-shan (Nei
Issan). "Poem on snowy night."
1315

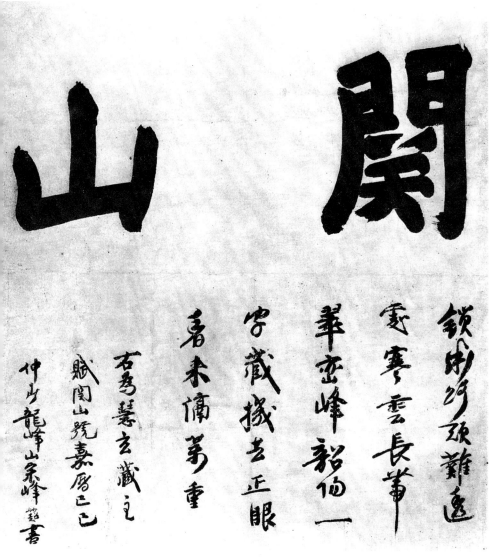

23. Calligraphy of Daitō Kokushi. "Kanzan," title which he gave to his disciple
    Early 14th century

24a. Calligraphy of Jiun Onkō. "Kan-gin" (leisurely humming). 18th century

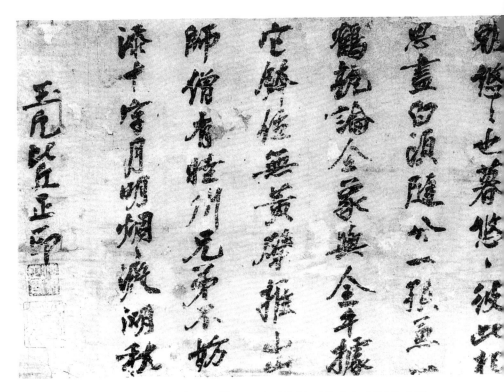

24b. Calligraphy of Yüeh-chiang Chêng-yin (Gekkō Shōin). Middle 12th century

25a. Calligraphy of Ikkyū. Late 15th century

25b. Calligraphy of Hakuin. Sanskrit characters
symbolizing Acala-vidyā-rāja
Middle 18th century

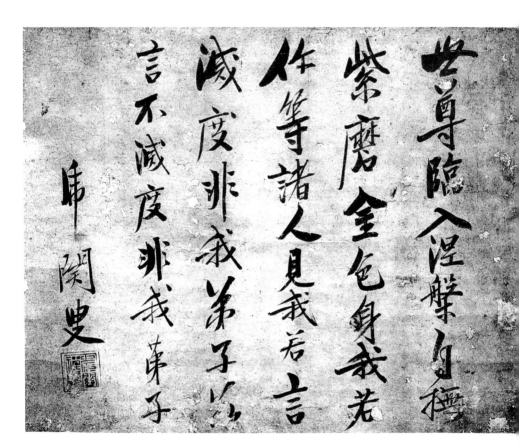

26. Calligraphy of Kokwan Shiren. Late 13th century

27. Kao Jan-hui (Kō Zenki). Sunrise in the mountains. 14th century

28. Artist unknown. Musō Kokushi
    Late 13th century

29. **Ma Kuei (Baki).** Yao-shan (Yakusan) the Zen
master, interviewing Li Ao (Ri Kō) the scholar
12th century

30. Bunsei. The three laughing sages at Hu-ch'i (Kokei)
Middle 15th century

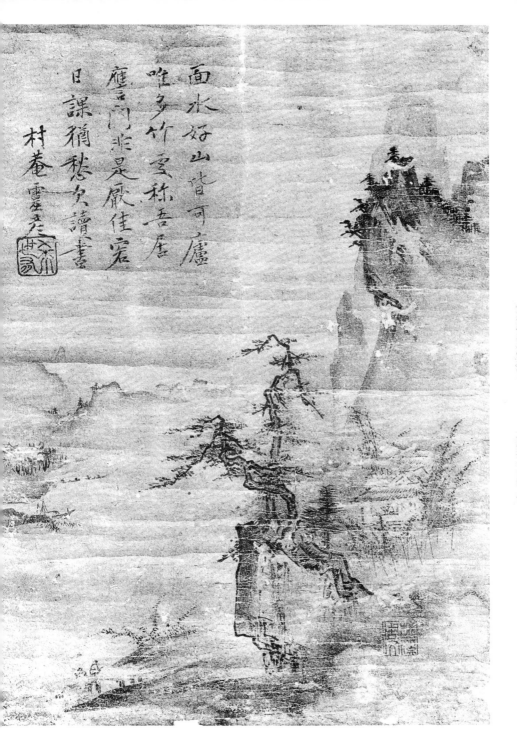

面水好山皆可廬
唯多竹更称吾廬
應言門非是嚴佳宅
日課猶愁欠讀書
村菴靈□

31. Shūbun. Landscape. Early 15th century

32. Sesshū. Landscape, autumn. Late 15th century

33. Sesshū. Landscape, winter. Late 15th century

34. Miyaguchi Ikkwansai the swordsmith at work (1957)

35. Artist unknown. Takuan the Zen master. Late 16th century

36a. Shi K'o (Sekkaku). A Zen master in meditation. 10th century

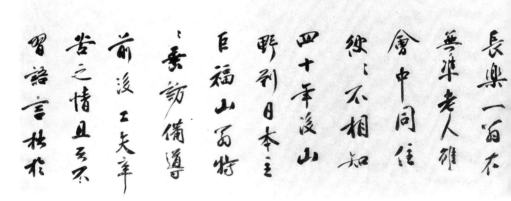

36b. Calligraphy of Bukkō Kokushi. Late 13th century

a. Shi K'o (Sekkaku). A Zen master and a tiger. 10th century

37b. Calligraphy of Takuan. Late 16th century

不然乎劔不失漢王左右手也小譬大豈萬人敵也若推而上之則準陰長是非妄也非幻也庶幾進可以學權攻則敗可謂一劔不藤二刀誠揚屈伸曲直得于心臁于手攀則曰二刀流其兩擊兩又措縱横抑劔客靳克玄信每一手持一刀鞴袖裏青蛇藜下者方士之幻術也旋風打連架打者異儻之姿詰也

38. Artist unknown. Miyamoto Musashi (Niten). Possibly a self-portrait
Early 17th century

39. Detail of 38

40. Hakuin's portrait, by one of his disciples, with an inscription by
Hakuin. Early 18th century

41. Miyamoto Musashi (Niten). Bodhidharma (Daruma)
   Early 17th century

42. Hakuin. Bodhidharma
 (Daruma)
 Early 18th century

43. Sengai. A traveling monk with a
    kyōku ("crazy poem")
    Late 18th century

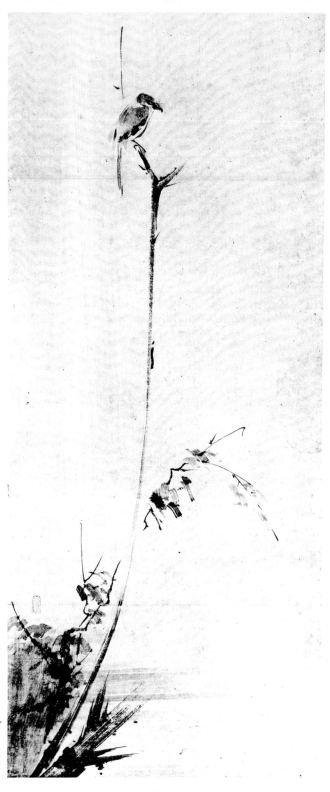

44. Miyamoto Musashi (Niten). A shrike on a dead
branch. Early 17th century

5. Ma Yüan (Bayen). Tung-shan (Tōzan) crossing the stream. 12th century

46. Kanō Motonobu. Ling-yün (Rei-un) viewing the
peach blossom. Early 16th century

47. Kanō Motonobu. Hsiang-yen (Kyōgen) and the bamboos. Early 16th century

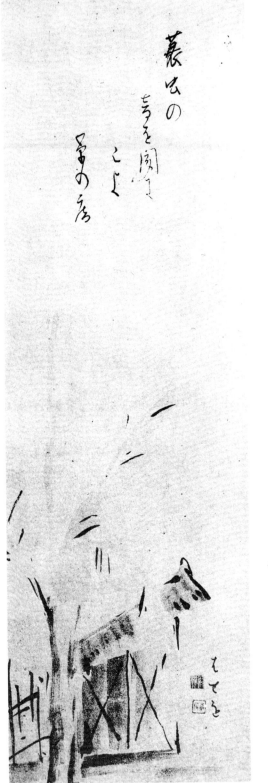

48. Bashō. A cottage and a banana plant, with a *haiku*
Late 17th century

49. Artist unknown.
Portrait of Bashō,
with his *haiku*
Late 17th century

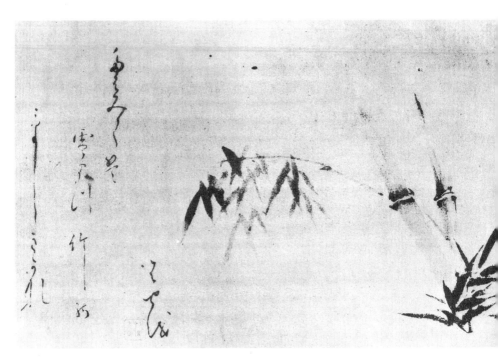

50. Bashō. Bamboos and a *haiku*. Late 17th century

51. Sengai. Banana plant and frog, with a *haiku*
    Late 18th century

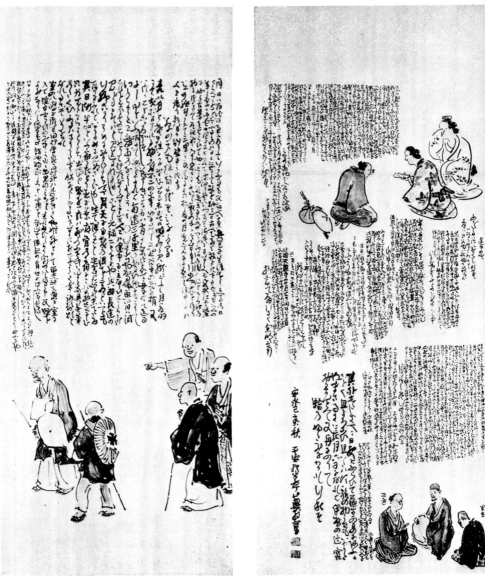

52. Yosa Buson. Panels of the screen illustrating Bashō's *Oku no Hosomichi*. 1779

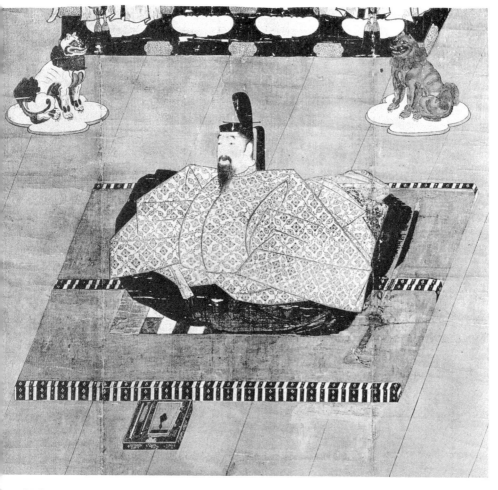

53. Unknown artist of the Yamatoye school. Emperor Godaigo (reigned 1318–39)
   Probably late 14th century

54. View of the garden attached to the Myōki-an Tearoom, Kyoto

55. Hakuin. Daitō Kokushi, founder of Daitokuji
Temple and teacher of Emperor Godaigo
Early 18th century

56. Artist unknown. Daitō Kokushi. 1334

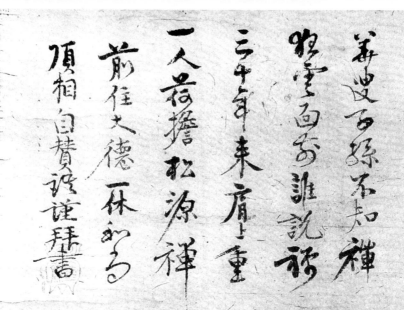

57. Bokusai. Ikkyū the Zen master (1394–1481). Late 15th century

なつ笑ふ契り包ぬ雲か
翔夕に抹ゆるとやら
谷の岩橋

58. Sengai. The three laughing sages at Kokei, with a thirty-one-syllable poem
   Late 18th century

豊国大明神

秀頼

徳川の栄えをうらやむ涙川
そのながれ
はやとなり
きへにけるとも
またのさかえをみるへき

59. Artist unknown. Toyotomi Hideyoshi (1536–98),
with inscription by Hideyoshi's son Hideyori
Early 17th century

60. Hakuin. The three sages tasting vinegar. Early 18th century

61. Enkai. Prince Shōtoku. 1069

62. Calligraphy of Ryōkwan. "Shin-gachi-rin" (Mind-moon-circle)
18th or early 19th century

63. Sengai. A contented man in the sum-
    mer evening with a *haiku*
    Late 18th century

64. Ascribed to Wu Tao-tzŭ (Godōshi). Kwannon
    Early 8th century

living on the other side of the River Sumida, who was known as Odagiri Ichiun. Whereas Tajima no kami was connected with the Tokugawa family, then at the height of its power, and was therefore enjoying power and wealth and a great reputation as teacher to the third Shōgun Iyemitsu, Ichiun remained almost unknown except among his intimate friends and disciples. Their social positions stood in great contrast. Judging from his writings, however, Ichiun was probably a much better swordsman as far as his personality was concerned. He despised all those profes sional masters who gathered around men of political influence and worldly renown, for they were what his teacher Sekiun char acterized as "the beastly-minded," because their life objective was for "name and gain" at the sacrifice of their profession.

What Ichiun and Yagyū had in common was their philosophy of swordsmanship, which was basically that of Zen Buddhism. In one sense, Ichiun was inclined to emphasize Zen more than studying the technique of the sword, which followed by itself when one understood what Zen was. Yagyū, on the other hand, seemed to pay some attention to the technique. It goes without saying that he also stressed the importance of Zen in the mastery of the art. Apparently, however, he did not go so far as Ichiun, who altogether ignored tactical skill as such. Ichiun openly declared that his was the sword of "non-action," of "no art," of "no technique," of "relying on nothing," with "no rhythmicality," lacking anything resembling what might be designated swordsmanship. Therefore, he remarked that if anyone witnessed his method of practical training, he would pronounce it "very strange, very extraordinary." Lastly, Ichiun characterized his sword as consisting not in *ai-uchi* but in *ai-nuke*.[24]

The following is an abstract, much shortened, of an eighteenth-century manuscript copy of the original writing prepared by

[24] *Ai-nuke* is a very important term in the philosophy of swordsmanship as expounded by Ichiun. It stands against *ai-uchi*, which is mutual killing, whereas *ai-nuke* is mutual escaping. For a little more explanation, see below, p. 172.

Odagiri Ichiun, disciple of Hariya Sekiun, who is claimed to have been the founder of the school called "The Sword of No-abiding Mind" (*Mujūshin-ken*). The manuscript starts with an account of the school, quoting the master and Ichiun's relation to him. It is of much significance in the history of swordplay for demonstrating the all-importance of what might be called spiritual training instead of merely learning the art as art, and for showing the position of a perfect personality on technical mastery and its crafty handling. Swordsmanship is, after all, not the art of killing; it consists in disciplining oneself as a moral and spiritual and philosophical being.

'THE SWORD OF NO-ABIDING MIND'
FOUNDED BY HARIYA SEKIUN

MY TEACHER, Sekiun, began his study of swordsmanship when he was about thirteen years of age, and later became a disciple of Ogasawara Genshin. Genshin was one of the four most prominent disciples of Kami-idzumi Ise no kami Hidetsuna (d. 1577), who was the founder of a new school known as Shinkage-ryū. Japanese swordsmanship may be said to have made a new development under Kami-idzumi. He was a great creative genius in the Japanese history of the sword. Ogasawara Genshin, after mastering Shinkage-ryū, went to China. While teaching the Chinese people the art, he happened to meet an expert in the use of a certain Chinese weapon known as the *hoko*. By studying under him, he improved his own technique to an extraordinary degree. On his return to Japan, he tried the new method out on his old friends and found that none of them could stand his offensive. Believing in the absolute superiority of his discovery, he taught it to a large number of pupils. After hard study, Sekiun finally succeeded in mastering all the secrets of the new school.

My teacher, however, did not feel fully satisfied with his accomplishment. He began to study Zen under a retired abbot of Tōfukuji, one of the chief monasteries in Kyoto. Under Kohaku, which was his name, my teacher made great advance in the understanding of Zen Buddhism. He ultimately came to this conclusion: none of the great professors of swordsmanship so far as he knew, including his own teacher Genshin and Genshin's teacher Kami-idzumi, could be called real masters of the art. For they utterly failed in understanding the fundamental principle of life; without it, however advanced their mastery of the technique, they were all slaves of delusive thoughts, worth absolutely nothing. They could not go beyond these three alternatives: (1) to defeat the inferior enemy; (2) to be defeated by the superior one; and (3) with an equal, to end in mutual striking-down or killing (*ai-uchi*).

Sekiun now employed himself in learning how to perfect the art of swordsmanship along the line of Heavenly Reason or Primary Nature in the state of as-it-is-ness. He was convinced that such a principle was applicable to the art. One day he had a great awakening. He discovered that there was no need in swordplay to resort to the so-called technicality. When a man is enthroned in the seat of Heavenly Reason, he feels as if he were absolutely free and independent, and from this position he can cope most readily with all sorts of professional trickery. When Sekiun, my teacher, tried his discovery with his teacher Ogasawara Genshin, Sekiun easily defeated Genshin even though Genshin exhausted all his secret arts. It was like burning bamboos in the flames of an angry fire.

Sekiun was then already past sixty when I, Ichiun, twenty-eight years old, came to him as pupil. During the five years of tutorship under Sekiun, I applied myself most earnestly and assiduously to the art of swordsmanship, which was now taught by the old master in the form newly synthesized with the principle and practice of Zen. When I thought I was finally ready to try my attainment with the master, I challenged him, and at each of the three contests we were engaged in, the outcome was what was called *"ai-nuke."*

[*Ai-nuke* is a new term in swordplay. When the contestants are of equal caliber and proficiency the game as it is generally played finishes with an *ai-uchi*, which, when it is carried on with real steel, means killing each other. An *ai-nuke*, however, does not at all involve any kind of killing or hurting each other, as *nuke* means, not "striking down" as *uchi* does, but "passing by," or "going through" unhurt. When, therefore, Ichiun had his tests with Sekiun, his teacher, neither of them was at all hurt though they were of equal attainment. There was no "striking down" on either side. Each "escaped" without being defeated in any sense of the word. Ichiun writes: "This was the feature most characteristic of our school, which was designated by Sekiun's Zen teacher, Kohaku, as the 'Sword of No-abiding Mind.' " [25] Ichiun continues:]

Soon after this my teacher passed away, and I was left to myself. For the six following years I was in retirement, quietly contemplating Heavenly Reason, and I had no idea of propagating my newly acquired art. Instead, I devoted myself to a life of introspection so that I forgot even to feel hunger and cold.

One significant fact I have to mention in connection with my contests with the master is that, after the third test, the master gave me a scroll containing words of testimony in which he fully recognized his disciple's realization of the principle of swordsmanship. The master then took out a rosary from his

---

[25] "No-abode" or "no-abiding" is a Buddhist term, *apratiṣṭhā* in Sanskrit. It equates with "emptiness" (*śūnyatā*) and sometimes with "non-attachment" (*anabhiniveśa*). It literally means "not to have any home where one may settle down"; its real meaning is "to settle down where there is no settling down." This is a kind of paradox as far as our ordinary sense of logic is concerned. But the Buddhists would tell us that life is more than logic and that logic ought to conform to life in order to be logical and not life to logic just for the sake of logic. When this—which the philosopher would designate as "absurdity"—is actually comprehended as we live our daily life, we are said to have realized the "abiding where there is no abiding." The swordsman is also asked to attain this in his art.

chest pocket, and, burning incense, turned toward me and bowed in the way the Buddhists generally do toward their object of reverence.

I really did not know what the master meant by this religious act. There is no doubt, however, that the master thereby paid to his young pupil the highest compliment one mortal could ever give to another.

Though I had no thought of advertising myself as teacher of the new school, some of my old friends found me out and urged me to initiate them into the new experiences. My name and school thus gradually came to be known among wider circles. Judging from the way they now follow the teaching and discipline of the school, it is likely that the school will go on prospering for some generations to come, and my late teacher's wonderful attainments in his late years will not be lost to the world. But it is advisable to put these things down in writing lest men of posterity understand the teaching each in his own way. They must be protected against any possible misinterpretation. . . .

[26] After thus introducing himself and his teacher, Ichiun mentions the thing of first importance for the swordsman's personality. He is to give up all desire for name and gain, all egotism and self-glorification, he is to be in accord with Heavenly Reason and observe the Law of Nature as it is reflected in every one of us. In Ichiun's words: "My teacher despised people of the worldly type, saying that they are defiled with the beastlike spirit, because like the lower animals they are always bent on finding something to eat—that is, always looking for the material welfare of their own selves. They do not know what is meant by human dignity and laws of morality which regulate our human life."

As to swordsmanship, Ichiun declares that the first principle of the art is not to rely on tricks of technique. Most swordsmen

[26] What follows is the author's interpretation of Ichiun's ideas, interpolated frequently with Ichiun's own words.

make too much of technique, sometimes making it their chief concern to sanctify their acquirements. Therefore, if one wishes to follow the teaching of the "Sword of No-abode," the first thing required is to discard any desire to turn swordsmanship into a kind of entertainment, a matter of mere accomplishment. Further, one is not to think of achieving a victory over the opponent. Let the swordsman disregard from the first what may come out of the engagement, let him keep his mind clear of such thoughts. For the first principle of swordsmanship is a thorough insight into Heavenly Reason, which works out according to the chance circumstances; the rest is of no concern to the swordsman himself.

When Heavenly Reason is present in us it knows how to behave on every occasion: when a man sees fire, his Reason knows at once how to use it; when he finds water, it tells him at once what it is good for; when he meets a friend, it makes him greet him; when he sees a person in a dangerous position, it makes him go right out to his rescue. As long as we are one with it, we never err in our proper behavior however variable the situation may be.

It exists even before we are born, it is the principle that regulates the universe morally as well as physically. That principle, which is creative, is divided into four aspects: *gen* (*yüan*, the "sublime"), *kō* (*hêng*, "success"), *ri* (*li*, "furthering"), and *tei* (*chên*, "perseverance").[27] When man is born by virtue of the Creative Principle, he partakes of these four aspects in the form of the four cardinal social virtues: *jin* (*jên*, "love"), *gi* (*i*, "justice"), *rei* (*li*, "propriety"), and *chi* (*chih*, "wisdom"). These four virtues constitute human nature, whereby man distinguishes himself as spiritual leader from the rest of creation.

The Primary Nature functions in its purest form in our

---

[27] These English terms are taken from the English translation by Cary F. Baynes of Richard Wilhelm's German version of the *I Ching*, or Book of Changes, one of the five Chinese classics.

infancy, when we are held in our mother's arms and fed from her breasts. As the baby is sufficient unto itself with the Nature, so even as adults we must be sufficient unto ourselves when the Nature is permitted to work in its own way with no interference from the side of relative consciousness. Unfortunately, as soon as we begin to grow up we are indoctrinated by every means accessible to us. Because of conceptualization, our sense-experiences inform us with an incorrect picture of the world. When we see a mountain, we do not see it in its suchness, but we attach to it all kinds of ideas, sometimes purely intellectual, but frequently charged with emotionality. When these envelop the mountain, it is transformed into something monstrous. This is due to our own indoctrination out of our "scholarly" learning and our vested interests, whether individual, political, social, economic, or religious. The picture thus formed is a hideous one, crooked and twisted in every possible way. Instead of living in a world presented to the Primary Nature in its nakedness, we live in an artificial, "cultured" one. The pity is that we are not conscious of the fact.

If the swordsman wants to know how this contorted world picture affects his acts, let him observe himself when he is engaged in the contest. He will find that all his actions are against the principle of the "Sword of No-abode" which from start to finish is to be in accord with the thinking and acting of the infant. According to this discipline in conformity with the Nature, the steps the swordsman may take when confronting the enemy will be neither quick nor slow nor indifferent. They are simply left to the Primary Nature as it sees fit in terms of the situation, which is subject to change from moment to moment. The swordsman is not to make a show of untoward bravery, nor is he to feel timid. He will also hardly be conscious of the presence of an enemy, or in fact of himself as confronting somebody. He will act as if he were conducting his everyday business—for instance, enjoying breakfast. Let the swordsman handle his sword as if he were handling his chopsticks, picking up a piece of food and putting it into the mouth and setting them down when the meal is finished. The handling of the sword does not require any more of his concern than sitting at the breakfast table. If he wants to do more than this, he is not a graduate of the school.

Ichiun continues: In order to explain the mysterious working of Heavenly Reason or of the Primary Nature in man, we make use of various expressions, but the main thing is to return to the innocence of the original man, that is, of infancy, which is often called Great Limit (*taikyoku; t'ai-chi* in Chinese), or Nature in its isness, or a state of no-action or emptiness. But most people, instead of looking directly into the fact, cling to words and their commentaries and go on entangling themselves further and further, finally putting themselves into an inextricable snare.

Let such people for once go back to their own infancy and see how the infant behaves. The great earth may crack, and he remains unconcerned. A murderer may break into the house and threaten to kill him, but he smiles at him. Does this not show great courage? Now let us see how he behaves toward worldly gain, for which we are almost ready to sacrifice our lives or shamelessly to employ our most demoniac cunning. Would the baby be overwhelmed with joy when the empire is given to him, or when he is decorated with a medal of great distinction? He will not even turn his head. We may say that the infant knows nothing of the world of grown-ups. But Ichiun will retort: "What is there of real worth in the adult's world? It is all vanity of vanities. What concerns the infant is the absolute present. He does not recollect the past, nor does he anticipate the future. Therefore, he is free, he knows no fear, no insecurity, no anxiety, no 'courage to be.' " What concerns the swordsman as well as every one of us, therefore, is to become conscious of this Heavenly Reason working in babes and sucklings. They are not conscious of it, but they act it, and it is for us to bring into full consciousness the Nature as it reveals Heavenly Reason in us. To reach maturity does not mean to become a captive of conceptualization. It is to come to the realization of what lies in our innermost selves. This is "true knowledge" (*ryōchi*), "sincerity" (*makoto*), "reverence" (*kei*), "unmistakableness" (*tanteki*). However old a man may grow, he will not find it outworn. "Infantism" is ever fresh, energizing, and inspiring.

For this reason, Ichiun's instruction to his disciples is the simplest and apparently easiest possible one. For he says: "When with a sword you confront the enemy, advance toward him, if the distance is too far, and strike. When from the first the distance is just right, strike him from where you are. No thinking is needed. With most swordsmen, however, the case is different. As soon as they stand against the enemy, they fix their glance on him; survey the distance between them; take up the position which they think will be most advantageous; measure the length of the sword; reflect on what kind of technical trickeries they will use—'giving,' 'taking away,' or 'slowing' of motion; and so on. Their mind works in the busiest possible way on how best to make use of all the tactics they have learned. They have no idea whatever of Heavenly Reason and its functioning under varying conditions. The great mistake in swordsmanship is to anticipate the outcome of the engagement; you ought not to be thinking of whether it ends in victory or in defeat. Just let the Nature take its course, and your sword will strike at the right moment."

Perhaps the most momentous advice Ichiun gives us, as the first step in the training of the swordsman, is that he is to start the contest with the idea of an *ai-uchi*, a "mutual striking down." This advice has an important psychological significance. *Ai-uchi*, in other words, means paying no attention whatever to the outcome of the contest, being concerned not at all with the question of coming out of it safely or not. When a man faces a deadly situation in this frame of mind, he is the most resolute, the most desperate, the most daring person, before whom no enemy can stand unless he himself has come to the same resolution.

Such instances have already been given in this book. But the idea of an *ai-uchi*, one must remember, is what we start with as the preliminary step in the mastery of swordsmanship and not the step with which it should finish. Let us heed what Ichiun, as an accomplished master and teacher of the "Sword of No-abode," would further advise us.

Ichiun's second lesson constitutes the core of his methodology and at the same time demonstrates what a deep insight he has into the dark corners of human psychology. He writes: "The idea of an *ai-uchi* may not seem difficult to cherish at the start of the game, but as it progresses the contestant is sure to raise the hope of victory, and this is what most assuredly interferes with the natural functioning of Heavenly Reason in him." So, Ichiun continues: "This is the moment for you to reflect: How is it that I seem to be double-minded? I start with the firm determination to end the contest in an *ai-uchi*, and nevertheless I begin to waver, wishing to be the victor. The reflection will now put your mind in the state of *kufū*.[28] When you go on

---

[28] The term *kufū* has been used several times before in the text, but I feel that it has not yet been fully explained. Hence the following explanation, perhaps for the last time. It is one of the most significant words used in connection with Zen and also in the fields of mental and spiritual discipline. Generally, it means "to seek the way out of a dilemma," or "to struggle to pass through a blind alley." A dilemma or a blind alley may sound somewhat intellectual, but the fact is that this is where the intellect can go no further, having come to its limit, but an inner urge still pushes one somehow to go beyond. As the intellect is powerless, we may enlist the aid of the will; but mere will, however pressing, is unable to break through the impasse. The will is closer to fundamentals than the intellect, but it is still on the surface of consciousness. One must go deeper yet, but how? This "how" is *kufū*. No teaching, no help from the outside is of any use. The solution must come from the inmost. One must keep on knocking at the door until all that makes one feel an individual being crumbles away. That is, when the ego finally surrenders itself, it finds itself. Here is a newborn baby. *Kufū* is a sort of spiritual birth pang. The whole being is involved. There are physicians and psychologists who offer a synthetic medicinal substance to relieve one of this pang. But we must remember that, while man is partially mechanistic or biochemical, this does not by any means exhaust his being; he still retains something that can never be reached by medicine.

with it for some years you will finally have an insight into Heavenly Reason, which never subjects itself to any form of mobility, that is, to any irresolution of mind. For Reason, or Nature, or Mind (*kokoro*), or Substance—all of which are synonyms—remains forever quiet, unmoved, and unchanging, and it is indeed because of this quality that it acts in infinite ways and beyond the reach of thought."

Before I quit this lengthy exposition of the teaching of the school of swordsmanship called "Sword of No-abode," I must not fail to mention four things in Ichiun's manuscript that characterize his Sword:

(*1*) The absence of a system of stereotyped techniques.

(*2*) The meekness of spirit (*kṣānti*), or nonresistance, or nonaction—these terms strongly remind us of the philosophy of Lao-tzŭ and Chuang-tzŭ.

(*3*) The conviction that "I am the only swordsman who has no peers in the world." This matches the declaration which, according to Mahāyāna tradition, the Buddha made at his birth: "Heavens above and earth below, I alone am the most honored one!" This matching of the two declarations is interesting in a double sense: Ichiun applauds "infantism" as incarnating the principle of swordsmanship, while it was the infant Buddha who made the bold declaration. Ichiun's "infant" is a fully matured swordsman who has gone through every stage of trials at the risk of his life. In either way, the spirit and teaching of Zen is discerned in Ichiun as well as in the legendary Buddha. Both want us to scratch away all the dirt our being has accumulated even before our birth and reveal Reality in its is-ness, or in its suchness, or in its nakedness, which corresponds to the Buddhist concept of emptiness (*śūnyatā*).

(*4*) I have to add another item which in all probability

This is where his spirituality lies, and it is *kufū* that finally wakes us to our spirituality, distinguishing us from mere animality as well as mere mechanicality.

originated with the "Sword of No-abode": the idea of *ai-nuke*. This is something no other schools of swordsmanship have ever taught. When the game is well matched, it generally ends in an *ai-uchi*, "mutual striking-down," while in the "Sword of No-abode" there is no such tragic culmination because the ending is an *ai-nuke* and not an *ai-uchi*. As I stated before, *nuke* literally means "not hitting," and therefore when this takes place neither hits the other and both escape unhurt. When either of the combatants is not a perfect master of the "Sword of No-abode," he invites, as it were, the real master's sword to fall on him, and he thereby commits a kind of suicide. As far as the master himself is concerned, he harbors no murderous intent in his mind. The inevitability of the situation has compelled him to face the enemy. It is the enemy who is filled with the evil spirit of killing, his mind is not at all free from the egoism of destruction. Therefore, when he comes before the master of the "Sword of No-abode," the evil spirit possesses him and he is killed by this evil spirit while the master is not even aware of having struck the opponent down. We can say that here Heavenly Reason punishes those who go against it, and that the master's "infantism" remains utterly innocent of all that has been going on about him.

After reading Ichiun, my impression is that the author is not just a professional swordsman but essentially a Zen master who happens to use swordplay. His sword is like the Zen-man's staff, which strikes the monk who would approach him with any undigested idea of Zen. Sekiun's sword inherited by Ichiun is really the sword of nonaction, that is, the sword of no-abode, which constitutes the essence of the philosophy of *Prajñāpāramitā* (*hannya-haramita*, in Japanese).

Toward the end of his treatise on swordsmanship, Ichiun sums up the significance of his sword in the following way: "There are at present many schools of swordsmanship—more

than two hundred—but they come primarily from the four principal disciples of Kami-idzumi Ise no kami. My teacher Sekiun
studied the art under one of these, Ogasawara Genshin. Genshin,
after visiting China and learning the use of a weapon characteristically Chinese, invented a new method of swordplay of his
own, which proved so ingenious that none of his former rivals
could beat him. Sekiun my teacher studied this under Genshin
and thoroughly mastered it. But later, when Sekiun came to
understand Zen, he gave up everything he had learned under
Genshin and took to the sword of nonaction. He now confronted
his former teacher with this sword of his own attainment to see
how it would work in practice against the old school, which
solely relied on the mastery of technique and on the superiority
of tactical cunning. The result was the defeat of the old school,
showing that it was then Sekiun my teacher whose swordsmanship stood supreme, for nobody now could beat him in seventeenth-century Japan."

Ichiun's conclusion: The reason even the best swordsman of
Japan could not defeat his teacher Sekiun after his study of
Zen was that all the other swordsmen of any school whatever
had one thing or another on which they built up their scheme of
technical superiority. Sekiun's sword, on the contrary, was one
of no-abode embodying Heavenly Reason itself and going beyond
the realm of human understanding. After his *satori* experience
in Zen, there was no doubt that Sekiun reached the stage of
holiness. For his "Sword of No-abode" has now nothing to do
with tactical movements, technical subtleties, indeed with anything that is at all connected with swordsmanship as it is ordinarily practiced. Besides, the sword is altogether independent of
all sorts of worldly interests and motivations that taint the
character of its wielder. And just because of the pure-heartedness
and "empty-mindedness" (*mushin, wu-hsin*) of the man, the
sword partakes of this quality and plays its role with the utmost
degree of freedom. It was for this reason, Ichiun concludes, that
no one could stand against it face to face unless he was of the

same degree of spiritual attainment. Swordsmanship is, after all, not a matter of petty technique but of highly developed personal spirituality. Hence Ichiun's declaration to the effect that there is no one who can be his equal.

8

WHAT MAKES swordsmanship come closer to Zen than any other art that has developed in Japan is that it involves the problem of death in the most immediately threatening manner. If the man makes one false movement he is doomed forever, and he has no time for conceptualization or calculated acts. Everything he does must come right out of his inner mechanism, which is not under the control of consciousness. He must act instinctually and not intellectually. At the moment of the most intensely concentrated struggle for life and death, what counts most is time, and this must be utilized in the most effective way. If there were the slightest moment of relaxation (suki) the enemy would feel it instantly and lose no time in making use of it, which means your annihilation. It is not a matter of mere defeat and humiliation.

The moment of intense concentration is the moment when a perfect identification takes place between subject and object, the person and his behavior. When this is not reached, it means that the field of consciousness has not yet been completely cleared up: that there still remains "a subtle trace of thought" (misai no ichinen) which interferes with an act directly and straightforwardly issuing from the person—that is, psychologically speaking, from the Unconscious. The result is surely calamitous, for the threatening sword will strike the interfering gap of consciousness.

This is the reason why the swordsman is always advised to be free from the thought of death or from anxiety about the outcome of the combat. As long as there is any "thought," of whatever nature, that will most assuredly prove disastrous. The Chinese saying runs: "When you act resolutely even the gods will shun you." Resolute-mindedness is the one thing that is urgently needed in swordsmanship. Without this there cannot be any sort of concentration, much less identification. Concentration, single-mindedness, one-pointed-ness (*ekāgratā*), resolute-mindedness—they all come to mean the same thing. When an act is to play the supreme role, it must be left all to itself. This moment is known in Zen as the state of "no-mind-ness" (*munen*), corresponding to "infantism," in which there is yet no inchoation of conceptualism.

Some may wonder: resolute-mindedness is a highly human quality. We cannot attain it unless our mind goes through a process of training and becomes fully matured, for it is a sign of well-developed mentality. Being so, how can one be asked to give up one's manly privilege and to return to the mental state of infancy? How can one go back to the start after having made the laborious journey? Or how can one identify a highly developed mind with the helplessness of a child? This is one way of looking at the matter, but we must not forget that there is another way in which the child excels him who is "fully developed." Let us see what that is.

Being in such a hurry to make ourselves "fully developed," we have utterly neglected the one most important quality the child has and we have, which is faith—a faith in an unknown being. The unknown may be called Heavenly Reason, the Nature, the True or Primary Mind, Tao, God, the Unconscious, or the Inmost Self. Inasmuch as the unknown, whatever the name we may give it, refuses to be brought up to the conscious field of the mind, or loses its isness or suchness the moment consciousness tries to hold it in its grasp, therefore it has been left behind in our race for "development" and "maturation"—so much so that we have forgotten its existence and the part it performs without making us conscious of its reality. When the swordsman or the religious talks about childlikeness or "no-mind," most of us fail to understand what it means. Or when we try to understand it, we bring it up or down (according to how we evaluate it) to the ordinary level of consciousness and discourse on it in the way we do with other things that are found there. As a result we distort it, twist it, truncate it, misshape it, and make it altogether lose its original whatness. When somebody else now refers to it, we can no longer recognize it. Resolute-mindedness applies to the work of restoration in which the "fully developed" are now engaged. It is not a question of developing what has already been developed but of recovering what has been left behind, though this has been with us, in us, all the time and has never been lost or distorted except for our misguided manipulation of it. But the swordsman, perhaps first instigated by the Zen masters and after a long trial experience of his own, has come to recognize the presence in himself and the importance of this "unknown quantity," which we now strive in every way to describe.

With this introduction, we may be able to comprehend better what follows, as given to us by various swordsmen who, though rich in practical experience, have not indulged much in philosophical presentation.

i. Adachi Masahiro

ONE ADACHI MASAHIRO of Kyoto, who claimed to be the founder of the school of swordsmanship called *Shimbu-ryū* (or *Jimmu-ryū*), wrote a work entitled *Heijutsu Yōkun* ("Essentials of Swordsmanship"), in two fascicles, dated 1790. It was first printed in the thirty-eighth year of Meiji (1905) as one of several treatises on cognate subjects compiled and edited by Arima Yūsei and Inouye Tetsujirō under the collective title *Bushidō Sōsho* ("Collection of Treatises on the Way of Samurai").

Adachi Masahiro emphasizes the importance of psychic [29] training. The physical training and the mastery of technique are no doubt essential, but he who lacks psychic training is sure to be defeated. While being trained in the art, the pupil is to be active and dynamic in every way. But in actual combat, his mind must be calm and not at all disturbed. He must feel as if nothing critical is happening. When he advances, his steps are securely on the ground, and his eyes are not glaringly fixed on the enemy as those of an insane man might be. His behavior is not in any way different from his everyday behavior. No change is taking place in his expression. Nothing betrays the fact that he is now engaged in a mortal fight.

To be able to act in this fashion when the swordsman meets his opponent and when his life is at stake with every movement means that the swordsman must have realized "the immovable mind." Physiologically speaking (as we would say today), he must have been thoroughly trained in keeping his *kokoro* way down in the abdominal region.[30] When this is interpreted in

---

[29] "Psychic" here does not refer to extrasensory phenomena. It includes all that is not material or physiological. The word "mental" is too psychological, and "spiritual" has some theological taint. I wish to make *psyche* stand here for the Japanese *kokoro* or *seishin*. *Kokoro* is a very comprehensive term. It first of all means the physical "heart," and then the true "heart" (conative and emotional), "mind" (intellectual), "soul" (in the sense of an animating principle), and "spirit" (metaphysical). In the case of the swordsman, the *kokoro* has rather a conative sense; it is the will in its deeper signification.

[30] The author has already distinguished two kinds of *kokoro:* one is the physical "heart" and the other is the true "heart." The heart susceptible to emotionality is the first kind. When it is kept down below the navel, it becomes immovable. Unless this takes place, all the skill the swordsman may have acquired is of no use. C. G. Jung writes (in "Fundamental Psychological Conceptions," a mimeographed report of five lectures given under the auspices of the Institute of Medical Psychology in London, 1935) in this connection: "The Pueblo Indians told me that all Americans are crazy, and of course I was somewhat astonished and asked them why. They said, 'Well, they say they think in their heads. No sound man thinks in the head. *We* think in the heart.' They are just about in the Homeric age, when the region of the diaphragm was considered the seat of psychical activity." (I am grateful to Dr. Gerhard Adler for the clarification of this passage.)

the modern way, it will mean that his diaphragm is to be kept downward so that his chest may have room enough for the lungs to breathe freely and the heart to beat unhindered. For one who feels excited in any sense over the situation, or one who calculates on overpowering the opponent by an aggressive exhibition of strength or by a cunning tactic designed to trip him up, is doomed to be outdone by the enemy who approaches the arena in a composed, well-balanced state of mind. From this it will be seen that in swordsmanship the technical skill is to be subordinate to the psychic training, which will finally raise the swordsman even to the level of high spirituality. When spirituality is attained, *myō* (*miao*) [31] is manifested, wherein we observe that swordplay is not just an art but has something of original creativity.

Spiritual attainment may not be expected of every swordsman, however well disciplined in the technique, but when he fully makes up his mind not to come out alive from the combat, he may prove himself to be a formidable opponent even for a highly trained swordsman. Fear of death or attachment of any kind is liable to affect the movement of the sword, and the enemy is sure to make use of the opportunity to his advantage.

What distinguishes the art of swordsmanship most characteristically from any other branch of art, as we now clearly see, is that it is most intimately connected with the ultimate problem of life and death. And it is here that swordsmanship has taken itself to be a close ally to the study of Zen and even to aspire to a spiritual attainment of high degree.

To illustrate what he means here, Adachi Masahiro gives the case of a desperate fighter who caused an expert swordsman to beat a retreat. The author gives this as a good example showing what a determined person, however unskilled in swordplay, can do.

Once, when the feudal system was still in being, a man belonging to the servant class happened to incur the great dis-

[31] See above, p. 142, n. 3.

pleasure of a certain politically influential personage. This digni-
tary demanded that the master surrender the servant, which
naturally meant that the unfortunate man was to be put to death.
The master had no choice but to yield to the demand of the
aggrieved one.

The master said to the servant: "It is a great pity that I
have to give you up to this official, who is most likely to punish
you with the death penalty. There is no help as far as I am concerned. Now I advise you to take up a sword and have a final
combat with me, and after killing me to surrender yourself
to the offended officer."

The servant replied, "That would be utterly unreasonable of
me. You are a first-class swordsman and a teacher of the art.
How could I expect to defeat you?—I, a mere servant, who have
never handled the sword."

The master, being a prominent professional swordsman, cherished a secret wish to try his sword with one who had no hope
of life whichever way he turned, and he said to the servant,
"You try your luck anyway, and let me see how I can meet you."

When they stood each armed with a drawn sword, ready to
have a deadly combat, the master swordsman found himself in
the worse position. He was forced to step back until he stood
against the wall, beyond which there was no room for further
retreat. He himself had to make up his mind for a final decision.
This was no joke nor matter of experiment. Thus cornered, with
no hope of improving the situation, the swordsman uttered a
cry of "Eh!" and struck down his opponent with one blow of
the sword.

Afterward, the master confessed to his pupils, "What a desperate fight it was! I was almost beaten by the servant, whose
fierce play with the sword was really irresistible. May you never
experiment with such a match. When even an awkward servant
can present such an irresistible front, how much more a swordsman of the first order!"

One of the pupils asked, "When you retreated step by step,

was it a tactic on your part, or were you really pressed so hard?"

The master acknowledged, "Yes, I was really hard pressed."

"When, uttering 'Eh!,' you struck down the servant, did you discover a *suki* [32] in him?"

"There was no *suki* at all, but the wonder (*myō*) was that he fell under the sword."

The story ends here. The author, Adachi Masahiro, comments: "The wonder (*myō*) here referred to is not due to the working of the swordsman's [conscious] mind, but to the 'immovable mind.' When one's will is fatally made up, even an unskilled hand can offer such resistance to an expert. . . . This being so, the swordsman is not to think lightly of anybody, nor is he to feel timid before a strong opponent. The main point is to forget yourself as well as the opponent and to let the *myō* [unconscious] work itself out."

Then Adachi quotes Uyesugi Kenshin (1530–78), one of the most famous generals of the sixteenth century: "Fate is in Heaven, the armor is on the breast, success is with the legs. Go to the battlefield firmly confident of victory, and you will come home with no wounds whatever. Engage in combat fully determined to die and you will be alive; wish to survive in the battle and you will surely meet death. When you leave the house determined not to see it again you will come home safely; when you have any thought of returning you will not return. You may not be in the wrong to think that the world is always subject to change, but the warrior may not entertain this way of thinking, for his fate is always determined."

Let me remark in passing that the warrior or samurai or the swordsman is, I am afraid, an advocate of determinism. As long as we are persuaded to think that there is a power of unknown source that breaks out in the midst of our humanly well-planned project and upsets the whole business, we cannot help

---

[32] See above, p. 143, n. 4. It means an opening in the line of concentration, which shows itself when the tension is relaxed owing to the intrusion of a disturbing idea or feeling.

acknowledging our limitations. Free will or freedom of knowledge and action is no more than our dream. But the queerest question we can ask is: What is it that makes us dream when in actuality we are limited all around? What is it that makes us detach ourselves from the realities of life as we really live it and reflect upon them as if they were of no concern to us? Where does the idea of limitedness itself come from if not from the limitless beyond?

ii. The Teaman and the Ruffian

WHAT FOLLOWS is the story of a teaman who had to assume the role of a swordsman and fight with a ruffian. The teaman generally does not know anything about swordplay and cannot be a match in any sense of the word for anybody who carries a sword. His is a peaceful profession. The story gives us an idea of what a man can do with a sword even when he has never had any technical training, if only his mind is made up to go through the business at the risk of his life. Here is another illustration demonstrating the value of resolute-mindedness leading up to the transcendence of life and death.

Toward the end of the seventeenth century, Lord Yama-no-uchi, of the province of Tosa, wanted to take his teamaster along with him on his official trip to Yedo, the seat of the Tokugawa Shogunate. The teamaster was not inclined to accompany him, for in the first place he was not of the samurai rank and knew that Yedo was not a quiet and congenial place like Tosa, where he was well known and had many good friends. In Yedo he would most likely get into trouble with ruffians, resulting not only in his own disgrace but in his lord's. The trip would be a most risky adventure, and he had no desire to undertake it.

The lord, however, was insistent and would not listen to the remonstrance of the teamaster; for this man was really great in his profession, and it was probable that the lord harbored the secret desire to show him off among his friends and colleagues. Not able to resist further the lord's earnest request, which was in fact a command, the master put off his teaman's garment [33] and dressed himself as one of the samurai, carrying two swords.

While staying in Yedo, the teamaster was mostly confined in his lord's house. One day the lord gave him permission to go out and do some sight-seeing. Attired as a samurai, he visited Uyeno by the Shinobazu pond, where he espied an evil-looking samurai resting on a stone. He did not like the looks of this man. But finding no way to avoid him, the teaman went on. The man politely addressed him: "As I observe, you are a samurai of Tosa, and I should consider it a great honor if you permit me to try my skill in swordplay with you."

The teaman of Tosa from the beginning of his trip had been apprehensive of such an encounter. Now, standing face to face with a *rōnin* [34] of the worst kind, he did not know what to do. But he answered honestly: "I am not a regular samurai, though so dressed; I am a teamaster, and as to the art of swordplay I am not at all prepared to be your opponent." But as the real motive of the *rōnin* was to extort money from the victim, of whose weakness he was now fully convinced, he pressed the idea even more strongly on the teaman of Tosa.

Finding it impossible to escape the evil-designing *rōnin*, the teaman made up his mind to fall under the enemy's sword. But he did not wish to die an ignominious death that would surely reflect on the honor of his lord of Tosa. Suddenly he remembered that a few minutes before he had passed by a swordsman's training school near Uyeno park, and he thought he would go and ask the master about the proper use of the sword on such occasions and also as to how he should honorably meet an inevitable death. He said to the *rōnin*, "If you insist so much,

[33] In the feudal days the teaman was dressed in his own fashion and did not carry any weapons about him. I may add, it is not clear to me why this teaman had to change his regular habit to that of a samurai.

[34] A *rōnin* is a samurai who has lost his attachment to a master for various reasons, somewhat corresponding to the term "free-lance."

we will try our skill in swordsmanship. But as I am now on my master's errand, I must make my report first. It will take some time before I come back to meet you here. You must give me that much time."

The *rōnin* agreed. So the teaman hastened to the training school referred to before and made a most urgent request to see the master. The gatekeeper was somewhat reluctant to acquiesce because the visitor carried no introductory letter. But when he noticed the seriousness of the man's desire, which was betrayed in his every word and in his every movement, he decided to take him to the master.

The master quietly listened to the teaman, who told him the whole story and most earnestly expressed his wish to die as befitted a samurai. The swordsman said, "The pupils who come to me invariably want to know how to use the sword, and not how to die. You are really a unique example. But before I teach you the art of dying, kindly serve me a cup of tea, as you say you are a teaman." The teaman of Tosa was only too glad to make tea for him, because this was in all likelihood the last chance for him to practice his art of tea to his heart's content. The swordsman closely watched the teaman as the latter was engaged in the performance of the art. Forgetting all about his approaching tragedy, the teaman serenely proceeded to prepare tea. He went through all the stages of the art as if this were the only business that concerned him most seriously under the sun at that very moment. The swordsman was deeply impressed with the teaman's concentrated state of mind, from which all the superficial stirrings of ordinary consciousness were swept away. He struck his own knee, a sign of hearty approval, and exclaimed, "There you are! No need for you to learn the art of death! The state of mind in which you are now is enough for you to cope with any swordsman. When you see your *rōnin* outcast, go on this way: First, think you are going to serve tea for a guest. Courteously salute him, apologizing for the delay, and tell him that you are now ready for the contest. Take off your *haori* [outer coat], fold it up carefully, and then put your fan on it just as you do when you are at work. Now bind your head with the *tenugui* [corresponding to a towel], tie your sleeves up with the string, and gather up your *hakama* [skirt]. You are now prepared for the business that is to start immediately. Draw your sword, lift it high up over your head, in full readiness to strike down the opponent, and, closing your eyes, collect your thoughts for a combat. When you hear him give a yell, strike him with your sword. It will probably end in a mutual slaying." The teaman thanked the master for his instructions and went back to the place where he had promised to meet the combatant.

He scrupulously followed the advice given by the swordmaster with the same attitude of mind as when he was serving tea for his friends. When, boldly standing before the *rōnin*, he raised his sword, the *rōnin* saw an altogether different personality before him. He had no chance to give a yell, for he did not know where and how to attack the teaman, who now appeared to him as an embodiment of fearlessness, that is, of the Unconscious. Instead of advancing toward the opponent, the *rōnin* retreated step by step, finally crying, "I'm done, I'm done!" And, throwing up his sword, he prostrated himself on the ground and pitifully asked the teaman's pardon for his rude request, and then he hurriedly left the field.

As to the historicity of the story I am in no position to state anything definite. What I attempt here to establish is the popular belief underlying the story cited here and others of similar character; this is that, underneath all the practical technique or the methodological details necessary for the mastery of an art, there are certain intuitions directly reaching what I call the Cosmic Unconscious, and all these intuitions belonging to various arts are not to be regarded as individually unconnected or mutually individually unrelated, but as growing out of one fundamental intuition. It is indeed firmly believed by Japanese generally that the various specific intuitions acquired by the swordsman, the teamaster, and masters of other branches of art and culture are no more than particularized applications of one great experience. They have not yet thoroughly analyzed this belief so as to give it a scientific basis; but the fundamental experience is acknowledged to be an insight into the Unconscious itself as source of all creative possibilities, all artistic impulses, and particularly as Reality above all forms of mutability beyond the *saṁsāra*-sea of birth-and-death. The Zen masters, ultimately deriving their philosophy from the Buddhist doctrine of *śūnyatā* and *prajñā,* describe the Unconscious in terms of life, that is, of birth-and-death which is no-birth-and-death. To the Zen masters, thus, the final intuition is the going beyond birth-and-death and the attaining to the state of fearlessness. His *satori* is to mature to this, when wonders are accomplished. For the Unconscious then permits its privileged disciples, masters of the arts, to have glimpses of its infinite possibilities.

iii. Yamaoka Tesshū

YAMAOKA TESSHŪ (1836–88), a great swordsman and a Zen-man, trained his pupils in a way characteristic of his Zen. The method apparently consists in leading them to a state of exhaustion physically as well as mentally. When they reach this state and are utterly unable to rise again, a certain stimulus is given which, working on them as a sort of electric shock, unexpectedly taps a new source of energy hitherto altogether hidden in them. The source may be regarded as corresponding to the Unconscious, which in the case of swordsmanship is perhaps the instinct of self-preservation, though not in its usual biological sense. The instinct is ordinarily intimately connected with the concept. The concept works in our consciousness as though it were the instinct itself, therefore with all the vitality attached to the instinct and reinforced emotionally by free association.

When the instinct alone, especially in its purely ontological status, acts without any conceptual interference, there is nothing to prevent its native virility. But when the concept enwraps and conditions it, it hesitates, looks around, and evokes the feeling of fear in its various forms, and the blind instinctual uncontrollability is curbed or greatly impaired. Since the awakening of consciousness, man has turned into a conceptual being who deals with abstract ideas in his daily living. Life itself is handled in terms of conceptualism. Though the instincts are not suppressed, they have lost much of their native irresistibility and impulse to violent outburst. In one case at least, instinct has been "sublimated," and its efflorescences have embellished human culture in various ways. I mean in the fields of intellect and utilitarianism, where conceptualization has produced great results. But in other fields where realities, including various instincts, are to be handled directly without mediatory interference, or handled as they are in their pristine state of suchness, our habit of concept-making has done great damage. The damage is principally revealed in all the kinds of mental maladies and spiritual insecurity that plague modern men and women, perhaps including cases of juvenile delinquency. In swordsmanship the situation it creates is so acute and im-mediate (in the sense of "no medium") as not to allow the interception of conceptual, consciously intellectual trickery. However instantaneously the sword may seem to be moving, when intellection interferes even an infinitesimal amount, time is wasted and the enemy has the chance (*suki*) to strike you right down. The swordsman faces reality and not conceptualization. Hence its partiality to the Zen training, as already treated under the sections on Odagiri Ichiun and Yagyū Tajima no kami.

Mr. Ogura Masatsune, one of my friends, who is a great authority on Japanese swordsmanship, writes in his memoirs [35] about the way Yamaoka Tesshū trained his pupils. Mr. Ogura

[35] *Ogura Masatsune Dansō* (Tokyo: Kōkō-an, 1955). Privately circulated.

quotes one of his friends who had personally gone through the
training of Yamaoka, in somewhat the following manner:

Yamaoka applied the teaching of Zen to his philosophy of
swordsmanship and disciplined his pupils by telling them to
discover by their personal experience the meaning of the "sword
of no-sword," which is based on the theory of absolute identity
as propounded by Zen teachers. He originated what is known
as *Seigwan-Geiko*. Seigwan is a Buddhist term meaning "vow"
or "prayer" and *geiko* or *keiko* is "disciplining"; it is also
called *Tachikiri-Geiko* [36] or *Kazu-Geiko*.[37] It consists in repeat-
ing contest after contest almost indefinitely, though the number
is generally limited to one hundred in the morning and another
hundred in the afternoon. Those who wish to go through this
trial will notify the master, but the permission will not be readily
given, because the master knows that the trial is one of the
utmost severity, which only the strong and the brave can go
through. When it is given, the public announcement is made
and contestants are free to challenge the candidate. The trial
may last from three days to a week. As the skin of the fingers
and hands, though protected by gloves, is apt to break and get
stained with blood, it is all to be wrapped in soft silk inside the
gloves. The candidate is kept standing throughout the contests
as the fresh combatants come up one after another, with no
intermission.

As for the candidate, the first day he is full of vigor, on the
second he begins to feel fatigued, and on the third his arms and
legs grow stiff and he can hardly hold his sword (made of split
bamboo) properly. While it is to be held up with the point at
about the level of the opponent's eyes, he finds that he has
ceased to be the master of his own limbs and his sword stands
vertically. As for his diet, he can now take only semiliquid or
liquid food, and his urine has turned reddish.

[36] *Tachikiri* means "to keep on standing."
[37] *Kazu* is "number" or "multiple."

The candidate, Mr. Kagawa Zenjiro, to whom Mr. Ogura is here referring, goes on to say that he was the first applicant to go through his test, and relates his experience in the following manner:

"On the third day of these strenuous exercises I could hardly raise myself from bed and had to ask my wife's help. When she tried to lift me she felt as if raising a lifeless corpse and unconsciously withdrew her hands which she had placed underneath my back. And then I felt her tears on my face. Hardening myself to the utmost I admonished her not to be so weak-hearted. Somehow I succeeded with her help in raising the upper part of my body.

"I had to use a cane to walk up to the training hall. I had also to be helped to put on my protecting equipment. As soon as I took my position, the contestants began to crowd in. After a while I noticed one member come in and approach the master to ask his permission to take part in the exercises. The master permitted him right away. I looked at him and at once realized that he was the one noted for his rascality, who, disregarding the swordsman's usage, would thrust his bamboo sword to the naked throat behind the protecting gorget and keep it up even after he was already struck over his head by his victorious opponent.

"When I saw him coming up to me, I made up my mind that this would be my last combat, for I might not survive the contest. With this determination I felt within myself the surging up of a new energy. I was quite a different person. My sword returned to its proper position. I approached him now fully conscious of my fresh inner surge and lifting up the sword over my head, was ready to strike him with one blow of it. At this moment came the master's emphatic command to stop, and I dropped my sword."

Mr. Kagawa added, writes Mr. Ogura, that Yamaoka at that moment saw his disciple come to the realization of "the sword of no-sword."

This is, indeed, a most strenuous and exhausting ordeal the swordsman had to go through under Yamaoka Tesshū's tutorship. Tesshū knew from his long experience in Zen that a man has to die, for once, to his ordinary consciousness in order to awaken the Unconscious. A swordplayer is generally a man of great physical prowess, able to stand a good deal of physical training, while his mind is not so badly harassed with all sorts of metaphysical problems as are those of most Zen followers. The physical method, therefore, may be regarded as the only one to be employed in the case of a swordsman who sincerely desires to master the art. "The great death" Zen-men talk so much about thus comes also to be experienced by him.

9

THESE historical examples supply us with enough material to draw this conclusion: When one is resolved to die, that is, when the thought of death is wiped off the field of consciousness, there arises something in it, or, rather, apparently from the outside, the presence of which one has never been aware of, and when this strange presence begins to direct one's activities in an instinctual manner wonders are achieved. These wonders are called *myō*. *Myō* is thus in some way related to instinct. When life is not intellectually and therefore consciously conditioned but left to the inner working of the Unconscious, it takes care of itself in an almost reflex automatic fashion, as in the case of the physiological functioning of an organic body.

Now, the question may be asked: Every living being has an instinctive hate of death, and how could we make the conscious resolution to die? Yes, even at the most critical moment, when death is inevitable, we make every attempt to save ourselves. We die only when we are exhausted. Suicide is rather an abnormality. But the fact is that it is only man who ever commits suicide, showing that there is something of more worth than

life the preservation of which we are most intently concerned
with. But we can ask again: Is it not only our conscious thought
of death that we can destroy, while our innate desire for life still
exists in our Unconscious? When we have erased the conscious
desire for life we imagine that we willingly embrace death, but
in point of fact is it not possible that we are still unconsciously
craving life? As is the case with the lower animals and plants,
they are not consciously asserting life, they just go on living and
striving to continue this state of things unconsciously. We human
beings are conscious of this striving, and because of this consciousness we carry on all kinds of imagination in regard to life
and death. And is it really this imagination, or, strictly speaking,
this delusion, and not the actuality of things as they are, that
creates in us every occasion for worries, fears, harrowing antic-
ipations? When this delusion is wiped away, would not life itself
look after its own welfare as it deems best? And would not this
be the way the swordsman lets his life-preserving instinct work
itself out in full accordance with Nature? Being freed from human interference, which consists mainly of conscious intellection
and self-deceiving deliberations, Nature now knows how best to
proceed. It is, no doubt, of the utmost difficulty to wipe out the
idea of death from the field of consciousness, but there is no
reason we cannot do it, seeing that the conscious field is our
deliberate cultivation, collective and individual. We need a strong
decisive will, aided by insight, but we know that the will is cul-
tivable. Especially the swordsman's life is devoted to this form of
discipline. He drives away his conscious notion of death from the
field of consciousness we ordinarily recognize and permits the
instinct of self-preservation to come forward, which then occupies the whole field of unconscious consciousness. The instinct is
now absolutely unconditioned, there are no impediments offered
by intellectual and emotional machination. Not only that, it
knows how to make use of the technique consciously acquired
by the man. When he reflects afterwards on the whole procedure
he is struck with its wonderful achievements not at all consciously

carried out, but as though by an agent outside himself. I believe this is on the whole the psychology of perfect swordsmanship.

The "Immovable Mind" referred to in the various works on
swordsmanship may be said in one sense to be the same thing
mentioned in the letter by Takuan to Yagyū Tajima no kami,
who was Takuan's lay disciple and teacher of the reigning
Shōgun, Iyemitsu. But Takuan's mind goes far deeper than the
swordsman's, for the latter generally stops at being psychological,
while Takuan, being a Zen master, sees into the very source of
reality, which we may call the metaphysical or cosmic Unconscious, though the term is liable to be misunderstood because of
its psychological connotation. The main point is that the swordsman's insight is limited: he carries a sword; he faces an opponent or opponents; he sees that his life is at stake though he is
not at all afraid of meeting the situation; his instinctual craving
for life, though quite unconscious, is not effaced; he has not
yet attained to the state of emptiness which comes upon one when
the reservoir of *ālayavijñāna* is completely broken up. He does
very well as far as his immediate business is concerned. But when
he comes back to his ordinary everyday life, his everyday consciousness also comes back, and he is again an ordinary man
with all his desires, attachments, and insecurities.

It is different with the Zen master. His start is with the fundamental problem of reality, with the ultimate significance of life,
with the totality of his personality. The swordsman is also confronted with the question of life and death, which almost covers
the whole extent of existence; but it is only when he feels an
urgent urge to go very much deeper that he and the Zen master
begin to walk hand in hand along the road to ultimate reality.
The swordsman stops short at the instinctual Unconscious,
whereas the Zen-man walks on until the whole universe, rather
the whole emptiness of space, is broken to pieces. Yagyū Tajima
no kami is right when he says: [38]

[38] A paraphrase.

"The Mind (*kokoro*) is Emptiness (*kū, k'ung, śūnyatā*) it-self, but out of this Emptiness an infinity of acts is produced: in hands it grasps, in feet it walks, in eyes it sees, etc. This Mind must once be taken hold of, though it is indeed very difficult to have this experience because we cannot get it from mere learning, from the mere listening to others talk about it. Swordsmanship consists in personally going through this experience. When this is done, one's words are sincerity itself, one's behavior comes right out of the Original Mind emptied of all ego-centered contents. The mind we generally have is defiled, but the Original Mind is pure—the Tao itself.

"I talk as though I have experienced all this, but really I am far from being a Tao-man. I note it down simply because all human life ought to be in conformity with this view of the Mind. If we are still unable to apply it to every phase of our life, as swordsmen we must have it at least in the exercise of our art."

Yagyū Tajima no kami is quite frank in acknowledging that he is still incapable of realizing the Mind as Emptiness, while he fully knows his position as regards swordsmanship. He must have thoroughly studied the instruction given him by his Zen master Takuan. Takuan was a well-seasoned master of Zen. Probably he never studied swordplay as the professional samurai did, but there was no doubt that he could take up the sword and acquit himself ably with any one of the experts, including Yagyū Ta-jima no kami, who was at the time conceded to be the best swordsman of Japan. Yagyū himself, however, must have real-ized that he was no actual match for Takuan, as we can see from the letter he left to his best disciples on swordsmanship, and also from some other sources that treat of the Zen master's encounter with professional swordsmen.[39]

Odagiri Ichiun's manuscript on swordsmanship, already the subject of a lengthy discourse above, throws more light in this connection. What I mean is the title of his school, which reflects the philosophy of the Mahāyāna school of Buddhism, especially

[39] See above, pp. 95 ff., 150 ff.

of the Zen teaching. Odagiri Ichiun, or rather Hariya Sekiun, who was Ichiun's teacher and the founder of the school, called it "The Sword of No-abiding Mind" (*Mujūshin-ken*). This phrase is taken from the Mahāyāna-Buddhist *Vimalakīrti Sūtra* (*Yuima Kyō*), one of the texts very much used by Zen-men. The *sūtra* describes the ultimate source of all things as "No-abode." "No-abode" or "having no abiding place anywhere" means that the ultimate source of all things is beyond human understanding, beyond the categories of time and space. As it thus transcends all modes of relativity, it is called "having no abode" to which any possible predications are applicable. The sword used by men of this school is, therefore, no ordinary sword with a form, or at least with a definitely designated form. Being swordsmen, they no doubt carry a sword in their hands when encountering an actual opponent, but the sword is a sword of formless form. When an enemy stands before it, therefore, he does not know how to cope with it, he cannot trace its movements, and before he can adjust himself he is already beaten down. The opponent can never understand how all this happened, because as soon as he appears before this "no-abiding" sword, we may say that his head is already no longer on his shoulders.

The reader may ask: What kind of sword could the Sword of No-abode be? Is not the swordsman holding an actual one in his hands that makes us bleed when we touch it?

Bukkō the National Teacher (1226–86), the founder of the Engakuji monastery in Kamakura, came to Japan at the invitation of Hōjō Tokimune in 1279. While still in China he was threatened by soldiers of the Mongolian armies overrunning southern China. No respecters of religion, they were about to strike down this solitary monk as he was devoting himself to meditation. The monk, not at all disturbed, recited a verse of his own composition:

> *There is not a room in the whole universe where*
> *one can insert even a single stick;*

> *I see the emptiness of all things—no objects, no persons.*
> *I admire the sword of the Great Yüan* [40] *three*
>   *feet in length:*
> *[When it cuts at all,] it is like cutting the spring*
>   *breeze with a flash of lightning.*

The sword in the hands of the Mongolian warriors was to the Zen monk no better than the blowing of the wind. It merely passed over his head, for his real being, filling up the whole universe, remains forever unchanged—no swords, no bombs of any sort could ever touch it. The soldiers were unable to understand what all this meant, and it is said that they left this quizzical monk unmolested, perhaps disgusted with his "immobility."

The sword of the Great Yüan, from the Zen monk's point of view, was a "Sword of No-abode," whether it was held in the hands of an enemy or in his own. The difference between Bukkō and Ichiun is that the latter holds the sword in his own hands while Bukkō is about to be struck with it; one is the subject while the other is the object. For Ichiun as well as Bukkō, the swinging of the sword is like cleaving the wind or the air.

In one of the poems left by Fu Daishi (Fu Hsi, 497–569), of the Liang dynasty, we have:

> *I hold a spade in my hands, and yet I hold it not;*
> *I walk and yet I ride on the water buffalo.*

What kind of spade can it be that is held in the hands and yet is not found there? It is no other than "the Sword of No-abode." Fu Daishi's garden implement and Ichiun's sword that gives life are not different from one another, they all come from the Mind that is no-Mind. Fu Daishi's spade was once in Adam's hands when he was still in the Garden of Eden; Ichiun's sword is the sword in the hands of Acala the Immovable and also the *Prajñā-*

---

[40] The Mongolian dynasty (1260–1367) that invaded China and replaced the Sung dynasty.

sword in the hands of Mañjuśrī the Bodhisattva. It kills and yet gives life, according to the frame of mind of him who approaches it.

Banzan Hōjaku (P'an-shan Pao-chi) was one of the great masters of Zen in the T'ang dynasty. He once gave this sermon: "[Zen is] like one's wielding the sword in the air, one does not ask whether it hits the object or not; the air is not cleft, the sword is not broken." On another occasion he said: "There are no dharmas [that is, objects] in the triple world, and where do we search for the Mind? The four elements are from the first empty, and where could the Buddha find his abode? The heavenly axle remains unmoved, all is quiet and no words are uttered. It is presented right to your face, nothing more is to be done."

Dōkyo Yetan (1641–1721) who is better known as Shōjū Rō-nin (Shōjū the Old Gentleman), was the teacher of Hakuin [40, 42, 60 (1685–1768), who is one of the great modern Zen masters of Japan. Shōjū Rōnin had once a swordsman visitor,[41] who said:

"I have been disciplined in swordsmanship since my younger days. For the past twenty years I have been assiduously employed in the study of it under teachers of different schools, and I am master of all their secrets. I now have a great wish to establish a school of my own and have been at it for some time. In spite of my most arduous search for the ultimate principle of a new school, I have not been able to take hold of it. All my efforts to realize the ultimate *myō* have so far been a complete failure. Is it possible for you to teach me the way to it?"

After attentively listening to this, Shōjū Rōnin stood up from his seat and struck the swordsman three times with both his fists, using all the strength in him. Not only this, the Rōnin kicked the man down onto the floor. It was indeed the roughest treatment

---

[41] The following story is taken from Imagita Kōsen (1817–93), *Life of Shōjū Rōnin.* First published independently and later incorporated in the *Collected Works of Hakuin and of the Zen Masters Related to Him* (Tokyo, 1935).

one can get from another, but it produced the desired effect on the swordsman, because he then had a *satori*. It is said that the experience opened up a new vista to his art.

The report of this interview caused a stir among the swordsmen in the neighborhood, and they began to visit Shōjū Rōnin inquiring how to make Zen work with their profession. One day they invited Shōjū Rōnin to tea and had him watch the contests among themselves. Finally, they said: "You are a great master of Zen, and as far as theory is concerned we cannot compete with you. But when the question comes to actual use of the sword, we are afraid that you cannot beat us."

Shōjū Rōnin said, "If you wish to strike me, just strike, but I am afraid that you cannot."

The swordsmen exchanged an ominous glance among themselves and said, "Would you really permit us to have a trial once with you?"

The Rōnin agreed.

They stood up and were ready to try the sword with the Zen master. The latter, however, refused to take a sword, saying, "I am a Buddhist. Here is a fan and it will be my weapon. Strike when you are ready. If you do, I will grant that you are a good swordsman."

Lifting their swords high up and uttering loud cries, they tried by every means to strike the master. But his fan was seen everywhere and there was no opening for them to let the weapon fall upon him. They at last had to acknowledge their defeat.

Later, there was a monk who asked Shōjū Rōnin, "As to Zen, I would not say anything, but how did you ever manage to play sword?"

The Rōnin said, "When the right insight is gained and knows no obstruction, it applies to anything, including swordplay. The ordinary people are concerned with names. As soon as they hear one name a discrimination takes place in their minds. The owner of the right eye sees each object in its own light. When he sees the sword, he knows at once the way it operates. He confronts the multiplicity of things and is not confounded."

Mr. Takano Shigeyoshi, now eighty years old, is one of the greatest swordsmen modern Japan has produced. While writing about a bamboo sword [42] in a short essay recently, Mr. Takano refers to the psychology of swordplay.

"When I have a bamboo sword most suited to my personal taste in respect of weight, formation, tone, etc., I can enter more readily into a state of identity where my body and the sword I hold become one. It goes without saying that as soon as one cherishes the thought of winning the contest or displaying one's skill in technique, swordsmanship is doomed. When all these thoughts are done away with, including also the idea of the body, one can realize the state of oneness in which you are the sword and the sword is you—for there is no more distinction between the two. This is what is known as the psychology of *muga* ('no-ego' or 'no-mind'). This perhaps corresponds to what Buddhism calls a state of emptiness. It is then that all thoughts and feelings, which are likely to hinder the freest operation of whatever technique one has mastered, are thoroughly purged, and one returns to one's 'original mind' divested of its bodily encumbrances.

"I sometimes feel that when the marionette master puts his mind wholly into the play his state of mind attains something of the swordsman's. He is then not conscious of the distinction between himself and the doll he manipulates. The play becomes really an art when the master enters into a state of emptiness.

[42] A wooden sword was used in practice before a bamboo one replaced it. The bamboo is split into slats, which are woven together and held by pieces of leather. Four well-seasoned bamboo strips make a good *shinai* (lit., "pliable") or *chikutō* (lit., "bamboo-sword").

The essay was published in the popular magazine *Bungei Shunjū* ("Literary Annals"; July, 1956).

Some may feel like seeing a difference between the marionette master and the swordsman, because of the latter's confronting a living personality who is aiming every moment at striking you down. But my way of thinking is different, inasmuch as both have realized the state of identity it must operate alike regardless of its objectives.

"When the identity is realized, I as swordsman see no opponent confronting me and threatening to strike me. I seem to transform myself into the opponent, and every movement he makes as well as every thought he conceives are felt as if they were all my own and I intuitively, or rather unconsciously, know when and how to strike him. All seems to be so natural."

What may be called Mr. Takano's "super-psychology" of self-identity fitly describes the perfect swordsman's mind when he actually confronts the opponent. As long as he is *conscious* of holding the sword and standing opposed to an object and is *trying to make use* of all the technique of swordplay he has *learned,* he is not the perfect player. He must forget that he has an individual body known as "Takano" and that a part of it holds the sword, which he is to employ against another individuated body. He now has no sword, no body. But this does not mean that all has vanished into a state of nothingness, for there is most decidedly a something that is moving, acting, and thinking. This is what Mr. Takano and other swordsmen, the Taoist and Buddhist philosophers, designate as "the original mind" (*honshin*), or "the mind of an infant" (*akago no kokoro*), or "the true man" (*shinjin; chên-jên* in Chinese), or "the perfect man" (*shijin; chih-jên*), or "the original face" (*honrai no memmoku; pên-lai mien-mu*).

This mysterious "non-existent" quiddity "thinks and acts" without thinking and acting, for according to Mr. Takano "he" perceives every thought that is going on in the mind of "one who stands opposed," as if it were his own, and "he" acts accordingly.

"He" is evidently not he, nor is "he" not-he, as we have in a world of opposites. When this not-he falls, he does not know that it is "he" or not-he. When all is over, "the original mind" comes back to itself, that is, to its own consciousness, and this is the awakening of "one thought" (*ichinen*), the separation of light from darkness, of subject from object, the rising of a dichotomous world. This is what Aśvaghoṣa, the author [43] of *The Awakening of Faith*, calls "the sudden awakening of thought" (in Chinese, *hu-jan nien ch'i*; in Japanese, *kotsunen nenki*). This is the situation in which Mr. Takano or Yagyū Tajima no kami, Odagiri Ichiun or Miyamoto Musashi, finds himself—standing with the sword before the fallen "enemy" so called.

Emerson's poem "Brahma" fittingly illustrates the perfect swordsman's psychology:

> *If the red slayer think he slays,*
> *Or if the slain think he is slain,*
> *They know not well the subtle ways*
> *I keep, and pass, and turn again.*
>
> *Far or forgot to me is near;*
> *Shadow and sunlight are the same;*
> *The vanished gods to me appear;*
> *And one to me are shame and fame.*
>
> *They reckon ill who leave me out;*
> *When me they fly, I am the wings;*
> *I am the doubter and the doubt,*
> *And I the hymn the Brahmin sings.*
>
> *The strong gods pine for my abode,*
> *And pine in vain the sacred Seven;*
> *But thou, meek lover of the good!*
> *Find me, and turn thy back on heaven.*

[43] Aśvaghoṣa, a great Indian exponent of Mahāyāna philosophy. The text has been translated by the present author from Chinese into English.

God creates the world and finds himself exclaiming "It is good." God has not committed any moral or immoral act. It is simply "good." And this "goodness" of things as they are is *sono-mama* in Japanese Zen and Shin terminology.

The following passage paraphrased from the *Chuang-tzŭ* (XIX) may be of interest:

A man called Sonkyū (Sun-hsiu) came to Henkei-shi (Pien Ch'ing-tzŭ) and said: "When I was in my native town there was nothing I did not practice in the way of morality, there was no difficult situation into which I was not courageous enough to plunge myself. And yet when I am engaged in my fields they do not yield good harvests; when I serve a master he does not show me any favor. I was driven away from my native town, I am an outcast from my province. What sins did I commit against Heaven? What kind of fate am I going to suffer?"

Henkei answered, "Have you never heard of how the perfect man (*chih-jên*) behaves himself? He forgets his own viscera, he is not conscious of his own bodily existence. He saunters away from a world of defilement as if he did not belong to it, he engages himself in every kind of activity as if he were not engaged in it at all. This is the meaning of the dictum: 'A work is accomplished and lay no claim to it; let things grow up by themselves and exercise no authority.' But in your case you make a show of your intelligence, which frightens the backward people; you take to moral discipline which brings out defects in others. You act as shiningly as if the sun or the moon is fully out. You had better congratulate yourself that you have preserved your body whole with all the nine orifices and have not in the meantime suffered the misfortune of turning deaf or blind or lame, and that you are still counted as human. What leisure is yours to rail against Heaven? Begone!"

One thing we have to notice in these accounts of swordsmanship given by the various writers on the subject is that the Japanese swordsman never thinks of defending himself but always of attacking, and thus that he is from the first advised not to think of coming out of the combat alive. Especially in the case of Odagiri Ichiun, he tells his disciples to meet the opponent with the idea of an *ai-uchi,* that is, with no thought of surviving the fight. This tactic of always being on the offensive and not the defensive may be a Japanese characteristic, and may account for their holding the sword in both hands, leaving nothing for defense. I do not know how early in the history of the Japanese weapons this usage dates. In any case, it is a significant fact that the Japanese sword has a long hilt, so that the warrior can seize it with both hands and strike the enemy with the full force of his being.

To be always on the offensive in a single-handed engagement means that one's mind is bent in any circumstances on striking the enemy regardless of one's own safety, absolutely free from the thought or fear of death. If there is anything in the mind that even remotely approaches this, one can never assume a positive attitude, for there would always be a residue of negativistic restraint arising from the instinct of self-preservation. The problem of death is from the very start to be discarded. Especially with Yagyū Tajima no kami, this is the reason the swordsman is most emphatically advised to be fearless or even reckless as regards his coming out of the combat alive. Once he stands against an opponent, he is positively to identify himself with the sword in his hands and to let the sword function as it will.

Psychologically stated, the sword now symbolizes the Unconscious in the person of the swordsman. He then moves as a kind of automaton. He is no more himself. He has given himself up to an influence outside his everyday consciousness, which is no other than his own deeply buried Unconscious, whose presence he was never hitherto aware of. But we must remember that it is no easy task to realize this state of mind, for a man has to go through a great deal of discipline, not only moral but highly spiritual. As Ichiun says, a first-class swordsman must also be a "perfect man"; he is not only to be great in his profession, but as a moral character he is also to be great in every way; the swordsman must be more than a mere technician who cannot think of anything else but displaying his skill in the art of killing. As long as the technician is impatient in the demonstration of his art he can never come out victorious in his combat. The encounter of one Umedzu with Toda Seigen [44] affords us a fine example of the sad fate met by an imperfect personality, and it also proves that the sword is after all the symbol of spirituality and not an instrument of wanton killing.

A swordsman called Umedzu, probably of the early seventeenth century, was known for his proficiency in the art of swordplay and was quite conscious of it himself. When he heard that Toda Seigen was coming to Mino, where Umedzu was teaching the art, he was anxious to try his skill with him. Seigen, however, was not at all eager to accept the challenge. He said, "The sword is used only when criminals are punished or when honor is involved. Neither of us is a criminal, nor is there any question of honor between us. What then is the use of a contest?" Umedzu took this for an excuse on Seigen's part to avoid defeat. He grew all the more arrogant and publicly asserted himself to that effect.

Saitō Yoshitatsu, lord of Mino, heard of the challenge and, getting interested in the matter, dispatched two of his retainers and courteously asked Seigen to accept. But Seigen refused to respond. The request was thrice repeated. Not being able to refuse any longer, he consented. An umpire was to be elected. The place and the date were settled.

Umedzu took the matter quite seriously and devoted two nights and three days in succession to practicing a religious rite of purification. Someone suggested to Seigen that he follow the example. But he quietly declined, saying, "I am always culti-

<hr>

[44] The story is quoted from a book called *Bubi Wakun*, by Katajima Takenori, who resided in Osaka early in the eighteenth century. The book, published in 1717, contains the general moral injunctions for the samurai.

vating a heart of sincerity. It is not something the gods will give
me in cases of emergency. I have no idea of hurting anybody.
I have simply accepted the challenge because I thought it was not,
after all, gentlemanly to keep on refusing so persistent a request
from the lord of the province."

When the day came, both combatants appeared in the appointed field. Umedzu was accompanied by a large number of
his pupils. He carried a wooden sword as long as three feet
six inches, while Seigen had a short one no longer than one foot
three inches. Umedzu then asked the umpire to permit the
use of a real sword. This was transmitted to Seigen who, however, declined the proposal, adding that if Umedzu wished he
was free to have a real sword instead of a wooden one in the
impending contest; as for himself, Seigen was contented with his
short wooden substitute. The umpire decided that each should
have a wooden piece and not the steel, though its length was left
to each to choose his own.

Both were now ready. Umedzu with his longer weapon acted
like a fierce lion trying to strike the opponent down with one
blow. Seigen looked quite nonchalant, like a sleepy cat about to
catch a rat. When they had been facing each other for a while,
Seigen uttered a cry and at once his short sword apparently
struck Umedzu's neck, for it began to bleed. Incensed with this
blow, Umedzu tried to crush the opponent with all his energy in
one sweeping stroke of his long heavy stick. But before this was
done Seigen gave another hard blow on his opponent's right
arm, which made Umedzu drop his weapon. It was broken into
two pieces under Seigen's feet. Umedzu now attempted to un-
sheath the sword in his belt, but his arm failed to obey his
will, and he fell to the ground. One of the onlookers later reported, "Seigen's action was like splitting a piece of bamboo—
so easy, so clear-cut, so indifferent."—And "so unobstructed,"
the Kegon Buddhists might add.

Seigen was no more a mere swordsman, he was Chuang-tzŭ's
"perfect man" who "could not be drowned in water nor burned

in fire." Umedzu was just the opposite. He knew nothing of the
moral and the spiritual side of his art that was really the essence
of it. His egotistic pride was boundless. He thought his self-assert-
ing aggressiveness, backed by his mastery of the technique, made
complete swordsmanship. He never realized that mere offensive-
ness, characterizing the Japanese method of swordplay, was after
all nothing unless something transcending the sportive spirit of
winning and losing controlled the entire procedure of combat.
Not only must the desire to be victorious or to be not defeated entirely absent itself from the consciousness of the combatant; the
philosophical problem of life and death must be fully settled,
not theoretically or conceptually, indeed, but in the most concretely practical way. For this reason Ichiun as well as Yagyū
Tajima no kami emphasized the importance of Zen training
whereby the swordsman would be able to transcend the limits of
his technique.

10

IN CONNECTION with swordsmanship, there is another psychological phenomenon that may be of interest to "parapsychol-
ogists." It is a sort of telepathy or mind reading that seems to
develop in some swordsmen. Yagyū Tajima no kami is said to
have had this "sixth sense." According to my view, this comes
out of a very much deeper source, and cannot be subsumed under
the category of an abnormal or extraordinary psychic phenomenon.

According to the author of the book *Gekken Sōdan*,[45] Tajima no kami took a walk in his garden one fine spring day and
seemed to be intensely absorbed in admiring the cherries now in
full bloom. He was accompanied by a boy attendant, who carried
his sword behind him. The boy secretly harbored the idea: "However skilled my lord may be in the art of swordplay, he might

[45] See above, p. 129.

easily be attacked from behind as he stands so enchanted by the cherry blossoms." Tajima no kami thereupon happened to look around him as if he wished to locate somebody hiding. Seeing nobody, he came back to his room. Leaning against a post, he stood quietly for some time, looking in every way as if he had gone altogether out of his mind. The attendants were all afraid of approaching him. One of them finally came forward and asked if the lord felt well and if they could help him in some way. Answered Tajima no kami: "I feel very well, but some strange incident has been troubling me for some time which I cannot explain. By virtue of my long training in swordplay, I can feel whatever thoughts might be moving in the mind of the one who stands against me, or is around me. While I was in the garden, most unexpectedly I became aware of a 'murderous air.' I looked around, but except for my boy attendant there was not even a dog in the neighborhood. I cannot give an account of my feeling. I am disgusted with myself. Hence this absent-mindedness."

The boy attendant, learning of this report, approached the lord, confessed all that had happened to him while standing behind the lord, and humbly asked for his forgiveness. This pleased Tajima no kami, who said, "It is all clear now."

The following story of animal intelligence is remarkable. If this could be subjected to experiment, it might give us an unusual insight into the monkey's instincts. We humans have lost most of the instincts that are frequently demonstrated by the so-called lower animals, and we are apt to imagine that such stories as this are entirely fictitious. The following one also comes from Yagyū Tajima no kami.

He used to keep two monkeys as pets. They were allowed to watch his pupils going through training. Being by nature extremely imitative, and being fond of sports, they apparently learned the way to handle the sword and engage in the game. They became experts, in a way. When a *rōnin* who was friendly with the lord expressed the wish to try his spearmanship with him, the lord suggested that the man first try it with one of his monkeys. The *rōnin* felt greatly hurt, for he thought he was humiliated. When they were ready to fight, the monkey with a *shinai* and the *rōnin* with a spear, the man, bent on striking the animal with one blow, fiercely thrust his spear against him. The monkey, however, in a most nimble manner dodging it, closed up to the *rōnin* and struck him. The *rōnin* then held the spear in a defensive attitude, but this was of no avail. The monkey leaped on the shaft. The spearman had to acknowledge his defeat.

When he came back blushing with shame to Tajima no kami, the lord remarked, "I was sure from the start of your inability to stand against the monkey."

The *rōnin* stopped visiting the lord. About half a year elapsed. Then, expressing the desire to have another contest with the monkey, he appeared again before the lord. The lord this time perceived that the monkey was no longer any match for him and refused to grant his request. But, as the *rōnin* was insistent, the monkey was brought in. As soon as they stood against each other ready for the fray, the monkey threw up his weapon and ran away crying. Tajima no kami concluded, "Was I not right?" Later he recommended the *rōnin* to the service of his colleague.

VII

Zen and Haiku

I T IS impossible to speak of Japanese culture apart from Buddhism, for in every phase of its development we recognize the presence of Buddhist feeling in one way or another. There are, in fact, no departments of Japanese culture which have not undergone the baptism of Buddhist influence, an influence so pervasive, indeed, that we who are living in its midst are not at all conscious of it. Since its introduction into our country officially in the sixth century, Buddhism has ever been a most stimulating formative agent in the cultural history of Japan. We can almost state that the very fact of its introduction was due to the wish, on the part of the ruling classes of the time, to make Buddhism the agency of cultural advancement and political consolidation.

However this may be, Buddhism rapidly and inevitably came to be identified with the State. While it is doubtful, from the purely religious point of view, whether or not such identification was really good for the healthy development of spiritual Buddhism, the historical fact is that Buddhism was thoroughly mixed up with the political power of the successive governments and helped them to further their policies in various ways. And as the sources of Japanese culture have generally been in the hands of the upper ruling classes, it was natural that Buddhism took for itself an aristocratic pattern.

If we want to see the degree to which Buddhism has entered into the history and life of the Japanese people, let us imagine that all the temples and the treasures sheltered therein were

completely destroyed. Then we should feel what a desolate place
Japan would be, in spite of all her natural beauty and kindly
disposed people. The country would then look like a deserted
house with no furniture, no pictures, no screens, no sculptures,
no tapestries, no gardens, no flower arrangements, no Nō plays,
no art of tea, and so on.

1

TO CONFINE myself to Zen and its influence on, or rather its
relationship to, Japanese culture, it is desirable once more,
though briefly, to touch on some features of Zen Buddhism that
specifically appeal to the Japanese mentality.

No doubt the philosophy of Zen is that of Mahāyāna Buddhism
in general, but it has its own characteristic method of realizing it.
This consists in seeing directly into the mystery of our own being,
which, according to Zen, is Reality itself. Zen thus advises us not
to follow the verbal or written teaching of Buddha, not to believe
in a higher being other than oneself, not to practice formulas of
ascetic training, but to gain an inner experience which is to take
place in the deepest recesses of one's being. This is an appeal to
an intuitive mode of understanding, which consists in experiencing what is known in Japanese as *satori* (*wu* in Chinese). Without *satori* there is no Zen. Zen and *satori* are synonymous. The
importance of this *satori* experience has thus now come to be
regarded as something exclusively related to Zen.

The principle of *satori* is not to rely upon concepts in order to
reach the truth of things, for concepts are useful in defining the
truth of things but not in making us personally acquainted with
it. Conceptual knowledge may make us wise in a way, but this
is only superficial. It is not the living truth itself, and therefore
there is no creativeness in it, being a mere accumulation of dead
matter. Zen in this respect perfectly echoes the spirit of Oriental
thinking.

There is truth in saying that the Oriental mind is intuitive while the Western mind is logical and discursive. An intuitive mind has its weaknesses, it is true, but its strongest point is demonstrated when it deals with things most fundamental in life, that is, things related to religion, art, and metaphysics. And it is Zen that has particularly established this fact—in *satori*. The idea that the ultimate truth of life and of things generally is to be intuitively and not conceptually grasped, and that this intuitive prehension is the foundation not only of philosophy but of all other cultural activities, is what the Zen form of Buddhism has contributed to the cultivation of artistic appreciation among the Japanese people.[1]

It is here then that the spiritual relationship between Zen and the Japanese conception of art is established. Whatever definitions are used, the relationship rises from an appreciation of the significance of life—or we may say that the mysteries of life enter deeply into the composition of art. When an art, therefore, presents those mysteries in a most profound and creative manner, it moves us to the depths of our being; art then becomes a divine work. The greatest productions of art, whether painting, music, sculpture, or poetry, have invariably this quality—something approaching the work of God. The artist, at the moment when his

---

[1] "Intuition" has various shades of meaning. Ontologically speaking, its most fundamental quality is to come directly in touch with Reality. The human mind is generally found to be chock-full of ideas and concepts. When a man sees a flower he sees clustered with it all kinds of associated analytical thoughts, and it is not the flower in its suchness. It is only when *prajñā*-intuition is exercised that "the flower is red and the willow is green." For a detailed exposition of the subject, see my *Studies in Zen*, under the heading "Reason and Intuition in Buddhist Philosophy."

Recently, however, I have come to think that "feeling" is a better term than "intuition" for the experience Zen claims to have—"feeling" in its deepest, broadest, and most basic sense, and not the "feeling" psychologists generally distinguish from other activities of the mind. The experience the human mind has when it is identified with the totality of things or when the finite becomes conscious of the infinite residing in it—this experience is the most primary feeling which lies at the basis of every form of psychic functioning we are capable of. An intuition in whatever form or sense still reminds us of an intellectual residue.

creativeness is at its height, is transformed into an agent of the creator. This supreme moment in the life of an artist, when expressed in Zen terms, is the experience of *satori*. To experience *satori* is to become conscious of the Unconscious (*mushin*, no-mind), psychologically speaking. Art has always something of the Unconscious about it.

The *satori* experience, therefore, cannot be attained by the ordinary means of teaching or learning. It has its own technique in pointing to the presence in us of a mystery that is beyond intellectual analysis. Life is indeed full of mysteries, and wherever there is a feeling of the mysterious, we can say there is Zen in one sense or another. This is known among the artists as *shin-in* (*shên-yün*) or *ki-in* (*ch'i-yün*), spiritual rhythm, the taking hold of which constitutes *satori*.

Satori thus refuses to be subsumed under any logical category, and Zen provides us with a specific method for its realization. Conceptual knowledge has its technique, that is, its progressive method, whereby one is initiated into it step by step. But this does not allow us to come in touch with the mystery of being, the significance of life, the beauty of things around us. Without an insight into these values it is impossible for one to be master or artist of anything. Every art has its mystery, its spiritual rhythm, its *myō* (*miao*), as the Japanese would call it. As we have seen, this is where Zen becomes most intimately related to all branches of art. The true artist, like a Zen master, is one who knows how to appreciate the *myō* of things.

Myō is sometimes called *yūgen* (*yu-hsüan*) or *gemmyō* (*hsüan-miao*) in Japanese literature. Some critics state that all great works of art embody in them *yūgen* whereby we attain a glimpse of things eternal in the world of constant changes: that is, we look into the secrets of Reality. Where *satori* flashes, there is the tapping of creative energy; where creative energy is felt, art breathes *myō* and *yūgen*.[2]

---

[2] *Yūgen* is a compound word, each part, *yū* and *gen*, meaning "cloudy impenetrability," and the combination meaning "obscurity," "unknowability," "mystery," "beyond intellectual calculability," but not "utter darkness." An

Satori has a specifically Buddhist ring about it, for it is to penetrate into the truth of the Buddhist teaching concerning the reality of things or the mystery and meaning of life. When *satori* artistically expresses itself, it produces works vibrating with "spiritual (or divine) rhythm" (*ki-in*), exhibiting *myō* (or the mysterious), or giving a glimpse into the Unfathomable, which is *yūgen*. Zen has thus greatly helped the Japanese to come in touch with the presence of the mysteriously creative impulse in all branches of art.

2

THE MYSTERIOUS is something which cannot be captured and made to work by means of intellectual analysis or systematization or conscious scheming, and therefore we may conclude that *satori* is to be an act of divine grace, as Christians would declare, and the monopoly of an artistic genius. Zen, however, has devised a method of its own to realize *satori*, to bring it within the reach of every ordinary mind, and this is where Zen is distinguished from other schools of Buddhism. But this Zen method is really no method in the usual sense of the word. It is sometimes a terribly "brutal" method, for it is unscientific and "inhuman."

object so designated is not subject to dialectical analysis or to a clear-cut definition. It is not at all presentable to our sense-intellect as this or that, but this does not mean that the object is altogether beyond the reach of human experience. In fact, it is experienced by us, and yet we cannot take it out into the broad daylight of objective publicity. It is something we feel within ourselves, and yet it is an object about which we can talk, it is an object of mutual communication only among those who have the feeling of it. It is hidden behind the clouds, but not entirely out of sight, for we feel its presence, its secret message being transmitted through the darkness however impenetrable to the intellect. The feeling is all in all. Cloudiness or obscurity or indefinability is indeed characteristic of the feeling. But it would be a great mistake if we took this cloudiness for something experientially valueless or devoid of significance to our daily life. We must remember that Reality or the source of all things is to the human understanding an unknown quantity, but that we can feel it in a most concrete way.

A few days after cubs are born to the mother lion, it is said, she throws them down the precipice to see if they are self-reliant and courageous enough to climb back up all by themselves. If they fail, she pays no further attention to them as unworthy of her race. Something of the mother lion will be noticed in the burglar's "inhuman" way of teaching his art to his son, so that the son can be worthy of the family profession. The story was told earlier in this book. The swordsman's system of training was also described there. The principle of Zen methodology is this: Whatever art or knowledge a man gets by an external means is not his own, does not intrinsically belong to him; it is only those things evolved out of his inner being that he can claim as truly his own. And his inner being opens up its deep secrets only when he has exhausted everything belonging to his intellect or his conscious deliberations. It is true that genius is born and not made. But it will never be brought out fully unless it goes through stages of serious severe disciplining. The Zen "genius" sleeps in every one of us and demands an awakening. The awakening is *satori*.

Generally speaking, *satori* breaks out when a man is at the end of his resources. He feels within himself that something remains to complete his mastership of the art, whatever it may be. He has nothing to learn as far as the techniques are concerned, but if he is really dedicated to his chosen field of work and sincere to himself, he is sure to have a feeling of uneasiness owing to something in his Unconscious, which is now disquietingly trying to move out into the open area of consciousness. In the case of Zen study as it is carried on nowadays, there are the master and the *koan* confronting the student. In the case of artistic disciplines individual experiences may vary, though there are a certain number of fixed patterns.

The following is an example of *satori* attained by a monk-spearman.

Experts of the Hōzōin school use a certain kind of spear that was invented by the school's founder, Inyei (1521–1607), a monk of the Hōzōin temple belonging to the Kegon sect of Buddhism. The spear has a crescent-shaped horn branching out at about the middle part of the spearhead. The idea of having this extra attachment came to the monk, it is said, in the following way. It was his habit to train himself in the use of the spear in the evening in the temple grounds. What engaged his mind most intently on these occasions was not the mastery of the technique of spearmanship, for he was already an expert. What he wanted was to realize a state of mind in which there was perfect unification of Inyei himself and his spear, of man and instrument, subject and object, actor and action, thought and deed. Such unification is called *samādhi* (*sammai* in Japanese), and its realization was the aim of the spearman-monk in his daily exercises. While thrusting his spear in and out, Inyei unexpectedly noticed one evening the reflection of a crescent moon crossing his glistening spearhead in the pond. This perception was the occasion of his breaking through his dualistic consciousness. Tradition says that after this experience he added the crescent form to his spearhead. However this may be, the point we make is his fact of realization and not the innovation.

The experience of the Hōzōin priest reminds me of the Buddha's experience. His Enlightenment took place when he looked up early one morning at the morning star. He had been engaged in meditation for many years; his intellectual research had given him no spiritual satisfaction; he was intensely occupied with discovering, if possible, something which went deeper into the ground of his personality. Looking at the star made him conscious of that something in himself which he had been in search of. He then became the Buddha.

[12, 45–47]

In the case of Hōzōin he penetrated into the secret of using the spear and became a *meijin* of his art. A *meijin* is a man who is more than an expert or a specialist, he is one who has gone even beyond the highest degree of proficiency in his art. He is

a creative genius. Whatever art he may pursue, his original individuality marks him out. Such a one is known as *meijin* in
Japanese. There is no born *meijin*, one becomes a *meijin* only
after experiencing infinitely painstaking discipline, for only such
a series of experiences leads to the intuition of the secret depths
of art, that is, of the lifespring.

Chiyo (1703–75), the *haiku* poetess of Kaga, wishing to improve herself in the art, called upon a noted *haiku* master of her
day who happened to visit her town. She was already known
among her friends as a fine composer of *haiku*. But she was not
satisfied with a merely local fame; not only that, what urged
her to see the traveling poet was the question of her creative
activity. She wished to know what constituted a genuine *haiku*,
a *haiku* really worth noting as such, a *haiku* of truly poetic inspiration. He gave her a subject about which she might write
a *haiku* poem. It was a conventional one, "the cuckoo." This
is one of the birds very much liked by the Japanese poets of
haiku as well as of *waka*;[3] one prominent characteristic of this
bird is that it sings in the night as it flies, and for this reason poets find it very difficult to hear it cry or see it fly. One of
the *waka* poems on the cuckoo reads:

Hototo-gisu	*Hearing a cuckoo cry,*
Nakitsuru kata wo	*I looked up in the direction*
Nagamureba,	*Whence the sound came:*
Tada ariake no	*What did I see?*
Tsuki zo nokoreru.	*Only the pale moon in the dawning sky.*[4]

Chiyo now tried several *haiku* on the subject given by her
master, but he rejected every one of them as merely conceptual
and not true to feeling. She did not know what to say, or how to
express herself more genuinely. One night she went on cogitating
on the subject so intently she did not notice at all that it was al-

---

[3] A *waka* or *uta* consists of thirty-one syllables $(5 + 7 + 5 + 7 + 7)$ and is
longer than a *haiku* (which has seventeen: $5 + 7 + 5$). Therefore, the poet can
put more objects or thoughts in it.

[4] I do not attempt to preserve the syllable count in the translations, but
to approximate it.

ready dawning and that the paper screens had begun to light up faintly, when the following *haiku* formed itself in her mind:

Hototogisu,	*Calling "cuckoo," "cuckoo,"*
Hototogisu tote,	*All night long,*
Akenikeri!	*Dawn at last!*

When this was shown to the master, he at once accepted it as one of the finest *haiku* ever composed on the cuckoo. The reason was that the *haiku* truly communicated the author's genuine inner feeling about the *hototogisu* and that there was no artificial or intellectually calculated scheme for any kind of effect; that is to say, there was no "ego" on the part of the author aiming at its own glorification. *Haiku,* like Zen, abhors egoism in any form of assertion. The product of art must be entirely devoid of artifice or ulterior motive of any kind. There ought not to be any presence of a mediatory agent between the artistic inspiration and the mind into which it has come. The author is to be an altogether passive instrument for giving an expression to the inspiration. The inspiration is like Chuang-tzǔ's "heavenly music" (*t'ien-lai*). The artists are to listen to the heavenly music and not to the human. And when it comes upon one, let him be a sort of automaton with no human interference. Let the Unconscious work itself out, for the Unconscious is the realm where artistic impulses are securely kept away from our superficial utilitarian life. Zen also lives here, and this is where Zen is of great help to artists of all kinds.

Chiyo's all-night meditation on the *hototogisu* helped to open up her Unconscious. What she used to do before this experience was to contemplate the subject she would use in composing a *haiku,* and for this reason whatever *haiku* she produced was always tinged with a certain amount of artificiality or mere cleverness that had really nothing to do with poetry in its proper sense. Chiyo for the first time realized that a *haiku,* as long as it is a work of poetical creativity, ought to be an expression of one's inner feeling altogether devoid of the sense of ego. The *haiku* poet in this sense must also be a Zen-man. The poet's *satori* is an artistic one, so to speak, while the Zen-man's grows out of a metaphysical background. The former may be said to be partial, while the latter covers the totality of one's being. The artistic *satori* may not penetrate the artist's entire personality, for it may not go any further than what I feel like calling the artistic aspect of the Unconscious.

Whatever aspects of the Unconscious there may be, they can never be tapped unless one experiences *samādhi* or *sammai*, which is the state of one-pointedness (*ekāgratā*), that is, of concentration. And this state is realized only when the artist, with his knowledge of all the technicality, is still sincerely and loyally looking for a complete mastery of the art. Without sincerity and loyalty no artist can claim to be original and creative. It is sincerity and loyalty or whole-hearted devotion that enables him to reach the highest rung of the ladder, for mere "genius" will never accomplish anything in the way of developing all of his being. Every one of us, however ordinary he may be, has something in him, in his Unconscious, that is hidden away from the superficial level of consciousness. To awaken it, to make it work out things of great value to our human world, we must exert ourselves to the utmost and thoroughly purge ourselves of all our selfish interests. To reach the bedrock of one's being means to have one's Unconscious entirely cleansed of egoism, for the ego penetrates even the Unconscious so called. Not the "Collective Unconscious" but the "Cosmic Unconscious" must be made to reveal itself unreservedly. This is why Zen so emphasizes the significance of "no-mind" (*mushin*) or "no-thought" (*munen*), where we find infinite treasures well preserved.

3

BEFORE we proceed, I must tell you more of what a *haiku* is. It is the shortest form of poem we can find in world literature.

It consists of seventeen syllables into which have been cast some of the highest feelings human beings are capable of. Some readers may, perhaps reasonably, wonder how such a short string of words could express any deep stirrings of the mind. Did not Milton write *Paradise Lost*? Did not even Wordsworth write "Intimations of Immortality"? But we must remember that "God" simply uttered, "Let there be light," and when the work was finished, he again simply remarked that the light was "good." And this was the way, we are told, that the world started, this world in which all kinds of dramatic events have been going on ever since it made its debut in such a simple style. "God" did not use even as many syllables as ten and his work was successfully carried out. When Moses asked God by what name he would transmit God's message to his people, God said, "My name is 'I am who I am,'" or "the God who is." And is this not the grandest utterance one can make in this world? Do not say that it was God and not Man who uttered these words. But I would say, it is Man and not God who recorded all these sayings of God's. The recorder is "I am who I am" and not the utterer, because the utterer belongs to the past, to the limbo of history. But the recorder is here forever. It is he, indeed, and no other, who is "I am who I am." In any event, the shortness of a *haiku* in the number of syllables has nothing to do with the significance of the content. At the supreme moment of life and death we just utter a cry or take to action, we never argue, we never give ourselves up to a lengthy talk. Feelings refuse to be conceptually dealt with, and a *haiku* is not the product of intellection. Hence its brevity and significance.

Let me give you a specimen or two of *haiku*. Bashō (1643–94), [49 founder of the modern school of *haiku*, has this, which is said to have been the start of his revolutionary movement:

Furu ike ya!   *The old pond, ah!*
Kawazu tobikomu,   *A frog jumps in:*
Mizu no oto.   *The water's sound!*

Nothing can be shorter than this, but some of us may ask, "Is this really poetry? Does it say anything that appeals to the depth of our being really worth communication? What have 'an old pond,' 'a jumping frog,' and 'the water's splash' to do with any poetic inspiration?"

To quote Dr. R. H. Blyth, an authority on the study of *haiku:* "A *haiku* is the expression of a temporary enlightenment, in which we see into the life of things." Whether "temporary" or not, Bashō gives in his seventeen syllables a significant intuition into Reality.

Dr. Blyth continues: "Each thing is preaching the law [Dharma] incessantly, but this law is not something different from the thing itself. *Haiku* is the revealing of this preaching by presenting us with the thing devoid of all our mental twisting and emotional discoloration; or rather, it shows the thing as it exists at one and the same time outside and inside the mind, perfectly subjective, ourselves undivided from the object, the object in its original unity with ourselves. . . . It is a way of returning to nature, to our moon nature, our cherry-blossom nature, our falling leaf nature, in short, to our Buddha nature. It is a way in which the cold winter rain, the swallows of evening, even the very day in its hotness and the length of the night become truly alive, share in our humanity, speak their own silent and expressive language." [5]

What Dr. Blyth calls the moon nature, the cherry-blossom nature, etc., are no more than the suchness of things. In Christian terms, it is to see God in an angel as angel, to see God in a flea as flea. Bashō discovered this in the sound of the water as a frog jumped into the old pond. This sound coming out of the old pond was heard by Bashō as filling the entire universe. Not only was the totality of the environment absorbed in the sound and vanished into it, but Bashō himself was altogether effaced from his consciousness. Both the subject and the object, *en-soi* and *pour-soi,* ceased to be something confronting and condi-

[5] *Haiku,* I, pp. 270 ff.

tioning each other. And yet this could not be a state of absolute annihilation. Bashō was there, the old pond was there, with all the rest. But Bashō was no more the old Bashō. He was "resurrected." He was "the Sound" or "the Word" that was even before heaven and earth were separated. He now experienced the mystery of being-becoming and becoming-being. The old pond was no more, nor was the frog a frog. They appeared to him now enveloped in the veil of mystery which was no veil of mystery. When he wished to communicate it to others, he could not avoid this paradox, but within himself everything was transparent, and no clouds of ambiguity enveloped him. *Haiku* and Zen, however, are not to be confused. *Haiku* is *haiku* and Zen is Zen. *Haiku* has its own field, it is poetry, but it also partakes of something of Zen, at the point where a *haiku* gets related to Zen.

Let me give a fine example of this relationship between a *haiku* and Zen. Bashō's "the old pond" may be interpreted as having almost too much of Zen in it, but the following expresses an exquisite interfusion of Zen and *haiku* and humanism characteristic of the author's personality. When Bashō was traveling on "the Narrow Road of Oku," he happened to meet two prostitutes on their way to the Ise Shrine, and they all stayed in the same inn. After listening to their tale of a wretched life which they abhorred, Bashō had his *haiku:*

Hitotsu ya ni	*Under one roof,*
Yūjo mo netari,	*Prostitutes, too, were sleeping;*
Hagi to tsuki.	*The hagi* [6] *flowers and the moon.*

It requires a great deal of interpretation to make the full meaning of this *haiku* clear to those readers who are not well acquainted with the Japanese social conditions of the seventeenth century and who also are ignorant of the flowering bush clovers in

---

[6] The bush clover (*Lespedeza striata*) blooms in early autumn and is liked very much by the Japanese people, especially by *haiku* and *waka* poets.

brightly shining autumn moonlight. Only let me say this much:
Here is a solitary wandering poet with something of Zen aloofness; he meets prostitutes bound for Ise, where they are planning to worship at the shrine dedicated to the ancestral spirits
of the Japanese race; he listens to their story of miseries and
woes and karmic retributions; the poet is in full sympathy with
them but does not know what to do in the condition in which
all are situated; human iniquities, moral indignation, individual
helplessness. With all this, Bashō is a nature poet. He sets the
prostitutes as well as himself together with the bush clovers and
the moon in the nature frame of transcendentalism. And the
outcome is the seventeen-syllable *haiku:*

> *Under one roof,*
> *Prostitutes, too, were sleeping;*
> *The bush clovers and the moon.*

The prostitutes are no more fallen specimens of humanity,
they are raised to the transcendentally poetic level with the
lespedeza flowers in their unpretentious beauty while the moon
impartially illuminates good and bad, comely and ugly. There
is no conceptualization here, and yet the *haiku* reveals the
mystery of being-becoming.

Before Bashō, the *haiku* men indulged in word play which
incited him to raise the dignity of *haiku* to a higher level. In
many ways *haiku* may be said to reflect the Japanese character.
First of all, the Japanese are not given to verbosity; they are
not argumentative, they shun intellectual abstractions. They are
more intuitional and wish to give out facts as facts without much
comment, emotional as well as conceptual. What is known as
Kami nagara no michi [6a] is their credo; "to leave things to the
will of the gods" and not to interfere with them with human
scheming coincides well with the Buddhist teaching of suchness
(*tathatā*), which is, in colloquial Japanese, *sono-mama. Sono-
mama* (or *kono-mama*) is the ultimate reality itself; we hu-

---

[6a] See *History of Philosophy Eastern and Western,* ed. S. Radhakrishnan
and others. I, 596 ff. (ch. XXV: "Japanese thought").

mans, however fiercely or desperately we may strive or struggle, can never go beyond this. All that we can do then is to write a *haiku* appreciating the fact, without asking why or how. This we may say is a kind of resignation. But the Japanese do not grumble, nor do they curse as most Western peoples do; they just accept cheerfully and with humor.

4

PERHAPS one most egregiously Japanese characteristic is to take notice of the small things of nature and tenderly take care of them. Instead of talking about great ideals or highly abstract thoughts, they cultivate chrysanthemums or morning-glories, and when the season comes they delight to see them bloom beautifully as they planned. If I enumerate the following subjects among many others taken up by the *haiku* poets for their cherished seventeen syllables, the readers may be tempted to look at them as not at all worthy of the dignified profession of poet. I wonder if the Western mind has ever come to be moved poetically by such insignificant creatures as the following?

(*1*) A tree frog on a banana leaf:

Amagaeru	*A little frog*
Bashō ni norite,	*Riding on a banana leaf,*
Soyogi keri.	*Trembling.*

Whatever Kikaku (1660–1707),[7] the author of this *haiku*, wished to depict here, I see first of all a broad expanding banana leaf perfectly green in color and vividly fresh about the time of year when the tree frog begins to jump around in the garden. It is spring, and it is probable that the frog has just come out of its shelter after a rainfall, though the frog family likes to be drenched in it. It now finds itself riding toward the

[7] One of the "Ten Disciples" of Bashō.

end of the leaf, which quivers under the weight of the little creature. The leaf is broad and strong enough to support the frog if the latter sits near the stem. The "riding" and "trembling" or "quivering," however, suggest a movement in a quiet spring garden where things are all green in a variety of shades, and it brings out the contrast between the greenness of the frog and that of the banana leaf.

(2) A monkey soaked in rain:

Hatsu shigure,	First winter rain:
Saru mo komino wo	The monkey also seems to wish
Hoshige nari.	For a little straw cloak.

In his traveling through the mountain paths, Bashō must have observed a little monkey sitting on a branch thoroughly wet with the cold rain. The pitiful sight moved Bashō's tender heart, but I like to feel here something deeper than mere sentimentalism. A poet of loneliness, though he himself is somewhat like the monkey wishing for a rain cloak, has full appreciation for the approach of the dreary chilly winter foretold by the drenching showers. According to Chinese philosophy, winter symbolizes the limit of the feminine principle when the universe, shorn of all its outward showiness, holds within itself all the creativity needed for the coming season. "A solitary traveler" who is Bashō feels something of himself in the approaching winter. This is a life of eternal longing.

(3) A "most inarticulate object" [8] such as a nameless insignificant plant in bloom:

Kusa mura ya:	Among the grasses,
Na mo shiranu,	An unknown flower
Shiroku saku.	Blooming white.

[8] Dr. Blyth in his Haiku, I, p. 289.

This is by Shiki (1869–1902), one of the most modern *haiku* poets. While Shiki is not a blind follower of Bashō and often depreciates Bashō as too much of a subjectivist, this *haiku* on a white-flowering plant has something similar to Bashō's on the *nazuna* herb. Though Shiki makes no reference to "a careful observation" (*yoku mireba*) as Bashō does, which may be said to be Bashō's subjectivism, Shiki's verse practically echoes Bashō's "sentimentalism," if this term is applicable to the spirituality of "the flower in the crannied wall" or of the Biblical "lilies of the field." "*Na mo shiranu*" means "the name unknown," "insignificant," "humble," and "being ready to feed the oven tomorrow." This is really an epithet we have to give to everything, great and small, existing in its own right, for it is a nothing, of no value whatever, until it stands connected with the totality of being—embraced in the divine grace, as Christians would say. Bashō observed his *nazuna* by the wild hedge in this light,[9] and I would like to see Shiki, too, observing "the white-blooming plant" among the grasses in the same light.

(4) The octopus in a jar:

Tako tsubo ni	*The octopuses in the jars:*
Hakanaki yume wo	*Transient dreams,*
Natsu no tsuki.	*The summer moon.*

I understand the fisherman sinks a jar into the sea, and the octopus, thinking it a fine shelter, gets into it. While it is sleeping there and perhaps enjoying an innocent dream, the crafty fisherman pulls up the jar together with its occupant or occupants, as the case may be. This is what we call human intelligence, by which we not only keep ourselves alive but to a greater or lesser extent destroy one another as intelligence grows up to "systematized knowledge." As to the poor octopuses entrapped, we think, they go on dreaming a "transient dream" under the

[9] See below, p. 263.

summer moon. But who would not say that men are of superior intelligence when they go on devising all sorts of "wonderful" weapons of mutual annihilation? Who would not call this "dreaming a transient dream under the summer moon," or in fact anywhere? *"Haka naki"* means not only "transient," but "vain," "inane," "futile," "useless," and it is not only the octopus snugly dreaming in the fisherman's jar, but every one of us including the fisherman himself keeps on dreaming idle vain dreams. If not for the moon of suchness, of any season, summer or winter, our existence here on earth could not be anything but "vanity of vanities." As Ecclesiastes cries, "What profit hath a man of all his labor which he taketh under the sun?"

(5) A firefly flying flickeringly:

Ō-botaru,	*A huge firefly,*
Yurari-yurari to,	*Waveringly,*
Tōri keri.	*Passes by.*

Yurari-yurari to is the original Japanese for "waveringly," which is Dr. Blyth's translation. I do not know whether or not this is a happy English word for *yurari-yurari to*. The word is one of those reduplicatives which appeal more to the feeling than to the intellect and therefore are not convertible into abstract conceptual terms. Both the Chinese and the Japanese languages abound with these reduplicatives, showing that the people who use these languages are not so used to the abstract way of thinking as are most of the Western peoples, and also that the Easterners live closer to the pristine experiences of reality than those peoples who have highly developed their systems of analysis and abstraction. Probably there is no one English word equivalent to *yurari-yurari to:* "waveringly," "unsteadily," "unreliably," "discontinuously," "fluctuatingly," "vibratingly," "unquietly," etc. are all conceptual, whereas *yurari-yurari to,* no doubt describing a discontinuous movement, is very much more than that; it suggests feelings of freedom, unconcernedness, dignity, not being hurried by anything external, leisurely taking one's own time. When these feelings are combined with the verb of action, *tōri keri*, the firefly, not a small one but a huge one, reminds us of a person living a life of freedom, fearlessness, and individual dignity, with an air of aloofness and transcendentalism. A firefly passing on through the air is not attached to the ground and its sordidness. Issa (1763–1827), the author of this *haiku*, is said to have spent some months revising it before he could settle on the present form, though it looks as spontaneous as if it were a work of instant inspiration.

Let me add, in this connection, a word about the liberal use of reduplicatives and other adverbial expressions of a similar nature, which give a great advantage to the Chinese and the Japanese languages in communicating a certain type of experience. When they are translated into conceptual and intellectually well-defined terms these expressions lose their rich personal flavor and imaginative depth, their beguiling vagueness. This will readily be understood when we compare the Chinese originals, for instance, of Lao-tzŭ's or Chuang-tzŭ's descriptions of the Tao-man, with the English versions [10] of the same. How

---

[10] There are a number of English translations of Lao-tzŭ's *Tao Tê Ching*, and Arthur Waley's is one of the best, I think. The following is culled from his version of Chapter XX, where the ideal man, "Tao-man," is described in the first person. ". . . All men, indeed, are *wreathed in smiles* (*hsi-hsi*). . . . I *droop and drift* (*ch'êng-ch'êng*) as though I belonged nowhere. . . . Mine is indeed the mind of a very idiot, *so dull* (*tun-tun*) am I. . . . They *look lively and self-assured* (*ch'a-ch'a*): I alone, *depressed* (*mên-mên*). I seem *unsettled* (*tan-hsi*) as the ocean; *Blown adrift* (*liao-hsi*), never brought to a stop." The italicized English phrases are equivalents for the Chinese given in parentheses.

Actually, the Chinese language ought never to be expressed other than in its ideograms. The Chinese mentality is so intimately ingrained in those rather clumsy-looking, but to my mind most expressive, sign-words. The Chinese thoughts and feelings and these ideograms are inseparable. For a practical purpose here, we have the sounds romanized. As to the original characters, the reader is referred to the Index. Incidentally I wish to remark that the English translator has not interpreted the last two lines properly. Lao-tzŭ's idea is: "I am serene as the ocean, I am mobile as the wind."

prosaic, uninteresting, and impersonal the latter read! The Oriental peoples are sometimes said to be deficient in the power of philosophical thinking and analytical preciseness. Perhaps they are, but they have a richer store of the experience of reality itself, which refuses to be so sharply defined that "yes" can never be "no" and "no" "yes." Nowadays, I am told, the physicists are trying to use the concept of complementarity, seeing that one theory in exclusion of an antagonistic one does not explain everything. Life goes on whether or not we logically comprehend and mechanically control it. Though this does not mean that we are to give up all such attempts, it is best to recognize that there is something in life whose mystery goes beyond our intellectual prehension. The *yurari-yurari* way of a huge firefly passing before my window contains in it all that defies our relativistic scrutiny.

(6) Fallen leaves under the water:

Mizu soko no	*Under the water,*
Iwa ni ochitsuku	*On the rock resting,*
Kono ha kana.	*The fallen leaves.*

This is by Jōsō (1661–1704), one of the chief disciples of Bashō. Superficially and ordinarily, most of us are liable to think nothing of the fallen leaves of autumn finding their final resting place on the rocks in the stream. They are now all discolored, showing none of the yellowish or reddish tinge they had while on the trees, but after being hurled up and down, here and there, in the corners of the garden, or upon the roofs of the house, they are finally settled under the water and safely over the rocks. Perhaps some further fate may be waiting for them, but as far as the poet sees they are quietly resting as if this were their final place. He does not venture to think of anything beyond. He just sees them there and gives no intimation as to what he has in his mind. It is this very silence of the poet that makes the verse all the more eloquent. We also stop here with the poet, yet we feel that there is something much more than we can expressly utter. This is where the *haiku* is at its best. Dr. Blyth sees here the suchness of things. I should like to see the mystery of being.

(7) Lice and fleas and the stable:

Nomi shirami,	Fleas, lice,
Uma no nyō suru	The horse pissing
Makuramoto.	Near my pillow.

A strange combination of things. If they are suggestive of anything, it is something disgusting, utterly annoying, repugnant. What else could Bashō feel in those circumstances? Is there anything at all evocative of poetic feelings? This will be what we would like to know.

The *haiku* has a prelude: Bashō happened to stop at a miserable shed in the mountains while traveling along "the narrow road of Oku." It rained continuously for three days. The poor lonely traveler had nothing else to do but to stay patiently at the stable. He was, however, a poet. Let me quote what Dr. Blyth has to comment about the situation and the poet; it is really illuminating, showing how much of the *haiku* spirit the commentator has imbibed.

"Bashō's verse is to be read with the utmost composure of mind. If there is any feeling of disgust and repugnance as a predominating element of the mind, Bashō's intention is misunderstood. Fleas are irritating, lice are nasty things, a horse pissing close to where one is lying gives one all kinds of disagreeable feelings. But in and through all this, there is to be a feeling of the whole, in which urine and champagne, lice and butterflies take their appointed and necessary place.

"This of course is not Bashō's meaning; this was certainly his experience, but we are concerned with his *poetical* experience, which is a different thing and yet somehow the same thing. Sometimes, not by any means always, the simple, elemental experiences of things, whether of lice or of butterflies, the pissing of horses or the flight of eagles, have a deep significance, not of something beyond themselves, but of their own essential nature. But we must lodge with these things for a night, for a day, for three days. We must be cold and hungry, flea-ridden and lonely, companions of sorrow and acquainted with grief. Bashō's verse is not an expression of complaint or disgust, though he certainly felt irritation and discomfort. It is not an expression of philosophic indifference nor an impossible love of lice and dirt and sleeplessness. What is it an expression of? It is the feeling 'These things too. . . .' But anyone who tries to finish this sentence does not understand what Bashō meant." [11]

These are a few of the subjects that have occupied the *haiku* poets of Japan. The moon and the sun, storms and waves, mountains and rivers—so-called bigger aspects of Nature—will also engage their attention, but what I wish to emphasize here is the Japanese sensitivity for the small things of Nature generally neglected by people of the West, and the fact that these insignificant and ignoble creatures are in intimate relationship with the grand totality of the cosmic scheme. Japanese mysticism will not leave them out as too mean for human or, for that matter, divine consideration. This is more than delicate feminine sentimentalism. And it is where Zen comes in and becomes associated with *haiku*.

5

Furu ike ya!   *The old pond, ah!* [12]
Kawazu tobikomu,   *A frog jumps in:*
Mizu no oto.   *The water's sound!*

T H I S is said to have been the first revolutionary alarm given by Bashō to the *haiku* world of seventeenth-century Japan. Before

48]

---

[11] *Haiku*, III, pp. 195–96.

[12] "Ah!" here stands for the Japanese *ya*. *Ya* is frequently an important particle in the composition of a *haiku* when the emphasis of the whole *haiku*

him, *haiku* had been mere plays on words with nothing deeper than pleasantry, and it was Bashō who gave them a new start by this utterance on the "old pond." The story as to how he came to compose it goes this way:

When Bashō was studying Zen under his master Bucchō, Bucchō one day paid him a visit and asked, "How are you getting on these days?"

Bashō said, "After the recent rain the moss has grown greener than ever."

Bucchō shot a second arrow to see the depths of Bashō's understanding of Zen, "What Buddhism is there even before the moss has grown greener?"

This question is tantamount to Christ saying, "I am even before Abraham was." The Zen master wants to know who this "I" is. With Christians probably the mere assertion, "I am," was enough, but in Zen the question must be asked and a more concrete answer must be forthcoming. For this is an essential part of Zen intuition. So Bucchō asked, "What is there even before the world came into existence?" That is to say, "Where is God even before he uttered, 'Let there be light'?" Bucchō the Zen master is not just talking about the recent rainfall and the green moss growing fresher; what he wants to know about is the cosmic landscape prior to the creation of all things. When is timeless time? Is it no more than an empty concept? If it is not, we must be able to describe it somehow for others. Bashō's answer was, "A frog jumps into the water, and hear the sound!"

Bashō's answer at the time it was uttered did not have the first line, "the old pond," which, it is reported, he added later on to make a complete *haiku* of seventeen syllables. We may ask now: Where is that something revolutionary in it which marked the beginning of modern *haiku* poetry? It is Bashō's insight into

turns on this one particle. But in the present *haiku* by Bashō the *ya* does not play such a very weighty role as it does in some other cases, for instance, in Chiyo's *"Asagao ya!"* "The old pond" here is used to indicate the place where "the sound" has been produced. For what is most significant in Bashō's *haiku* here is "the sound" itself, as I try to explain in the text.

the nature of life itself, or into the life of Nature, which forms
the background of his verse. He really penetrated into the depths
of the whole creation, and what he saw there came out as depicted
in his *haiku* on the old pond.

Let me try to give a little more intelligible account of Bashō
whereby we, with our prosaic too-modern minds, may understand him. Most of us are liable to interpret the *haiku* on the
old pond as describing a scene of solitude or tranquillity. According to them, the following is the line of imagination they
would pursue: "An ancient pond is likely to be located in some
old temple grounds, filled with many stately trees. Around the
pond also there are odd-looking shrubs and bushes with outstretching branches and thickly-grown leaves. Such surroundings
add to the tranquillity of the unrippled surface of the pond. When
this is disturbed by a jumping frog, the disturbance itself en-
hances the reigning tranquillity; the sound of the splash rever-
berates, and the reverberation makes us all the more conscious
of the serenity of the whole. However, this consciousness is
awakened only in him whose spirit is really in consonance
with the world spirit itself. It took Bashō, the truly great *haiku*
poet, to give voice to this intuition or inspiration."

Let me repeat. To understand Zen as a gospel of quietism is
not at all in the right, nor is it the way to interpret Bashō's
haiku, for it is far from being an appreciation of tranquillity. A
double mistake is thus committed. As regards Zen, I have had
occasion to give my views in my several books on the subject
and will confine myself here to the correct interpretation of
Bashō. First of all, we must know that a *haiku* does not express
ideas but that it puts forward images reflecting intuitions. These
images are not figurative representations made use of by the poetic
mind, but they directly point to original intuitions, indeed,
they are intuitions themselves. When the latter are attained,
the images become transparent and are immediate expressions of the experience. An intuition in itself, being too intimate, too personal, too immediate, cannot be communicated to

ZEN AND HAIKU 241

others; to do this it calls up images by means of which it becomes transferable. But to those who have never had such an experience it is difficult, even impossible, to reach the fact itself merely through images, because in this case images are transformed into ideas or concepts, and the mind then attempts to give them an intellectual interpretation, as some critics do with Bashō's *haiku* on the old pond. Such an attempt altogether destroys the inner truth and beauty of the *haiku*.

As long as we are moving on the surface of consciousness, we can never get away from ratiocination; the old pond is understood as symbolizing solitude and tranquillity, and a frog jumping into it and the sound thereof are taken for instruments whereby to set off and also to increase the general sense of eternal quietness. But Bashō the poet is not living there as we are, he has passed through the outer crust of consciousness away down into its deepest recesses, into a realm of the unthinkable, into the Unconscious, which is even beyond the unconscious generally conceived by the psychologists. Bashō's old pond lies on the other side of eternity, where timeless time is. It is so "old," indeed, that there is nothing more ancient. No scale of consciousness can measure it. It is whence all things come, it is the source of this world of particulars, yet in itself it shows no particularization. We come to it when we go beyond the "rainfall" and "the moss growing greener." But when this is intellectually conceived, it becomes an idea and begins to have an existence outside this world of particulars, thus making itself an object of intellection. It is by intuition alone that this timelessness of the Unconscious is truly taken hold of. And this intuitive grasp of Reality never takes place when a world of Emptiness is assumed outside our everyday world of the senses; for these two worlds, sensual and supersensual, are not separate but one. Therefore, the poet sees into his Unconscious not through the stillness of the old pond but through the sound stirred up by the jumping frog. Without the sound there is no seeing on the part of Bashō into the Unconscious, in which lies the source of creative activities and upon which all true artists draw for their inspiration. It is difficult to describe this moment of consciousness where polarization ceases or rather starts, for these contradictory terms are applicable there without causing logical inconvenience. It is the poet or the religious genius who actually has this kind of experience. And, according to the way this experience is handled, it becomes in one case Bashō's *haiku* and in the other a Zen utterance.

The human mind can be considered to be made up, as it were, of several layers of consciousness, from a dualistically constructed consciousness down to the Unconscious. The first layer is where we generally move; everything here is dualistically set up, polarization is the principle of this stratum. The next layer below is the semiconscious plane; things deposited here can be brought up to full consciousness any time they are wanted; it is the stratum of memory. The third layer is the Unconscious, as it is ordinarily termed by the psychologist; memories lost since time immemorial are stored up here; they are awakened when there is a general mental upheaval; memories buried nobody knows how long ago are brought out to the surface when a catastrophe takes place designedly or accidentally. This unconscious layer of the mind is not the last layer; there is still another which is really the bedrock of our personality, and may be called "collective unconscious," corresponding somewhat to the Buddhist idea of *ālayavijñāna*, that is, "the all-conserving consciousness." The existence of this *vijñāna* or unconscious may not be experimentally demonstrated, but the assumption of it is necessary to explain the general fact of consciousness.

Psychologically speaking, this *ālayavijñāna* or "collective unconscious" may be regarded as the basis of our mental life; but when we wish to open up the secrets of the artistic or religious life, we must have what may be designated "Cosmic Unconscious." The Cosmic Unconscious is the principle of creativity, God's workshop where is deposited the moving force of the universe. All creative works of art, the lives and aspirations of

religious people, the spirit of inquiry moving the philosophers
—all these come from the fountainhead of the Cosmic Unconscious, which is really the store-house (*ālaya*) of possibilities.

Bashō came across this Unconscious, and his experience was
given an expressive utterance in his *haiku*. The *haiku* is not just
singing of a tranquillity imagined to be underneath the superficial tumult of the worldly life. His utterance points to something
further below, which is at the same time something we encounter
in this world of pluralities, and it is on account of this something that our world gains its value and meaning. Without reckon-
ing on the Cosmic Unconscious, our life, lived in the realm of
relativities, loses its moorings altogether.

We now can understand why it is not necessary for the Japanese *haiku* to be long and elaborate and intellectual. It avoids
an ideational or conceptual construction. When it appeals to
ideas, its direct pointing to the Unconscious is warped, marred,
interrupted, its refreshing vitality forever gone. Therefore, the
haiku attempts to offer the most appropriate images in order to
make us recall the original intuition as vividly as possible. The
images thus held up and arranged in a *haiku* may not be at all
intelligible to those whose minds have not been fully trained to
read the meaning conveyed therein. As in the case of Bashō's
haiku, what can most people who are not educated to appreciate
a *haiku* generally see in the enumeration of such familiar objects
as an old pond, a jumping frog, and the sound resulting therefrom? It is true that these objects are not merely enumerated;
there are also an exclamatory particle *ya* and a verb of motion
tobikomu. But I am afraid that the uninitiated may not be able
to recognize anything poetically enlivening in those seventeen
syllables so loosely strung. And yet what a deep truth of intuition is herein given utterance—a truth which cannot be expressed
so inspiringly even with a formidable array of ideas!

The religious intuitions are usually communicated in simple
terms; they are direct, straightforward utterances without equivocation, though in Zen we find a great number of poetical quota-

tions, including *haiku*. But as soon as they are subjected to intellectual analysis, the philosophers and theologians have to vie with one another in writing volume after volume on the subject. In a similar manner, the poetical intuitions and aspirations that move the *haiku* poet may easily be occasions for longer and more elaborate pieces of poetry when they are delivered into the hands of another type of poet. As far as original inspiration is concerned, Bashō is just as great a poet as any of the West. The number of syllables has nothing to do with the true quality of the poet. The instrument made use of by poets, which is quite accidental, may vary, but we judge things as well as people not by what is accidental but by what essentially constitutes them.

43, 50, 51, 58, 63]

By way of a postscript, I wish to add Sengai's characteristic comment on Bashō and his frog. Sengai (1750–1837) was the abbot of Shōfukuji in Hakata, Kyūshū. He was not only a fine Zen master but a painter, calligrapher, and poet, full of humor and wit, and was loved by people of all classes, men and women, young and old. He once painted a picture of a banana plant and a frog crouching under it. *Bashō* is banana plant in Japanese and the poet's *nom de plume* "Bashō" comes from it. Sengai now writes over the picture a *haiku*—so to speak, a frog's soliloquy:

Ike araba,	*If there were a pond* [*around here*],
Tonde bashō ni	*I would jump in, and let Bashō*
Kikasetai.	*Hear* [*the plop*]!

6

Asagao ya!	*Ah! Morning-glory!*
Tsurube torarete	*The bucket taken captive!*
Morai mizu.	*I begged for water.*

THIS is the *haiku* composed by the poetess Chiyo of Kaga (1703–75), the author of a *haiku* on the cuckoo.[13] Bashō's frog

[13] See above, p. 224.

produced a sound by jumping into the old pond, and this gave him a chance to commune with the spirit of the old pond—the pond as old as Eternity itself. In Chiyo's case, it was the morning-glory that acquainted her with the spirit of beauty.

An explanation is needed here, I believe, to show the connection between morning-glory and bucket and water-begging. In olden days, a well supplying water for daily household use was generally situated outside the house, especially in the countryside. The water was drawn up by means of a bucket attached to a certain device we know as a shadoof.[14] One late summer morning, Chiyo the poetess found the bucket entwined by the morning-glory vine, which bore a flower. She was so deeply struck by its beauty that she forgot her mission for some little while. When she recovered, she thought of the water she wanted for her morning work, probably in the kitchen. She had no idea of disturbing the flower, and so she went to her neighbor. This is one of the simple incidents in our daily life that might take place any late-summer morning anywhere.

Some may say there is no poetry in it, and would argue in this way: As to the morning-glory, it is such a common flower in Japan and especially in the countryside, where no particular care is taken of the plant, that the flowers can be nothing but most ordinary, and there is nothing in them which would evoke a poet's admiration. As to going to the neighbor for water, it is quite stupid of Chiyo. Why did she not unwind or cut the vine and release the bucket? It is the easiest thing in the world. And then as to composing a *haiku* on this most prosaic event, how could one extract anything romantic from it? There is nothing extraordinary here worth even seventeen syllables.

In answer to this matter-of-fact interpretation of Chiyo's *haiku* on the morning-glory I would say: To the prosaic, everything is prosaic and practical. They forget the fact, or they are unable

[14] This contrivance was already in use in ancient China at the time of Chuang-tzŭ (*c.* 369–286 B.C.). It is still used in some parts of Japan as well as in Egypt, whence its name, as the dictionary tells us.

to appreciate it, that when one is in a certain mood—I would say, a certain divine mood—even the most ordinary thing that we pass by in our daily life, without paying it any attention whatever, incites a deep religious or spiritual feeling one has never experienced before. This is the time one becomes a poet in spite of oneself. Chiyo was already one and left the immortal *haiku* to us.

The point I wish to make here is that at the time Chiyo perceives the morning-glory early in the morning, which is the best time to see the flower, she is so absorbed in its unearthly beauty that the whole universe, including herself, is transformed into one absolute morning-glory blooming all by itself. This is the time, as Zen would declare, when Chiyo really sees the flower and the flower in turn sees the poetess. This is a case of perfect identification between subject and object, seer and seen: the whole universe is one flower, one real flower that stands here defying all change and decay. There is no one seeing it and admiring it. It is the flower seeing itself, absorbed in itself. At this supreme moment, to utter even a word would be altogether out of place. Chiyo, however, is human, she recovers herself from the reverie and murmurs, "Ah! Morning-glory!" She can say nothing more for a while. It takes her some more time to find room in her mind for any thought—that she is out to get water for her daily necessities. Even then she does not feel like touching the flower, for this would be a deed of desecration. This is the feeling shared by a number of pious souls, one [15] of whom made this *waka*:

> *If I break them off*
> *My hands may defile them;*
> *Let them alone as they stand in the field;*
> *And let me reverently offer these flowers*
> *To all the Buddhas of the past, present, and future.*

[15] The *Sōjō Henjō* (816–90) in one of the *waka* collections compiled by the Imperial orders.

The thought never occurred to Chiyo that she should untwine the vine in order to free the bucket for her use. Hence she went to the neighbor for water. A *haiku* generally is not explicit about what has been going on in the mind of the author. He does not go any further than barely enumerating, as it were, the most conspicuous objects that have impressed or inspired him. As to the meaning of such objects in their collective totality, it is left to the reader to construct and interpret it according to his poetic experiences or his spiritual intuitions. It is likely that this kind of interpretation frequently differs from the one intended by the author, but this does not matter very much. The original *haiku* is right before us, and we are free to use our own judgments concerning its artistic merit. We cannot in any way go beyond ourselves. To the pure-minded everything is pure. The world is, after all, our own subjective construction. There is no such thing as what can be called an absolutely objective reality as long as each of us has his own inner life. This we can say is in the nature of a *haiku* and constitutes its beauty.

When Chiyo saw the flower, this put her outside herself; but when she came back to her everyday plane of consciousness, she found herself with a pail in her hand, and remembering what she was about she went to her neighbor. If her psychology moved around an axis other than the way *haiku*-mindedness moves, her *haiku* might have shown an orderly disposition of ideas with a detailed description of her heavenly vision. But in this case it would not be a *haiku* of seventeen syllables, it would be a form such as we find in Western poetry. Chiyo was a Japanese born to the environment of her ancestral culture and naturally could not help expressing herself in the *haiku* as we have it. *Haiku* is the poetic form most natural and most appropriate and most vital for the Japanese genius in giving vent to his or her artistic impulses; and for this reason, perhaps, it takes a Japanese mind to appreciate fully the value of a *haiku*; foreign critics, whose way of feeling is not in accord with the

Japanese way because they were not born in this climate and brought up with its cultural tradition, may fail to enter into the spirit of a *haiku*. To understand the spirit of Zen along with *haiku*, a thorough acquaintance with Japanese psychology and surroundings is essential.

7

TO ILLUSTRATE how desirable it is to have a thorough knowledge of Japanese surroundings, physical, moral, aesthetic, and philosophical, let me cite another *haiku*, this time by Buson (1716–83), who was also a fine painter, of the late Tokugawa era. It runs thus:

> *Tsuri-gane ni*   *On the temple bell*
> *Tomarite nemuru*   *Perching, sleeps*
> *Kochō kana*   *The butterfly, oh!*

The full aspect of this verse will not be very easy to apprehend unless we know all about the temple bell and the butterfly as they appeal to the Japanese imagination. The *haiku*, as far as the season is concerned, evidently belongs to the early summer, for the butterfly generally comes out at that time of year and becomes noticeable as an object of poetic imagination. The butterfly is then associated with flowers, and flowers are now in bloom in the temple grounds where the bell is located. The imagination now leads us to a mountain monastery far away from the cities, to the monks given up to meditation, to the old trees, the wild mountain flowers, and perhaps to the murmuring of the rivulet: all is suggestive of a quiet unworldly atmosphere undisturbed by human affairs of greed and strife.

The belfry is not far above the ground, and the bell is exposed to view and approachable. It is of solid bronze, cylindrical in shape, somber and grave in color. As it hangs down from the beam it is the symbol of immovability. When it is struck at the bottom with a strong piece of wood (about five inches in diameter and six feet or more long) suspended horizontally, it gives out a series of soul-quieting sound waves. The boom is altogether characteristic of the Japanese temple bell, and sometimes one is made to feel that the spirit of Buddhism vibrates through this resonance sent out from the belfry, especially when the birds are wearily coming back to their nests after the day's labor.

Let us now observe in this setting, natural and historical and spiritual, a little white butterfly perched on the bell and gone to sleep. The contrast at once strikes us in various ways; the butterfly is a small evanescent creature, its life does not extend beyond the summer, but while living it enjoys itself to the highest degree, fluttering from flower to flower and occasionally basking in the relaxing sun; and now it is found dozing contentedly at the edge of the large awe-inspiring temple bell, symbolic of eternal value. In magnitude and dignity, the insect stands in great contrast to the bell; in color, too, the dainty little white creature, delicate and fluttering, is set off markedly against the heavy darkish background of the bronze. Even from a purely descriptive point of view, Buson's *haiku* is poetic enough as it beautifully depicts an early summer scene in the mountain monastery grounds. But if it went no further than that, it would be just a pretty piece of wording. Some people may think that the poet was somewhat playfully inclined, putting the sleeping butterfly on a temple bell that may be struck by a thoughtless monk at any moment, when its booming vibration will surely frighten the poor little innocent thing away. This utter unconsciousness of events to come, good or bad, is also typical of human life: we dance over a volcano altogether unaware of the possibility of a sudden explosion, just like Buson's butterfly. And for this reason, some expect to read in Buson a certain moral warning aimed at our frivolous habits of living. This interpretation is not impossible. The uncertainty of fate always accompanies this life of ours on earth. We nowadays try to avert it by means of the so-called sciences, but our greed is there, always ready to assert itself, most frequently in a violent way, and all "scientific" computations are upset. If Nature does not destroy us, we destroy ourselves. In this respect we are far worse off than the butterfly. The little "science" we are so proud of makes us conscious of all kinds of uncertainties surrounding us and urges us to dispel them by means of observation, measurement, experiment, abstraction, systematization, etc. But there is one great Uncertainty, born of Ignorance and productive of all other uncertainties, which defies all our "scientific" calculations; and before this Uncertainty, this Insecurity, Homo sapiens is no better than the butterfly sleeping on the temple bell. The humorous playfulness to be detected in Buson, if there is really any, is directed against ourselves. It is a reflection pointing to the awakening of the religious consciousness.

But to my mind there is in Buson's *haiku* another side, revealing his deeper insight into life. By this I mean his intuition of the Unconscious as it is expressed by the images of the butterfly and bell. As far as the inner life of the butterfly, as Buson sees it, is concerned, it is unconscious that the bell exists separate from itself; in fact, it is not conscious of itself. When it lighted on the bell and went on dozing, as if the bell were the very foundation of all things, the place where they find their last shelter, did the butterfly make, humanlike, a discrimination beforehand? When, feeling the vibration created by the monk announcing noontime, the butterfly detaches itself from the bell, does it regret having made a miscalculation? Or is it taken aback by the "unexpected" booming? Are we not here reading too much of human intellection into the inner life of the butterfly, indeed into our own inner life, or rather into Life itself? Is life really so connected with the analysis which occupies our superficial consciousness? Is there not in every one of us a life very much deeper and larger than our intellectual deliberation and discrimination—the life of the Unconscious itself, of what I call the "Cosmic Unconscious"? Our conscious life gains its real significance only when it becomes connected with something more fundamental, namely, the Unconscious. Being so, the inner life, which is our religious life as represented by the butterfly in Buson's *haiku*, knows nothing of the bell being eternity symbolized, nor is it at all troubled by the sudden booming. It has been fluttering over the beautifully scented flowers profusely decorating the mountainside; it is now fatigued, the wings long for a rest after carrying about the tiny body of the life form commonly designated by ever-discriminating human beings as a butterfly; the bell is idly hanging, it perches on it, and being tired it goes to sleep. It now feels vibrations that were neither expected nor unexpected. As it feels them as an actuality, it flies away as unconcernedly as before. It makes no "discriminations"; therefore it is perfectly free from anxieties, worries, doubts, hesitations, and so on; in other words, it lives a life of absolute faith and fearlessness. It is the human mind that makes the butterfly live a life of "discrimination" and hence of "little faith." Buson's is a *haiku* truly laden with religious intuitions of the weightiest importance.

We read in the *Chuang-tzŭ:* "Once upon a time, I, Chuang-tzŭ, dreamt I was a butterfly, fluttering hither and thither, to all intents and purposes a butterfly. I was conscious only of following my fancies as a butterfly, and was unconscious of my individuality as a man. Suddenly I awoke, and there I lay, myself again. Now I do not know whether I was then a man dreaming I was a butterfly, or whether I am now a butterfly dreaming I am a man. Between a man and a butterfly there is necessarily a mutuality. This is called Becoming."

Whatever "mutuality" (*fên*) and "becoming" (*wu-hua*) may mean, Chuang-tzŭ is Chuang-tzŭ while he is Chuang-tzŭ, and the butterfly is a butterfly while it is a butterfly; "mutuality" and "becoming" are human terms, not at all appropriate in the world of Buson and Chuang-tzŭ and butterfly.

The type of intuition given out by Buson is also traceable in Bashō's *haiku* on the cicada:

Yagate shinu	*Of an early death,*
Keshiki wa miyezu,	*Showing no signs,*
Semi no koye.	*The cicada's voice.*

This is understood by most critics and commentators to mean that life is transient and that we, not fully realizing it, are given up to enjoyments of various kinds just like the cicada singing vociferously at the top of its voice, as if it were going to live forever. Bashō is said to be giving us here a moral and spiritual admonition with a concrete familiar example. But, so far as I can see, this kind of interpretation altogether mars Bashō's intuition of the Unconscious. The first two lines (or first twelve syllables) are no doubt a human reflection on the transitoriness of life, but this reflection is a mere preface to the closing phrase, "*semi no koye,*" the cicada's singing, "*jyū, jyū, jyū . . . !*" wherein lies the entire weight of the *haiku*. The "*jyū, jyū, jyū . . . !*" is the way the cicada asserts itself—that is, makes its existence known to others—and while this goes on here the cicada is perfect, content with itself and with the world, and nobody can contradict this fact. It is our human consciousness and reflectiveness whereby the idea of transitoriness is introduced and asserted against the cicada as if he were not thoughtful of its approaching destiny. As far as the cicada itself is concerned, it knows no human worries, it is not vexed with its short life, which may end at any moment as the days grow colder. As long as it can sing it is alive, and while alive here is an eternal life and what is the use of worrying about transitoriness? The cicada may be laughing at us when our reflection leads us to take thought for things of the morrow which is not here yet. The cicada will surely cite for us the divine injunction: "If God so clothe the grass of the field which today is, and tomorrow is cast into the oven, shall he not much more clothe you, O ye of little faith?" (Matthew 6 : 30.)

Faith is another word for intuition of the Unconscious. The Bodhisattva Avalokiteśvara (Kwannon Bosatsu) is the "giver

64]

of fearlessness," and those who believe in him are given fearlessness, which is faith and intuition. All the *haiku* poets are worshipers of Kwannon and in possession of fearlessness, and therefore they can understand the inner life of the cicada and of the butterfly, which are never fearful of the morrow and of things belonging to it.

I hope I have cleared up at least one aspect of the relationship existing between the Zen experience of *satori*, of nondiscrimination, and the *haiku* poets' intuitions of the Unconscious. We can also see that the *haiku* is a poetic form possible only for the Japanese mind and the Japanese language, to the development of which Zen has contributed its respectable quota.

8

IN THE following chapter on the art of tea I have occasion to refer to what is known mostly among the tea-men as *wabi* or *sabi*, which really constitutes the spirit of tea. Now, this *wabi*, which literally means "solitariness," "aloneness," and more concretely, "poverty," is, we might say, what characterizes the entirety of Japanese culture reflecting the spirit of Zen. I mean poverty not only in its economic sense but also in its spiritual sense. In truth, all religion upholds the life of poverty. Christ emphasizes the importance of being poor in spirit, because Heaven is for those who are such. The so-called Lord's Prayer echoes a life of poverty as something blissful. References to "daily bread," "debts," "debtors," as well as "take no thought for the morrow," "one fed on the crumbs which fall from the master's table," "the stone which the builders rejected," "babes and sucklings ordaining strength," "a camel going through the eye of a needle," and so on—all these demonstrate how Christians incline to the virtues of poverty, materially as well as spiritually. Zen also naturally inclines to poverty, for as long as we are attached to something, as long as we are possessed by the idea of possession, we can never be free spirits. Even life is to be dispossessed, for "he that finds his life shall lose it, and he that loses his life for my sake shall find it." Poverty is Zen [16] and so is *haiku*. We cannot imagine a *haiku* rich in ideas, speculations, and images. *Haiku* is loneliness itself. Bashō was an incarnation of this spirit.

First of all, he was a great wandering poet, a most passionate lover of Nature—a kind of Nature troubadour. His life was spent in traveling from one end of Japan to another. It was fortunate that in those days there were no railways. Modern conveniences do not seem to go well with poetry. The modern spirit of scientific analysis and mechanization leaves no mystery unraveled, and poetry and *haiku* do not seem to thrive where there are no mysteries, no feelings of wonderment. The trouble with science is that it tries to leave no room for uncertainties or indefiniteness, it wants to see everything laid bare, it hates to leave anything unanalyzed and unexposed. Where science rules, the imagination beats a retreat. But fortunately science is not omniscient, nor is it omnipotent, and there will always be room enough for *haiku*, and poetry goes on thriving.

We of modern times are all made to face so-called "hard" facts, or what are generally known as "objective truths," which tend to ossify our minds. Where there is no tenderness, no subjectivity, poetry departs; where there is a vast expanse of sand, no verdant vegetation is possible. In Bashō's day, life was not yet so prosaic and hard pressed. One bamboo hat, one cane stick, and one cotton bag were enough for the poet in his wandering life. He would stop for a while in any hamlet, or anywhere that struck his fancy, and enjoy whatever experiences came to him, though these were likely to include the hardships of primitive traveling, too. But we must remember that, when traveling is made too easy and comfortable, its spiritual meaning is lost. This may be called sentimentalism, but a certain sense of loneliness engendered by traveling leads one to reflect upon the meaning of life, for life is after all a traveling from one un-

[16] Cf. Kyōgen's stanza on "Poverty," which is quoted on p. 296.

known to another unknown. The period of seventy, eighty, or even ninety years allotted to us is not meant to uncover the veil of mystery. A too-smooth course over this period robs us of this sense of Eternal Aloneness.

That Bashō had an irresistible desire for traveling is seen from one of the prefaces to his travel diaries called *Oku no Hosomichi*, "The Narrow Road of Oku": [52

"The sun and the moon [17] are eternal wayfarers; so are the seasons, coming and going, year after year. Those who pass their lives on the floating boat and those who grow old taking hold of the horse's bridle—for such, traveling is their daily occupation, it is in fact their own habitat. Of old there were many who died while journeying.

"I do not remember when, but I have conceived the strong desire for a wandering life, giving myself up to the destiny of a solitary cloud as it is wafted in the wind. After spending some time along the seashore, I settled last autumn for a while in a tumbledown hut that stands by the river. The old cobwebs were swept away and the shelter was made somewhat habitable.

"But as the year approached its end, my wandering spirit violently asserted itself once more. It was as if I were pursued by a supernatural being whose temptation was more than I could resist. I was possessed with the idea of visiting the frontier district of Shirakawa under the foggy sky of the coming spring. Peace left my heart. My leggings were hurriedly patched, my traveling hat had its strings renewed, and my shins were treated with moxa burning.[18] Finally, giving up my hut to a friend, I started

---

[17] "The sun and the moon" stand for Time, and the whole sentence means that "Time flies, with us behind his car."

[18] "Moxa" comes from *mogusa* in Japanese, meaning "burning herb." It is made of young dried leaves of the herb called *yomogi* (*Artemisia moxa*), and looks like a soft woolly clump, easily combustible. It is applied to the skin and made to burn, acting as a kind of counter-irritant. Moxa burning has developed into a system in Japan and is used to cure various physical ailments.

on the northern trip, my heart filled with the moonlight that
would soon greet me at Matsushima."

The predecessor of Bashō was Saigyō (1118–90), of the
Kamakura period. He was also a traveler-poet. After quitting
his official career as a warrior attached to the court, he devoted
his life to traveling and poetry. He was a Buddhist monk. Whoever has traveled through Japan must have seen the picture of
a monk in his traveling suit, all alone, looking at Mount Fuji.
I forget who the painter was, but the picture suggests many
thoughts, especially about the mysterious loneliness of human
life, which is, however, not the feeling of forlornness, nor the de-
pressive sense of solitariness, but a sort of appreciation of the
mystery of the Absolute. The poem then composed by Saigyō
runs:

> *The wind-blown*
> *Smoke of Mount Fuji*
> *Vanishing far away!*
> *Who knows the destiny*
> *Of my thought wafting with it?*

Bashō was not a Buddhist monk but was a devotee of Zen. In
the beginning of autumn, when it begins to shower occasionally,
Nature is the embodiment of Eternal Aloneness. The trees become bare, the mountains begin to assume an austere appearance, the streams are more transparent, and in the evening when
the birds weary of the day's work and fly homeward, a lone traveler grows pensive over the destiny of human life. His mood
moves with that of Nature. Sings Bashō:

> *Tabi-bito to*   *A traveler—*
> *Waga na yobareru*   *Let my name be thus known—*
> *Hatsu shigure.*   *This autumnal shower.*

We are not necessarily all ascetics, but I do not know if there is
not in every one of us an eternal longing for a world beyond this

of empirical relativity, where the soul can quietly contemplate its own destiny.

Haiku before Bashō was mere wordplay, without contact with life. As we have observed, Bashō, who was questioned by his master about the ultimate truth of things, happened to see a frog leaping into the old pond, its sound making a break into the serenity of the whole situation. He grasped once for all where the source of life starts from a beginningless beginning and goes on to an endless end. After that he became an artist, watching every mood of his mind as it came in contact with a world of constant becoming, and the result was that he bequeathed to us a great many seventeen-syllable poems. Bashō was a poet of Eternal Aloneness.

Another of his *haiku* is:

Kare eda ni	*A branch shorn of leaves,*
Karasu no tomari keri,	*A crow perching on it—*
Aki no kure.	*This autumnal eve.*

Simplicity of form does not always mean triviality of content. There is a great Beyond in the lonely raven perching on the dead branch of a tree. All things come out of an unknown abyss of mystery, and through every one of them we can have a peep into the abyss. You do not have to compose a grand poem of many hundred lines to communicate the feelings thus awakened by looking into the abyss. When a feeling reaches its highest pitch, we remain silent, because no words are adequate. Even seventeen syllables may be too many. In any event, Japanese artists, more or less influenced by the way of Zen, tend to use the fewest words or strokes of the brush to express their feelings. When feelings are too fully expressed, no room is left for the unknown, and from this unknown start the Japanese arts.

According to Bashō, what is here designated as the spirit of Eternal Aloneness is the spirit of *fūga* (or *fūryū*, as some would have it). *Fūga* means "refinement of life," but not in the modern sense of raising the standard of living. It is the chaste enjoyment of life and Nature, it is the longing for *sabi* or *wabi*, and

not the pursuit of material comfort or of sensation. A life of
fūga starts from the identification of one's self with the creative
and artistic spirit of Nature. A man of *fūga*, therefore, finds his
good friends in flowers and birds, in rocks and waters, in rains
and the moon. Bashō, in the following passages taken from the
foreword to one [19] of his journals, classifies himself as belonging to the group of such artists as Saigyō (1118–90), Sōgi
(1421–1502), Sesshū (1421–1506), and Rikyū (1521–91), who
were all *fūrabō*,[20] lunatics," as far as their love of Nature went.
Bashō's foreword reads:

"There is something in this body composed of one hundred
members and nine orifices, which is called provisionally a
fūrabō. Does it refer to a thin robe in tatters, flapping in the
wind? This fellow has for a long while been an ardent composer
of *kyōku*,[21] for he thought that this was his life mission. Sometimes, however, becoming tired of it, he wants to throw it overboard; sometimes, cherishing the positive ambition to excel
others in it, his mind is distracted very much with worldly concerns; and for this reason he feels uneasy. Indeed, he often aspires to a worldly position, but [his liking for *haiku*] suppresses
the thought. After all this, he is now an ignoramus with no ac-
complishments whatever except that he holds steadily to the pursuit of one line only, which is in truth the line uniformly followed by Saigyō in his *waka*, by Sōgi in his *renga*,[22] by Sesshū in
his paintings, and by Rikyū in his art of tea. One spirit activates
all their works. It is the spirit of *fūga*; he who cherishes it accepts Nature and becomes a friend of the four seasons. Whatever objects he sees are referred to the·flowers; whatever
thoughts he conceives are related to the moon. When objects are

[19] The *Yoshino Journal*.
[20] *Fū* = wind, *ra* = thin fabric, and *bō* = monk. The name taken as a whole
means "an old monk who wanders about fluttering like a thin piece of fabric in the wind."
[21] Literally, "mad phrase," meaning *haiku*.
[22] *Waka* is a Japanese poem of thirty-one syllables. *Renga* is a form of *waka*
running in a series.

not referred to the flowers, one is a savage; when thoughts are not related to the moon, one resembles the lower animals. Therefore, I declare: Go beyond savagery, be separated from the lower animals, and accept Nature, return to Nature."

Bashō calling himself *fūrabō*, "a man whose life is like a wind-blown piece of gauzy fabric," evokes an interesting link of associations, since of old the wind has been full of unknowabilities. One does not know where it comes from or where it blows itself away to. But while it goes on it brings forth all kinds of strange unpredictable phenomena. Chuang-tzŭ gives a fine description of it as "earthly music." Christ compares the wind to the Spirit: "The wind blows where it will, and you hear the sound of it, but you do not know whence it comes or whither it goes; so it is with every one who is born of the Spirit." (John 3 : 8.) A Japanese poet writes:

> *Autumn is come!*
> *Though not visible*
> *So clearly to the eyes,*
> *One knows it by the sound*
> *Of the wind as it blows.*

Lieh-tzŭ, the great Taoist philosopher, has a mystical conception of the wind. I quote the whole story, as it is pregnant with typical Taoist ideas that have been instilled into the Zen way of feeling and thence into the *haiku* poet's attitude towards life.

"Lieh-tzŭ had Lao-shang for his teacher, and Po Kao-tzŭ for his friend. When he had mastered the system of these two philosophers, he rode home on the wings of the wind.

"Yin-shêng heard of this, and became his disciple. He dwelt with Lieh-tzŭ for some months without visiting his own house. When he had an opportunity, he begged to be initiated into his arts. Ten times he asked, and each time received no answer. Becoming impatient, Yin-shêng announced his departure, but Lieh-tzŭ still gave no sign. So Yin-shêng went away; but after some months his mind was still unsettled, so he returned and became his follower once more.

"Lieh-tzŭ said to him: 'Why this incessant going and coming?'

"Yin-shêng replied: 'Some time ago, I sought instruction from you, Sir, but you would not tell me anything. That made me vexed with you. But now I have got rid of that feeling, and so I have come again.'

"Lieh-tzŭ said: 'Formerly, I used to think you were a man of penetration, and have you fallen so low? Sit down, and I will tell you what I learned from my Master. After I had served him, and enjoyed the friendship of Po Kao, for the space of three years, my mind did not venture to reflect on right and wrong, my lips did not venture to speak of profit and loss. Then, for the first time, my Master bestowed one glance upon me—and that was all.

" 'At the end of five years a change had taken place; my mind was reflecting again on right and wrong, and my lips were speaking again of profit and loss. Then, for the first time, my Master relaxed his countenance and smiled.

" 'At the end of seven years, there was another change. I let my mind reflect on what it would, but it no longer occupied itself with right and wrong. I let my lips utter whatsoever they pleased, but they no longer spoke of profit and loss. Then, at last, my Master led me in to sit on the mat beside him.

" 'At the end of nine years my mind gave free rein to its reflections, my mouth free passage to its speech. Of right and wrong, profit and loss, I had no knowledge, either as touching myself or others. I knew neither that the Master was my instructor, nor that the other man was my friend. Inside and outside were emptied. After that, there was no distinction between eye and ear, ear and nose, nose and mouth: all were the same. My mind was concentrated, my body in dissolution, my flesh and bones all melted away. I was wholly unconscious of what my body was resting on, or what was under my feet. I was borne this way and that on the wind, like dry chaff or leaves falling from a tree. In fact, I knew not whether the wind was riding on me or I on the wind. Now, you have not spent one whole season in your teacher's house, and yet you have lost patience two or three times already. Why, at this rate, the atmosphere will never support an atom of your body, and even the earth will be unequal to the weight of one of your limbs! How can you expect to walk in the void or to be charioted on the wind?'

"Hearing this, Yin-shêng was deeply ashamed. He could hardly trust himself to breathe, and it was long ere he ventured to utter another word." [23]

Chuang-tzŭ is, however, not quite satisfied with Lieh-tzŭ, for the latter has to wait for the wind for his ride. Chuang-tzŭ [24] would have nothing to do with the wind, indeed, not with anything that is external:

"As to Lieh-tzŭ's riding on the wind and moving about as he wished, it is all very well. He sometimes stayed away even as long as fifteen days. Among those who have attained happiness his is really a rare case. Though he has freed himself from walking [being attached to the earth], he still has to wait for something to turn up. But if he, riding upon the eternal reason [25] of the universe and controlling the six elements of Nature, could leisurely roam about in the realm of the Infinite, what would he have to wait for?"

Whatever the Taoist philosopher may say, Lieh-tzŭ and Chuang-tzŭ are saying the same thing, for they are both wanderers in the realm of the Unlimited, where all things start and return. Bashō must surely have been acquainted with those mystical writings. The Chinese mind is practical enough, but frequently it aspires to break through all the barriers that keep it within the rules of conventionalism; but the Japanese mind is so attached to

[23] *Taoist Teachings from the Book of Lieh Tzu,* tr. Lionel Giles, pp. 39–42. Slight changes have been made in the text by the author.

[24] Book I.

[25] The original term for "eternal reason" is *chêng,* meaning "a state of things as they are": fire burns, water flows, wind blows, stone falls, gas rises, etc.

the earth that it would not forget, however mean they may be, the grasses growing under the feet. Bashō has no doubt a great deal of Taoism in him, but at the same time he does not fly away on the wings of the wind or neglect things in his intimate surroundings or lose daily touch with his mundane life.

One of the favorite sayings of Zen runs:

After so many years of hardship my robe is in tatters
And a half of it is now all blown away with the wind.

9

THESE considerations lead me to take up some of the *haiku* in their relation to the Japanese character. While the *haiku* masters are poets of poverty, they are not at all ego-centered, as indigence sometimes disposes people to be. If they were they could not be poets. For the poet first of all must be selfless so that he can broaden himself out to embrace the whole universe in his arms. It was Ryōkwan of Echigo (1758–1831) who suffered all the lice to infest his undergarments and even gave them occasional airings when "his black robe of monkhood was not wide enough to take in all the poor people." This may be an extreme case, but the *haiku* poet, if he at all aspires to be one, cannot have his self assertive in any circumstance.

Yamaji kite	*Coming along the mountain path,*
Naniyara yukashi	*I am somehow mysteriously moved*
Sumire-gusa.	*By these violets.*

This is Bashō's *haiku*. "Mysteriously" is made to stand for the Japanese "*naniyara yukashi*," but the English is far from giving the original feeling. I am not sure what word has an equivalent value for *yukashi*. *Naniyara* means "without knowing why," and "somehow" may do. As to *yukashi*, I may choose for it such words as "charming," "sweet," "dainty," "attractive." The Japanese has all these, but it means something more, something deeper, something mysteriously impressive and attracting, but in a sense keeping one away from approaching too near or too familiarly, as it demands a certain reverence.

Bashō must have had a long, dreary, tiresome treading over a rugged mountain pass when he came across a few violets in bloom among the wild bushes. They are not very assuming flowers, not much demanding attention; they are in a way homely, and in this very homeliness there is something sweet and attractive, yet holding a dignity that forbids one's too familiar approach. Their unobtrusive dignity and unaffected homeliness must have mysteriously impressed Bashō. Hence the phrase "*naniyara yukashi sumire-gusa.*"

Bashō has another *haiku* on an humble flower, a white flowering herb known in Japan as *nazuna*. This is not at all pretty and charming; it is quite insignificant compared with the violet, and I doubt if it had ever been elevated to an object demanding a kind of poetic treatment for any reason. Its English name is shepherd's-purse. Bashō is probably the first one who picked it up as an herb worth while for a *haiku* inspiration:

Yoku mireba	*When closely inspected,*
Nazuna hana saku,	*The nazuna is flowering*
Kakine kana.	*By the hedge.*

Apparently the *haiku* does not say much about the herb in its unpretentious flowering by a neglected countryside hedge. Bashō's attention was first awakened by something white by the roadside. Wondering, he approached, and carefully examined it, and discovered that it was the flowering *nazuna*, ordinarily unnoticed by most passers-by. The discovery must have called up a variety of feelings, on which he is not at all explicit in his seventeen syllables. He leaves the pleasure of discovery and appreciation to the readers. How shall we then interpret this *haiku?*

Wordsworth, in his "Intimations of Immortality," has this:

—But there's a Tree, of many, one,
A single Field which I have looked upon,
Both of them speak of something that is gone:
The Pansy at my feet
Doth the same tale repeat:
Whither is fled the visionary gleam?
Where is it now, the glory and the dream?

Did the shepherd's-purse revive for Bashō the memory of a paradise lost? Wordsworth mentions a pansy; the pansy is full of colors, not at all like the *nazuna*. I wonder if the *nazuna* would ever
attract the English poet so as to make him bend over it and give
it a close inspection.

Tennyson, another great English poet, has his famous "Flower
in the Crannied Wall," which reads:

Flower in the crannied wall,
I pluck you out of the crannies,
I hold you here, root and all, in my hand,
Little flower—but if I could understand
What you are, root and all, and all in all,
I should know what God and man is.

Tennyson is here quite inquisitive, philosophically speaking. He
thinks, if he could know what he has in his hand—the little
flower, root and all—he would also know what God and man is.
Did Bashō have the same inquisitive mind? No, his mind was far
from being so. In the first place, he would never think of merci-
lessly plucking the poor *nazuna* with "its root and all" and holding it in his hand and asking of himself any question. Bashō
knew better than Tennyson. He was no scientist bent on analysis
and experiment, nor was he a philosopher. When he saw the
white-flowered *nazuna*, so humbly, so innocently, and yet with all
its individuality, growing among other vegetation, he at once realized that the herb was no other than himself. If it is arrayed
better than "Solomon in all his glory," Bashō is also glorified in

the same style. If it is "alive today and tomorrow thrown into the oven," Bashō, too, has the same destiny. A Zen master declares that he can turn one blade of grass into the Buddha-body sixteen feet high and at the same time transform the Buddha-body into a blade of grass. This is the mystery of being-becoming and becoming-being. This is the mystery of self-identification and universal interpenetration or interfusion.

One day Mañjuśrī, ordering Sudhana to bring him a medicinal herb, added, "Search for a herb that is not medicinal." Sudhana went out and searched for one such, but in vain. He came back and announced, "There is not a herb in the field that is not medicinal." Mañjuśrī said, "Bring then what is medicinal." Sudhana just picked any herb growing around there and handed it over to Mañjuśrī, who took it up and made this declaration: "This herb is medicinal: it takes life, it also gives life." Bashō and the *nazuna* herb as well as the one in Mañjuśrī's hand— each has this mysterious power in itself. Did this occur to Bashō when the *nazuna* under the old hedge was scrutinized by him?

By way of a postscript I wish to add a few words here. What we can say generally about Western poetry on nature is that it is dualistic and personal, inquisitive and analytical. When a poet sees the "primrose by the wayside" he asks,[26]

> *Can anything so fair and free*
> *Be fashioned out of clay?*

When he sees a rose he wonders and thinks of the giver as performer of miracles:

> *We muse on miracles who look*
> *But lightly on a rose!*
> *Who gives it fragrance or the glint*
> *Of glory that it shows?*

[26] All that follows is taken from *Masterpieces of Religious Verse*, ed. James D. Morrison, pp. 19–21. (The first three poets quoted are Anna Bunston de Bary, Edith Daley, and Ralph Hodgson.)

Wordsworth may gaze at "a violet by a mossy stone half hidden from the eye," but his interest is not in the violet as such. It comes to his notice only when he thinks of the fate of a country maid who lives and dies unknown and unpraised. The violet may bloom unknown and unpraised, it may wither unknown and unpraised. The poet would pay no attention to it. It is only when he thinks of the maid he loves. His romantic contemplation of it comes only in connection with a human interest.

The snowdrop flowering "close to sod . . . in white and green" is seen "unmarred, unsoiled" only when "a thought of God" is brought in. If not for God, it would not be "so holy and yet so lowly." If not for God, it would never "cleave the clay," and it is surely subject to "destruction" and will never make you "fall on your knees" beside it.

Another poet sings of the rose:

> He came and took me by the hand
> Up to a red rose tree,
> He kept His meaning to Himself
> But gave a rose to me.

> I did not pray Him to lay bare
> The mystery to me.
> Enough the rose was Heaven to smell
> And His own face to see.

Why must the poet bring "Him" into the rose in order "to smell Heaven" in it and to see "His own face"? Is not the rose "the mystery" in its isness or in its suchness, without making it rely on a stranger? Bashō has no need for dualism and personalism.

While some other flowers, such as the daffodil, violet, hyacinth, lily, daisy, verbena, pansy, etc., have not escaped the notice of Western poets, it is the rose that has attracted them most strongly. The following poem on the rose by G. A. Studdert-Kennedy bespeaks in various ways characteristic Western and Christian feeling:

.   .   .   .   .

All mysteries
In this one flower meet
And intertwine,
The universal is concrete,
The human and divine,
In one unique and perfect thing, are fused
Into a unity of Love,
This rose as I behold it;

.   .   .   .   .

The tears
Of Christ are in it
And His Blood
Has dyed it red,
I could not see it but for Him
Because He led
Me to the Love of God,
From which all Beauty springs.
I and my rose
Are one.

In the first part of the quotation the author is philosophical; in
the second, perhaps, he is religious. But such images or symbols
as blood and tears are required to realize the oneness of the rose
and myself!

VIII

Zen and the Art of Tea

I

1

WHAT is common to Zen and the art of tea is the constant attempt both make at simplification. The elimination of the unnecessary is achieved by Zen in its intuitive grasp of final reality; by the art of tea, in the way of living typified by serving tea in the tearoom. The art of tea is the aestheticism of primitive simplicity. Its ideal, to come closer to Nature, is realized by sheltering oneself under a thatched roof in a room which is hardly ten feet square but which must be artistically constructed and furnished. Zen also aims at stripping off all the artificial wrappings humanity has devised, supposedly for its own solemnization. Zen first of all combats the intellect; for, in spite of its practical usefulness, the intellect goes against our effort to delve into the depths of being. Philosophy may propose all kinds of questions for intellectual solution, but it never claims to give us the spiritual satisfaction which must be accessible to every one of us, however intellectually undeveloped he may be. Philosophy is accessible only to those who are intellectually equipped, and thus it cannot be a discipline of universal appreciation. Zen—or, more broadly speaking, religion—is to cast off all one thinks he possesses, even life, and to get back to the ultimate state of being, the "Original Abode," one's own father or mother. This can be done by every one of us, for we are what we are because of it or him or her, and without it or him or her we are nothing. This is to be called the last stage of simplification, since things cannot be reduced to any simpler terms. The art of tea symbolizes simplification, first of all, by an inconspicuous, solitary, thatched hut erected, perhaps, under an old pine tree, as if the hut were part of nature and not specially constructed by human hands. When form is thus once for all symbolized it allows itself to be artistically treated. It goes without saying that the principle of treatment is to be in perfect conformity with the original idea which prompted it, that is, the elimination of unnecessaries.

Tea was known in Japan even before the Kamakura era (1185–1338), but its first wider propagation is generally ascribed to Eisai (1141–1215), the Zen teacher, who brought tea seeds from China and had them cultivated in his friend's monastery grounds. It is said that his book on tea, together with some of the tea prepared from his plants, was presented to Minamoto Sanetomo (1192–1219), the Shōgun of the time, who happened to be ill. Eisai thus came to be known as the father of tea cultivation in Japan. He thought that tea had some medicinal qualities and was good for a variety of diseases. Apparently he did not teach how one conducts the tea ceremony, which he must have observed while at the Zen monasteries in China. The tea ceremony is a way of entertaining visitors to the monastery, or sometimes a way of entertaining its own occupants among themselves. The Zen monk who brought the ritual to Japan was Dai-ō the National Teacher [1] (1236–1308), about half a century later than Eisai. After Dai-ō came several monks who became masters of the art, and finally Ikkyū (1394–1481), the noted abbot of Daitokuji, taught the technique to one of his disciples, Shukō (1422–1502), whose artistic genius developed it and succeeded in adapting it to Japanese taste. Shukō thus became the originator of the art of tea and taught it to Ashikaga Yoshimasa (1435–90), Shōgun of the time, who was a great patron of the arts. Later, Jō-ō (1504–55) and especially Rikyū further improved it and gave a finishing touch to what is now known as *cha-no-yu*, generally translated "tea ceremony" or "tea cult." The original tea ceremony as practiced at Zen monasteries is

57]

[1] Returned from China in 1267.

carried on independently of the art now in vogue among the general public.

I have often thought of the art of tea in connection with Buddhist life, which seems to partake so much of the characteristics of the art. Tea keeps the mind fresh and vigilant, but it does not intoxicate. It has qualities naturally to be appreciated by scholars and monks. It is in the nature of things that tea came to be extensively used in the Buddhist monasteries and that its first introduction to Japan came through the monks. If tea symbolizes Buddhism, can we not say that wine stands for Christianity? Wine is used extensively by the Christians. It is used in the church as the symbol of Christ's blood, which, according to the Christian tradition, was shed for sinful humanity. Probably for this reason the medieval monks kept wine-cellars in their monasteries. They look jovial and happy, surrounding the cask and holding up the wine cups. Wine first excites and then inebriates. In many ways it contrasts with tea, and this contrast is also that between Buddhism and Christianity.

We can see now that the art of tea is most intimately connected with Zen not only in its practical development but principally in the observance of the spirit that runs through the ceremony itself. The spirit in terms of feeling consists of "harmony" (*wa*), "reverence" (*kei*), "purity" (*sei*), and "tranquillity" (*jaku*). These four elements are needed to bring the art to a successful end; they are all the essential constituents of a brotherly and orderly life, which is no other than the life of the Zen monastery. That the monks behaved in perfect orderliness can be inferred from the remark made by Tei Meidō (Ch'êng Ming-tao in Chinese), a Confucian scholar of the Sung, who once visited a monastery called Jōrinji (Ting-lin Ssŭ): "Here, indeed, we witness the classical form of ritualism as it was practiced in the ancient three dynasties." The ancient three dynasties are the ideal days dreamed of by every Chinese scholar-statesman, when a most desirable state of things prevailed and people enjoyed all the happiness that could be expected of a good government. Even now, the Zen monks are well trained individually and collectively in conducting ceremonies. The Ogasawara school of etiquette is thought to have its origin in the "Monastery Regulations" compiled by Hyakujō [2] and known as *Hyakujō Shingi*. While Zen teaching consists in grasping the spirit by transcending form, it unfailingly reminds us of the fact that the world in which we live is a world of particular forms and that the spirit expresses itself only by means of form. Zen is, therefore, at once antinomian and disciplinarian.

2

THE CHARACTER for "harmony" also reads "gentleness of spirit" (*yawaragi*), and to my mind "gentleness of spirit" seems to describe better the spirit governing the whole procedure of the art of tea. Harmony refers more to form, while gentleness is suggestive of an inward feeling. The general atmosphere of the tearoom tends to create this kind of gentleness all around—gentleness of touch, gentleness of odor, gentleness of light, and gentleness of sound. You take up a teacup, handmade and irregularly shaped, the glaze probably not uniformly overlaid, but in spite of this primitiveness the little utensil has a peculiar charm of gentleness, quietness, and unobtrusiveness. The incense burning is never strong and stimulating, but gentle and pervading. The windows and screens are another source of a gentle prevailing charm, for the light admitted into the room is always soft and restful and conducive to a meditative mood. The breeze passing through the needles of the old pine tree harmoniously blends with the sizzling of the iron kettle over the fire. The entire environment thus reflects the personality of the one who has created it.

"What is most valuable is gentleness of spirit; what is most essential is not to contradict others"—these are the first words of

[2] Pai-chang Hui-hai (720–814), a great Zen master of the T'ang dynasty.

the so-called "Constitution of Seventeen Articles," compiled by
Prince Shōtoku in 604.[3] It is a kind of moral and spiritual admonition given by the Prince Regent to his subjects. But it is
significant that such an admonition, whatever its political bear-
ings, should begin by placing unusual emphasis on gentleness of
spirit. In fact, this is the first precept given to the Japanese consciousness to which the people have responded with varying degrees of success during centuries of civilization. Although Japan
has lately come to be known as a warlike nation, this concept is
erroneous with respect to the people, whose consciousness of
their own character is that they are, on the whole, of gentle nature. And there is good reason to presume this, for the physical
atmosphere enveloping the whole island of Japan is characterized
by a general mildness, not only climatically but meteorologically.
This is mostly due to the presence of much moisture in the air.
The mountains, villages, woods, etc., enwrapped in a somewhat
vaporous atmosphere, have a soft appearance; flowers are not as
a rule too richly colored, but somewhat subdued and delicate;
while the spring foliage is vividly fresh. Sensitive minds brought
up in an environment like this cannot fail to imbibe much of it,
and with it gentleness of spirit. We are, however, apt to deviate
from this basic virtue of the Japanese character as we come in
contact with various difficulties, social, political, economic, and
cultural. We have to guard ourselves against such subversive influences, and Zen has come to help us in this.

When Dōgen (1200–1253) came back from China after some
years of study of Zen there, he was asked what he had learned.
He said, "Not much except soft-heartedness (*nyūnan-shin*)."
"Soft-heartedness" is "tender-mindedness" and in this case means
"gentleness of spirit." Generally we are too egotistic, too full of
hard, resisting spirit. We are individualistic, unable to accept
things as they are or as they come to us. Resistance means friction, friction is the source of all trouble. When there is no self,
the heart is soft and offers no resistance to outside influences.

[3] Cf. p. 305 and n. 17.

This does not necessarily mean the absence of all sensitivities or emotionalities. They are controlled in the totality of a spiritual outlook on life. And in this aspect I am sure that Christians and Buddhists alike know how to follow Dōgen in the appreciation of the significance of selflessness or "soft-heartedness." In the art of tea the "gentleness of spirit" is spoken of in the same spirit enjoined by Prince Shōtoku. Indeed, "gentleness of spirit" or "soft-heartedness" is the foundation of our life on earth. If the art of tea purports to establish a Buddha-land in its small group, it has to start with gentleness of spirit. To illustrate this point further, let us quote the Zen Master Takuan (1573–1645).

TAKUAN ON THE ART OF TEA (CHA-NO-YU)

THE PRINCIPLE of *cha-no-yu* is the spirit of harmonious blending of Heaven and Earth and provides the means for establishing universal peace. People of the present time have turned it into a mere occasion for meeting friends, talking of worldly affairs, and indulging in palatable food and drink; besides, they are proud of their elegantly furnished tearooms, where, surrounded by rare objects of art, they would serve tea in a most accomplished manner, and deride those who are not so skillful as themselves. This is, however, far from being the original intention of *cha-no-yu*.

Let us then construct a small room in a bamboo grove or under trees, arrange streams and rocks and plant trees and bushes, while [inside the room] let us pile up charcoal, set a kettle, arrange flowers, and arrange in order the necessary tea utensils. And let all this be carried out in accordance with the idea that in this room we can enjoy the streams and rocks as we do the rivers and mountains in Nature, and appreciate the various moods and sentiments suggested by the snow, the moon, and the trees and flowers, as they go through the transformation of seasons, appearing and disappearing, blooming and withering. As visitors are greeted here with due reverence, we listen quietly to the boiling water in the kettle, which sounds like a breeze passing through the pine needles, and become oblivious of all worldly woes and worries; we then pour out a dipperful of water from the kettle, reminding us of the mountain stream, and thereby our mental dust is wiped off. This is truly a world of recluses, saints on earth.

The principle of propriety is reverence, which in practical life functions as harmonious relationship. This is the statement made by Confucius when he defines the use of propriety, and is also the mental attitude one should cultivate as *cha-no-yu*. For instance, when a man is associated with persons of high social rank his conduct is simple and natural, and there is no cringing self-deprecation on his part. When he sits in the company of people socially below him he retains a respectful attitude toward them, being entirely free from the feeling of self-importance. This is due to the presence of something pervading the entire tearoom, which results in the harmonious relationship of all who come here. However long the association, there is always the persisting sense of reverence. The spirit of the smiling Kāśyapa and the nodding Tsêng-tzŭ must be said to be moving here; this spirit, in words, is the mysterious Suchness that is beyond all comprehension.

For this reason, the principle animating the tearoom, from its first construction down to the choice of the tea utensils, the technique of service, the cooking of food, wearing apparel, etc., is to be sought in the avoidance of complicated ritual and mere ostentation. The implements may be old, but the mind can be invigorated therewith so that it is ever fresh and ready to respond to the changing seasons and the varying views resulting therefrom; it never curries favor, it is never covetous, never inclined to extravagance, but always watchful and considerate for others. The owner of such a mind is naturally gentle-mannered and always sincere—this is *cha-no-yu*.

The way of *cha-no-yu*, therefore, is to appreciate the spirit of a naturally harmonious blending of Heaven and Earth, to see the pervading presence of the five elements (*wu-hsing*) by one's fireside, where the mountains, rivers, rocks, and trees are found as they are in Nature, to draw the refreshing water from the well of Nature, to taste with one's own mouth the flavor supplied by Nature. How grand this enjoyment of the harmonious blending of Heaven and Earth!

[*Here ends Takuan*]

————

Had the art of tea and Zen something to contribute to the presence of a certain democratic spirit in the social life of Japan? In spite of the strict social hierarchy established during her feudal days, the idea of equality and fraternity persists among the people. In the tearoom, ten feet square, guests of various social grades are entertained with no discrimination; for, once therein, the commoner's knees touch those of the nobleman, and they talk with due reverence to each other on subjects in which they both are interested. In Zen, of course, no earthly distinctions are allowed, and its monks have free approach to all classes of society and are at home with them all. It is, indeed, deeply ingrained in human nature that it aspires once in a while to throw off all the restraints society has artificially put on us and to have free and natural and heart-to-heart intercourse with fellow beings, including the animals, plants, and inanimate objects so called. We, therefore, always welcome every opportunity for this kind of liberation. No doubt this is what Takuan means when he refers to "the harmonious blending of heaven and earth," where all angels join in the chorus.

"Reverence" is fundamentally and originally a religious feeling—feeling for a being supposed to be higher than ourselves who are, after all, poor human mortals. The feeling is later transferred to social relationships and then degenerates into mere formalism. In modern days of democracy so called, everybody is just as good as everybody else, at least from the social point of view, and there is nobody specially deserving reverence. But when the feeling is analyzed back to its original sense, it is a reflection on one's own unworthiness, that is, the realization of one's limitations, physical and intellectual, moral and spiritual. This realization evokes in us the desire for transcending ourselves and also for coming into touch with a being who stands to us in every possible form of opposition. The desire frequently directs our spiritual movements toward an object outside us; but when it is directed within ourselves, it becomes self-abnegation and a feeling of sin. These are all negative virtues, while positively they lead us to reverence, the wish not to slight others. We are beings full of contradictions: in one respect we feel that we are just as good as anybody else, but at the same time we have an innate suspicion that everybody else is better than ourselves—a kind of inferiority complex.

There is a Bodhisattva in Mahāyāna Buddhism [4] known as Sadāparibhūta (Jōfukyō Bosatsu), "one who never slights others." Perhaps when we are quite sincere with ourselves— that is, when we are all alone with ourselves in the innermost chamber of our being—there is a feeling there which makes us move toward others with a sense of humiliation. Whatever this may be, there is a deeply religious attitude of mind in reverence. Zen may burn all the holy statues in the temple to warm itself on a cold wintry night; Zen may destroy all the literature containing its precious legacies in order to save its very existence as the truth shorn of all its external trappings, however glamorous they appear to outsiders; but it never forgets to worship a storm-broken and mud-soiled humble blade of grass; it never neglects to offer all the wild flowers of the field, just as they are, to all the Buddhas in the three thousand chiliacosms. Zen knows how to revere because it knows how to slight. What is needed in Zen

[4] *The Saddharmapuṇḍarīka Sūtra*, tr. H. Kern, p. 356.

as in anything else is sincerity of heart, and not mere conceptualism.

Toyotomi Hideyoshi was the great patron of the art of tea in his day and an admirer of Sen no Rikyū (1521–91), who was virtually the founder of the art. Although he was always after something sensational, grandiose, and ostentatious, he seems to have understood finally something of the spirit of the art as advocated by Rikyū and his followers, when he gave this verse to Rikyū at one of the latter's "tea parties":

> *When tea is made with water drawn from the depths of*
>   *Mind*
> *Whose bottom is beyond measure,*
> *We really have what is called cha-no-yu.*

Hideyoshi was a crude and cruel despot in many ways, but in his liking for the art of tea we are inclined to find something genuine beyond just "using" the art for his political purposes. His verse touches the spirit of reverence when he can refer to the water deeply drawn from the well of the mind.

Rikyū teaches that "the art of *cha-no-yu* consists in nothing else but in boiling water, making tea, and sipping it." This is simple enough as far as it goes. Human life, we can say, consists in being born, eating and drinking, working and sleeping, marrying and giving birth to children, and finally in passing away— whither, no one knows. Nothing seems to be simpler than living this life, when it is so stated. But how many of us are there who can live this kind of matter-of-fact or rather God-intoxicated life, cherishing no desires, leaving no regrets, but absolutely trustful of God? While living we think of death; while dying we long for life; while one thing is being accomplished, so many other things, not necessarily cognate and usually irrelevant, crowd into our brains, and divert and dissipate the energy which is to be concentrated on the matter in hand. When water is poured into the bowl, it is not the water alone that is poured into it—a variety of things go into it, good and bad, pure and impure, things about which one has to blush, things which can never be poured out anywhere except into one's own deep unconscious. The tea water when analyzed contains all the filth disturbing and contaminating the stream of our consciousness. An art is perfected only when it ceases to be art: when there is the perfection of artlessness, when the innermost sincerity of our being asserts itself, and this is the meaning of reverence in the art of tea. Reverence is, therefore, sincerity or simplicity of heart.

"Purity," estimated as constituting the spirit of the art of tea, may be said to be the contribution of Japanese mentality. Purity is cleanliness or sometimes orderliness, which is observable in everything everywhere concerned with the art. Fresh water is liberally used in the garden, called *roji* (courtyard); in case natural running water is not available, there is a stone basin filled with water as one approaches the tearoom, which is naturally kept clean and free from dust and dirt.

Purity in the art of tea may remind us of the Taoistic teaching of Purity. There is something common to both, for the object of discipline in both is to free one's mind from the defilements of the senses.

A teamaster says: "The spirit of *cha-no-yu* is to cleanse the six senses from contamination. By seeing the *kakemono* in the *tokonoma* (alcove) and the flower in the vase, one's sense of smell is cleansed; by listening to the boiling of water in the iron kettle and to the dripping of water from the bamboo pipe, one's ears are cleansed; by tasting tea one's mouth is cleansed; and by handling the tea utensils one's sense of touch is cleansed. When thus all the sense organs are cleansed, the mind itself is cleansed of defilements. The art of tea is after all a spiritual discipline, and my aspiration for every hour of the day is not to depart from the spirit of the tea, which is by no means a matter of mere entertainment." [5]

[5] By Nakano Kazuma in the *Hagakure*. *Hagakure* literally means "hidden under the leaves," that is, "to be unostentatious in practicing a life of goodness," or "not to be 'as the hypocrites [who] love to pray standing in the

In one of Rikyū's poems we have this:

> *While the roji is meant to be a passageway*
> *Altogether outside this earthly life,*
> *How is it that people only contrive*
> *To besprinkle it with dust of mind?*

.Here as in the following poems he refers to his own state of mind while looking out quietly from his tearoom:

> *The court is left covered*
> *With the fallen leaves*
> *Of the pine tree;*
> *No dust is stirred,*
> *And calm is my mind!*

> *The moonlight*
> *Far up in the sky,*
> *Looking through the eaves,*
> *Shines on a mind*
> *Undisturbed with remorse.*

It is, indeed, a mind pure, serene, and free from disturbing emotions that can enjoy the aloneness of the Absolute:

> *The snow-covered mountain path*
> *Winding through the rocks*
> *Has come to its end;*
> *Here stands a hut,*
> *The master is all alone;*
> *No visitors he has,*
> *Nor are any expected.*

synagogues and in the corners of the streets'" (Matt. 6 : 5). It contains wise sayings given by Yamamoto Jōchō, a recluse Zen philosopher, to his disciple, Tashiro Matazaemon, both of whom lived on the feudal estate of Lord Nabeshima. It consists of eleven fascicles, compiled between 1710 and 1716. The book is also known as the "Nabeshima Rongo" in imitation of the Confucian *Analects* (*Rongo*).

In a book called *Nanbō-roku,* which is one of the most important, almost sacred, textbooks of the art of tea, we have the following passage, showing that the ideal of the art is to realize a Buddha-land of Purity on earth, however small in scale, and to see an ideal community gathered here, however temporary the gathering and however few its members:

"The spirit of *wabi* is to give an expression to the Buddha-land of Purity altogether free from defilements, and, therefore, in this *roji* (courtyard) and in this thatched hut there ought not to be a speck of dust of any kind; both master and visitors are expected to be on terms of absolute sincerity; no ordinary measures of proportion or etiquette or conventionalism are to be followed. A fire is made, water is boiled, and tea is served: this is all that is needed here, no other worldly considerations are to intrude. For what we want here is to give full expression to the Buddha-mind. When ceremony, etiquette, and other such things are insisted on, worldly considerations of various kinds creep in, and master and visitors alike feel inclined to find fault with each other. It becomes thus more and more difficult to find such ones as fully comprehend the meaning of the art. If we were to have Jōshu [6] for master and Bodhidharma, the first Zen patriarch, for a guest, and Rikyū and myself picked up the dust in the *roji,* would not such a gathering be a happy one indeed?"

We see how thoroughly imbued with the spirit of Zen is this statement of one of the chief disciples of Rikyū.

The next section will be devoted to the elucidation of *sabi* or *wabi,* the concept constituting the fourth principle of the art of tea, "tranquillity." In fact, this is the most essential factor in the tea art, and without it there can be no *cha-no-yu* whatever. It is in this connection, indeed, that Zen enters deeply into the art of tea.

[6] An old Chinese Zen master reputed for his saying, "Have a cup of tea." See my *Introduction to Zen Buddhism,* p. 80, and also pp. 34 f. of the present book.

3

I HAVE used the term "tranquillity" for the fourth element making up the spirit of the art of tea, but it may not be a good term for all that is implied in the Chinese character *chi,* or *jaku* in Japanese. *Jaku* is *sabi,* but *sabi* contains much more than "tranquillity." Its Sanskrit equivalent, *śānta* or *śānti,* it is true, means "tranquillity," "peace," "serenity," and *jaku* has been frequently used in Buddhist literature to denote "death" or "nirvāṇa." But as the term is used in the tea, its implication is "poverty," "simplification," "aloneness," and here *sabi* becomes synonymous with *wabi.* To appreciate poverty, to accept whatever is given, a tranquil, passive mind is needed, but in both *sabi* and *wabi* there is a suggestion of objectivity. Just to be tranquil or passive is not *sabi* nor is it *wabi.* There is always something objective that evokes in one a mood to be called *wabi.* And *wabi* is not merely a psychological reaction to a certain pattern of environment. There is an active principle of aestheticism in it; when this is lacking poverty becomes indigence, aloneness becomes ostracism or misanthropy or inhuman unsociability. *Wabi* or *sabi,* therefore, may be defined as an active aesthetical appreciation of poverty; when it is used as a constituent of the tea, it is the creating or remodeling of an environment in such a way as to awaken the feeling of *wabi* or *sabi.* Nowadays, as these terms are used, we may say that *sabi* applies more to the individual objects and environment generally, and *wabi* to the living of a life ordinarily associated with poverty or insufficiency or imperfection. *Sabi* is thus more objective, whereas *wabi* is more subjective and personal. We speak of a *wabi-zumai,* "the *wabi* way of living," but when a vessel such as a tea caddy or a bowl or a flower vase comes in for appraisal, it is often characterized as having a *"sabi* taste," or *kan-mi. Kan* and *sabi* are synonymous, while *mi* is "taste." The tea utensils are, as far as I know, never qualified as being of *"wabi* taste."

Of the following two verses the first is considered expressive of the idea of *wabi,* while the second gives the idea of *sabi:*

> *Among the weeds growing along the wall*
> *The crickets are hiding, as if forsaken,*
> *From the garden wet with autumnal showers.*

> *The yomogi herbs in the garden*
> *Are beginning to wither from below;*
> *Autumn is deepening,*
> *Its colors are fading;*
> *Not knowing why, my heart is filled with*
>   *melancholy.*

The idea of *sabi* is said to come primarily from *renga* masters, who show great aesthetic appreciation for things suggestive of age, desiccation, numbness, chilliness, obscurity—all of which are negative feelings opposed to warmth, the spring, expansiveness, transparency, etc. They are, in fact, feelings growing out of poverty and deficiency; but they have also a certain quality lending themselves to highly cultivated aesthetic ecstasy. The teamen will say that this is "objectively negated but subjectively affirmed," whereby external emptiness is filled with inner richness. In some ways, *wabi* is *sabi* and *sabi* is *wabi;* they are interchangeable terms.

Shukō (d. 1502), a disciple of Ikkyū (1394–1481) and teamaster to Ashikaga Yoshimasa (1435–90), used to teach his pupils about the spirit of the tea with this story. A Chinese poet happened to compose this couplet:

> *In the woods over there deeply buried in snow,*
> *Last night a few branches of the plum tree burst out in*
>   *bloom.*

He showed it to his friend, who suggested that he alter "a few branches" into "one branch." The author followed the friend's advice, praising him as his "teacher of one character." A solitary

branch of the plum tree in bloom among the snow-covered woods
—here is the idea of *wabi*.

On another occasion, Shukō is reported to have said: "It is
good to see a fine steed tied in the straw-roofed shed. This being
so, it also is specially fine to find a rare object of art in an ordinarily furnished room." This reminds one of the Zen phrase, "To
fill a monk's tattered robe with a cool refreshing breeze." Outwardly there is not a sign of distinction, appearances all go
against the contents, which are in every way priceless. A life of
wabi can then be defined: an inexpressible quiet joy deeply hidden beneath sheer poverty; and it is the art of tea that tries to
express this idea artistically.

But if there is anything betraying a trace of insincerity, the
whole thing is utterly ruined. The priceless contents must be
there most genuinely, they must be there as if they were never
there, they must be rather accidentally discovered. In the beginning there is no suspicion of the presence of anything extraordinary, yet something attracts—a closer approach, a tentative examination, and, behold, a mine of solid gold glitters from among
the unexpected. But the gold itself remains ever the same, discovered or not. It retains its reality, that is, its sincerity to itself,
regardless of accidents. *Wabi* means to be true to itself. A master
lives quietly in his unpretentious hut, a friend comes in unexpectedly, tea is served, a fresh spray of flowers is arranged, and
the visitor enjoys a peaceful afternoon charmed with his conversation and entertainment. Is this not the tea rite in its reality?

Parenthetically, some may ask: "In these modern times how
many of us are situated like the teamaster? It is nonsense to
talk about leisurely entertainment. Let us have bread first, and
fewer working hours." Yes, it is true that we have to eat bread in
the sweat of our face and to work a number of hours as the slave
of machinery. Our creative impulses have thus been miserably
downtrodden. It is not, however, just for this reason, I believe,
that we moderns have lost the taste for leisureliness, that we find
no room in our worrying hearts for enjoying life in any other

way than running after excitement for excitement's sake. The question is: How have we come to give ourselves up to such a life as to try to keep the inner worries only temporarily suppressed? How is it that we no longer reflect on life more deeply, more seriously, so that we can have a realization of its inmost meaning? When this question is settled, let us if necessary negate the entire machinery of modern life and start anew. I hope our destination is not the continual enslaving of ourselves to material wants and comforts.

Another teamaster writes: "From Amaterasu Ōmikami [7] starts the spirit of *wabi*. Being the great ruler of this country, he was free to erect the finest palaces, inlaid with gold and silver and precious stones, and nobody would dare to speak ill of him, and yet he dwelt in a reed-thatched house and ate unpolished rice. In every possible way, besides, he was self-sufficient, modest, and ever-striving. He was truly a most excellent teamaster, living a life of *wabi*."

It is interesting to see that this writer regards Amaterasu Ōmikami as the representative teaman, who lived a life of *wabi*. This, however, shows that the tea is the aesthetic appreciation of primitive simplicity; in other words, that the tea is an aesthetic expression of the longing which most of us seem to feel in the depths of our hearts to go as far back to Nature as our human existence will permit and to be at one with her.

Through these statements, the concept of *wabi* is, I think, becoming clearer. We can say that, in a way, with Sōtan, a grandson of Rikyū, real *wabi* life starts. He explains that *wabi* is the essence of the tea, corresponding to the moral life of the Buddhists:

"It is a great mistake, indeed, to make an ostentatious show of *wabi* while inwardly nothing is consonant with it. Such people construct a tearoom as far as appearances go with all that is

[7] The Ōmikami is really the sun-goddess in Japanese mythology, but the writer seems to understand her to be a male deity and, anachronistically, associates her with the art of tea.

needed for *wabi;* much gold and silver is wasted on the work; rare objects of art are purchased with the money realized by the sale of their farms—and this just to make a display before visitors. They think a life of *wabi* is here. But far from it. *Wabi* means insufficiency of things, inability to fulfill every desire one may cherish, generally a life of poverty and dejection. To halt despondently in one's course of life because of his inability to push himself forward—this is *wabi.* But he does not brood over the situation. He has learned to be self-sufficient with insufficiency of things. He does not seek beyond his means. He has ceased to be cognizant of the fact that he is in tight circumstances. If, however, he should still abide with the idea of the poverty, insufficiency, or general wretchedness of his condition, he would no more be a man of *wabi* but a poverty-stricken person. Those who really know what *wabi* is are free from greed, violence, anger, indolence, uneasiness, and folly. Thus *wabi* corresponds to the Pāramitā of Morality as observed by the Buddhists."

In *wabi,* aestheticism is fused with morality or spirituality, and it is for this reason that the teamasters declare the tea to be life itself and not merely a thing for pleasure, however refined this may be. Zen is thus directly connected with the tea; indeed, most ancient teamasters studied Zen in real earnest and applied their attainment in Zen to the art of their profession.

Religion can sometimes be defined as a way of escape from the humdrum of this worldly life. Scholars may object to this, saying that religion aspires not to escape but to transcend life in order to reach the Absolute or the Infinite. But, practically stated, it is an escape where one finds a little time to breathe and recuperate. Zen as a spiritual discipline does this, too, but as it is too transcendental, as it were, too inaccessible for ordinary minds, the teamasters who have studied Zen have devised the way to put their understanding into practice in the form of the art of tea. Probably in this, to a great extent, their aesthetic aspirations asserted themselves.

When *wabi* is explained as above, readers may think that it is more or less a negative quality, and that its enjoyment is meant for people who have been a failure in life. This is true in some sense, perhaps. But how many of us are really so healthy as not to need medicine or a tonic of one kind or another at some time in their lives? And then every one of us is destined to pass away. Modern psychology gives us many cases of active business-men, strong physically and mentally, who will suddenly collapse when they retire. Why? Because they have not learned to keep their energy in reserve; that is to say, they have never become aware of a plan to retreat while still working. The Japanese fighting man in those old days of strife and unrest, when he was most strenuously engaged in the business of war, realized that he could not go on always with nerves at the highest pitch of vigilance and that he ought to have a way of escape sometime and somewhere. The tea must have given him exactly this. He retreated for a while into a quiet corner of his Unconscious, symbolized by the tearoom no more than ten feet square. And when he came out of it, not only did he feel refreshed in mind and body, but very likely his memory was renewed of things of more permanent value than mere fighting.

Thus we see that "tranquillity," which is the fourth and chief factor making up the spirit of the tea, ultimately means a kind of aesthetic contemplation of poverty in the Eckhartian sense, which the teamen call *wabi* or *sabi* according to the objects to which they apply the term.[8]

[8] In Part II, I touch on the same subjects, but from a somewhat different approach. It is an elaboration of a lecture given in 1954 to a group of the foreign residents of Yokohama. It will help, I hope, make clearer the points I have treated of in Part I.

IX

Zen and the Art of Tea

II

1

TWO Zen-men were discussing Zen. One, named Chōkei (Ch'ang-ch'ing Hui-ling, 853–932), said, "Even a fully enlightened arhat may be proclaimed to be still harboring something of the three poisonous passions,[1] but as to the Buddha, he never makes an equivocal statement. Whatever he asserts is absolute truth. What do you say to this?"

Hofuku (Pao-fu Ts'ung-chan, d. 928) asked, "What then is the Buddha's statement?"

Chōkei said, "The deaf cannot hear it."

This was criticized by Hofuku: "You are coming down onto a secondary level."

"What then is the Buddha's statement according to your judgment?"

"Have a cup of tea, O my brother-monk."[2]

Tea-drinking is quite an innocent deed, and we practice it in our everyday life, especially in the East, but when it is taken up by the Zen-men it turns out to be a momentous event that leads directly up to Buddhahood and its absolute truth. Ordinary-minded people may well wonder how such a transformation could take place even by subtle verbal tricks of the Zen masters. But the fact is that their world is not the same as the one in which ordinary-minded, sense-bound people live. This does not mean

---

[1] Greed, anger, and folly.

[2] *Dentōroku* ("Transmission of the Lamp"), fasc. 19, under "Hofuku." The book has never been translated into any other language.

that a tree is not a tree in one world and is a tree in the other world, though there is something almost like this in the Zen world. For in the latter what is is at once what is and what is not. The mountain confronting us, you and me, is a mountain and not a mountain; the pen I hold in my hand is a pen and not a pen. The Zen-man sees things from this point of view. To him, therefore, the tea-drinking is not just drinking tea; it comes directly from and goes deeply down into the roots of existence. According to Eckhart, "A flea, as it is in God, ranks above the highest angel in himself. Thus, in God all things are equal and are God himself." [3]

When Shōzan (Sung-shan) the Zen teacher and Hō (P'ang Chü-shih) the Zen layman, both of the eighth century (T'ang dynasty), were enjoying tea, Hō raised the *takusu* [4] and said, "Each one of us has his, and why cannot he say something about it?"

Shōzan said, "It is just because each one of us has his that he is unable to say something about it."

Hō retorted, "How is it then that you seem to be able to say something about it?"

Shōzan protested, "One cannot remain without saying something."

Hō said, "There you are!"

To these two Zen-men, too, the *takusu* was not just a *takusu*, it had a far deeper signification than the one we, the ordinary-minded, usually attach to it.

It is for this reason, briefly, that the Japanese make so much of tea-drinking, as if it were something mysteriously touching the very foundation of reality. In all likelihood it is not "as if" but the thing itself, and from the art of tea we have an insight into the spirit of Oriental culture.

[3] *Meister Eckhart*, ed. Pfeiffer, Sermon 96, p. 311.

[4] Something like a saucer, but made of wood with a base. The story is from the *Dentōroku*, fasc. 8.

2

THE TEA-DRINKING that is known as *cha-no-yu* in Japanese and as "tea ceremony" or "tea cult" in the West is not just drinking tea, but involves all the activities leading to it, all the utensils used in it, the entire atmosphere surrounding the procedure, and, last of all, what is really the most important phase, the frame of mind or spirit which mysteriously grows out of the combination of all these factors.

The tea-drinking, therefore, is not just drinking tea, but it is the art of cultivating what might be called "psychosphere," [5] or the psychic atmosphere, or the inner field of consciousness. We may say that it is generated within oneself, while sitting in a small semi-dark room with a low ceiling, irregularly constructed, from handling the tea bowl, which is crudely formed but eloquent with the personality of the maker, and from listening to the sound of boiling water in the iron kettle over a charcoal fire. Let time pass for a while, and as one feels more composed, one begins to notice another kind of sound coming from outside the windows. It is the water dripping from a bamboo trough that conducts it from somewhere on the mountainside. The dripping is neither scanty nor excessive, it is just enough to lead the mind to a state of tranquil passivity. But the mind is really active to the extent that it can fully appreciate the synthetic effect of things surrounding the tearoom outside as well as in.

What constitutes the frame of mind or "psychosphere" thus generated here is the realization of the spirit of poverty devoid of all forms of dichotomy: subject and object, good and evil, right and wrong, honor and disgrace, body and soul, gain and loss, and so on. Kyōgen Shikan (Hsiang-yen Chih-hsien), a Zen

---

[5] That is to say, the structure or pattern of consciousness into which all one's psychic activities fall, partaking of the general coloring or tonal quality of the structure itself. It corresponds to what is known in Buddhist psychology as *cittagocara* ("mental or consciousness field"). In Chinese, it is *ching-chieh* or *ching-ai* (both *kyōgai* in Japanese) or simply *ching* (*kyō*).

master of the late T'ang dynasty, gives his idea of poverty (*hin* in Japanese, *p'in* in Chinese) in the following stanza:

Last year's poverty was not yet perfect;
This year's poverty is absolute.
In last year's poverty there was room for the head of a gimlet;
This year's poverty has let the gimlet itself disappear.[6]

The poverty that permits no room for anything, even for the point of a needle, is what is known in the philosophy of *Prajñāpāramitā* (*hannya, pan-jo*) as "Emptiness" (*śūnyatā, kū, k'ung*), and the principle of the tea ceremony is based on it, for *sabi* or *wabi* [7] is no other than the aesthetic appreciation of absolute poverty.

3

IN PASSING, it is of interest to note in this connection that Meister Eckhart's notion of poverty (*armut*) exactly coincides with Kyōgen's cited just above. In one of his sermons Eckhart refers to one who is "godly poor, for God can find no place in him to work in." "This man is object-free in time and in eternity. . . . There are two objects: one is otherness, the other is a man's own proper self." [8] This kind of man who is free of objects, that is, free of the dichotomy of subject and object, is an "abodeless man" living in Emptiness. "True poverty of spirit requires that man shall be emptied of God and all his works, so that if God wants to act in the soul, he himself must be the place in which he acts." [9]

It is out of this absolute poverty cherished by Meister Eckhart that we also have the philosophy of tea. It is, indeed, out of the

[6] *Dentōroku*, fasc. 11.
[7] See above, pp. 284 ff., as to the different uses of these two important terms.
[8] Tr. Evans, I, pp. 122–23.
[9] Tr. Blakney, p. 230.

Emptiness where there is no place (*stätte*) not only for God's creatures but for God himself—because the Emptiness is God and God is the Emptiness—in other words, out of nowhereness and no-time-ness, that Jōshu,[10] Hofuku, Hō, and the other masters of Zen sip their cup of tea. The philosophy of tea is thus the philosophy of poverty, of *śūnyatā*, or Emptiness. When this is understood, we know where the Japanese enjoyment and appreciation of the tea originates.

4

IN THIS respect the ancient Japanese poem by Fujiwara Sadaiye, which is often quoted by the teamen as their motto, is significant:

> *As I look around,*
> *No flowers, no maple leaves,*
> *This fishing village,*
> *This autumnal eve!*

The desolation, however, is not just a stretch of sand and wilderness; one is not standing against an expanse of illimitable sea. For something of spring is already seen awakened behind the deserted boats and under the torn dragnets aired along the seabeach:

> *To those who are forever longing for flowers,*
> *How I wish to point out green patches in the snow,*
> *Fully expressive of the early spring!*

To an observing and discerning eye, the desolate wilderness of the late autumn already promises something of the coming spring, and every fallen leaf piling up on the ground, every withering blade of grass which had sheltered all forms of the singing insects, is already seen preparing or renewing life. As Rikyū says,

[10] See pp. 34 f.

the water that fills the kettle is drawn from the well of mind whose bottom knows no depths, and the Emptiness which is conceptually liable to be mistaken for sheer nothingness is in fact the reservoir (*ālaya*) of infinite possibilities. In the desolation of the late autumn we detect bits of what Secchō (Hsüeh-tou Chung-hsien, 980–1052), Zen poet of the Sung dynasty, sings of:

The spring mountains covered with layers of most variegated colors,
And the spring streams fancifully laden with the reflecting images.

The teaman sitting alone in his tearoom is the one whom Secchō continues to depict as

> *Standing by himself between heaven and earth,*
> *Facing infinitude of beings.*

Primarily, the spirit of tea is aloneness, "the sitting all alone at the summit of Mount Mahāvīra" as stated by Hyakujō. Sake, which is thought of as the opposite to tea, is for sociability and mostly for conviviality and frequently for boisterousness. Tea is aristocratic, sake is democratic. Tea is not so expanding and non-individualistic as sake. It is introvert and self-collective. Rihaku (Li Po), the great poet of the T'ang, was addicted to sake and could not produce his creative poems without its aid. When the teaman is inspired his works are concentric or centripetal, full of contemplative thought. So sake is best imbibed in company with sympathetic friends, but tea will be sipped all alone in the traditional room, ten or even six feet square, in a secluded corner away from the crowded places.

5

THE FOLLOWING description of a tearoom is from my article on the subject which appeared in *The Cultural East* (1945): "The tearoom is symbolic of certain aspects of Eastern culture,

especially of Japanese culture. In it we find in a most strongly
and deeply concentrated form almost all the elements that go to
make up what is characteristic of the Japanese mind statically
viewed. As to its dynamic aspects, there are only a few signs be-
tokening them in the tearoom, where even movements are so
controlled as to add to the quietude generally prevailing here.

"The room is small and the ceiling not at all high even for the
stature of an average Japanese. It is devoid of decorations, except in the alcove (*tokonoma*),[11] where a *kakemono* [12] is hung
and before which stands a flower vase containing perhaps a solitary flower not yet in full bloom. As I look around, in spite of
its obvious simplicity the room betrays every mark of thoughtful
designing: the windows are irregularly inserted; the ceiling is
not of one pattern; the materials used, simple and unornamented,
are of various kinds; the room is divided by a post obliquely
setting off one corner for tea utensils; the floor has a small
square opening as fireplace where hot water is boiling in an
artistically-shaped iron kettle.

"The papered *shōji* covering the windows admit only soft
light, shutting off all the direct sunshine, which, when it is too
strong for the teamen's sensibility, is further screened by a rustic *sudare* hanging just outside one of the windows. As I sit
here quietly before the fireplace, I become conscious of the burning of incense. The odor is singularly nerve-soothing; the fragrant flower produces a contrary effect on the senses. The incense wood, I am told, comes from tropical countries, and is
taken from old trees lying buried for a long time in water.

"Thus composed in mind, I hear a soft breeze passing through
the needle-leaves of the pine tree; the sound mingles with the
trickling of water from a bamboo pipe into the stone basin. The
flow and the breeze are rhythmical and soothing to the mind of

---

[11] *Tokonoma* is a sort of alcove occupying a corner of the room where a *kakemono* is hung. The principal guest sits before this honored corner.

[12] A *kakemono* is a hanging scroll of either painting or calligraphy, which
decorates the corner.

the sitter inside the hut. In fact, they stimulate his meditative mood to move on to the bedrock of his being."

Thus we can see that the spirit of tea is deeply steeped with the *Prajñā* [13] philosophy of Emptiness as taught by Zen. While the Emptiness may sound too abstract for the teaman sipping the green-colored beverage from a handmade bowl, the Emptiness is in truth no less than the concreteness of reality itself. It all depends on how a man looks into the nature of things. If his senses are alerted on the plane of relativity only, he can never rise from it. The man who sees with the eyes and hears with the ears cannot go any further than that. Unless one makes the eyes hear and the ears see, he has to stay confined within the senses. It is only when he goes out of them that he can achieve miracles by plunging into the realm of Emptiness, for Emptiness is the fountain of infinite possibilities. Daitō Kokushi, the founder of Daitokuji, Kyoto, once had this to say:

> *If your ears see,*
> *And eyes hear,*
> *Not a doubt you'll cherish—*
> *How naturally the rain drips*
> *From the eaves!*

6

T H I S we can best understand when we know the history of tea. Tea was first imported from China to Japan toward the end of the twelfth century by a Zen monk, who had studied it in China. He brought not only tea seeds but the ceremony the Chinese Zen

[13] This Sanskrit term is generally translated as "transcendental wisdom." It is a kind of intuitive knowledge in its deepest sense. When this is awakened, one has the enlightenment-experience that constitutes the center of Buddhist philosophy.

followers performed in offering a cup of tea to their first patriarch, Bodhidharma. Tea then came to be closely associated with Zen. In fact, there is something in the taste of tea that connects the teaman with the transcendentalism of Zen. As I said before, sake leads us to sociability and conviviality, and not infrequently even to the animal exhibition of energy it releases.

It was in the Ashikaga era that tea-drinking as an art came out of the Zen monastery and began to be appreciated by people principally of the samurai class. When the Shōgunate government lost its control over the feudal lords, Oda Nobunaga (1534–82) proved the strongest and was on the point of unifying the country under his generalship. He encountered a tragic death, however, and was succeeded by Toyotomi Hideyoshi (1536–98), [59 the ablest of his lieutenants. The work of unification was carried out by Hideyoshi. Both Hideyoshi and Nobunaga were great patrons of the art of tea, which had achieved great development by that time, especially under Hideyoshi. The man who contributed most to this and is properly regarded as the founder of the art of tea was Sen no Rikyū (1521–91).

One might say it was no more than an historical accident, but to my mind it was inevitable that the life of Rikyū came to illustrate all the contradictions and tragedies, the aestheticism and heroism, absurdities and rationalities, buried in the abysmal depth of Emptiness. Rikyū happened to be born in the period of political chaos and disorganization. He belonged to the merchant class, whose importance was keenly felt by the warring feudal lords. Gradually and quietly, Rikyū came to perform a secret political function in connection with his artistic genius and personality. He became in time a great friend of Hideyoshi's. Hideyoshi, who acquired a position of power through his superior generalship and political sagacity, was in a way a crude unlettered warrior, but he seems to have understood the art of tea. The strange thing is that, in spite of the utmost strenuousness in the atmosphere enveloping the whole Momoyama period, the warriors conceived a great taste for tea. They would occasionally seclude themselves in the tearoom and, meditatively sipping a cup of tea, breathe the air of quietism and transcendentalism. Temporarily, at least, their minds would be in the realm of Emptiness. Rikyū, great master of the art, seems to have awakened this spirit in those warlike samurai, who, while to a great extent unlettered, were ever ready to look into a world of great artistic traditions. On the other hand, Rikyū, though of the merchant class, came to be influenced by the spirit of the samurai. He thus came to symbolize at least one aspect of the Japanese life as displayed in the Momoyama period.

Where power rules, the slightest suspicion of its infringement is swept away with utmost swiftness. When Hideyoshi was informed, falsely or truly, of a supposed intrigue on the part of Rikyū, the latter had immediately to submit himself to the despot's almighty will: he was to die by his own hand, a privilege allowed to an honorable samurai. The last scene is dramatically depicted by Okakura Kakuzo (1862–1913), author of *The Book of Tea,* in the following manner (pp. 114–16):

"On the day destined for his self-immolation, Rikyū invited his chief disciples to a last tea ceremony. Mournfully at the appointed time the guests met at the portico. As they look into the garden path the trees seem to shudder, and in the rustling of their leaves are heard the whispers of homeless ghosts. Like solemn sentinels before the gates of Hades stand the gray stone lanterns. A wave of rare incense is wafted from the tearoom; it is the summons which bids the guests to enter. One by one they advance and take their places. In the *tokonoma* hangs a *kakemono*—a wonderful writing by an ancient monk dealing with the evanescence of all earthly things. The singing kettle, as it boils over the brazier, sounds like some cicada pouring forth his woes to departing summer. Soon the host enters the room. Each in turn is served with tea, and each in turn silently drains his cup, the host last of all. According to established etiquette, the chief guest now asks permission to examine the tea equipage. Rikyū places the various articles before them with the *kakemono*. After all have expressed admiration of their beauty, Rikyū presents one of them to each of the assembled company as a souvenir. The bowl alone he keeps. 'Never again shall this cup, polluted by the lips of misfortune, be used by me.' He speaks, and breaks the vessel into fragments.

"The ceremony is over; the guests with difficulty restraining their tears take their last farewell and leave the room. One only, the nearest and dearest, is requested to remain and witness the end. Rikyū then removes his tea gown and carefully folds it upon the mat, thereby disclosing the immaculate white death robe which it had hitherto concealed. Tenderly he gazes on the shining blade of the fatal dagger, and in exquisite verse thus addresses it:

> *"Welcome to thee,*
> *O sword of eternity!*
> *Through Buddha*
> *And through Dharma alike*
> *Thou hast cloven thy way.*[14]

"With a smile upon his face Rikyū passed forth into the unknown."

How would we ever connect the escapism of the art of tea with the tragic ending of the teamaster? How could one expect to see the solitary sword of Emptiness fly heavenward, killing both Buddhas and Māras (devils), friends and foes, tyrants and slaves? When Hideyoshi once wanted to see Rikyū's morning-glories,

[14] This poem in Chinese has given much trouble to followers of Rikyū with respect to how properly to understand it. It contains, for one thing, a quotation from a Chinese source (the last three lines) which itself is not very clear. I have given my rendering under "Rikyū and Other Teamen," p. 319, below. It will be interesting for the reader to know that nine years after (1598), Hideyoshi himself had to die in the midst of the Korean campaign, and his swan song was:

> *Like a dewdrop, settled,*
> *Like a dewdrop, fading away—*
> *Alas, this, my life!*
> *As to the affairs of Naniwa,*
> *A dream in a dream!*

Rikyū chopped down all the flowers in the garden; and when Hideyoshi entered the tearoom he saw just one single flower in the vase—all the rest were sacrificed for the one. And now even this One was to be sacrificed by the same hands which mowed down the hundred others. But was it really sacrificed? Did it altogether disappear from the cultural history of Japan? No, there still "stands the one sword glittering cold against the sky."

7

AS I SAID before, the spirit of tea is poverty, solitariness, and absolutism, which concretizes the philosophy of Emptiness. When, therefore, the tearoom begins to be filled even with a few people, its spirit is violated and some "regulating principles" come to be established. As Lao-tzŭ says, "The great Tao obliterates itself when benevolence and righteousness assert themselves." The tearoom is really reserved for one person who, all by himself, sits there with the same spirit which inspired Buddha at his birth to exclaim: "Heavens above, heavens below, I alone am the most honored one!" When a second person enters, the One splits itself and there starts a dualism out of which we have a world of multitudinousness. The tearoom then demands rules whereby somehow the original peace is to be preserved. The art of tea, or tea ceremony so called, is a degeneration, but this was in fact the way the warriors in the Warring Period (1467–1590) learned to get a glimpse into a realm of transcendentalism or of Emptiness. The tearoom then became a spiritual training station and the art a disciplining technique for the samurai.

Generally, the principles regulating the tearoom are four: (1) Harmony (wa), (2) Reverence (kei), (3) Purity (sei), and (4) Tranquillity (jaku). The first two are social or ethical, the third is both physical and psychological, and the fourth is spiritual or metaphysical.

When one goes over these four items, one will see that here

are represented the four schools of Oriental teaching: Confucianism is for the first two, Taoism and Shintoism for the third, and Buddhism and Taoism for the fourth.

Harmony, the first, may also be regarded as Taoist, because one of its practical teachings is to retain a harmonious relationship with Nature, that is, between the male and the female principles. It is due to this harmony that the world goes on forever (*ch'ang*) without exhausting its energy.[15] The baby may cry all day, but it will retain its voice without getting hoarse. The crying is apparently no sign of inharmony, according to Lao-tzŭ. Therefore, harmony is called eternity, or infinity.[16]

Harmony is referred to in Prince Shōtoku's "Constitution" [17]   [61
as "the thing most estimable." This is no doubt political, reflecting the state of affairs which existed in his day.

Purity, the third "principle," is no doubt Shinto; the handwashing and mouth-rinsing remind us of ablution. But when it goes beyond mere superficiality and acquires a deeper sense it touches upon Taoism. "Heaven is pure because of its oneness."[18] The purification of the heart is Buddhist. But the art of tea is here more concerned with general cleansing and orderliness, which tend to make the mind free from unnecessary psychological encumbrances.

Tranquillity, which is the last "principle" governing the art of tea, is the most pregnant one; where this is lacking, the art will

[15] *Tao Tê Ching*, Ch. 42.

[16] Ibid., Ch. 55.

[17] Cf. p. 275. Shōtoku Taishi, 574–622. "The Constitution" consists of seventeen articles based on Buddhist and Confucian ethics and philosophy. It opens with a statement about harmony. The Chinese character for harmony (*ho*) also means "softness" (*juan ho ho ti*) as was already explained on p. 274. It also is "warmth" (*nuan ho ho ti*). As a man stands in the soft warm relaxing spring breeze, he is to feel much in the same style in the tearoom. In whatever sense the compiler of "The Constitution" wished to have *wa* (or *ho*) understood by his subjects, there is no doubt that the teaman's idea of *wa* is to see a soft, tender, conciliatory, yielding atmosphere pervade the room, barring all the arrogant, individualistic, self-assertive spirit, so characteristic of modern Japanese young men.

[18] *Tao Tê Ching*, Ch. 49.

lose its significance altogether. For each particular performance that goes to a successful conduct of the art is so contrived as to create the atmosphere of tranquillity all around. The massing of rocks, the trickling of water, the thatched hut, the old pine trees sheltering it, the moss-covered stone lantern, the sizzling of the kettle water, and the light softly filtering through the paper screens—all these are meant uniformly to create a meditative frame of mind. But, in reality, the principle of tranquillity is something that emanates from one's inner consciousness as it is especially understood in the art of tea. This is where Zen Buddhism enters and turns the whole situation into an intimate relationship with the larger sphere of reality. The tearoom is a sense organ for the teaman to express himself. He makes everything in it vibrate with his subjectivity. The man and the room become one, and each speaks of the other. Those who walk into the room will at once realize it. Here is the art of tea.

The teaman is generally very sensitive to anything jarring in his environment. His nerves are in this respect very well trained, indeed, sometimes too well. But to appreciate and enjoy the tea, it is not really necessary to be too critical about such things. Let the mind be not concerned with details; let it be in a receptive frame so as to take in the trickling of the water and the rustling of the pine needles, and it will then be able to breathe a spirit of tranquillity into all the surrounding objects. Purity may belong to the subject as well as to the object, but tranquillity or serenity is a spiritual quality. When the hands are washed and the mouth is cleansed, the physical person of the teaman may be regarded as purified and fit to enter the tearoom. But this kind of purity does not ensure his tranquillity. Environment has a great deal to do with the molding of a man's character and temperament, but he is also the molder and even the creator of his environment, for man is at once creature and creator. So tranquillity is something man adds to his environment from his inner self.

The tearoom, the *roji* (garden), the stone basin, the evergreens surrounding the hut, may be most meticulously arranged in every detail to yield the total effect of tranquillity, and yet the teaman's spirit may be found wandering somewhere else. With this most important spiritual quality wanting, the art of tea cannot be anything but a farce.

8

THE ART of tea is a syncretism of all the philosophical thoughts that were thriving throughout the Ashikaga (1338–1568), the Momoyama (1568–1615), and the Tokugawa (1615–1867) periods, when the cult attained its highest degree of perfection. If Japan did not produce any philosophical system of her own, she was original enough to embody in her practical life all that could profitably be extracted from Confucianism, Taoism, and Buddhism, and to turn them into the material for her spiritual enhancement and artistic appreciation. The Japanese, we can say, did not develop all the implications of Indian and Chinese thought in such a way as to demonstrate their intellectual possibilities. On the contrary, they strove to melt them into the humdrum of their workaday life, thereby transforming this into something enjoyable on a higher artistic plane. The Japanese genius so far failed to assert itself on the intellectual and rationalistic plane, but can we not say that it was manifested more on the side of the art of living? It seems to me that the Japanese are great in changing philosophy into art, abstract reasoning into life, transcendentalism into empirical immanentism. For this reason the tearoom can be said to be the syncretism of the three great schools of Oriental religio-philosophical thought. The Chinese mind is differently constructed. When it came in contact with the Indian way of thinking as represented in Buddhism, it was stirred to the depths of its intellectual powers; it worked out on the one hand the philosophy of Kegon (*Hua-yen*), Tendai

(*T'ien-t'ai*), and Sanron (*San-lun*); and on the other hand it created the philosophy of the Sung dynasty known as Rigaku (*Li-hsüeh*), which is the Chinese elaboration in response to the Zen-Kegon interpretation of Mahāyāna Buddhist thought. The Japanese thinkers so far have not intellectually taken up foreign stimulations, though there are ample indications now that promise a fruitful future for rationalistic thinking in Japan. Ultranationalism has unfortunately set a check on the growth of vigorous original thought among the Japanese. Instead of expressing themselves by free inquiry and healthy reflection on life itself, the Japanese rather sought to escape from the feudalistic oppression by such devices as the Nō dance, the art of tea, literature, and other social and artistic entertainments. The Japanese political system, I think, is to be held responsible for the impotence or lame development of the Japanese philosophical genius.

9

TRANQUILLITY is *par excellence* Buddhistic. The character (*jaku* in Japanese, *chi* in Chinese) has a special connotation in Buddhism. Originally, and nowadays also, *jaku* means "to be quiet," or "to be lonely," but when it is used in the Buddhist and especially in the Zen sense, it acquires a deep spiritual significance. It points to a life transcending mere worldliness, or to a realm beyond birth and death, which men of penetrating spiritual insight alone are able to inhabit. The Buddhist stanza generally found affixed at the end of a Mahāyāna sūtra reads:

> All composite things are impermanent,
> They belong in the realm of birth and death;
> When birth and death is transcended,
> Absolute tranquillity is realized and blessed are we.

In Buddhism, *jaku* is generally coupled with *metsu* (*mieh*), and the combination means "absolute tranquillity." This is frequently understood as a state of complete annihilation or of absolute nothingness, and Buddhists are criticized for their nihilism or acosmism. That this is due to the critics' not having a clear enough insight into the deepest recesses of Buddhist thought will easily be recognized by all students who have seriously studied this subject. This is not, however, the place for this kind of discussion, and I will make no further comments on it.

I have said that the art of tea was discovered as a way of escape from feudalistic regimentation, but it may be better to say that we all have an innate desire to transcend ourselves, whether we are living under a feudalistic political system or in a liberal democratic country. In whatever political and social environment we may be situated, we are ever seeking a new life which looms up before us. Thus urged, we are never satisfied with what we actually have, but are forever seeking a new era of culture, and for its creation we never relax our efforts. When a new one is found not to be in correspondence with our spiritual needs and to give us no promise for its future development, it is doomed.

If the art of tea stopped short at Confucianism and Taoism, it would be no more than a mere pastime, a quiet entertainment for the bourgeoisie, and we should fail to find in it anything contributing to the enhancement of our spiritual life. It was, therefore, up to the teaman to introduce into the art something of Buddhist metaphysics. He found it in the Buddhist idea of *jaku,* "tranquillity," not as an environmental attribute but as an idealistic disposition which every teaman, if he really desires to recover a vision, ought to cultivate.

Tranquillity, therefore, in the art of tea is a spiritual quality transcending birth and death, and not a mere physical or psychological one. This must carefully be kept in mind when the tea is spoken of as a step toward devoting one's life to a higher level from which one is to view our ordinary world and to live in it as if not in it. The following is the view on the tea held by Seisetsu (1746–1820), a Japanese Zen master of the late Tokugawa era:

"My Tea is No-tea, which is not No-tea in opposition to Tea.

What then is this No-tea? When a man enters into the exquisite realm of No-tea he will realize that No-tea is no other than the Great Way (*ta-tao*) itself.

"In this Way there are no fortifications built against birth and death, ignorance and enlightenment, right and wrong, assertion and negation. To attain a state of no-fortification is the way of No-tea. So with things of beauty, nothing can be more beautiful than the virtue of No-tea.

"Here is a story: A monk came to Jōshu (Chao-chou Ts'ung-shên), who asked, 'Have you ever been here?' The monk said, 'No, Master.' Jōshu said, 'Have a cup of tea.' Another monk called, and the master again asked, 'Have you ever been here?' 'Yes, Master,' was the answer. The master said, 'Have a cup of tea.'

"The same 'cup of tea' is offered to either monk regardless of his former visit to Jōshu. How is this? When the meaning of such a story as this is understood to its depths, one enters into the inner sanctuary of Jōshu and will appreciate the bitterness of tea tempered with the salt of sweetness. Well, I hear a bell ringing somewhere."

10

SEISETSU'S "No-tea" is a mysterious variation of the tea. He wants to reach the spirit of the art by the way of negation. This is the logic of *Prajñā* philosophy, which has sometimes been adopted by the Zen masters. As long as there is an event designated as "Tea" this will obscure our vision and hinder it from penetrating into "Tea" as it is in itself. This is particularly the case with what may be called the psychology of the tea. When a man is all the time conscious of performing the art called tea-serving, the very fact of being conscious constrains every movement of his, ending in his artificially constructing a "fortification." He always feels himself standing against this formidable thing which starts up a world of opposites, right and wrong, birth and death, "Tea" and "No-tea," *ad infinitum*. When the teaman is caught in these dualistic meshes, he deviates from the Great Way, and tranquillity is forever lost. For the art of tea is of the Great Way; it is the Great Way itself.

This transcendentalistic conception of the art of tea is not to be understood as something undiscoverable in our prosaic workaday life. To interpret the tea in this light is not in accord with its spirit. Tranquillity is at the basis of every movement as the teaman takes the powdered tea out of the caddy and stirs it in the bowl with a bamboo whisk. Tranquillity is to be dynamically conceived. Otherwise, it splits the mind in two and makes the teaman sit outside himself: the man and the work are bifurcated and the tea ceases to be the "No-tea." As long as there is any consciousness of a split between act and actor, the opposition causes friction and friction builds up "fortifications." The *Prajñā* philosopher would say: "Tea is Tea only when Tea is No-tea." So long as there is any kind of "fortification" there will be no "unobstructed flowing." The principle of tranquillity which makes up the art of tea will be violently negated.

Plotinus has his own way of expressing this idea: "There were not two; beholder was one with beheld; it was not a vision compassed but a unity apprehended. The man formed by this mingling with the Supreme must—if he only remember—carry its image impressed upon him: he is become the Unity, nothing within him or without inducing any diversity; no movement now, no passion, no outlooking desire, once this ascent is achieved; reasoning is in abeyance and all Intellection and even, to dare the word, the very self: caught away, filled with God, he has in perfect stillness attained isolation; all the being calmed, he turns neither to this side nor to that, not even inwards to himself; utterly resting he has become very rest." [19] The Plotinian "rest" is no other than the teaman's *jaku*.

The *Bhagavad Gītā*'s way of expressing this is rather strong

[19] Plotinus, tr. Stephen MacKenna, VI, 9, 11.

and deeply breathes the spirit Rikyū exhaled at his last moment
by throwing his sword skyward:

> *But he whose mind dwells*
> *Beyond attachment,*
> *Untainted by ego,*
> *No act shall bind him*
> *With any bond:*
> *Though he slay these thousands*
> *He is no slayer.*[20]

Objectively and relatively speaking, this may stagger some of
our readers; but we must remember that the author of the *Gītā*
has his own viewpoint, which evades our intellectually limited
measurement. Emerson must have been influenced by this when
he wrote "Brahma," the first four lines of which run:

> *If the red slayer think he slays,*
> *Or if the slain think he is slain,*
> *They know not well the subtle ways*
> *I keep, and pass, and turn again.*

Why? Because

> *Far or forgot to me is near;*
> *Shadow and sunlight are the same;*
> *The vanished gods to me appear;*
> *And one to me are shame and fame.*

Rikyū's sword that opened up his own bowels is also the one
that slays Buddhas and patriarchs, saints and sinners, creator
and created. When the art of tea reaches this height of enlightenment, the Zen master's "Tea of No-tea" is realized.

To quote Eckhart:

"Then how shall I love him [God]?

"Love him as he is: a not-God, a not-spirit, a not-person, a

---

[20] The *Bhagavad Gītā*, tr. Swami Prabhavananda and Christopher Isherwood,
XVIII, 17.

not-image; as sheer, pure, limpid one, alien from all duality. And in this one let us sink down eternally from nothingness to nothingness." [21]

If I may add an unnecessary comment, to drink tea as no-tea, as recommended by Seisetsu the Japanese Zen master, is no other than "to love God as a not-God (*niht got*) . . . to sink (*versinken*) eternally from nothingness to nothingness." "The principle of tranquillity" is to be understood in this sense.

11

S O M E of my readers may blame me for making a mountain of a molehill: "Tea-drinking is a matter of insignificant importance; to develop it into something of the highest thought that engages the human mind is altogether out of proportion; if we have to take up every little incident of life in this fashion, we will not have anything enjoyable, free from perplexing and wearing thoughts. What has tea-drinking, after all, to do with metaphysics of a most annoying sort? Tea is tea and cannot be anything else. When we are thirsty we have a cup of it, and that is enough. What is the use of making a strange art out of it? Oriental people are too fussy. We of the West have no time for such trivialities."

Now let me ask: Is a funeral ceremony a more significant event than tea-drinking? Has a wedding a more moral or metaphysical meaning than tea-drinking? From the point of view of "God's isness" or "a flea's isness," death is what inevitably follows from birth; there is nothing ominous about it. So with marriage. Why then do we make so much of it? If we wanted to, it could be reduced easily to the level of eating a morning meal or going to one's business office. We turn it into a grand ceremony because we just want it so. When we think life is too monotonous, we break it into several occasions and get sometimes excited, sometimes depressed. We all like vicissitudes and

[21] *Meister Eckhart,* tr. Evans, I, pp. 247–48.

mutations. When a universe comes to an end, a Zen monk asks, "Does this go with it?" One master replied, "Yes," while another one said, "No." [22] Which is in the right? "Both are right," Zen would declare, and, so declaring, it will go its own way, celebrating or lamenting its ending, or nonchalantly disregarding states of becoming.

As far as life itself is concerned, time and space are not of much consequence, though they are the mediums whereby life expresses itself from our human point of view. Our senses and intellect are so constructed as to interpret objectivity along the line of space and time. For this reason, we are really interested in quantitative estimates. We think eternity is something beyond our sensuous measurements, but from the innerness of life one minute or one second is just as long, just as important, as one thousand years. The morning-glory lasting only a few hours of the summer morning is of the same significance as the pine tree whose gnarled trunk defies wintry frost. The microscopic creatures are just as much manifestations of life as the elephant or the lion. In fact, they have more vitality, for even if all the other living forms vanish from the surface of the earth, the microbes will be found continuing their existence. Who would then deny that when I am sipping tea in my tearoom I am swallowing the whole universe with it and that this very moment of my lifting the bowl to my lips is eternity itself transcending time and space? The art of tea really teaches us far more than the harmony of things, or keeping them free from contamination, or just sinking down into a state of contemplative tranquillity.

[22] The *Hekigan-shū* ("Blue Rock Collection"), case 29: "Taizui Hōshin on the Universe." See also Appendix I.

X

Rikyū and Other Teamen

IT MAY not be inopportune to give here a very short sketch of the life of Sen no Rikyū. He is the founder of the art of tea as it is practiced in Japan today, and every teamaster gets his or her certificate as qualified for the profession from the hands of Rikyū's descendants. The art of tea in these modern days may not transmit exactly the spirit that animated its earlier masters, and there may not be so much of Zen in it as in the day of Rikyū. This is perhaps inevitable.

Sen no Rikyū (1521–91) was born the son of a well-to-do merchant in Sakai. Sakai, in Idzumi province, was in that day a flourishing port for foreign trade, and it was among its wealthy merchants that the art of tea seems to have developed first. For them it was a form of recreation; as they were rich, they were owners of many fine pieces of earthenware, chiefly imported from Korea, China, and southern Asia, which they used in connection with the art of tea. In all likelihood the teaman's unusual penchant for rare objects of art thus started with the merchants of Sakai, who in this respect also reflected Ashikaga Yoshimasa's aestheticism. Later, I will give a few anecdotes from the history of the tea, in which we find illustrated an extraordinary or inordinate attachment to tea utensils, as shown not only by teamen themselves but by the feudal lords of all degrees. They were willing to pay exorbitant prices for rare bowls or tea caddies, and the owners of such wares were objects of genuine envy among the lords, merchants, and men of culture.

Rikyū began to learn the art early in his life, and when he was about fifty he was universally recognized as one of the most accomplished masters in the art. The Emperor Ōgimachi gave him a special Buddhist name by which he has been known ever since in history, that is, Rikyū. Oda Nobunaga was a great patron of the art and specially favored Rikyū. After the death of Nobunaga, Rikyū came to be befriended by Toyotomi Hideyoshi, who followed Nobunaga and finally succeeded in consolidating his position as the most influential power, political as well as military, in the Japan of that day. Hideyoshi gave him three thousand *koku* of rice for his service to him as teamaster. Even in his various campaigns against his military opponents, Hideyoshi was accompanied by Rikyū. In those days of unrest, the tea was so much a favorite pastime with the feudal lords that they could not do without it even while occupied with military affairs. The "tea party" was frequently a political camouflage, and one can suspect the important political dealings transacted by the generals closeted in the four-and-a-half-mat room. Rikyū must have been a silent party to this. He was a man quite capable of the task.

Rikyū studied Zen at Daitokuji, one of the "Five Mountains" in Kyoto. He knew that the idea of *wabi* which he espoused in the tea rite was derived from Zen, and that without Zen training he could not capture the spirit of his art. While he was in actual life not a man of *wabi*, "insufficiency," but one endowed with material wealth, political power, and an unusual amount of artistic genius, he longed deep in his heart for a life of *wabi*. Circumstances, however, conspired otherwise: in spite of himself he was more and more drawn into worldly entanglements; and in some unknown way he incurred the great displeasure of his despotic master. He was commanded by Hideyoshi to commit suicide. The reasons given out for this capital punishment were trivial, and we suspect that there must have been something much graver, perhaps political, going on beneath the surface.

Rikyū was then over seventy. When he received the order,

he retired to his room, made his last tea, quietly enjoyed it, and wrote his farewell words in both Chinese and Japanese. The Chinese verse, roughly translated, is:

> *Seventy years of life—*
> *Ha ha! and what a fuss!*
> *With this sacred sword of mine,*
> *Both Buddhas and Patriarchs I kill!* [1]

The Japanese runs:

> *I raise the sword,*
> *This sword of mine,*
> *Long in my possession—*
> *The time is come at last—*
> *Skyward I throw it up!*

This tragic death, closing a brilliant life devoted to the tea and the idealization of *wabi*, took place on the twenty-eighth day of the second month in the nineteenth year of Tensho (1591).

The following stories told of Rikyū, whether historical or fictional, are interesting, and they shed light on the character of the man.

1

WHEN Hideyoshi learned of the beautifully blooming morning-glories at Rikyū's, he intimated his wish to see them. When the next morning Hideyoshi entered Rikyū's garden, there was not a morning-glory—not a shadow of one. He thought this was strange but did not say anything about it. When he stepped into the tea-room, lo and behold, there was one solitary flowering morning-glory.

---

[1] See above, p. 303, for Okakura's version, which is evidently based on a different text.

2

ONE DAY Hideyoshi, wishing to outwit Rikyū, brought out a gold basin filled with fresh water and a spray of plum blossoms, and requested Rikyū to arrange it. Rikyū without a moment's hesitation took up the spray in his hands and, scraping the blossoms, let them fall pell-mell into the basin. Buds and full-blown flowers scattered against the gold presented a most beautiful sight.

3

WHEN, one day in the spring, Hideyoshi was entertained by Rikyū, he was shown to a small room, one mat and three-quarters wide, which is in modern measurement less than six feet square. As he was about to enter, he noticed some full-blown branches of drooping cherry blossoms hanging from a vase suspended from the ceiling. The flowers filled the room even up to the entrance opening. This pleased Hideyoshi very much; for, in spite of his liking for the tea, he was secretly inclined toward luxurious extravagances. He stayed outside for a while admiring the gorgeous flowering cherry blossoms, which literally filled the room.

4

WHEN Rikyū was still apprentice at the art of tea, his master told him to sweep the *roji*—the court attached to the tearoom. The *roji* had already been swept clean by the master himself. When Rikyū came out, not a speck of dust was to be found, but he at once read the master's mind. Shaking a tree a little, he let a few leaves fall on the ground. This pleased the master.

5

RIKYŪ had a mind extremely sensitive to beauty from the
point of view of *wabi* or *sabi*. He detected the smallest thing
that went against it. When Rikyū was invited to a first winter tea
party somewhere, he was accompanied by his son-in-law. When
they stepped into the court, they noticed the gate hung with
an ancient-looking door. The son-in-law remarked that it savored
highly of *sabi*. But Rikyū smiled somewhat sarcastically: "This
is far from savoring of *sabi*, my son; it is on the contrary a most
expensive piece of work. Look here closely. Such a door as this
is not to be found in this vicinity. It must have come from a remote mountain temple far away from the human world. Think of
the amount of labor to bring it here, for which the master must
have paid dearly. If he had understood what genuine *sabi* is,
he would have searched for a suitable door ready-made or
made to order among the neighboring dealers, and would have
had it pieced together with an old board found about his premises.
Then the door fixed here would certainly savor of *wabi*. The
taste shown before us is not a genuine one." It was thus the
son-in-law was taught the art in a practical way.

6

RIKYŪ attended a *cha-no-yu* given by his eldest son. When he
stood in the *roji*, he said to the friend accompanying him,
"Among these steppingstones there is one just a trifle higher
than the rest. My son does not seem to have noticed it." This
remark was overheard by his son, who said to himself, "I have
been thinking of it myself for some time. What a quick intuitive
mind is my father's!" While the guests were taking a little rest
after the first tea, Rikyū's son quietly slipped out to the *roji*
and, digging a little underneath the stone in question, set it down

to the proper level. To conceal the new work, he sprinkled fresh water around. Later, when Rikyū again went over the stepping-stones on his way home, the alteration done with all subtlety did not escape his eye, for he remarked, "Well, well! Dō-an [which was his son's name] must have overheard my criticism, but how readily he took it to his heart and remedied it even before our departure!"

7

R I K Y Ū was once invited to tea, accompanied by a few friends. They found the court filled with splendid *kashi* trees and the passage covered with fallen leaves, and they felt as if they were walking on a mountain pass. "How fine!" Rikyū said. After a little reflection, however, he continued, "I am afraid that the master will sweep the passage clean, as he has yet no idea about *sabi*." Surely enough, when they went in again after the first service, they found that the leaves were all too completely swept up. Rikyū then explained to his friends how things were to be arranged on such occasions. Later, while instructing one of his pupils in the care of the *roji*, he quoted the following verse by Saigyō as expressing his notion of it:

> *Leaves of the kashi trees,*
> *Even before they were tinged,*
> *Are all scattered*
> *Along the path to the mountain*
>   *monastery—*
> *Along the path, lone and desolate.*

(That rocks and mosses and lichens are among the chief features of Japanese gardening, especially of that connected with the tearoom, is noteworthy; for they are suggestive of the Zen monk's life in the mountains and of the principle of *sabi*, which rules everything associated with the art of tea. The use of stones as they come from mountains, valleys, riverbeds, and other localities adds a great deal to the atmosphere of solidity, solitude, and ancientness pervading the *roji*. The moss, in large variety, covering the rocks and the ground, creates a feeling of the mountainous region far away from the life of the city. This feeling is essential to the tearoom, for the main object of the tea is to escape from commercialism and all that savors of it.)

8

T H A T Rikyū was the authority on *wabi* is shown in the following story. A teaman of Sakai owned a caddy of a special pattern entitled "Unzan Katatsuki." As the ware was quite well known among teamen and prized by them, the owner was naturally proud of it. One day he invited Rikyū to tea and used this caddy. But Rikyū did not seem to be very much concerned about it and left the house with no comments. The owner was upset over this, and immediately broke it to pieces by striking it against the *gotoku*, and sighed, "What is the use of keeping these days an article not at all approved of by Rikyū?"

A friend of the owner's later collected the broken pieces of the caddy and glued them together carefully so as to restore the original pattern. The work was done with a great deal of skill, and he thought the mended caddy was after all not a poor specimen. He conceived the idea of inviting Rikyū to tea and using the caddy again to see what Rikyū would say about it.

While the tea was being served, Rikyū's keen eye at once detected the same old caddy now pieced together. He said, "Is this not the same caddy I saw elsewhere some time ago? When it is repaired like this, it has really turned into a piece of *wabi*." The friend was exceedingly pleased with the remark and returned the caddy to its former owner.

After changing owners many times, this once-broken and now perfectly pieced-together "Katatsuki" fell into the hands of a certain feudal lord. Kyōgoku Anchi, one of the most famed tea-men in Kyoto in those days, fancied it very much. A physician-friend of his, learning of it, visited the lord, and apparently quite accidentally referred to the wish of Kyōgoku Anchi to have the caddy. The lord was amused and jokingly said, "If he is willing to pay two loads of gold for it, I may part with it."

The physician took this seriously and reported the matter to Anchi, who said, "If that is the case, I wish you would see to it that I have it for two loads of gold."

When the lord was notified of Anchi's readiness to pay the gold, he was thunderstruck and said, "From the first I had no intention to part with it for whatever amount of money one might pay for it." This confused the matter. The physician, who voluntarily acted as a go-between, did not know what to do. There was much going back and forth between Anchi and the lord. Each of the parties concerned, taking it up as affecting his sense of honor, assumed a stiffer attitude than ever toward the affair. All the teamen became interested in it, and extended their good offices to smooth the complications. By means of great diplomacy they finally succeeded in making the arrange-ment that two loads of gold would be paid to the lord by the other party, not indeed as the price for the disputed treasure, but as a kind of relief fund for the poor and needy in the feudal estate of the lord, and that the treasure itself would be a free gift from the lord to Anchi. Two loads of gold were equivalent in the currency of the time to 12,000 *ryō,* which must be in modern money at least 100,000 yen.[2]

Anchi was perfectly satisfied with the way the matter was settled, though this no doubt meant a great cut into his own exchequer. He was not, however, quite satisfied with the caddy itself, for he thought he could improve on the way it was patched. He consulted with Kobori Yenshū, another great tea-master and authority of the time, as to replacing certain pieces. But Kobori Yenshū was a wiser critic and said, "It was just

[2] Today, nearly $30,000.

because of those oddities that it appealed to Rikyū so much and
became an object of reputation among the teamasters. You
would do best to leave them exactly as they stand."

9

IN JAPANESE architecture the alcove (*tokonoma*) performs
a significant office in various ways. This recess cut into the
wall of a principal room originally comes from Zen architecture, where it was meant for a sacred picture or statue. Nowadays
any *kakemono* may be found here, but the presence of a flower
vase and a censer in the alcove still tells its former history. In
any event, the flower vase is an essential feature of the *tokonoma*, and no tearoom is complete without it. When Toyotomi
Hideyoshi was engaged in besieging the Odawara castle commanded by Hōjō, the latter offered a stubborn resistance, and
some months passed without achieving much. Hideyoshi wanted
to have tea parties by way of recreation for his generals. But
there was no available flower vase for the room. He told Rikyū
to get one. Rikyū thought of making one out of a stalk of
bamboo; this was quite an original idea with him, for hitherto
no vases of this kind had ever been devised and put into practical use. He visited the neighboring bamboo groves to find
suitable material, which found, he made into a vase himself.
As the bamboo dried, it showed a crack, and this crack became
the characteristic mark of the vase, and it has been known ever
since as the "Onjōji vase." The Onjōji is an historical Buddhist
temple by Lake Biwa, and its bell has earned its reputation from
having a crack in it. It was due to this coincidence that Rikyū's
vase acquired its name.

Rikyū's homely-looking bamboo vase became a sacred treasure
among teamen, not only because of its artistic value but because of its historical associations. When its envied owner was
one Iyehara Jisen, his friend Nomura Sōji, of Nagoya, came up

to Kyoto with the special object of viewing the vase. Jisen, however, refused and asked him to wait for a year. In the meantime, Jisen busied himself with constructing a new tearoom in which no bamboo was used in any form. The vase in the *tokonoma* was the only bamboo in sight. Sōji was then invited and shown the treasure in a most appropriate setting. When Sōji's request to see it the year before had been refused, he was chagrined, but when he saw what was then in the mind of his friend, he felt grateful and fully appreciated his artistic attitude of reverence for Rikyū and his work.

Fuyuki, a rich merchant of Fukagawa, Yedo, wished to acquire the vase for his own tearoom, but Jisen would not part with it. Later, when Jisen found himself in adverse circumstances, he thought of Fuyuki, who was once willing to pay 500 *ryō* for the bamboo vase, and sent a messenger to Yedo with the message that Jisen would sell it now for 50 *ryō* less, that is, for 450 *ryō*. Fuyuki sent his messenger back with no answer, but ordered his own messenger to follow Jisen's, carrying 500 *ryō* instead of 450 *ryō*. Fuyuki's messenger respectfully carried the vase back with him to Yedo. The idea was not to slight the value of such a treasure, but, apart from the commercial interests, to treat it with due respect.

Then, still later, its ownership went to Lord Fumai (1751–1819), another feudal baron of the Tokugawa regime, who loved the tea cult and had very fine taste for *sabi*. When he was using the vase in his tearoom to entertain his friends, his attendant noticed that water dripped from the crack, thus wetting the mat underneath. He asked the master if he would not have a kind of cylindrical receptacle made for it. Lord Fumai, however, said, "The *fūryū* [or *sabi*] of this bamboo vase consists in the very fact of this leakage."

10

KANŌ TANNYŪ the painter (1602–74) is a name I believe
to be very well known to lovers of Japanese art, and it may not
be altogether inappropriate to introduce him in connection with
the tea, as he was also greatly interested in it. He studied it
under the instruction of Sōtan, grandson of Rikyū and a great
advocate of *wabi*, probably in this respect greater than Rikyū.
Tannyū was still young when he began to visit Sōtan, hardly
over twenty years of age. When he saw the blank screens fitted
up in Sōtan's newly built tearoom, he had an irresistible desire
to paint them with his own brush. But his teamaster would not
listen to the request, for he thought his young pupil was still
not experienced enough to do the work. Tannyū did not press
the idea that day.

Some time later, he accidentally dropped into Sōtan's new
room. The master was absent. The screens still remained blank.
He considered the opportunity the rarest one, as his former ambition asserted itself once more. In fact, he had been planning
for some time what picture would be suitable to try his skill here.
He took out the brushes and started at once with his work. It
was to be "The Eight Sage Drinkers." As he proceeded, he
grew ever more enthusiastic about it, and the picture was nearly
finished when he heard somebody approaching. He felt that this
must be the master himself. It would be quite awkward if he
were caught in the act. He wanted to finish hurriedly. The
steps became more and more distinct. What remained to be done
now was the hands of one figure. He somehow finished them
and left the room as Sōtan stepped into it. Sōtan was surprised
to see such a fine work from the brush of such a young artist,
whose proficiency he had not thought very highly of before.
However, as he examined the work closely, he found the hands
of one figure wrongly attached, that is, the left hand to the right
and the right one to the left. But he did not say much about it.

The picture remains there as it was executed even to the present day.

Later when Tannyū's reputation as the greatest painter of the day, the one favored by Iyeyasu the Shōgun, spread far and wide throughout the country, his old picture with hands wrongly adjusted called out fresh interest among art lovers.

Tannyū owned a "Katatsuki" caddy known as "Tanemura," an object of great admiration among teamen. He thought the world of it. When the great fire of the Meireki (A.D. 1657) reduced Tannyū's house to ashes, he told one of his servants to carry the caddy away from destruction. But when the spread of the fire threatened his own life, the trusted servant threw away the precious treasure and ran off to save himself. After the fire, a goods carrier from Kyoto happened to discover it on the roadside. He picked it up and on his return to Kyoto he sold it to an art dealer. The Mayor Makino Chikashige heard of the find and bought it from the dealer, when it proved on examination to be the "Tanemura Katatsuki."

Some time later Chikashige invited Tannyū and treated him to tea. When he innocently referred to the caddy Tannyū told him that he was unspeakably grieved over the loss and wished him not to make any further mention of it. Chikashige told his attendant to bring the article in question before the guest, remarking guilelessly, "Here is a Tanemura duplicate." Tannyū was indeed overjoyed and did not know how to express his feelings. The mayor was gallant enough to part with it for the price he paid to the dealer, with the request that he would like to have twelve views of Mount Fuji painted by Tannyū to compensate his good will. Tannyū, of course, agreed. But it was a difficult proposition, and the painter had to spend much thought and skill upon the execution of the pictures, which, when finished after great pains, proved to be among his masterpieces.

XI

Love of Nature

I

1

THE JAPANESE love of Nature, I often think, owes much
to the presence of Mount Fuji in the middle part of the main
island of Japan. Whenever I pass by the foot of the mountain
as a passenger on the Tokaido railway line, I never fail to have
a good view of it, weather permitting, and to admire its beautiful
formation, always covered with spotless snow and "rising sky-
wards like a white upturned folding fan," as it was once described by a poet [1] of the Tokugawa period. The feeling it
awakens does not seem to be all aesthetic in the line of the
artistically beautiful. There is something about it spiritually pure
and enhancing.

One [2] of the earlier poets of Japan who sang of Mount
Fuji has this:

> *To the beach of Tago*
> *I come, and, behold,*
> *In pure whiteness enveloped*
> *There rises Mount Fuji—*
> *Snowing it seems above us!* [3]

---

[1] Ishikawa Jōzan (1583–1672).

[2] Yamabe no Akahito (d. *ca.* 736) in the *Mannyōshū*, "Collection of Ancient
Poems."

[3] As I have remarked before, in these translations of Japanese poetry no
attempt is made to reproduce the original rhythm. They are mostly literal ren-
derings, with the fewest additions necessary to make the sense somewhat more
intelligible to English readers.

Another poet,[4] who has more religious feelings than Akahito of the Nara period, sings in the *Mannyōshū:*

> *Extending over Suruga and Kai,*
> *Mount Fuji lifts its summit high.*
> *Even the clouds of heaven, struck with awe,*
> *Dare not pass over that steep peak;*
> *Even the birds attempt in vain*
> *To soar over its giddy heights.*
>
> .   .   .   .
>
> *It is a god that watches over Japan—*
> *Over Yamato, the Land of the Sunrise—*
> *It is her sacred treasure and her glory:*
> *Upon the peak of Fuji in Suruga*
> *Long may we gaze and gaze and never weary.*

Saigyō's poem on Fuji has a mystical vein which is quoted elsewhere. In his day, that is, in the twelfth century, Fuji must still have been a live volcano, at least emitting smoke now and then. Such a sight is always inspiring. To see a solitary drifting cloud over a high peak carries one's thoughts away from earthly affairs.

It was not the poets alone who were impressed with Fuji. Even a warrior had a feeling for it, expressing himself thus:

> *Each time I see Fuji*
> *It appears changed*
> *And I feel I view it*
> *Ever for the first time.*
>
> *How shall I describe Fuji*
> *To those who have not yet seen it?*
> *It is never seen twice alike,*
> *And I know no one way*
> *Of describing the sight.*

[4] Anonymous (in the *Mannyōshū,* V, III), also of the Nara period. The translation (slightly modified) is by Asatarō Miyamoto.

The singer is Daté Masamune [5] (1565–1636), one of the most renowned generals at the time of Hideyoshi and Iyeyasu. He was a dauntless fighter, winning many fierce battles in which he personally took part. He was made the feudal lord of the district of Sendai, which is in the northeastern section of Japan. Who would imagine such an active soldier in the warlike days of the sixteenth and seventeenth centuries finding room in his brain to appreciate Nature and write poems on it? But such was actually the fact, and in it we recognize how innate the love of Nature is in the Japanese heart. Even Hideyoshi, who rose from the peasant class—in his days a class badly downtrodden and hopelessly ignorant—composed poems and was a patron of the arts. His time is known as the Momoyama period in the history of Japanese art.

Fuji is now thoroughly identified with Japan. Wherever Japan is talked or written about, Fuji is inevitably mentioned. Justifiably so, because even the Land of the Rising Sun would surely lose much of her beauty if the sacred mountain were erased from the map. The mountain must be actually seen in order to impress. Pictures and photographs, however artistic, cannot do justice to the real view. As Masamune sings, it is never the same, it is ever changing in its features, as it is affected by atmospheric conditions, and also as it is viewed topographically from different angles and at different distances. To those who have never seen it, even Hiroshige (1797–1858) fails to convey the real artistic value of the mountain, about which Yamaoka Tesshū (1836–88) [6] writes another poem from another point of view than Masamune:

[5] He is well remembered in Japanese history as the one who sent an envoy to the Pope in 1613.

[6] It is possible that the poem is not Tesshū's original composition. But I remember having read it among his innumerable calligraphic works. He was not a poet by profession; he was one of the great modern swordsmen, who deeply delved into the study of Zen and applied his understanding to swordsmanship. See also pp. 193 ff., above.

In fair weather,
In cloudy weather,
Beautiful indeed
And never changing—
This peak of Fuji!

In these prosaic days of ours, there is a craze among the young men of Japan for climbing high mountains just for the sake of climbing; and they call this "conquering the mountains." What a desecration! This is a fashion no doubt imported from the West along with many others not always worth while learning. The idea of the so-called "conquest of nature" comes from Hellenism, I imagine, in which the earth is made to be man's servant, and the winds and the sea are to obey him. Hebraism concurs with this view, too. In the East, however, this idea of subjecting Nature to the commands or service of man according to his selfish desires has never been cherished. For Nature to us has never been uncharitable, it is not a kind of enemy to be brought under man's power. We of the Orient have never conceived Nature in the form of an opposing power. On the contrary, Nature has been our constant friend and companion, who is to be absolutely trusted in spite of the frequent earthquakes assailing this land of ours. The idea of conquest is abhorrent. If we succeed in climbing a high mountain, why not say, "We have made a good friend of it"? To look around for objects to conquer is not the Oriental attitude toward Nature.[7]

Yes, we climb Fuji, too, but the purpose is not to "conquer" it, but to be impressed with its beauty, grandeur, and aloofness; it is also to worship a sublime morning sun rising gorgeously from behind the multicolored clouds. This is not necessarily an act of sun worship, though there is nothing spiritually degrading in that. The sun is the great benefactor of all life on earth, and it is only proper for us human beings to approach a benefactor

[7] Cf. my article "The Role of Nature in Zen Buddhism," in *Studies in Zen,* pp. 176 ff.

of any kind, animate or inanimate, with a deep feeling of gratitude and appreciation. For this feeling is granted to us only;
lower animals seem to be wanting in this delicate sentiment.
Some of the high mountains of popular interest in Japan are
nowadays provided with a system of cable railway, and the
summit is easily reached. The materialistic utilitarianism of
modern life demands all such contrivances, and perhaps there
is no escape from them; for I myself often resort to them, for
instance, when I go up to Hiei in Kyoto. Nevertheless my feelings are revolted. The sight of the track lighted up at night by
electricity reflects the modern spirit of sordid gain and pleasure-
hunting. That Mount Hiei, to the northeast of the ancient capital
of Japan, which Dengyō Daishi (767–822) first consecrated
with his Tendai monastery and other institutions [8] of his order,
is to be treated with such ruthless commercialism is no doubt a
cause of grief to many a pious-hearted countryman. In the wor-
shipful attitude toward Nature there is a highly religious feeling
that I should like to see even in these days of science and
economics and war.

2

O N E may see how much in love with Nature the Japanese is, in
spite of his modern assertion of the conquest idea, if he builds
a study, or rather a meditation room, somewhere in the mountain
woods. It is not much of a building by the Western way of
measurement, for it will be no more than a four-and-a-half-mat
or six-mat room (about ten or fifteen feet square). It is thatched
with straw, and it probably stands under a huge pine tree, protected by its outstretched branches. When viewed from a

[8] Recently (1956), one of the buildings (called the "Lecture Hall") making
up the group was burned maliciously by one of the caretakers. This is an ir-
reparable loss not only to the followers of Tendai but to the cultural history of
Japan. The incident is one of the bad examples reflecting the modern spirit of
wanton vandalism.

distance, the hut forms an insignificant part of the landscape, but it appears to be incorporated in it. It is by no means obtrusive, it belongs somehow to the general scheme of the view. As the master sits in this simple room—where there are no cumbrous pieces of furniture, perhaps only a table, a cushion, a flower vase, an incense burner—he finds that it is in no special way separated from the surroundings, from Nature that encircles the hut. A cluster of plantain trees is growing near one of the oddly shaped windows; some of their broad leaves are irregularly torn by a recent storm, and now they look like a monk's robe all in tatters. And for this reason they appear more suggestive of the Zen poems of Kanzan.[9] It is not only the formation of these leaves which is poetic, but the way they—in fact, all plants—grow out of the earth, that makes the observer feel that he, too, is living the life they are living. The floor of the meditation room is not raised too far from the ground, just enough to keep the occupant from dampness and yet to feel the common source from which all life shoots forth.

A hut so constructed is an integral part of Nature, and he who sits here is one of its objects like every other. He is in no way different from the birds singing, the insects buzzing, the leaves swaying, the waters murmuring—nor even from Mount Fuji, looming up on the other side of the bay. Here is a complete merging of Nature and man and his work, illustrated in a practical manner. As I speak of Fuji again, I am reminded of a poem by Ōta Dōkwan (d. 1486), a general of the fifteenth century. When he was asked by the Emperor Gotsuchimikado as to his residence, the general answered in verse:

My hut is on the beach
Lined with pine trees,
And the high peak of Fuji
Looms up above the eaves.

[9] Han-shan, a lunatic monk of the T'ang dynasty. He was always in company with Jittoku (Shih-tê) and left many poems. Cf. pls. 6, 18, 19, and p. 25, above.

The emperor living in Kyoto had never seen the mountain in actuality, hence the poet-soldier's special reference to it. And is it not interesting to notice here the way he describes his residence as a hut (*ihori* or *iho* in Japanese)? Being the warrior-general who first established his headquarters at the present site of Tokyo before Iyeyasu had his grand castle, Ōta Dōkwan's residence must have been of no mean magnitude. Yet he describes it as an *ihori*, with which we ordinarily associate the humble straw-thatched cottage of a recluse. His poetical, nature-loving spirit revolted against anything highly savoring of human artificiality. His "hut" naturally fits in with the stretch of pine trees, the wave-washed beach, and the snow-covered Fuji. In this respect, Dōkwan truly reflects the love of Nature that is the predominant note in the Japanese character.[10]

A grandly constructed building [11] is too obtrusive an object

[10] I sometimes wonder if any of the great Western soldiers ever turned into a poet. Can we imagine, for instance, in recent times, that General MacArthur or General Eisenhower would compose a poem upon visiting one of those bomb-torn cities? General Nogi, of the Russo-Japanese war, after a great battle fought around Port Arthur, in which he lost his two sons, wrote this poem in Chinese:

> How dreary and unconsolable they look—mountains and
> rivers, trees and grasses.
> The battlefield, newly won, for as much as ten miles around,
> is filled with an atmosphere odorous of spilt blood.
> The steed refuses to move on and the man, grim and silent,
> Stands all alone outside the fortress of Chinchow in the
> shadow of the setting sun.

[11] The American liking for high buildings is no doubt economically necessitated and, I believe, in some cases topographically also. But I suspect there is a certain psychological element in this fondness for tall architecture of any kind. Fundamentally, it is the desire to free oneself from the earth, for in one sense the earth symbolizes bondage, constriction, enthrallment, restraint of whatever kind from freedom and independence. In reality, one can never be free from the earth, for however high one may fly, one has finally to come down to earth. But since the development of the intellectual powers, man has conceived the idea of pushing this as far as it can go even at the expense of his other and possibly weightier interests. The towering architecture is the symbolization of the intellect, and modern man has forgotten or is as yet unconscious of the fact that this intellectualization is one of the causes contributing to all sorts of mental disturbance that we see about us. When I was in Chicago recently, I met the

to keep company with the surrounding objects of Nature. From the practical point of view, it may serve its purpose well, but there is no poetry in it. Any artificial construction, with its object too prominent, detracts from its artistic value. It is only when it is in ruins and no more serves its original purpose that it is transformed into a object of Nature and appreciated as such, though even in this appreciation there is much that has to do with the historical significance of the ruins themselves.

Again, the Emperor Gotsuchimikado must have heard of the Musashino prairie, where Dōkwan had his castle. Japan is a mountainous country with few plains, and the Musashino, where now stands the capital of the country, is one of the largest. The emperor, who had probably never left his mountain-encircled Kyoto, was curious to know how wide the Musashino was. So he asked Dōkwan about it, and Dōkwan replied in verse:

> *No dewdrops are seen around my hut,*
> *Though a summer shower has just passed*
> *Over the plain of Musashino—*
> *Far wider it must be than the rain clouds.*

This pleased the emperor immensely, and he gave the following reply to the much talented warrior-poet from the wild East:

> *I thought the Musashino was only a prairie*
> *With nothing but wild thistles;*
> *How pleasantly surprised I am*
> *To find such words in bloom!*

architect of a tall modern building, who lives on the top floor of the same building. When I admired the fine views of the city and the lake it commands, for the room is well provided with large glass windows, the architect said, "That is true, but I have to confess that I have a feeling of insecurity, though I don't know why." The feeling of insecurity—is this not the ailment most modern people suffer from, not only socially but internationally? The intellect presses the button, the whole city is destroyed, and hundreds of thousands of human souls are crushed ignominiously to the ground. And the intellect will not have any compunction whatever. All is done mechanically, logically, systematically, and the intellect is perfectly satisfied, perhaps even when it destroys itself together with its victims. Is it not high time for us all to think of ourselves from another point of view than that of mere intellectuality? Do we not have to be much closer to the earth, where the nature lover's hut humbly stands?

Dōkwan is one of the most popular heroes with the Japanese. Unfortunately, he lived in the age when the Ashikaga Shōgunate was fast approaching its end, and the country was on the verge of general disorder. Dōkwan was cravenly assassinated with a spear by his treacherous enemy. His farewell song was:

Until yesterday this body of mine,
Like a hemunashi [12] bag,
Was the depository of wrong attachments—
Is it now for the last time burst?

3

THE POET-GENERAL Ōta Dōkwan was fortunate to enjoy the mountain in white snow against the foaming waves of the blue ocean; but the hearts of the host and hostess of the dilapidated Ugetsu hut were torn between the moon and the autumnal rain drops, and they were greatly puzzled, not knowing what to do. Yet, in this not knowing what to do with the hut—this time a really humble one—we recognize as much poetry as in the case of Dōkwan, perhaps more of it. The Japanese love of Nature is here graphically depicted. The story, in short, runs as follows:

Ugetsu, meaning "Rain and Moon," is one of the Nō plays adapted from an incident taking place in one of Saigyō's wanderings in Japan. Saigyō (1118–90), the monk-poet of the early Kamakura period, came one evening to a solitary house and asked for a night's lodging. An old couple was living there, and the house looked quite dilapidated. The old man refused to respond to the monk's request on the ground that the accommodations were not good enough for him; while his wife, seeing the traveler was a Buddhist monk, wished to give him lodging. But the fact remained the same: the hut was in no proper condition to entertain a stranger. The reason was this: The old lady loved

---

[12] *Hemunashi* or *hennashi* means "no edge" or "no hem." The bag therefore is an "unhemmed bag," perhaps a worn-out or worthless bag, in the usage of fifteenth-century Japan.

the moonlight so much that the leaking roof was left unrepaired according to her desire; but the old gentleman loved to listen to the rain drops beating against the roof, which could not happen if the roof were left out of repair as it now was. Is the hut to be roofless for the moon? Or is it to be put in order for the rain? The autumn is already here. The finest moon season is approaching, and at the same time the autumnal showers are so enjoyable when one sits quietly listening to them. As long as this problem was not decided, it would be highly inhospitable on the part of the host and the hostess to take any stranger into their house. They thought:

> Our humble hut—
> Is it to be thatched, or not to be thatched?

Saigyō exclaimed, "Here is a good poem already half composed!" "If you understand poetry," said the old couple, "complete the stanza, and we will give you lodging, whatever it may be." Saigyō immediately responded:

> Is the moonlight to leak?
> Are the showers to patter?
> Our thoughts are divided,
> And this humble hut—
> To be thatched, or not to be thatched? [13]

The monk-poet was now invited in. As the night advanced, the moon grew brighter, illuminating the faraway fields and mountains and shedding its light even inside the hut. But, listen, showers are coming! Trees are rustling! No, it is the dead leaves that are beating against the house, sounding like the rain drops. A wind is up, but the sky is clear as ever. It is a shower of falling leaves in the moonlight.

---

[13] Saigyō has another poem to similar effect:

> The hut leaks when it rains,
> And I am wet;
> I think of the kindly visits of the moonlight.

When the dead leaves are falling thick,
As I sit quietly at night in my room,
Difficult it is to judge
Whether it is showering,
Or whether it is not showering.[14]

The falling leaves in autumn have often awakened the poetic sensibility of the nature-loving Japanese. The scene is suggestive of solitude and induces one to a meditative mood. Saigyō was also deeply impressed with it. While alone in his humble hermitage somewhere in the mountains, he was awakened during the night by the falling leaves striking showerlike against the roof and the *amado*,[15] which no doubt greatly added to the feeling of aloneness, which is the spirit of autumn-nature. The following poem is not merely descriptive, it reflects the mood of the season.

May it be a passing shower
That keeps me awake in bed?
No, it is the autumn leaves falling
Resistlessly before a squall.

From the practical point of view, rain is an inconvenient thing, but in Japanese and also in Chinese poetry much reference is made to rain—especially to a gentle rain such as we have in Japan—as whispering to us the inner secrets of Reality. Listen to Saigyō again:

Completely imprisoned in the spring rain,
I am all alone in the solitary hut,
Unknown to humankind.

To really understand the poetry and philosophy of the spring rain one must live in Japan in a small straw-thatched house,

[14] By Minamoto no Yorizane, of the thirteenth century.

[15] Literally, "rain door." The Japanese house has practically no windows in the Western sense. It is all doors—sliding doors which serve to partition the rooms, admit light, protect the house against rain, snow, wind, etc. The *amado* are outside sliding doors, which are closed regularly at night or when the weather is inclement.

perhaps with a stretch of lawn and a little pond before one's six-mat room. "Unknown to humankind," but thoroughly acquainted with Nature was the poet.

Dōgen (1200–1253) was the founder of the Sōtō branch of Zen Buddhism in Japan. The following is the most celebrated of his poems, worth while quoting in this connection:

How we go like clouds drifting through births and deaths!
The path of ignorance and the path of enlightenment—we walk
  dreaming!
There's one thing only still in my memory even after waking:
The sound of a rainfall to which I listened one night while at
  my Fukakusa retreat!

Thoreau, in *Walden*, gives an inkling of what is sometimes designated as cosmic consciousness or cosmic feeling, which he cherished as he listened to rainfall:

"I have never felt lonesome, or in the least oppressed by a sense of solitude, but once, and that was a few weeks after I came to the woods, when, for an hour, I doubted if the near neighborhood of man was not essential to a serene and healthy life. To be alone was something unpleasant. But I was at the same time conscious of a slight insanity in my mood, and seemed to foresee my recovery. In the midst of a gentle rain, while these thoughts prevailed, I was suddenly sensible of such sweet and beneficent society in Nature, in the very pattering of the drops, and in every sound and sight around my house, an infinite and unaccountable friendliness all at once like an atmosphere sustaining me, as made the fancied advantages of human neighborhood insignificant, and I have never thought of them since. Every little pine needle expanded and swelled with sympathy, and befriended me. I was so distinctly made aware of the presence of something kindred to me, even in scenes which we are accustomed to call wild and dreary, and also that the nearest of blood to me and humanest was not a person nor a villager, that I thought no place could ever be strange to me again." (Ch. 5, "Solitude.")

4

LET US note here, in passing, how Oriental thoughts and feelings filtered into the American mind in the nineteenth century. The Transcendentalist movement begun by the poets and philosophers of Concord is still continuing all over America. While the commercial and industrial expansion of America in the Far East and all the world over is a significant event of the twentieth century, we must acknowledge at the same time that the Orient is contributing its quota to the intellectual wealth of the West— American as well as European. In 1844, Emerson wrote, in response to Carlyle's chiding of his otherworldliness, in these remarkable terms: "You sometimes charge me with I know not what sky-blue, sky-void idealism. As far as it is a partiality, I fear I may be more deeply infected than you think me. I have very joyful dreams which I cannot bring to paper, much less to any approach to practice, and I blame myself not at all for my reveries, but they have not yet got possession of my house and barn. . . . I only worship Eternal Buddha in the retirements and intermissions of Brahma."

Emerson's allusion to "sky-void idealism" is interesting. Apparently he means the Buddhist theory of *śūnyatā* ("emptiness" or "void"). Although it is doubtful how deeply he entered into the spirit of this theory, which is the basic principle of the Buddhist thought and from which Zen starts on its mystic appreciation of Nature, it is really wonderful to see the American mind, as represented by the exponents of Transcendentalism, even trying to probe into the abysmal darkness of the Oriental fantasy. I am now beginning to understand the meaning of the deep impressions made upon me while reading Emerson in my college days. I was not then studying the American philosopher but digging down into the recesses of my own thought, which had been there ever since the awakening of Oriental consciousness. That was the reason why I had felt so familiar with him— I was, indeed, making acquaintance with myself then. The same can be said of Thoreau. Who would not recognize his poetic affinity with Saigyō or Bashō, and his perhaps unconscious indebtedness to the Oriental mode of feeling towards Nature?

To finish this part of my thesis, let me introduce to you a Zen master whose remark on rain is well-known among the followers of Zen. It was raining one day, and Kyōshō (d. 937) the master said to a monk, "What is the sound outside the door?" The monk answered, "The pattering of rain drops, master." This was an honest answer, and the master knew it from the first. His verdict, however, was: "All beings are confused in mind, they are pursuing outside objects always, not knowing where to find the real self." This is a hard hit. If the outside pattering is not to be called rain, what is it? What does it mean to pursue the outside objects, and to be confused in the notion of the ego? Secchō comments:

An empty hall, and the sound of pattering rain!
Indeed, an unanswerable question even for an accomplished master! [16]

The American Transcendentalist's attitude toward Nature has no doubt a great mystical note, but the Zen masters go far beyond it and are really incomprehensible. But we will drop the rain for a while, for it is now time to see into the teaching of Zen.

---

[16] From the *Hekigan-shū* ("Blue Rock Collection"), case 46.

II

1

TO UNDERSTAND the cultural life of the Japanese people
in all its different aspects, including their intensive love of Nature, which we have spoken of just now, it is essential, as I
have repeatedly stated, to delve into the secrets of Zen Buddhism.
Without some knowledge of these the Japanese character is difficult to appreciate. This does not, of course, mean that Zen is
everything in the molding of the character and general culture
of the Japanese people. What I mean is that, when Zen is
grasped, we can with some degree of ease get into the depths
of their spiritual life in all its varied expressions.

This fact is recognized, consciously or unconsciously, by
scholars and by men in the street. The former recognize it in
an analytical and critical manner worthy of their profession;
the latter appreciate it by actually living it, in the delight they
feel in listening to tales and traditions traceable somehow to the
teaching of Zen Buddhism.

That Zen has had a great deal to do in the building of Japanese
character and culture is pointed out also by foreign writers on
Japan, among whom we may mention the following.

The late Sir Charles Eliot, who most unfortunately passed
away without personally revising his valuable book, *Japanese
Buddhism,* writes (p. 396): "Zen has been a great power in the
artistic, intellectual, and even the political life of the Far East. To
a certain extent it has moulded the Japanese character, but it is

also the expression of that character. No other form of Buddhism is so thoroughly Japanese." The one significant point here is that Zen is the expression of the Japanese character. Historically, Zen started in China about fifteen hundred years ago, and it was not until the latter part of the Sung dynasty (961–1280), that is, in the earlier part of the thirteenth century, that Zen was brought to Japan. Thus the history of Zen in Japan is far younger than in China, but it was so adaptable to the character of the Japanese people, especially in its moral and aesthetic aspects, that it has penetrated far more deeply and widely into Japanese life than into Chinese. Hence we see that the statement made by the author of *Japanese Buddhism* is not at all an exaggeration.

Sir George Sansom, another capable English writer on Japan, makes the following observation on Zen in his *Japan, A Short Cultural History* (p. 336): "The influence of this school [i.e., Zen Buddhism] upon Japan has been so subtle and pervading that it has become the essence of her finest culture. To follow its ramifications in thought and sentiment, in art, letters and behaviour, would be to write exhaustively the most difficult and the most fascinating chapter of her spiritual history. . . ." While I may have occasion later to criticize this writer's view on the Japanese love of Nature, the point he makes here is accurate, and I am in full agreement with him.

What are the characteristic features of Zen as distinguished from the other forms of Buddhism? It will be necessary to know them before we proceed to see the relationship between Zen and the Japanese love of Nature. Naturally, it is outside our scope of study here to enter in detail into what really and essentially constitutes Zen. Much has already been done along this line, directly and indirectly, in the preceding sections. Therefore, let the following brief statements here suffice concerning the teaching and discipline of Zen, as regards its four aspects: religious, moral, aesthetic, and epistemological.

2

IN THE first place, let me state that Zen is not a mere ascetic discipline. When we see a monk living in a humble hut and sustaining himself on rice and pickles and potatoes, we may imagine him to be a world-fleeing recluse, whose principle of life is self-abnegation. True, there is a certain side in his life tending to this, as Zen teaches a form of detachment and self-control. But if we imagine there is nothing more in Zen, we entertain a very superficial view of it. The Zen insights go far deeper into the source of life, where Zen is truly religious. By this I mean Zen is in close touch with Reality; indeed, Zen takes hold of it and lives it, and this is where Zen is religious.

Those who are acquainted only with the Christian or some Indian Bhakti forms of religion may wonder where really in Zen is that which corresponds to their notion of God and their pious attitude toward him; Reality sounds to them too conceptual and philosophical and not devotional enough. In fact, Buddhism uses quite frequently more abstract-sounding terms than Reality, for instance, "suchness" or "thusness" (*tathatā*), "emptiness" or "void" (*śūnyatā*), "limit of reality" (*bhūtakoṭi*), etc. And this is sometimes what leads Christian critics and even Japanese scholars themselves to regard Zen as the teaching of a quietistic, meditative life. But with the followers of Zen these terms are not conceptual at all, but quite real and direct, vital and energizing—because Reality or Suchness or Emptiness is taken hold of in the midst of the concrete living facts of the universe, and not abstracted from them by means of thought.

Zen never leaves this world of facts. Zen always lives in the midst of realities. It is not for Zen to stand apart or keep itself away from a world of names and forms. If there is a God, personal or impersonal, he or it must be with Zen and in Zen. As long as an objective world, whether religiously or philosophically or poetically considered, remains a threatening and annihilating power, standing against us, there is no Zen here. For Zen makes "a humble blade of grass act as the Buddha-body sixteen feet high,[1] and, conversely, the Buddha-body sixteen feet high act as a humble blade of grass." Zen holds the whole universe, as it were, in its palm. This is the religion of Zen.

Zen is often thought to be a form of pantheism. Apparently it is, and Buddhists themselves sometimes ignorantly subscribe to this view. But if this is taken as truly characterizing the essence of Zen, it altogether misses the point; for Zen is most decidedly not pantheistic in the same measure as Christianity is not. Read this dialogue between Ummon (Yün-mên, d. 949) and his disciple.

Monk: "What is the Pure Body of the Dharma?"

Master: "The hedgerow."

Monk: "What is the behavior of the one who thus understands?"

Master: "He is a golden-haired lion." [2]

When God is the hedgerow dividing the monastery grounds from the neighboring farms, there is perhaps a faint suggestion of pantheism, we may say. But what about the golden-haired lion? The animal is not a manifestation of anything else, he is supreme, he is autonomous, he is king of the beasts, he is complete as he is. No idea is suggested here of the manifestation of anything in any form.

"The golden-haired lion," as it stands in Ummon's statement, may not be quite intelligible, even with this short explanatory comment, to those who are not used to the Zen way of expression. To help them I may quote another Zen *mondo:*

Monk: "I understand that when a lion seizes upon his opponent, whether it is a hare or an elephant, he makes an exhaustive use of his power. Pray tell me what this power is."

---

[1] The Buddha-body is traditionally regarded as gold-colored and sixteen feet in stature.

[2] *Hekigan-shū,* case 39.

Master: "The spirit of sincerity" (literally, the power of not-deceiving).[3]

"Sincerity," that is, "not-deceiving" or "putting forth one's whole being," is, according to Rinzai,[4] "the whole being in action" (zentai sayū), in which nothing is kept in reserve, nothing is expressed under disguise, nothing goes to waste. When a person lives like this, he is said to be a golden-haired lion; he is the symbol of virility, sincerity, whole-heartedness; he is divinely human; he is not a manifestation but Reality itself, for he has nothing behind him, he is "the whole truth," "the very thing."

This Zen way of understanding life and the world must be distinctly comprehended, as it is important when later the fact is demonstrated that there is nothing of symbolism in the Japanese love of nature.

If it is necessary to apply to Zen some form of classification, Zen may be pronounced a polytheism, although this "many" (polys) is to be taken as corresponding to the "sands of the Gaṅgā" (gaṅgānadīvālukā). Not a few thousands of gods, but hundreds of thousands of koṭis of gods. In Zen, each individual is an absolute entity, and as such he is related to all other individuals: this nexus of infinite interrelationships is made possible in the realm of Emptiness because they all find their being here even as they are, that is, as individual realities. This may be difficult to grasp for those who are not trained in the Buddhist way of thinking. But I have here no time to stop and explain the whole system from its beginning, and I must hurry on to the main subject.

In short, Zen has its own way of handling Reality, and this Zen way of handling Reality constitutes the inner meaning of the

---

[3] Dentōroku ("Transmission of the Lamp"), fasc. 27. The master's name is missing.

[4] Sayings of Rinzai Gigen. Rinzai Gigen (Lin-chi I-hsüan, d. 867) was one of the greatest Zen masters of the T'ang dynasty, and his analects known as the Rinzai-roku (Lin-chi Lu) are considered by some the supreme specimen of Zen literature.

Japanese love of Nature. For the Japanese love of Nature is not to be understood in the sense in which it is ordinarily understood. This will be made clearer as we proceed.

3

ZEN is ascetic when it plays the role of a moral discipline in the sense that it aims at simplicity in all its forms. It has something of the stoicism in which the samurai class of Japan has been reared. The simplicity and frugality of the Kamakura life under the Hōjō regime in the thirteenth century no doubt owes its initial motives to the influence of Zen. Furthermore, the moral courage and indomitable spirit of Hōjō Tokimune (1251–84), without whom the history of Japan would probably have taken quite a different course, were fostered by the teaching of Zen under the Chinese masters, who, by the invitation of the Hōjō government, found their shelter then in Japan. Tokiyori (1227–63), father of Tokimune, was also a great Zen devotee, and it was, indeed, under his direction that Tokimune visited the Zen monasteries, where he went through a moral and spiritual training, making himself thereby one of the greatest figures in the annals of Japan.

In Zen we find Chinese pragmatism solidly welded with Indian metaphysics and its high-soaring speculations. Without this perfect welding of the two highest forms of Oriental culture, it is very unlikely that Zen could have grown even in the congenial and, therefore, fruitful soil of Japan. And Zen came to Japan at the most opportune time in its history, because it was then that the old schools of Buddhism in Nara and Kyoto had proved ineffectual to usher in a new spiritual era. It was most fortunate for Zen that it found in the very beginning of its career in Japan such able disciples as Hōjō Tokiyori and Tokimune. So far, the meaning of the part the Hōjō family played in the cultural, political, and economic history of Japan has not been fully appreciated. This was chiefly due to those of militaristic bias, who tried to interpret history in their own crooked style. As Japanese scholars, however, begin to study it from a new point of view, which is now possible through the tragic experience of recent years, they will surely come to realize the significance of the Kamakura era, of which Yasutoki, Tokiyori, and Tokimune were the most remarkable representatives. And the significance of Zen in this period, as one of the most effective molding agencies of the Japanese character, will also be understood.

What is the most specific characteristic of Zen asceticism in connection with the Japanese love of Nature? It consists in paying Nature the fullest respect it deserves. By this it is meant that we may treat Nature not as an object to conquer and turn wantonly to our human service, but as a friend, as a fellow being, who is destined like ourselves for Buddhahood. Zen wants us to meet Nature as a friendly, well-meaning agent whose inner being is thoroughly like our own, always ready to work in accord with our legitimate aspirations. Nature is never our enemy standing always against us in a threatening attitude; it is not a power which will crush us if we do not crush it or bind it into our service.

Zen asceticism consists not necessarily in curbing or destroying our desires and instincts but in respecting Nature and not violating it, whether our own Nature or the Nature of the objective world. Self-mortification is not the proper attitude we may take toward ourselves, nor is selfish utilization the justifiable idea we may conceive toward Nature in any sense. Therefore, Zen asceticism is not at all in sympathy with the materialistic trends so much in evidence all over the world, in science, industrialism, commercialism, and many other movements of thought.

Zen purposes to respect Nature, to love Nature, to live its own life; Zen recognizes that our Nature is one with objective Nature, not in the mathematical sense, but in the sense that Nature lives in us and we in Nature. For this reason, Zen asceticism advocates simplicity, frugality, straightforwardness, virility, making no attempt to utilize Nature for selfish purposes.

Asceticism, some are afraid, lowers the standard of living. But, to speak candidly, the losing of the soul is more than the gaining of the world. Are we not constantly engaged in warlike preparations everywhere in order to raise or maintain our precious standard of living? If this state of affairs continues, there is no doubt of our finally destroying one another, not only individually but internationally. Instead of raising the so-called standard of living, will it not be far, far better to elevate the equality of living? This is a truism, but in no time of history has such a truism been more in need of being loudly declared than in these days of greed, jealousy, and iniquity. We followers of Zen ought to stand strongly for the asceticism it teaches.

4

THE AESTHETIC aspect of Zen teaching is closely related to Zen asceticism in that there is in both the absence of selfhood and the merging of subject and object in one absolute Emptiness (*śūnyatā*). This is a strange saying, but, as the basic teaching of Zen, it is reiterated everywhere in Zen literature. To explain this is a great philosophical task, full of intellectual pitfalls. Not only does it require arduous and sustained thinking, but frequently this very thinking is apt to lead to grave misconceptions of the true meaning of Zen experience. Therefore, as already hinted, Zen avoids abstract statements and conceptual reasoning; and its literature is almost nothing but endless citations of the so-called "anecdotes" or "incidents" (*innen* in Japanese) or "questions and answers" (known as *mondo*). To those who have not been initiated into its mystery, it is a wild and unapproachable territory of briars and brambles. The Zen masters, however, are not yielding; they insist on having their own way of expressing themselves; they think that in this respect they know best, and they are in the right because the nature of their experience is determinative as regards their method of communication or demonstration. If I cite the following *mondo* to illustrate Zen aestheticism, I hope you will not take me as purposely mystifying my position.

While Rikkō (Lu Kêng), a high government official of the T'ang dynasty, had a talk with his Zen master Nansen,[5] the official quoted a saying of Sōjō,[6] a noted monk-scholar of an earlier dynasty:

Heaven and earth and I are of the same root,
The ten-thousand things and I are of one substance

and continued, "Is not this a most remarkable statement?"

Nansen called the attention of the visitor to the flowering plant in the garden and said, "People of the world look at these flowers as if they were in a dream."

This "story" or *mondo* eloquently describes the aesthetic attitude of Zen toward objects of Nature. Most people do not really know how to look at the flower; for one thing they stand away from it; they never grasp the spirit of it; as they have no firm hold of it, they are as if dreaming of a flower. The one who beholds is separated from the object which is beheld; there is an impassable gap between the two; and it is impossible for the beholder to come in touch inwardly with his object. Here is no grasping of actual facts as we face them. If heaven and earth, with all the manifold objects between them, issue from the one root which you and I also come from, this root must be firmly seized upon so that there is an actual experience of it; for it is in this experience that Nansen's flower in its natural beauty appealed to his aesthetic sense. The so-called Japanese love of

[5] Nan-ch'üan (748–834). *Hekigan-shū*, case 40.

[6] Sêng-chao (384–414). Sêng-chao, one of the four principal disciples of Kumārajīva (who came from Kucha, Central Asia, to Ch'ang-an, China, in 401), wrote several essays on Buddhism. The quotation is from one of them. Its source is in the *Chuang-tzŭ*, II.

Nature becomes related to Zen when we come to this experience of Nature appreciation, which is Nature-living.

Here we must remember that the experience of mere oneness is not enough for the real appreciation of Nature. This no doubt gives a philosophical foundation to the sentimentalism of the Nature-loving Japanese, who are thus helped to enter deeply into the secrets of their own aesthetic consciousness. Sentimentalism to that extent is purified, one may say. But the feeling of love is possible in a world of multiplicity; Nansen's remark falls flat where there is only sameness. It is true that people of the world are dreaming, because they do not see into the real foundation of existence. The balancing of unity and multiplicity or, better, the merging of self with others as in the philosophy of the Avataṃsaka (Kegon) is absolutely necessary to the aesthetic understanding of Nature.

Tennyson says:

> *Little flower—but if I could understand*
> *What you are, root and all, and all in all,*
> *I should know what God and man is.*

The beauty of the little flower in the crannied wall is really appreciated only when it is referred to the ultimate reason of all things. But it goes without saying that this is not to be done in a merely philosophical and conceptual way, but in the way Zen proposes to accomplish it: not in a pantheistic way, nor in a quietistic way, but in the "living" way as has been done by Nansen and his followers. To do this and to appreciate Nansen truly, one must first greet Rikkō and be friendly with him; for it is in this way that one can feel the force of the remark made by Nansen. The genuine beauty of the flower as he saw it is for the first time reflected in one's soul-mirror.

The aesthetic appreciation of Nature always involves something religious. And by being "religious" I mean being "super-worldly," going beyond the world of relativity, where we are bound to encounter oppositions and limitations. The oppositions and limitations which confront every movement of ours, physical and psychological, put a stop, also, to the free flow of our aesthetical feeling toward its objects. Beauty is felt when there is freedom of motion and freedom of expression. Beauty is not in form but in the meaning it expresses, and this meaning is felt when the observing subject throws his whole being into the bearer of the meaning and moves along with it. This is possible only when he lives in a "superworld" where no mutually excluding oppositions take place, or rather when the mutually excluding oppositions of which we are always too conscious in this world of multiplicities are taken up even as they are into something of a higher order than they. Aestheticism now merges into religion.

Sir George Sansom makes this comment concerning the Zen love of Nature (*Japan, A Short Cultural History*, p. 392): "But the Zen artists and the Zen poets—and it is often hard to say where their poetry ends and their painting begins—feel no antithesis between man and Nature, and are conscious even of an identity rather than a kinship. What interests them is not the restless movement on the surface of life, but (as Professor Anezaki puts it) the eternal tranquillity seen through and behind change." This is not Zen at all. Both Professor Anezaki and Sir George Sansom fail to grasp the true Zen attitude toward Nature. It is not an experience of identification, nor is it the feeling of "eternal tranquillity" they dream of. If the poets and the artists linger with that which is felt "through and behind change," they are still walking hand in hand with Rikkō and Sōjō, they are far, far from being friends of Nansen. The real flower is enjoyed only when the poet-artist lives with it, in it; and when even a sense of identity is no longer here, much less the "eternal tranquillity."

Thus I wish to emphasize that Zen does not see any such thing as is designated "the restless movement on the surface of life." For life is one integral and indivisible whole, with neither surface nor interior; hence no "restless movement" which can be separated from life itself. As was explained in the case of Um-mon's "golden-haired lion," life moves in its complete oneness, whether restlessly or serenely, as you may conceive it; your interpretation does not alter the fact. Zen takes hold of life in its wholeness and moves "restlessly" with it or stays quietly with it. Wherever there is any sign of life at all, there is Zen. When, however, the "eternal tranquillity" is abstracted from "the restless movement on the surface of life," it sinks into death, and there is no more of its "surface" either. The tran-quillity of Zen is in the midst of "the boiling oil," the surging waves, and in the flames enveloping the god Acala.

Kanzan (Han-shan) was one of the most famous poet-lunatics of the T'ang dynasty—Zen often produces such "lunatics"—and one of his poems reads:

> *My mind is like the autumnal moon;*
> *And how clear and transparent the deep pool!*
> *No comparison, however, in any form is possible,*
> *It is altogether beyond description.*

Superficially, this poem may suggest the idea of tranquillity or serenity. The autumnal moon is serene, and its light uniformly pervading the fields and rivers and mountains may make us think of the oneness of things. But this is where Kanzan hesi-tates to draw any comparison between his feelings and things of this world. The reason is sure to take the pointing finger for the moon, as our worthy critics frequently do. To tell the truth, there is here not the remotest hint of tranquillity or serenity, nor of the identity of Nature and man. If anything is suggested here, it is the idea of utmost transparency which the poet feels through and through. He is entirely lifted out of his bodily existence, in-cluding both his objective world and his subjective mind. He has no such interfering mediums inside and outside. He is thoroughly pure, and from this position of absolute purity or transparency he looks out on a world of multiplicity so called. He sees flowers and mountains and ten thousand other things, and will pronounce them beautiful and satisfying. "The restless movements" are appreciated just as much as "the eternal tranquillity." It goes entirely against the spirit of Zen and the Japanese idea of love of Nature to imagine that the Japanese Zen poets and artists avoid the restlessness of a world of multiplicity in order to get into the eternal tranquillity of abstract ideas. Let us first get an experience of transparency, and we are able to love Nature and its multifarious objects, though not dualistically. As long as we harbor conceptual illusions arising from the separation of subject and object and believe them final, the transparency is obscured, and our love of Nature is contaminated with dualism and sophistry.

To quote another poet of Zen, this time a Japanese and the founder of a great Zen monastery called Eigenji in the province of Ōmi—his name is Jakushitsu (1290–1367):

The wind stirs the flying waterfall and sends in refreshing music;
The moon is risen over the opposite peak and the bamboo shadows are cast over my paper window:
As I grow older, the mountain retreat appeals all the more strongly to my feeling;
Even when I am buried, after death, underneath the rock, my bones will be as thoroughly transparent as ever.

Some readers may be tempted to read into this poem a sense of solitude or quietness, but that this altogether misses the point is apparent to those who know at all what Zen is. Unless the Zen artist is saturated with the feeling Jakushitsu graphically expresses here, he cannot expect to understand Nature, nor can he truly love Nature. Transparency is the keynote to the Zen understanding of Nature, and it is from this that its love of Nature starts. When people say that Zen has given a philosophical and religious foundation to the Japanese love of Nature, this Zen attitude or feeling must be taken fully into consideration. When Sir George Sansom surmises that "they [aristocrats, monks, and artists] were moved by a belief that all nature is permeated by one spirit," and that "it was the aim of the Zen practitioner in particular, by purging his mind of egotistic commotions, to reach a tranquil, intuitive realization of his identity with the universe" (p. 392), he ignores the part Zen has really contributed to the Japanese aesthetic appreciation of Nature. He cannot shake off the idea of "eternal tranquillity" or of a spiritual identity between subject and object.

The idea of "spiritual identity" by which our egotistic commotions are kept quiet and in which eternal tranquillity is experienced is an alluring idea. Most students of Oriental culture and philosophy grasp at it as giving them the key to the inscrutable psychology of the Eastern peoples. But this is the Western mind trying to solve the mystery in its own way—in fact, it cannot do anything else. As far as we Japanese are concerned, we are unable to accept without comment this interpretation offered by the Western critics. Plainly speaking, Zen does not acknowledge "one spirit" permeating all Nature, nor does it attempt to realize identity by purging its mind of "egotistic commotions." According to the author of this statement, the grasping of "one spirit" is evidently the realization of identity that is left behind when the purgation of egotism is effected. While it is difficult to refute this idea convincingly as long as we are arguing along the logical line of Yes and No, I will try to make my point clearer in the following paragraphs.

5

IT IS NOW necessary to say something about Zen epistemology. The term may sound too philosophical, but my object here is to make some plain statements about the facts of Zen intuition. What Zen is most anxious to do in its own characterization is to reject conceptual mediumship of any kind. Any medium that is set up before Zen in its attempt to understand the facts of experience is sure to obscure the nature of the latter. Instead of clarifying or simplifying the situation, the presence of a third party always ends in creating complexities and obscurations. Zen therefore abhors mediums. It advises its followers to have direct dealings with their objects, whatever they may be. We often speak of identification in our Zen discipline, but this word is not exact. Identification presupposes original opposition of two terms, subject and object, but the truth is that from the very first there are no two opposing terms whose identification is to be achieved by Zen. It is better to say that there has never been any separation between subject and object, and that all the discrimination and separation we have or, rather, make is a later creation, though the concept of time is not to be interposed here. The aim of Zen is thus to restore the experience of original inseparability, which means, in other words, to return to the original state of purity and transparency. This is the reason conceptual discrimination is discredited in Zen. Followers of identity and tranquillity are to be given the warning: they are ridden by concepts; let them rise to facts and live in and with them.

Chōsha,[7] of the T'ang dynasty, one day came back from a walk in the mountains. When he reached the monastery gate, the head monk asked, "Where have you been all this time, Reverend Sir?"

Replied the master, "I am just back from my mountain walk."

The monk pursued, "Where in the mountains?"

"I first went out in the field scented with grasses and then walked home watching the flowers fall."

Is there any expression here suggestive of "tranquillity that is behind and through change"? or of identity that is perceptible between Chōsha and the grasses and flowers among which he walked up and down?

Chōsha one evening was enjoying the moonlight with his friend

---

[7] That is, Chōsha Keishin (Chang-sha Ching-ts'ên), a disciple of Nansen. The story is from the *Hekigan-shū,* case 36.

Kyōzan.[8] Kyōzan, pointing at the moon, said, "Each person with-out exception has this, only that he fails to use it." (Is this a suggestion of "one spirit" or of "tranquillity"?)

Chōsha said, "Just as you say; and may I ask you to use it?" (As long as "identity" or "tranquillity" blinds your eyesight, how can you "use" it?)

Kyōzan: "Let me see how you use it." (Did he then enter into Nirvāṇa eternally serene?)

Chōsha then kicked his brother-monk down to the ground. Kyōzan, quietly rising, remarked, "O brother-monk, you are in-deed like a tiger." (When this tiger, like the golden-haired lion, roars, one ghostly "spirit" so valued by the critics vanishes, and "tranquillity" is no more.)

A strange yet lively scene enacted by the Zen poets, who were supposed to be enjoying the serenity of a moonlit eve, makes us pause and think about the significance of Zen in regard to its relation to the Japanese love of Nature. What is really here that stirs up the two apparently meditative and nature-loving monks?

The epistemology of Zen is, therefore, not to resort to the mediumship of concepts. If you want to understand Zen, under-stand it right away without deliberation, without turning your head this way or that. For while you are doing this, the object you have been seeking for is no longer there. This doctrine of immediate grasping is characteristic of Zen. If the Greeks taught us how to reason and Christianity what to believe, it is Zen that teaches us to go beyond logic and not to tarry even when we come up against "the things which are not seen." For the Zen point of view is to find an absolute point where no dualism in whatever form obtains. Logic starts from the division of subject and ob-ject, and belief distinguishes between what is seen and what is not seen. The Western mode of thinking can never do away with this eternal dilemma, this or that, reason or faith, man or God,

---

[8] Kyōzan Ejaku (Yang-shan Hui-chi, 814–90) was a disciple of Isan Reiyū (Kuei-shan Ling-yu, 770–853). Ibid., Yengo's notes.

etc. With Zen all these are swept aside as something veiling our insight into the nature of life and reality. Zen leads us into a realm of Emptiness or Void where no conceptualism prevails, where rootless trees grow and a most refreshing breeze sweeps over all the ground.

From this short characterization of Zen we can see what Zen's attitude toward Nature is. It is not a sense of identity nor of tranquillity that Zen sees and loves in Nature. Nature is always in motion, never at a standstill; if Nature is to be loved, it must be caught while moving and in this way its aesthetic value must be appraised. To seek tranquillity is to kill nature, to stop its pulsation, and to embrace the dead corpse that is left behind. Advocates of tranquillity are worshipers of abstraction and death. There is nothing in this to love. Identity is also a static condition and decidedly associated with death. When we are dead, we return to the dust where we started, we are then identified with the earth. Identification is not the thing to covet highly. Let us destroy all such artificial barriers we put up between Nature and ourselves, for it is only when they are removed that we see into the living heart of Nature and live with it—which is the real meaning of love. For this, therefore, the clearing away of all conceptual scaffolds is imperative. When Zen speaks of transparency, it means this clearing away, this thorough wiping of the surface of the mind-mirror. But, in point of fact, the mirror has never been obscured, and no need has ever been felt for wiping it clean; but because of such notions as identity, tranquillity, one spirit, egotistic commotions, and so on, we are compelled to set up a general sweeping operation.

After these interpretations, some may declare Zen to be a form of Nature mysticism, a philosophical intuitionism, and a religion advocating stoical simplicity and austerity. However this is, Zen gives us a most comprehensive outlook on the world, because the realm of Zen extends to the very limits of thousands of *koṭis* of chiliacosms, and even beyond them all. Zen has a most penetrating insight into Reality, because it sounds the very depths of all existence. Zen knows a most thoroughgoing way of appreciating the genuinely beautiful, because it lives in the body of the beautiful itself, known as the golden-colored Buddha-body with the thirty-two major and eighty minor marks of super-humanity. With these as the background, the Japanese love of Nature unfolds itself as it comes in contact with its objects.

III

1

THE LOVE of Nature the Japanese people originally had was no doubt their innate aesthetic sense for things beautiful; but the appreciation of the beautiful is at bottom religious, for without being religious one cannot detect and enjoy what is genuinely beautiful. And there is no denying that Zen gave an immense impetus to the native feeling for Nature, not only by sharpening it to the highest degree of sensitiveness but also by giving it a metaphysical and religious background. In the beginning, probably, the Japanese were naïvely attracted to the beautiful which they saw about them; it is possible that they regarded all things in Nature as uniformly animated with life, after the manner of primitive people who look upon even nonsentient things from their animistic point of view. But as they cultivated themselves in the Zen teaching, their aesthetic and religious sensitiveness was further nourished. And this nourishment came in the form of an exalted moral discipline and a highly spiritual intuition.

That is to say, the snow-crowned peak of Fuji is now seen as rising from the background of Emptiness; the pine trees ornamenting the monastery grounds are ever fresh and green because they are "rootless" and "shadowless"; the rain drops pattering on the roof of my humble hut transmit the echo of the ancient days when Kyōshō and Secchō, Saigyō and Dōgen made their comments on the sound. The moonlight that "leaked" into the empty room of Kanzan and of the old couple in the Ugetsu house will also this evening visit your hotel with all its modern conveniences. You may say, the universe remains ever the same with Zen or without Zen. But my solemn proclamation is that a new universe is created every moment Zen looks out from its straw-thatched four-and-a-half-mat retreat. This may sound too mystical, but without a full appreciation of it not a page of the history of Japanese poetry, Japanese arts, and Japanese handicrafts would have been written. Not only the history of the arts, but the history of the Japanese moral and spiritual life would lose its deeper significance, if detached from the Zen way of interpreting life and the world. Otherwise, it would have been perhaps impossible for the Japanese people to stand against the unprecedented onslaught of modern science, machines, and commercial industrialism.

Let me illustrate the spirit of Zen as lived by Ryōkwan (1758–1831), a Buddhist monk who passed his unpretentious life in the province of Echigo early in the nineteenth century. His having been a monk does not weaken, as one may suppose, the strength of my statement that Zen has deeply entered into the life of the Japanese people; for all those who came to associate with him, that is, the entire community in which he moved, approved of his life and saw in it something of permanent worth. To judge the direction of the wind it is enough to look at a single blade of grass. When we know one Ryōkwan, we know hundreds of thousands of Ryōkwans in Japanese hearts.

2

RYŌKWAN was a Zen monk belonging to the Sōtō school.[1] His hut was built in the northern part of the country facing the Sea of Japan. From the ordinary worldly point of view he was a "big fool" and a lunatic; he lacked what is known as common sense, of which we people of the world have too much. But he was very

[1] Founded by Dōgen in the Kamakura era (1185–1338).

much liked and respected by his neighbors, and quarrels and other annoying incidents which sometimes darken our daily life cleared off if he happened to appear in the midst of them. He was an accomplished poet in Chinese and Japanese and also a great calligrapher. Villagers and townspeople pursued him for his autograph, which he found very hard to refuse, for they devised many contrivances to get from him what they wanted.

I said he was a lunatic and "a great fool"—this latter being his own literary name. But he had a most sensitive heart for all things human and natural. Indeed he was love incarnate—a manifestation of Kwannon Bosatsu.[2] His solitary retreat on a mountain away from the village was once (or twice?) broken into by a burglar. The burglar must have been a complete stranger to the neighborhood, otherwise he would never have singled out this poor man's shelter to plunder. Naturally, there was nothing to carry away. He was greatly disappointed. Seeing this, Ryōkwan's heart was touched, and he gave him the clothes he had on. The burglar hastily left him with the outside *amado* open, from which a bright moon poured its light into Ryōkwan's room. The poet in him asserted itself:

> *A burglar failing to carry off the moon,*
> *It shines in from the window!*

Another poem by him reads:

> *Where, I wonder, is he passing the night,*
> *This cold freezing night,*
> *When it is even beginning to storm—*
> *A lonely wayfarer in a world of darkness?*

This is also said to have been composed by the recluse and lover of humanity after another unwelcome visit by a stranger. The visited one himself must also have suffered the freezing night in the lonely hut. Sure enough, he came the following

[2] The Bodhisattva Avalokiteśvara.

morning to his parental home with a flowing nose and shivering with cold, to ask for bedding.

He was also good to beggars. On his way home from his own begging tour, he was ready to give up everything he had to any unfortunate fellow being he might happen to meet. The following must have been composed on one of those occasions:

> *If my robe dyed black*
> *Were wide and broad enough,*
> *I would cover all the poor people of the world*
> *Under my sleeves.*

He had very few desires as far as he was concerned. When one of the feudal lords in the neighboring districts once visited his hut in order to take him along to his own town, and perhaps build a temple for his shelter and religious practices, this beggar-poet remained silent for a while. When politely pressed for an answer, he wrote this:

> *As much fuel as I need,*
> *Is supplied by the wind—*
> *These fallen leaves I gather!*

So blessed in poverty, the Zen poet was a great troubadour of poverty. His poems, especially in Chinese, are full of these sentiments. He must have been an ardent admirer of Kanzan (Han-shan), of the T'ang dynasty, for his poems remind us at once of the highly spiritual atmosphere in which Kanzan moved. Here is one singing of poverty:

> *In tatters, in tatters,*
> *Again in tatters—this my life:*
> *For food I pick herbs by the roadside;*
> *In the moonlight I sit meditating all night long;*
> *Looking at the flowers I forget to return home—*
> *This primitive life I have come to adopt*
> *Ever since my association with the Buddhist Brother-*
> *   hood.*

3

WHAT lessons did he learn of the Buddhist Brotherhood? Some
of them are here:

The past is already past,
The future is not yet here,
The present never abides;
Things are constantly changing, with nothing on which to
depend;
So many names and words confusingly self-created—
What is the use of wasting your life thus idly all day?
Do not retain your timeworn views,
Nor pursue your newly-fashioned imaginations:
Sincerely and wholeheartedly make inquiries and also re-
flect within yourself;
Inquiring and reflecting, reflecting and inquiring,
Until the moment comes when no further inquiries are pos-
sible;
For this is the time when you will realize that all your past
has been in the wrong.

This shows how assiduously Ryōkwan had employed himself in
the study of Buddhism, before he came to lead his "primitive
life" in an eternal stream of Karma.

Whence is my life?
Whither does it depart?
I sit alone in my hut,
And meditate quietly yet earnestly;
With all my thinking I know no whence,
Nor do I come to any whither:
So is it with my present,
Eternally changing—all in Emptiness!
In this Emptiness is the Ego for a while,
With its Yeas and Nays;

I know not just where to set them up,
I follow my Karma as it moves, with perfect
contentment.

What is the practical outcome of this philosophy of "not knowing anything" and of leaving Karma, whatever this may be, to its own working? In short, what is Ryōkwan's life of absolute passivity or dependence or emptiness? His grass hut was a most unpretentious one, indeed, just large enough for himself. Hence "Gogō," which means half a *shō* (less than one quart) of rice—an amount considered enough for one full-grown man for a day's support.

This solitary hut named "Gogō-an"
Resembles a hanging bell in shape;
It stands surrounded by the cedars growing thick,
While a few poems decorate the inside walls;
The cooking-pot is sometimes found covered with dust,
And smoke often fails to issue from the hearth;
The lonely visitor is an old man of the Eastern Village,
Who occasionally knocks at the door when the moon is
bright.

One autumnal eve I was wakeful,
Took a staff, and went out of doors;
The crickets were singing under the ancient tiles,
The dead leaves were fast falling off the shivering trees;
Far away the stream was heard murmuring,
The moon was slow to rise above the high peak:
All conspired to draw me on to a deep meditation,
And it was some time before I found my robe heavily wet
with dew.

4

THIS apostle of poverty and solitude—or would it be better to call him a grand Nature-mystic?—had a very warm heart for

B. Artist unknown. The Buddha entering into Nirvāṇa. Early 18th century

Nature and all objects of Nature, plants and animals. As he makes allusions in his poems to a bamboo grove surrounding his hut, many bamboo shoots must have been growing there. He liked them very much, I suppose, for food, but chiefly for their growing straight, for their being freshly green all the year round. Their roots are firmly set in the ground, while the trunk is hollow, symbolizing Emptiness. Ryōkwan liked this character in the bamboo. Once, it is said, a young growing shoot began to break through the floor of his closet. He took interest in it. At last, seeing it grow too tall for the enclosure, he started to remove the roof for it. He tried to burn the roof with a candle. Did he think it the easiest way to accomplish the work? Perhaps he had no such design in his mind, he simply wanted to give room to the young plant, and seeing the candle most available at the time he began the work. But unfortunately the roof caught fire more extensively than was first intended, and the whole structure, together with the bamboo itself, I believe, was burned down. The height of stupidity, indeed, this burning of a roof for the sake of a bamboo shoot—I mean from our practical point of view. But I feel like condoning or, rather, admiring his stupidity. There is something so genuine, or, shall I say, so divine in his feeling for the bamboo shoot. There is something like this in every genuine act of love. We as human beings, so given up to all kinds of practical and sordid considerations, are unable to follow every pure impulse of kindly feeling. How often do we deliberately suppress or repress the impulse? In us the impulse may not always be so thoroughly undefiled as in our poet-lunatic, and this may be our conscious reason for repression or suppression. If so, our life ought to be purged of all impurities before we criticize Ryōkwan.

Ryōkwan's love for pine trees appears in his poems. He does not seem to have been much of a talker or writer; everything that went through his sensitive mind was caught up in his poems, which took various forms according to his mood at the time, either in Chinese, or in classical Japanese of thirty-one syllables, or in the shorter form of seventeen syllables, or in the style of folk song, or in the *Mannyō* style of many syllables. He was quite an expert in all these compositions, but not conventionally bound by literary rules, which he frequently ignored. The other favorite form in which he gave expression to his inner life was calligraphy.[3] In our case, his literary products will better lead us into his inward sentiments. He sings of a solitary old pine tree at Kugami:

> *At Kugami,*
> *In front of the Otono,*
> *There stands a solitary pine tree,*
> *Surely of many a generation;*
> *How divinely dignified*
> *It stands there!*
> *In the morning*
> *I pass by it;*
> *In the evening*
> *I stand underneath it,*
> *And standing I gaze,*
> *Never tired*
> *Of this solitary pine!*

There must have been something intensely fascinating about this ancient tree. In fact, every old tree of any sort inspires a beholder with a mystic feeling which leads him to a faraway world of timeless eternity.

There was another pine tree at Iwamuro which deeply stirred his feeling of pity. The tree must have been a young one, with no stately outstretching branches. It was raining hard, and Ryōkwan saw it all drenched:

> *At Iwamuro,*
> *In the middle of the field*
> *A solitary pine stands;*
> *How I pity this solitary pine,*

[3] One example is given in plate 62.

Standing all alone
Thoroughly drenched in showers;
If it were a human being,
I would give him a raincoat,
I would help him with a rainhat:
Pitiful, indeed, this solitary tree!

Japan is the country of pine trees and cedars. The latter are seen to their best advantage in a group or in a row, and the former are fine when they stand singly. The Japanese species of the pine known as *matsu* generally spreads its branches irregularly and the trunk is gnarled. A solitary old pine tree growing for ever so many years in front of your room is such a consoling friend for the scholar or monk. Ryōkwan's attitude toward the tree in the field drenched in rain was naturally that of pity, but with Saigyō the tree stood in a different environment, and the man was of a different type of character, at least in a different mood of spirit at the time. Hence the following poems of Saigyō:

For a long time to come,
Stand here as thriving as ever,
And remember our companion days,
Even after my death, O Pine!
For I am the one who lives in the world
Unknown, unloved.

Tired of staying here
If I start my wandering again,
O Pine, would you not be solitary?

5

RYŌKWAN, the lover of trees, was also a great friend of the louse, perhaps also of the flea, of the mosquito, and so on. He had a tender human feeling for all beings. One interesting, though not quite engaging, incident recorded of him is his care for the louse. The story is illustrative of his general attitude toward other forms of life. He was often seen, during the early warm winter days, giving the lice a sun bath and exercise in the air. By taking them out one by one from his underwear onto sheets of paper, he exposed them in the sun. Before it begins to be too cool in the afternoon, they will be picked up and taken back into his own *fudokoro*, as he says:

> *O lice, lice,*
> *If you were the insects*
> *Singing in the autumn fields,*
> *My chest (fudokoro) would really be*
> *For you the Musashino prairie.*

The subject may not be very edifying, I am afraid, but his genuine, unadulterated love for such creatures has in it something tender and touching. Our modern idea of hygienic cleanliness has much to say about harboring beings of this class, but it was not very long ago, I am told, that in England gentlemen and ladies of the higher classes were not exempt from vermin, that the wearing of wigs over their heads was indeed partly due to their annoying presence, and that even these wigs were often full of nits. One scientist notes that "even long into the eighteenth century, lice were regarded as necessities." [4] Further, he notes that George Washington in his fourteenth year copied a paragraph on "Rules of Civility" which contains the following remarkable statements: "Kill no vermin, as Fleas, lice, tics, etc. in

[4] Dr. Hans Zinsser, "History of the Louse," in the *Atlantic Monthly,* January, 1935.

the sight of others, if you See any filth or thick Spittle, put your foot Dexterously upon it: if it be upon the Cloths of your Companions, put it off privately, and if it be upon your own Cloths, return thanks to him who puts it off." [5]

Ryōkwan was a great lover of children, as might be expected of such a character as he who was himself a child. He liked to play with them, he played hide-and-seek, he played *temari* ("handball"), too. One evening it was his turn to hide, and he hid himself well under a strawstack in the field. It was growing darker and the children not being able to locate him left the field. Early in the following morning a farmer came and had to remove the strawstack to begin his work. Finding Ryōkwan there, he exclaimed, "O Ryōkwan sama, what are you doing here?" The poet-lunatic answered, "Hush! don't talk so loud! The children will find me." Did he wait for the children all night under the straw? Did it never occur to him that the young ones were just as deceiving and untrustworthy as the grownups? But to reason like this is our human way in this world of unrealities; he perhaps followed another order of reasoning, that of burning the roof to save the bamboo shoot. It was his simplicity that made him spend the whole night in the open field with the controlling idea of hiding from his young, guileless, but occasionally mischievous, friends. The story being somewhat extreme, its genuineness may be suspected, but the fact that it has been in circulation conclusively proves his readiness at any moment to follow this pattern of action.

These days we live under such varied rules of convention. We are really slaves to ideas and notions, fashions and traditions, which constitute the psychological background or what is now popularly called the ideology of modern people in the organization. We can never act as Whitman advises. We are in a state of complete slavery, although we may not realize it or, rather, are not willing to admit it. When we see Ryōkwan giving himself up to the free movement of his feelings, which are

[5] Ibid.

thoroughly purged, to follow the conventional parlance of all egotistically oriented defilements, we feel as refreshed as if we were transported into another world. In his love of children we recognize the same psychological trait of independence and spontaneity that was exhibited in his feeling for a solitary pine tree and a bamboo shoot breaking through the floor. His love of playing *temari* and *otedama* with children is also indicative of his free playful spirit, which we all have but are constrained from indulging in, imagining that such playing is below the dignity of grownups.

While playing *temari* and *otedama*,[6] winnings are reckoned by singing a popular ditty. The bouncing of the *temari*, the turning of hands, and the rhythmic chant of voices—however simple, they perhaps help to give expression to Ryōkwan's simple and undeceiving spirit. This is of a piece with his liking to dance a primitive village dance on festival occasions. He was once found dancing with the villagers, disguised as a young woman. One of the dancers nearby, recognizing Ryōkwan, made a remark about his or rather her being a good dancer, purposely audible enough for Ryōkwan to overhear it. It is said that Ryōkwan later mentioned it to his friends with a feeling of elation.

6

THERE IS in every one of us a desire to return to a simpler form of living, which includes simpler ways of expressing feelings and also of acquiring knowledge. The so-called "way of the gods" points to it. Although I do not know exactly what signification the advocates of *Kaminagara no michi* want to give to this term, it seems to be certain to my mind that by this they wish to mean going back to or retaining or reviving the way in which the gods are supposed to have lived before the arrival

---

[6] These games were formerly played mostly by little girls.

of humankind. This way was one of freedom, naturalness, and spontaneity. How did we go astray from this? Here lies a great fundamental religious problem. Its solution gives the key to understanding some aspects of Zen Buddhism and of the Japanese love of Nature. When we speak of being natural, we mean first of all being free and spontaneous in the expression of our feelings, being immediate and not premeditating in our response to environment, not making any calculation as to the effect of our doings either on others or on ourselves, and conducting ourselves in such a way as not to leave room for thought of gain, value, merit, or consequence. To be natural means, therefore, to be like a child, though not necessarily with a child's intellectual simplicity or its emotional crudity. In a sense, the child is a bundle of egotistic impulses, but in its assertion of these it is altogether "natural," it has no scrupulousness, no deliberation as regards practical and worldly merit or demerit. In this respect the child is angelic, even divine. It ignores all the social devices that keep grownups decent and conventional and law-abiding. It is living under no such artificial, human-made constraints. The practical outcome of such behavior may not always be acceptable to the taste of so-called cultivated, refined, sophisticated people of the world. But the question here is not one of such practical considerations but of the genuineness of motive, the disinterestedness of feeling, and the immediateness of response. When there is thus no crookedness in one's heart, we say that one is natural and childlike. In this there is something highly religious, and angels are represented sometimes as babies with wings. And this is the reason why the Zen artists have a special liking for painting Kanzan and Jittoku, or Hotei with a group of children.

Going back to Nature, therefore, does not mean going back to the natural life of primitive and prehistoric peoples. It means a life of freedom and emancipation. The one thing that hampers and complicates our modern life, especially, is the concept of teleology, which we are all made to feel in every phase of our life. The concept is all right as far as our moral, economic, intellectual, and terrestrial existence is concerned, but this existence of ours means far more than all these considerations; for we never feel completely satisfied with them, we seek for something going really far deeper than the merely moral and intellectual. As long as we are on the plane of the teleological conception of existence, we are in no way free. And not being free is the cause of all the worries, all the miseries, all the conflicts, that are going on in this world.

To be thus free from all conditioning rules or concepts is the essence of the religious life. When we are conscious of any purpose whatever in our movements, we are not free. To be free means purposelessness, which of course does not mean licentiousness. The idea of a purpose is something the human intellect reads into certain forms of movement. When teleology enters into our life, we cease to be religious, we become moral beings. So with art. When purpose is too much in evidence in a work of art, so called, art is no longer there, it becomes a machine or an advertisement. Beauty runs away, ugly human hands become altogether too visible. Suchness in art consists in its artlessness, that is, purposelessness. In this, art approaches religion; and Nature is a perfect specimen of art inasmuch as there is no visible purpose in the waves rolling on from the beginningless past in the Pacific Ocean, and in Mount Fuji covered with ancient snow, standing absolutely pure high against the sky. In the flower we, as beings obsessed with utilitarian ideas, may read its going to seed, and in seeds the harboring of a life for the coming years; but from the religious aesthetical angle of observation, flowers as flowers are red or yellow, and leaves as leaves are green, and in this all utilitarian and teleological or biological conceptions are excluded.

We admire a machine most exquisitely and most delicately balanced and most efficiently working, but we have no feeling of going toward it; it is a thing altogether distinct from us, which stands here ready to obey our commands. Not only that, we know every part of it mechanically and the purpose for which it is set to work; there is no mystery, as it were, in the whole construction of it; there are no secrets, there is no autonomous creativeness here; everything is thoroughly explainable, subject to laws discovered by physics or dynamics or chemistry or some other science. Yet an ink sketch composed of a few strokes of the artist's brush—apparently very crudely executed—awakens in us the deepest of feelings and engages the attention of our whole being. In the same way, when we face nature, our whole being goes into it and feels every pulsation of it as if it were our own. To speak of an identification is a desecration, for it is a mechanical and logical conception, which does not apply to this phase of our life. And this is where Zen Buddhism has its realm, it is the corner from which people like Ryōkwan survey the world.

[64

7

I CANNOT help making reference in this connection to the Nirvāṇa picture of the Buddha. This may not seem to be a fit subject to be introduced here. What has the Nirvāṇa picture to do with the Japanese love of Nature or with Zen Buddhism, one may argue? But what I wish to see in the picture, as it is generally painted in Japan, has some significant bearing on the Buddhist attitude toward Nature. And as the picture has much to do with the Zen monasteries in Japan, and further as the picture has an unusual fascination for the Japanese generally, I will point out here one or two facts regarding the Nirvāṇa scene of the Buddha.

[B

I have not yet been able to trace the historical development of the Nirvāṇa conception as we have it today. As tradition ascribes the first idea or rather the first authorship of the picture to Wu Tao-tzŭ, the well-reputed painter of the T'ang era, it is likely that it originated first in China. But I have at present no means of ascertaining how far and how strongly it has taken hold of the imagination of the Chinese people. It is certainly in Japan that it has entered deeply into the religious consciousness of the people. The picture has come to be intimately connected with the Buddhist life of Japan, especially with Zen. There must be something in it which appeals powerfully to us all.

The one prominent feature of the Nirvāṇa picture is, naturally, the central figure and his quiet passing away, surrounded by his disciples. Contrast this with the crucifixion of Christ, with blood oozing from the head and the side. He is stretched upright against the cross, with an expression of the utmost pain and suffering, whereas the Buddha looks as if contentedly asleep on the couch, with no signs of distress. The vertical Christ represents an intense spirit of fight, but the horizontal Buddha is peaceful. When we look at the latter, everything that goes against the spirit of contentment is excluded from our consciousness.

The Buddha lies contented, not only with himself but with all the world and with all its beings animate and inanimate. Look at those animals, those gods, and those trees that are weeping over his parting. To my mind this is a scene pregnant with meaning of the utmost significance. Is it not a strong demonstration of the fact that the Buddhists are not at war with Nature, but that they and Nature are one in living the life of the Dharma?

This idea and the real feeling of living one and the same life in the Dharma makes the Buddhists feel at once at home with surrounding Nature. When they listen to the crying of a mountain bird they recognize the voice of their parents; when they see the lotus flowers in the pond, they discover in them the untold glory and magnificence of the Buddha-Kṣetra, or Buddha-realm. Even when they encounter an enemy and take his life for the sake of a greater cause, they pray for him so as to have their own merit turn toward his future salvation.

This is, further, the reason why they have the so-called soul-consoling rite performed for the morning-glories which are weeded out to give room to the better-qualified kind, or for all kinds of poor animals who are killed for various reasons to help humanity, or for the painters' worn-out brushes which served them in so many useful ways to produce their master-pieces in varied styles. The love of Nature of the Japanese is thus seen to be deeply colored with their religious insight and feeling. The Nirvāṇa picture in this respect is illuminating, as it sheds much light on the Japanese psychology.

It was due, I am told, to the genius of the Sung Zen monk-artists that the Buddha or Bodhisattvas came to be painted [C along with the animals and plants. Until then, the Buddha and Bodhisattvas were represented as beings transcending the reach of human feelings; they were supernatural beings, as it were. But when Zen came to control the religious consciousness of the Chinese and the Japanese people, it took away from Buddhist figures that aloof, unconcerned, rather unapproachable air which had hitherto characterized them. They came down from the transcendental pedestal to mingle with us common beings and with common animals and plants, rocks and mountains. When they talked, stones nodded their heads, and plants pricked up their ears. That is the reason why the Buddha's Nirvāṇa is so intimately shared by all forms of being as we observe in the picture.

The famous Nirvāṇa picture of the Tōfukuji Zen monastery, at Kyoto, was painted by one of its monks, Chō Densu (1352–1431), one of the greatest painters of Japan. It is one of the largest hanging pictures of this class in Japan, measuring about 39 by 26 feet. It is said that, at the time of a civil war which devastated the greater part of Kyoto early in the sixteenth century, the army of the Hosokawa family utilized this Nirvāṇa picture for screening their camp from the winds. There is a legend in connection with the production of this renowned picture which is characteristic of the Buddhist philosophy of life.

When Chō Densu was engaged in this grand work, a cat used to visit him and sit by him watching the progress of the picture. The artist, who wanted ultramarine in mineral form, playfully remarked, "If you are good enough to bring me the stuff I want, I will have your picture in this Nirvāṇa." The cat had been generally missing, for some unknown reason, in Nirvāṇa pictures executed until then. Hence Chō Densu's remark. And, miraculously enough, the following day the cat brought him the painting ingredient he wanted and, besides, led him to the place where it could be found in abundance. The artist's delight was beyond measure, and to keep his word he painted the cat in his Nirvāṇa picture, for which that cat has ever since had a nationwide reputation. Is it not a strange story? And it well illustrates the Buddhist attitude toward animals, which is also that of the Japanese people.

8

IN FACT, Japanese literature abounds with stories of this kind. But instead of citing more stories, it will suit our purpose better to give just a few more references from the history of Japanese culture, wherein an intense appreciation of the objects of Nature is expressed by our poets and artists. And the significant fact is that these objects are not necessarily confined to things commonly considered beautiful or those suggestive of an order beyond this evanescent and ever-changing world. Changeability itself is frequently the object of admiration. For it means movement, progress, eternal youthfulness, and it is associated with the virtue of non-attachment, which is characteristically Buddhistic as well as an aspect of Japanese character.

The morning-glory is one of the most common flowering plants in Japan. It is quite an art in the cultivators to make the plant yield to their artistic treatment, and competitive exhibitions take place early in summer everywhere in Japan. There are so many changing conditions to be taken into consideration when one hopes for fine large flowers on the vine. But ordinarily it will bloom profusely throughout the summer, over the country fences, walls, hedges, and anywhere. The one peculiarity is that it blooms fresh every morning, and there are never any of yesterday's flowers. However splendid the flowers are this morning, they fade even before noon of the same day. This evanescent glory has appealed very much to the Japanese imagination.

I do not know whether this momentaristic tendency in Japanese psychology is in their native blood or is due in some measure to the Buddhist *Weltanschauung;* but the fact is, beauty is something momentary and ever-fleeting, and if it is not appreciated while it is fully charged with life, it becomes a memory, and its liveliness is entirely lost. This is exemplified in the morning-glory:

> *Each morn as the sun rises,*
> *The flowers are newly fashioned,*
> *Glorious in their first awakening to life;*
> *Who says the creeper is short-lived?*
> *It keeps on blooming so long.*

Beauty is ever alive, because for it there is no past, no future, but the present. You hesitate, turn your head, and it is no more. The morning-glory must be admired at its first awakening as the sun rises; so it is with the lotus. This is the way the Japanese people have learned from Zen teaching how to love Nature, how to be in touch with the life running through all objects including human beings.

Another poem runs thus:

> *The pine tree lives for a thousand years,*
> *The morning-glory but for a single day;*
> *Yet both have fulfilled their destiny.*

There is no fatalism in this. Each moment pulsates with life both in the pine tree and in the morning-glory. The worth of this moment is not measured by the one thousand years of the one and the single day of the other, but by the moment itself. For this is absolute in each of them. Therefore, beauty is not to be spoiled by the thought of fatalism or of evanescence.

When Chiyo (1703–75), the *haiku* poetess to whom reference has already been made in a previous section, found the morning-glory blooming around the well, her mind was so occupied with its beauty and with a feeling of holiness that she had no desire to disturb the flower for any practical purpose. The plant could easily and quietly have been removed from the rope or pole around which it probably was entwined. But the idea never occurred to her. The sense of beauty and holiness was something that should not be defiled by mundane hands. Hence her poem (see pp. 244 ff.). What may be called a divine inspiration flashes upon our consciousness at the sight of an object of nature—which is not necessarily beautiful but may even be ugly, from the so-called common-sense point of view. When this takes place, we are so raised from our earthly occupations that merely giving vent to the experience may sound curiously factual and prosaic and even sacrilegious. It is only when we are elevated to the same height that we can grasp the full meaning of the utterance and see into the secrets that are concealed in the poet's feeling for nature.

The frog does not ordinarily seem a beautiful creature, but when it is found perching on a lotus or *bashō* leaf still fresh with the morning dew, it stirs the *haiku* poet's imagination.

> *A solitary frog drenched in rain*
> *Rides on a bashō leaf,*
> *Unsteadily.*

A quiet summer scene is depicted by means of a green-backed amphibious animal. To some, an incident like this may seem too insignificant to call out any poetical comment, but to the Japanese, especially to the Buddhist Japanese, nothing that takes place in the world is insignificant. The frog is just as important as the eagle or the tiger; every movement of it is directly connected with the primary source of life, and in it and through it one can read the gravest religious truth. Hence Bashō's poem on a frog leaping into the ancient pond in his park. This leap is just as weighty a matter as the Fall of Adam, for there is here, too, a truth revealing the secrets of creation.

> By a little kitten
> Sniffed at,
> Creeps the slug unconcerned.

Here is also a bit of human playfulness and sweetness. References to such happenings in Nature are constantly met with throughout Japanese literature, but especially in *haiku* poetry, which developed wonderfully during the Tokugawa period. The *haiku* is singularly concerned with little living things, such as flies of all kinds, lice, fleas, bugs, the singing insects, birds, frogs, cats, dogs, fishes, turtles, and so on. It is also deeply concerned with vegetables, plants, rocks, mountains, and rivers. And, as we know, the *haiku* is one of the most popular methods used by the Japanese people to express their philosophical intuitions and poetic appreciation of Nature. In the feeling compressed within the smallest number of syllables, we detect the soul of Japan transparently reflected, showing how poetically or intuitively sensitive it is toward Nature and its objects, non-sentient as well as sentient.

It goes without saying that the *haiku* embodies the spirit of the Bashō, its modern founder, and that the spirit of Bashō is the spirit of Zen expressing itself in the seventeen syllables. This has already been fully explained and illustrated in the section on the *haiku* and Zen.

9

PROBABLY the best way to illustrate the Japanese love of Nature in relation to the spirit of Zen Buddhism is to analyze the various concepts that have entered into the construction of the tearoom or teahouse where the art of tea, so called, is conducted in accordance with a set of rules. The rules have not by any means been arbitrarily compiled, but they have gradually and unconsciously grown out of the artistically trained minds of the teamasters; and in the composition of these minds we find the Japanese instinct for Nature thoroughly disciplined in the philosophy of Zen, morally, aesthetically, and intellectually. When we know all about the tea—its history, its practice, its conditions, its spiritual background, and also the moral atmosphere radiating from it—we can say that we also comprehend the secrets of Japanese psychology. The subject is highly interesting, but as it requires a lengthy treatment, it is deferred to another occasion.[7]

Let me describe a tearoom in one of the temples attached to Daitokuji, the Zen temple which is the headquarters of the tea. Where a series of flagstones irregularly arranged comes to a stop, there stands an insignificant-looking straw-thatched hut, low and unpretentious to the last degree. The entrance is not by a door but by a sort of aperture; to enter through it, a visitor has to be shorn of all his encumbrances, that is to say, both his swords, long and short, which in the feudal days a samurai used to carry all the time. The inside is a small semi-lighted room about ten feet square; the ceiling is low and of uneven height and structure. The posts are not smoothly planed and finished, they are mostly of natural wood. After a little while,

---

[7] Something of the art of tea has been said in the previous sections; cf. pp. 271 ff., above. They by no means exhaust all that is meant by the art of tea. To treat the subject fully would be quite a serious piece of work.

Crane

however, the room grows gradually lighter as our eyes begin
to adjust to the new situation. We notice an ancient-looking
kakemono in the alcove, with some handwriting or a picture
of *sumiye*. An incense burner emits a smoke of fragrance,
which has the singular effect of soothing one's nerves. The
flower vase does not contain more than a single flower stem, not
at all gorgeous or ostentatious; but, like a little white lily
blooming under a rock surrounded by the somber pines, the
humble flower in these surroundings is enhanced in beauty and
attracts the attention of the small gathering.

Now we listen to the sound of boiling water in the kettle,
resting on a tripod over a fire in the square hole cut in the
floor. The sound is not actually that of boiling water but comes
from the heavy iron kettle, and it is most appropriately likened
by the connoisseur to a breeze that passes through the pine
grove. It adds greatly to the serenity of the room, for a man
here feels as if he were sitting alone in a mountain hut where a
white cloud and the pine music are his only consoling companions.

To take a cup of tea with friends in this environment, talking
probably about the *sumiye* sketch in the alcove or some artistic
topic suggested by the tea utensils in the room, lifts the mind
above the perplexities of life. The warrior is saved from his
daily occupation of fighting, the businessman from his ever-
present idea of moneymaking. Is it not something, indeed, to
find in this world of struggles and vanities a corner, however
humble, where a man can rise above the limits of relativity and
have even a glimpse of eternity?

IV

THE FOLLOWING verses on the cherries are freely culled from Japanese poetry in order to show how passionately the people of Japan are attached to flowers, in fact to all objects of Nature. This feeling is not necessarily connected with the teaching of Zen, but, as I have said elsewhere, Zen helped a great deal to deepen the aesthetic sensibility of the Japanese mind and finally to root it in the religious intuitions that rise from a mystic understanding of Nature.

As before, the translations are almost literal, with just enough explanation to make the original sense intelligible in the English dress. Like poems in any language, those in Japanese cannot be rendered into a foreign language with all their subtle sentiments and literary artistries. Incidentally, let me remark that, as with *sumiye* painting, the Japanese mind has managed to express its poetic feelings in the fewest possible number of words. The *waka* of thirty-one syllables has become the *haiku* of seventeen. Some think that the Japanese mind has not yet quite differentiated philosophy from life and ideas from immediate experiences; that is to say, it has not yet attained to the highest degree of intellectuality; and that for this reason it is still satisfied with the shortest poetic form, such as the *waka* or *haiku,* in which no marshaling of ideas, no intellectual unfolding of highly developed feelings, is practicable. Others state that the Japanese vocabulary is poor and limited and that with such a medium no great poetry is produced. These criticisms may be true as far as they go, but all generalizations are only expressive of partial truth. The reason for Japanese poetry still awaits adequate analysis in various terms, including the psychological, philosophical, and historical background in which it has thrived.

One thing at least that I may remark about Japanese poetry is that, being short, it omits making specific references to ideas, experiences, and surroundings leading up to its composition and also to those derivable from it. These omissions are to be supplied by the reader, who, therefore, must be very well acquainted with the physical and psychological setting in which the poet lives. The genius consists in selecting a few significant reference points by which he is able to make the reader effectively conjure up all the poetic associations contained in his seventeen syllables. But we must remember that the secrets of the *haiku* are not necessarily in its mere suggestibility.

To give a few examples. Ryōta, of the eighteenth century, has a *haiku* expressing his feeling for the moon which, after having been hidden from him night after night because of so many continuous spring rainfalls, appears softly and unexpectedly through the pine trees. This must have been a most delightful surprise to him. The rainy season in Japan is very gloomy and trying to those who love the spring moonlight in the evening, when its tender, mellow, relaxing shadow is cast all over the hazy, vaporous earth.

> *In the June rains,*
> *One night, as if by stealth*
> *The moon, through the pines.*

The *haiku* as it stands in Japanese is no doubt unintelligible to most English readers, while its Chinese translation in four lines, with five characters to each line, gives a fuller idea:

> *'Tis midsummer, and my grass hut is dreary;*
> *Every evening I fall asleep to the sound of rain.*
> *Suddenly the full moon hangs [in the sky],*
> *And the shadow of the pine tree on my garden.*[1]

[1] Tr. Basil Hall Chamberlain, in "Bashō and the Epigram," pt. iv of his *Japanese Poetry*.

Tentoku's humanitarianism called out the following *haiku,* which has now become a proverb:

> *First snow this!*
> *That also man's child,*
> *Barrel-picker.*

This is to all appearance nonsensical. To the Japanese who know the first snow of the year and also what a barrel-picker in feudal days means, the present *haiku* is full of pathos. The day of the first snowfall is probably the first cold day of winter, but it is at the same time the day for the leisure class to have a friendly little sake party at a suburban restaurant with a fine garden. The poet was also in all likelihood on his way to such a party when he saw a poor boy picking up small sake casks thrown out in the streets. The boy was not warmly clad— in tatters probably—and barefooted. This called forth the poet's sympathy. The boy is also a man's child, and why should he have to suffer so when there are many others of the same age luxuriating in rich idleness? The sense of justice asserts itself. If he had been a Hood he would surely have written a "Song of the Shirt."

A *waka* or *uta* has thirty-one syllables and can express somewhat more than a *haiku*, but words of comment are often found necessary to connect merely suggested thoughts. One of the reasons why *waka* did not expand into more syllables is that when the Japanese poet wanted to express himself more fully he had recourse to what may be called a "prose poem," of which we have various forms in Japanese literature.

The following poems on the cherry are divided into four headings: the first (A) is concerned chiefly with the wind and rain, which are always apt to scatter the flowers too soon. They are not lasting flowers in any way, only about a week in bloom. They all burst out suddenly early in April, when the mountains and the riverbanks appear to be masses of flowers. This is especially noticeable, as most trees are still bare then. The second group (B) sings of the glorious sight when the cherry blooms are all out. It is really a magnificent view to see—for instance, the whole mountain of Yoshino covered with gorgeous flowers, mostly pink. Let a warm relaxing sun shine on them through the hazy atmosphere, and the whole populace of Tokyo or Kyoto will altogether lose their heads. The third group (C) refers to the spirit of the flower in whatever way it may be interpreted by the poets. The last group (D) depicts their anxious hopes that the cherries bloom. One thing, at least, which makes the Japanese think so much of them is that they are to us the symbol of the spring. When they are in bloom, the season reaches its height, days grow longer, and we are glad that winter is really behind.

A

Where is the shelter of the flower-scattering Wind?
Can anyone tell me?
For I want to see him at his home,
And lodge my complaint.

SŌSEI THE MONK (Tenth Century)

I thought this was the frontier gate,[2]
Where no winds were allowed to pass [as the name
indicates];
But, lo, the mountain path is strewn
With the fallen petals of the cherries!

MINAMOTO YOSHIIYE (1051–1108) [3]

[2] This was composed at the Na-ko-so frontier gate. *Na-ko-so* literally means "do not come."

[3] Yoshiiye of the Minamoto clan was a great soldier, especially skilled in archery and understanding *fūryū*. When he defeated Abe Sadatō at the Fort of Robes, he sent to him the following in verse form:

Ah, your Fort of Robes
Is at last reduced to tatters!

Not to be defeated in this, Sadatō immediately responded:

What a pity!
Long usage has caused
The threads to wear out.

What a pity, O cherry blossoms, so hurriedly scattering
   away!
Why not follow the spirit of Spring,
So peaceful, so relaxing, so eternally contented?

FUJIWARA TOSHINARI (1114–1204)

Let us not blame the wind, indiscriminately,
That scatters the flowers so ruthlessly;
I think it is their own desire to pass away before their
   time has come.

JIYEN THE MONK (1155–1225)

Nowhere is the spring now.
I blame neither the wind nor the world;
For even in the remotest parts of Yoshino
The cherries are visible no more.

FUJIWARA SADAIYE (1162–1241) [4]

B

Advanced in age, I'm old indeed—
No gainsaying this—
But as I look at these blossoming cherries,
How cheered up I feel in spirit!

FUJIWARA YOSHIFUSA (804–72)

There comes a wood-gatherer
Walking down the meandering mountain path:
"Tell me, O my friend,
Those on the peak, are they cherry blossoms,
   or clouds?"

MINAMOTO NO YORIMASA (1104–80)

---

[4] One of the compilers of *Shin Kokinshū*. This new collection of *waka* poems, containing the best specimens in the time of the ex-Emperor Gotoba, was edited in 1205 under the personal superintendence of the ex-Emperor.

The long-cherished desire of my heart, year after year,
To see the Yoshino cherries in bloom—
Fulfilled today!

TOYOTOMI HIDEYOSHI (1536–98) [5]

How radiant, yet how peaceful and relaxing,
The spirit of Spring is!
Surely out of this spirit
All these blossoming mountain cherries burst.

KAMO NO MABUCHI (1697–1769)

Would that all people inhabiting this globe
Come to this land of ours,
Come to this mountain of Yoshino,
And look at the cherries in full bloom!

KAMO NO MABUCHI

Choosing these long spring days as most opportune,
The cherries have their blooming season;
As I gaze at them, I think of the ancient days of
  the gods—[days of contentment].

ISHIKAWA YORIHIRA (1791–1859)

Yoshino-yama behind the mists—
  I know not how it is;
But, as far as my sight extends,
There's nothing but a mass of blossoming cherries.

HATTA TOMONORI (1799–1874)

Dressed in scarlet-colored armor, and wearing
  an ancient sword,
I would be a more appropriate sight
Amidst these mountain cherries in full glory.

OCHIAI NAOBUMI (1861–1903)

[5] For his liking for the art of tea, see pp. 301 ff. and 318 ff. in the section on the art of tea.

Saigyō, to whom frequent references have already been made in the present work, is an indelible name not only in the history of Japanese literature but in that of Buddhist influence on Japanese culture. He belongs to the pre-Zen period, but his spirit, his understanding of Nature, and his ardent aspiration to live with Nature, to be always one with Nature, connect him closely with Sesshū, Rikyū, Bashō, and many others. In fact Bashō groups himself with Saigyō as belonging to the same class. Saigyō's love for the cherries was such as to make him utter this:

> *My prayer is to die underneath the*
> *   blossoming cherry,*
> *In that spring month of flowers,*
> *When the moon is full.*

In Japan and China, the death of the Buddha is recorded as having taken place on the fifteenth day of the second moon (of the lunar calendar). Hence Saigyō's wish to die about that time, when the cherries are also likely to be blooming. The second moon generally corresponds to late March or early April of our calendar. Saigyō's prayer was fulfilled, for he died on the sixteenth day of the second moon in the first year of Kenkyū (1190). His attachment to the cherries went even beyond his grave, for his request was:

> *Make the offering to Buddha of cherry blossoms,*
> *If people of the future should think of me.*

Among other poems on the cherries, Saigyō has these, showing how passionately he was in love with them as well as with other objects of Nature:

> *Unknown and unadmired, even I live on in*
> *   this world;*
> *Why do these cherries then pass away*
> *So heartlessly from the sight of the admiring*
> *   crowds?*

At this late date, no flowers could forget the
    Spring;
They will soon be out, no doubt.
Leisurely awaiting then, I would pass this day
    under these trees.

I feel deeply concerned to find
On which mountaintops
The cherries begin to flower first:
How I long to see them!

He was also, as most Japanese are, a great lover of the moon. The moonlight singularly attracts the Japanese imagination, and any Japanese who ever aspired to compose a *waka* or a *haiku* would hardly dare leave the moon out. The meteorological conditions of the country have much to do with this. The Japanese are lovers of softness, gentleness, semi-darkness, subtle suggestiveness, and everything in this category. They are not fiercely emotional. While they are occasionally surprised by earthquakes, they like to sit quietly in the moonlight, enveloped in its pale, bluish, soul-consoling rays. They are generally averse to anything glaringly bright and stimulating and too distinctive in its individuality. The moonlight is illuminating enough, but owing to the atmospheric conditions all objects under it appear not too strongly individualized; a certain mystic obscurantism pervades, and this seems to appeal to the Japanese generally. Saigyō, all alone in his mountain retreat, communes with this spirit of Luna, of whom he cannot help thinking even after his death, or because of whom he is loath to pass away from this life although he may have no other attachments here. In fact, a Land of Purity is no other than the supermundane projection of such aesthetic-spiritual appreciations.

Not a soul ever visits my hut
Except the friendly light of the moon,
Peeping through the woods.

Some day I may have
To pass away from this world, alas!
For ever with a longing heart
For the moon, for the moon!

C

To the mountain village, this spring eve,
I come and listen to the monastery bell,
Watching the cherries in bloom,
And petals softly falling.

Nōin the Monk (Tenth Century)

This ancient capital of Shiga is dilapidation
  itself now,
Except for the mountain cherries,
Blooming as gloriously as ever.

Taira no Tadanori (1144–84)

The evening is come:
I make a lodging under yonder cherry tree,
The flower will then be my host tonight.

Taira no Tadanori

Blooming, and then scattering,
And leaving all to rain and wind—
The cherries are no more now!
But their spirit for ever remains unruffled.

Date Chihiro (1803–77)

D

"When the cherries begin to bloom,
Let me know at once":

The mountain-man has not forgotten my word;
I hear him come. "Saddle the horse, quick!"

MINAMOTO NO YORIMASA

When at Yoshino the cherries are about to bloom,
My heart is anxiously drawn to the white clouds
Veiling the mountaintops these spring mornings.

SAKAWADA MASATOSHI (1580–1643)

APPENDICES

I

TWO MONDO FROM THE
'HEKIGAN-SHŪ'

T O I L L U S T R A T E further the way Zen treats of some
important religio-philosophical problems, the following two
examples are quoted from a Zen textbook [1] which is extensively
used and highly appraised by all Zen students.

1

A M O N K asked Taizui Hōshin (Ta-sui Fa-chên), of the T'ang
dynasty, who was a disciple of Taian (Ta-an, d. 883) of Fuku-
shū (Fu-chou): "When the kalpa-end fire breaks out and con-
sumes all the worlds, I wonder if 'this' too is destroyed?"
  Taizui: "Yes, destroyed!"

---

[1] *Hekigan-shū* or *Hekigan-roku* (*Pi-yen Chi* or *Pi-yen Lu*), meaning "Blue
Rock Collection" or "Blue Rock Records," is a composite work of Secchō
Jūken (Hsüeh-t'ou Chung-hsien, 980–1052) and Yengo Bukkwa (Yüan-wu Fo-
kuo, 1062–1135), of the Sung dynasty. Secchō selected one hundred "cases"
from the history of Zen and wrote a kind of commentary on each of them in
verse form. He had great literary talents, and his verses were very much admired. Later, Yengo, in response to his disciples' request, lectured on Secchō's
one hundred cases together with the verses in at least two different localities.
Yengo, as far as records go, had no intention of compiling a book out of his
lectures or comments. But his monks took notes of them and kept the manuscript among themselves. There were at least two attempts among his disciples
—each quite independent of the other—to bring their notes together and put
them in good order. The first took place in 1124 and the second in 1128.
Apparently they worked in different localities. The text at present in circulation
is probably based on the book printed in 1304 under the Yüan dynasty.

Monk: "If so, does 'it' follow the rest?"
Taizui: "Yes, 'it' does." [2]

On this *mondo,* Yengo gives his comments in the following manner:

Hōshin of Taizui was a disciple of Taian and a native of Entei (Yen-t'ing), in Tosen (Tung-ch'uan). He studied Zen under more than sixty masters. While under Isan (Kuei-shan), he served in the kitchen, taking care of the fire (*huo-t'ou*). One day Isan asked him, "You have been here with me for some years, but you do not seem to know how to ask me a question and see how it goes." Taizui said, "But what question should I ask you after all?" Isan proposed this, "If you don't know, just ask, 'What is the Buddha?'" Then Taizui at once put his hand over the master's mouth and shut him up. Thereupon Isan remarked, "If you act like that, you may not get even one who will sweep the ground for you."

Taizui later returned to his native town, and at the foot of Mount Hōkō (Pêng-k'ou) he erected a little booth where he served tea to the passers-by for three years. Later, he was called to open up Mount Taizui, where a monastery was built. [Hence his name "Taizui."] One of the monks once asked him, "When the kalpa-end fire burns up all the worlds, will 'this' [3] be destroyed or not?"

This question comes from a Buddhist scripture in which the physical history of the universe is given as going through the four stages: "Coming to existence," "Continuing to exist," "Destruction," and finally "Disappearance." When conflagration takes place at the end of the kalpa ("age"), the flames rise up even to the third *dhyāna* heaven. This monk does not really know the ultimate sense of the story as it is told in the scripture.

[2] *Hekigan-shū*, case 29. See also *Dentōroku* ("Transmission of the Lamp"), fasc. XI.
[3] *Shako* in Japanese, *chê-ko* in Chinese.

D. Kuzumi Morikage. A family of three under the gourd

llis, looking at the summer moon. Middle 17th century

Let us ask: "What is really meant by 'this' alluded to in the question?" Some give to it an intellectual interpretation, saying, "this" is the original nature of all beings. Taizui answered, "Yes, destroyed!" The monk further asked, "Does 'it' then follow the rest?" Taizui said, "Yes, 'it' does." This is misunderstood by a number of people who are unable to get at its true signification, because they are given up to conceptualization. When Taizui declares that "this" is to follow the rest, where does it really go? If Taizui, on the other hand, said, " 'This' does not follow the rest," what then? Therefore, do we not have an ancient master stating that if you really wish to get intimately to the point, you should not ask any questions? [4]

Later, there was another monk who asked the headmaster of Shuzan (Hsiu-shan): "When the kalpa-end fire breaks out, all the worlds are destroyed, and will 'this' be destroyed or not?"

The master said, "No, not destroyed!"

The monk asked again, "Why not?"

"Because 'this' and all the worlds are identical" was the master's answer.

Indeed, whether you say "this" will be destroyed or whether you say "this" will not be destroyed—the outcome is the same; both statements are enough to stop the breath.

The first monk who failed to understand Taizui was very much worried over the matter and went to Tōsusan (T'ou Tzŭ-shan) of Joshū (Shu-chou), where he wished to solve the question with the help of the master there.

Tōsu the master asked, "Where do you come from?"

Monk: "From Taizui of Western Shoku (Shu)."

Tōsu: "What has Taizui to say?"

The monk then recited the whole proceeding which took place at Mount Taizui regarding the destiny of "this." Tōsu rose from his seat and, burning incense and reverently bowing toward Mount Taizui, remarked, "A Buddha has appeared in Western Shoku; you make haste and go back to Mount Taizui."

[4] Cf. St. Augustine's idea of time: *Confessions*, Book XI, 17.

The monk thereupon turned his steps back to Shoku, but when he reached Mount Taizui again—what a pity!—he found that his old master had already passed into Nirvāṇa.

Later in the T'ang, there was a monk by the name of Keijun (Ching-tsun), who visited Mount Taizui and composed the following poem in memory of Hōshin the Master:

All is cleared up! Absolutely alone!
Who says that Enō had his seal of transmission? [5]
The dictum "It follows the rest"
Has made the poor monk run over mountain after mountain.
The crickets are chirping this cold night on the stone wall;
The ghosts are seen worshiping in the shadow of the darken-
    ing lantern.
All is quiet and serene now around the lonely shrine,
And I find myself walking up and down deeply absorbed
    in thoughts inexpressible.

[Secchō, as we see below, makes use of two lines of this poem in his versified comment on the puzzled monk. Says Yengo:] At this moment I warn you not to take "it" as de-structible or not-destructible. "Where are we, then, ultimately?" you may ask. Keep your eyes open and see directly into the matter! Secchō comments:

In the midst of the flaming kalpa-fire, a question is asked;
The monk still hesitatingly stands against the dilemma.
What a pity! the one phrase "it follows the rest" is proving
    fatal,
Making him wander about all by himself with no end what-
    ever.

[5] This refers to the story of Enō (Hui-nêng, d. 713), the sixth patriarch, who was given the mind-seal of transmission by Gunin (Hung-jên, 602–675), the fifth patriarch, certifying Enō's understanding of orthodox Zen. The idea is that there cannot be any such thing as transmitting the Dharma from one individual to another. In the realm of "absolute emptiness" (śūnyatā), no dichotomies are possible.

Secchō's verse is altogether opportune and exactly hits the mark, for he knows how to get through the dilemma, on whichever horn he may be caught. It is all right when one says, "Destroyed!" It is all right, too, when the other says, "Not destroyed!" The only point that is absolutely important is to take hold of the truth itself, which transcends a dualistic interpretation of any sort. Otherwise, we shall have to follow the poor monk who travels back and forth over mountains and mountains with no time to rest.

2

A MONK asked Hyakujō Yekai (Pai-chang Huai-hai, 720–814): "What is the most miraculous event in the world?"

Hyakujō answered: "I sit here all by myself."

The monk then made a bow to the master, who struck him.

Yengo comments: [6] He who has a discerning eye has no hesitation in risking himself when necessary; for unless you venture into the tiger's lair you can never capture a cub. Hyakujō is a great master; he is like a winged tiger. But this monk defying death was not afraid of touching the tiger's whiskers. Hence his question: "What is the most miraculous event in the world?" He has a discerning eye, so Hyakujō takes the trouble to answer: "I sit here all by myself." The monk makes a bow. This will be understood when one can go back to the time even prior to the monk's questioning. The monk's bow is not an ordinary one, the monk knows Hyakujō thoroughly. But good friends sometimes act as if they did not know each other, they refrain from giving expression to all that they have within themselves. The bow is followed with a stick. Here we see that when the master lets out, everything is at once set to right; when he draws in, all is wiped out and not a trace is left.

[6] *Hekigan-shū*, case 26.

Let us ask: What is the idea of the monk's bowing? Is this properly done? If so, what is Hyakujō's motive for striking him? If the bowing were not proper, where is the point that is not proper? When we come to this we find that a trained mind is needed, while standing at the highest peak, to distinguish between black and white, fair and foul. The monk's bowing is like bearding the lion in his den, he knows where and how to turn his body about. It was fortunate that Hyakujō the old master was not to be deceived by the tricky behavior of the monk; he had an eye on his forehead and a charm under his arms, and this enabled him to detect at once what was in the mind of the one who was bowing before him, and he wielded his stick effectively. If it were somebody less than Hyakujō, he could not have done anything with the monk.

This monk [on the other hand] knows how to meet a challenge with challenge of whatever sort it may be. Hence his bowing.

Nansen Fugwan (Nan-ch'üan P'u-yüan, 748–834) once told his Brotherhood: "In the middle of last night, Mañjuśrī and Samantabhadra cherished the thought of Buddha, cherished the thought of the Dharma, and I gave each of them twenty blows of my stick and chased them away to the other side of the Mountains." At the time, Jōshu Jūshin (Chao-chou Ts'ung-shên, 778–897) came out of the congregation and said, "Who is going to be hit by your stick?" Nansen replied, "What fault do you find with this old man that I am?" Jōshu bowed.

The fully qualified Zen master very rarely overlooks where his opposing party stands, and, therefore, as soon as he notices a sign of something moving he at once starts his activity in the briskest manner. My old teacher Goso Hōyen (Wu-tsu Fa-yen, d. 1104) used to say: "It is like the game of wrestling—no time for deliberation is allowed. All that comes in through the senses, all that belongs to the realm of seeing and hearing, have them all at once put aside. When thus you take hold of yourself and become master of yourself, you will be able to see where Hyakujō is."

But what would happen if you let go? Let us see what
Secchō would say on this point:

Look at the Pegasus that freely gallops all over the patri-
archal fields!
When he comes down in the world of multitudes, rolling up,
spreading out, how free and how altogether independent
he is!
Like a flash of lightning, like a spark of flint striking steel,
each knows how to react to the situation:
Beware of the tiger that permits no one to touch his whisk-
ers.

[From Yengo's comments on this *gāthā* I give the following
extracts, which may shed light in understanding the whole
procedure between Hyakujō the master and the monk:]

A monk asked Baso Dōichi (Ma-tsu Tao-i, d. 788),[7] "What
is the ultimate teaching of Buddhism?" Baso struck him, saying, "If I did not strike you, the whole world would laugh at
me!"

Another monk asked, "What is the meaning of Bodhidharma
coming from the West?"[8] Baso said, "You come up nearer to
me and I'll tell you." When the monk approached him, the
master slapped the monk's ear, saying, "The secrets are difficult
to guard!"

Yengo further quotes Gantō Zenkatsu (Yen-t'ou Ch'üan-huo,
828–889), who once said this: "The best is to reject objects,
while to run after them is the worst." When one finds oneself
engaged in a combat, one is to be always master of the situation,
whatever way it may turn. Says Secchō: "The wheel of

[7] Ma-tsu, or Baso as he is generally called in Japan, is one who helped
Zen to develop along a new line in the history of Buddhism in China. He had
many disciples, and Hyakujō, who is the master in the story cited here, was
one of the most prominent. Yengo brings in Baso in order to illustrate Hyakujō's
masterful treatment of the monk.

[8] This amounts to asking the ultimate teaching of Buddhism. Bodhidharma
is the first Zen patriarch of China, who brought Buddhism from India.

becoming ever remains unmoved. Once moved, however, it surely runs in two directions [subject and object]." Indeed, if it did not move at all, it would be of no use whatever. If one is really of manly stature, one ought to detect where the slightest movement takes place, for this is the way to be one's own master. People of the present day are altogether too busy running after somebody else. When they go on like this, their noses will be firmly held by others, and how can they expect to attain their end? The monk knew well even in the midst of a lightning flash how to turn himself about and make a bow to the master. Secchō here compares Hyakujō to a fierce tiger and says that the monk's parry was like trying to play with the tiger's beard—an altogether dangerous trick.

3

TO THOSE who have not been initiated into the secrets of the Zen way of dealing with these religio-philosophical problems, the above *mondo* and comments will be complete enigmas, I believe. But one thing, at least, they will notice here is that Zen does not follow the ordinary rules of ratiocination; Zen has another way of viewing and judging realities. We may ask, "Why is not Zen more explicit in demonstrating this particular point instead of shrouding it, as it appears to some of us, with unnecessary 'mysteries'?" The answer will be: It is not that Zen purposely practices this mystification, so to speak, but in the nature of things there is no other way of demonstrating Zen than the one adopted by the successive masters in China and Japan. If they, like philosophers, followed the logical or dialectical method so called, there would be no Zen; in fact, the masters are doing their best to express themselves in the most vital and most pertinent manner they can possibly follow. To say that their behavior is inevitable is more to the point. When the fruit ripens it falls on the ground. When life is ready, it takes another form than the one it has so far been assuming. When spring comes, the field is green and we feel relaxed; when frost covers it, we shiver and see the trees all shorn of leaves. It is not that we have logic first and apply it to nature to make the latter obey its laws. Logic is a later product, and it is we who have constructed it. Where logic is not available, we must construct another which is "logical." Zen is prior to logic so called, and its masters are guiding us to an interview with a God who has not yet uttered "Let there be light."

To take up the first *mondo,* regarding the fate of "this" when the whole universe goes to destruction, one master says that "that" follows the fate of the rest—which we may take to mean that the soul distinguishable from the body disappears with the disappearance of the latter. But there is another master who apparently contradicts this assertion, for he says that the soul does not follow the destiny of the body. His second statement when asked "Why?" is: "The soul is the body and the body is the soul, and as they are identical there is no destruction of either." Or one may understand this master's view in the following way: It is a mistake from the start to distinguish soul from body, mind from world, thinker from thought, seer from seen, actor from action, subject from object, *meum* from *tuum, en-soi* from *pour-soi,* as is generally done by most philosophers as well as by men in the street; and because of this initial error we become involved in an endless series of logical difficulties. The best way to come to a real understanding of the matter is "not to ask a question," for this is where Zen is. Let the question be raised: "Is 'this' destroyed?" or "Is 'this' not destroyed?" and then we have an endless series of complications. If it is said that "this" is destroyed, we get worried over the destiny of our precious "soul" or anything which we hold to be dear to us. If it is said, on the other hand, that "this" is not destroyed, we worry just the same over its "wherefore," or its "whereabouts," or its "whither."

The second *mondo* cuts off all these logical complications

and physical worries, for Hyakujō is in the most positive manner affirmative and conclusive: "I sit here all by myself!"

The philosopher according to whom *cogito ergo sum* is generally weak-minded. The Zen master has nothing to do with such dialectical quibbles, he straightaway gives his final irrevocable pronunciamento: "I sit here all by myself!" He does not "think"; he is, in fact, where the thinking has not yet started. If he begins to do it, he is too late. Therefore, he goes straight to "I am," or just "am" or "is." The Zen master is a most impatient man; he will not wait for us to ask a question, for he says: "If you want to be intimate [with Reality] no questions need be asked, for the answer is where they have not yet been raised." "A flash of lightning" or "the spark of flint striking steel" does not necessarily mean instantaneity but im-mediacy. When you ask a question or when you think at all, this means mediation or time. Zen abhors mediation of any kind, it is always straightforward and wants to handle Reality in its nakedness or in its isness or suchness. Questioning and answering, or thinking or logicizing, is mediation and therefore takes time, which irritates the Zen master, who is always after im-mediacy. He does not want a pair of tongs to grasp fire, he wants us to grasp it with the naked hands, and the wonderful thing is that when grasped it does not burn the hands. This is the meaning of the saying: "Whoever loses his life will preserve it."

Is this not the most miraculous event in the world? And that Zen takes a firm hold of this miracle and asks no questions about it—is this not also a most wonderful fact in our experience? For indeed no questions are possible here. This is not the conclusion we reach after laborious reasoning. Hyakujō gives us here the whole truth without any reservation, and we have to accept it in the same spirit, wholeheartedly and unhesitatingly. But if we stopped here, there would not have been any Zen. Fortunately, if we can say so, the monk bowed and the master struck. This is something we find nowhere in the cultural history of mankind. And this is where real Zen is.

"I sit here all by myself" may be compared to Luther's "Here I stand," or to Christ's "I am before Abraham was," or to Yahveh's "I am that I am." But how about the bowing in this connection? The bowing is by no means an unconscious thing, but what does it mean here as a reaction to Hyakujō's diction? Zen gives no explanation, at least verbally. Besides, how should we have it related to the master's striking? The bowing becomes a veritable enigma.

And then the striking? Yengo parallels it with Baso's striking his questioners and praises Hyakujō very highly, saying that he is really the master of the whole situation and knows perfectly well how to cope with every phase of its shifting. To the outsiders, all this is beyond comprehension. What religion is this? What philosophy is this, if there is anything intelligible in it? I would not, however, go any further here except to state that Zen is the most intimate personal experience and that all these enigmatical behaviors are directly and inevitably related to it.

II

THE VIMALAKĪRTI SŪTRA

THE *Vimalakīrti Sūtra*, one of the most remarkable Mahāyāna texts, was produced in India probably around the beginning of the Christian era. It is remarkable that it bears the title "sūtra" in spite of the fact that it was given by a Buddhist philosopher and not by the Buddha himself, though the story is concerned with an incident in the life of the Buddha. It is in fact a philosophic-dramatic discourse in which the Mahāyāna doctrines are presented in the way characteristic of the Hindu psychology in contrast to the Chinese. To those who are accustomed to the Zen way of demonstrating Reality, the sūtra will certainly appear too circumlocutory and highly supernatural. But the stage on which the whole drama is enacted is fantastically grand and full of marvelous episodes which go altogether beyond the Chinese imagination, which paints things of Heaven in drab, colorless earthliness, while the Indians would transform our mundane everyday life into a glorious Elysian field. However this may be, there are many routes to the peak, as there are many mansions in "my Father's house."

The sūtra is called in Japanese the *Yuima Kyō*, and it was one of the first three Mahāyāna texts studied and commented upon by Prince Shōtoku (574–622) early in the seventh century. That Buddhism came to Japan to stay and molded the character of her people in more ways than one was due to this Prince, who is justly regarded by the Buddhists as the father of Japanese Buddhism. He was great not only as a pious Buddhist student but also as a statesman, educator, architect, social worker, and promoter of various branches of art. The Hōryūji at Nara is the monument immortalizing his memory. One of the ways to approach Zen philosophy will then be to get acquainted with the contents of the *Yuima Kyō*.

The *Yuima Kyō* was translated first by Kumārajīva, who came to China in A.D. 401. Owing to its deep philosophical and religious insight and also probably to its dramatic setting and fine literary quality, the sūtra has wielded great spiritual and intellectual influence not only in Japan but in China. The knowledge of its teaching will surely facilitate our understanding of Buddhism. It is not exactly known when this sūtra was compiled in India. This much we can say, that the compilation took place prior to Nāgārjuna, that is, some time at the beginning of the Christian era. The principal figure of the sūtra is Yuima, who is described as a wealthy householder of Vaiśālī in the time of the Buddha. He was thoroughly versed in Mahāyāna philosophy; he was a great philanthropist and an astute Buddhist philosopher. Although living in the world as a layman, his immaculate conduct elicited universal admiration. One time he was seen indisposed. This was one of his *hōben*, "skillful means" or "mysterious ways" (*upāyakauśalya*), whereby he wanted to teach his people regarding the transitoriness of life. The whole town of Vaiśālī, including the great lords, Brāhmans, officials, and other classes of people, hastened to visit him, anxiously inquiring after his health.

The Buddha, learning of this, wanted to send one of his disciples to Yuima. But they all refused to comply with the Buddha's wish, excusing themselves on the ground that none of them was equal to the task of interviewing the great Mahāyāna philosopher-saint. They had all had at least one experience previously with him, in which they were miserably worsted and had failed to carry on their line of argument against his. It may be interesting to cite one or two examples of such religio-philosophical interviews between Yuima and the disciples of

Buddha, for herein we can see what kind of discourse Yuima
advances to defeat the Hīnayāna followers of Buddha.

The great Kāśyapa was once going around begging for his
food among the poor. Yuima came to him and said, "You
need not purposely avoid the rich. When you go out begging,
your mind must be entirely detached from such discriminations,
your heart must be filled with impartial love. Food should be
received as if it were not received at all. To harbor the
thought of reception is a discrimination. Rising above the ideas
of self and not-self, of good and evil, of gain and loss, you are
able then for the first time to make offerings to all the Buddhas
and Bodhisattvas with one bowlful of food received from your
donors. Unless you attain this state of spirituality, you are a
wasteful consumer of food which you try to gather from the
poor, thinking that they might thus be given the chance to be
charitable."

When Subhūti was asked to visit Yuima, he made this con-
fession and excused himself as not worthy of the mission:
"When I once called at the old philosopher's residence for my
food, he filled my bowl with food and said: 'Only such a one is
worthy of this food as has no attachment to it, for to him all
things are equal. While in the midst of all forms of worldly
entanglements, he is emancipated; he accepts all existences as
they are, and yet he is not attached to them. Do not listen to
the Buddha, nor do you see him, but follow your heretical
teachers and go wherever they go; if they are destined for hell,
you just go with them; and when, by doing this, you feel no
hesitancy, no reluctance, then you are permitted to take this
food. Donors do not accumulate merit; charity is not the cause
of bliss. Unless you are able to go in company with devils and
work with them, you are not entitled to this food.' When I
heard this, I was thunderstruck and at the point of running
away from him without the bowl. But he said: 'All things are
after all like phantom existences, they are but names. It is only

the wise who without attachment go beyond logic and know what Reality is. They are emancipated and therefore never alarmed.' This being the case, I realize that I am not the person to go and inquire after his health."

To quote one more example from many others. When the turn came to Maitreya, he had this to say. "When I was formerly in the Tuṣita Heaven, discoursing before the Lord of Heaven and his followers on a life of nonretrogression, Yuima appeared and talked to me in this wise. 'O Maitreya, I understand that Śākyamuni the Buddha prophesied your attaining the supreme enlightenment in the course of one life. Now I wish to know what this one life really means. Is it your past, your future, or your present one? If it is the past one, the past is past and no more; if future, the future is not yet here; if present, the present is 'abodeless.' [That is to say, the present has no fixed point in time. When you say this is the present, it is here no longer.] This being the case, the so-called present life as it is lived this very moment by every one of us is taught by the Buddha as something not to be subsumed in the categories of birth, old age, and death.

" 'According to Buddha, all beings are of suchness (*tathatā*), and are in suchness; not only all wise and holy persons but every one of us—of course including yourself, O Maitreya. If you are assured by Buddha of attaining the supreme enlightenment and realizing Nirvāṇa, all beings sentient and nonsentient ought also to be sure of their enlightenment. For as long as we are all of suchness and in suchness, this suchness is one and the same; and when one of us attains enlightenment all the rest too share it. And in this enlightenment there is no thought of discrimination. Where do you, O Maitreya, put your life of nonretrogression when there is really neither attainment nor nonattainment, neither body nor mind?'

"O Blessed One, when Yuima gave this discourse in the Tuṣita Heaven, the two hundred deva-lords at once realized the

'kṣānti in the unborn dharma.'[1] For this reason I am not qualified to do anything with this old philosopher of Vaiśālī."

In this way one after another of Buddha's disciples at this
assembly refused to comply with his request which was full of
grave significance. Finally, Mañjuśrī accepted the mission.
Accompanied by eight thousand Bodhisattvas, five hundred
Śrāvakas, and hundreds of thousands of deva-lords, he entered
the city of Vaiśālī. Yuima, knowing this, had his room emptied
of all the furniture, leaving just one couch, on which he laid
himself down; nor was he attended by any of his followers. He
was all alone in his ten-foot-square room.

The interview of this wily philosopher-saint and the Bodhisattva whose wisdom had no peer among Buddha's disciples began in this manner:

Yuima: "O Mañjuśrī, you are welcome indeed. But your coming is no-coming, and my seeing is no-seeing."

Mañjuśrī: "You are right. I come as if not coming, I depart
as if not departing. For my coming is from nowhere, and my
departing is no-whither. We talk of seeing each other, and yet
there is no seeing between us two. But let us put this matter
aside for a while, for I am here commissioned by Buddha to
inquire after your condition. Is it improving? How did you become ill? And are you cured?"

Yuima: "From folly there is desire, and this is the cause of
my illness. Because all sentient beings are sick I am sick, and
when they are cured of illness, I too shall be cured. A Bodhisattva assumes a life of birth-and-death for the sake of all
beings; as long as there is birth-and-death, there is illness."

While the conversation between Yuima and Mañjuśrī is going

---

[1] *Anutpattika-dharma-kṣānti* in Sanskrit. This is one of the key terms in
the teaching of Mahāyāna Buddhism, but unfortunately it has been misunderstood by some of the early translators of Sanskrit Buddhism. *Kṣānti* does not
here mean "patience" or "endurance" as it generally does. It means "ac-
ceptance," "recognition," or "acknowledgment," and the "unborn" (*anutpat-
tika*) refers to Reality itself (*dharma*), which is not subject to birth and death.
The whole phrase, therefore, is synonymous with the supreme enlightenment
(*samya-sambodhi*).

on in this strain there take place one or two episodes in regard
to Śāriputra, one of the most intelligent hearers (*śrāvaka*) among
Buddha's followers gathered here.

Śāriputra happens to notice Yuima's room devoid of all furniture except the couch and wonders how the host is going to seat
all the Bodhisattvas and disciples who have come with Mañjuśrī. Yuima, reading the mind of Śāriputra, asks whether
Śāriputra is come for the sake of the Dharma or for the sake
of the seat. Assured of his coming for the sake of the Dharma,
Yuima tells him how to seek the Dharma. "Seeking the Dharma
consists in not seeking anything, not getting attached to anything; for when there is any seeking or attachment, from it
grows every form of hindrance, moral and intellectual, and one
will be inextricably involved in meshes of contradictions and
altercations. Hence no end of illness in this life."

Yuima learns from Mañjuśrī where to find the best seats as
the latter in his spiritual pilgrimage has visited every possible
Buddha-land in the entire chiliacosm. Yuima at once sends for
thirty-two thousand seats from that Buddha-land. Every one of
the seats is elaborately ornamented, high and broad, and fit
for any august Bodhisattva to sit on. The apparently small room
of Yuima accommodates all these seats, each of which is as high
as Mount Sumeru. All the visitors are asked to sit. The Bodhisattvas sit easily, but the Śrāvakas are unable to climb up to
the chairs, which are altogether too high for them. Realizing
how small the room is where this entire crowd is asked to sit,
Śāriputra still wonders how that can be accomplished, because
no one mustard seed can hold in it all the mountains of the
world, and also because no one pore of the skin (*romakūpa*)
can absorb all the four oceans together with their fishes, tortoises,
crocodiles, etc. This refers to the teaching of the Kegon Sūtra
(*Gaṇḍavyūha* or *Avataṃsaka*) constituting the foundation of
what is known as Kegon philosophy, which developed in China
in the seventh century.

Another incident happened to Śāriputra that is illustrative of the whole trend of this sūtra,—I mean his encounter with a celestial maiden. She was among the assembly, listening to the grand discourse carried on between Yuima and Mañjuśrī. She made a shower of heavenly flowers fall over the audience. The flowers slipped off the bodies of all the Bodhisattvas but remained stuck to those of the Śrāvakas, among whom was Śāriputra. He tried to brush them off, but in vain. The goddess asked him why he did that.

Replied Śāriputra: "This is not in accordance with the Dharma."

The goddess: "Do not say so; these flowers are free from discrimination. But, owing to your own discrimination, they adhere to your person. Look at the Bodhisattvas. As they are entirely free from this fault, no flowers stay on them. When all thoughts born of discrimination are removed, even evil spirits are unable to take advantage of such beings."

Śāriputra: "How long have you been in this room?"

The goddess: "As long as the length of your own emancipation."

After some further dialogues in this vein, Śāriputra is surprised at the intelligence of this fair celestial debater, and finally asks her why she does not transform herself into a male figure. The goddess at once retorts: "I have been for these twelve years seeking for the femininity of my person, but I have not succeeded in this. Why should I then go through a transformation?"

These dialogues are, however, side issues, and we must now follow the chief characters of the sūtra, Yuima and Mañjuśrī. Their conversation turns on the subject of nonduality, that is, advaitism; Yuima wants to have it defined by every one of the chief Bodhisattvas assembled. After each has given his own view, Yuima wants Mañjuśrī to express his. Mañjuśrī says: "As I understand it, when there is not a word to utter, not a sign to see, nothing to take cognizance of, and when there is complete detachment from every form of questioning, then one enters the gate of *advaitam* ("nonduality")."

Mañjuśrī asks: "O Yuima, what is your view now that we have all expressed ourselves on the subject?" Yuima remains silent and does not utter a word. Thereupon, Mañjuśrī makes this remark: "Well done, well done, indeed, O Yuima! This is really the way to enter the gate of *advaitam*, which no words, no letters can explain!"

This question of *advaitam* constitutes the main topic of the *Yuima Sūtra*, but there is another episode following this. The busy Śāriputra thinks of the meal time approaching, wondering how Yuima is going to feed these Bodhisattvas and other beings gathered in his ten-foot-square room. Perceiving what is occupying the mind of Śāriputra, Yuima announces that supernatural food will presently be served to every one of the assembly. He enters into a meditation and by means of his divine powers he transverses all the worlds numbering as many as the sands of forty-two Gangā rivers. Reaching thus a Buddha-land called "The Fragrant," Yuima asks the Buddha presiding over the land to let him have some of his food. The request is granted, Yuima comes back with his food to the assembly, and every one of them is sufficiently fed though the amount is exceedingly small. The feeding, however, does not consist in partaking of a gross material meal; it is an ethereal one, and to smell its fragrant odor is sufficient to appease whatever feeling of hunger all these strange beings may have.

After this they all, including Yuima the great philosopher-saint, appear before the Buddha, who then tells them about the country from which Yuima comes. The country is called Abhirati, the "Land of Perfect Joy," which is presided over by the Buddha Akṣobhya ("Immovable"). At the Buddha's request, Yuima miraculously brings the whole country of Abhirati right before the whole assembly. It is seen with its presiding Buddha Akṣobhya, Bodhisattvas, Śrāvakas, all classes of devas, and nāgas, and other spiritual beings, with its mountains and rivers and oceans, with its plants and flowers, with its inhabitants of both sexes. One of the peculiar features of this Buddha-country is that it is provided with three sets of staircases down to this world. The assembly is delighted with the sight and wishes to be born into this land of Akṣobhya. The sūtra concludes with the usual request of the Buddha for the continuance of the Dharma on this earth and the promise of all those who are present at the assembly to follow the Buddha's injunctions.

III

'YAMA-UBA,' A NŌ PLAY

THE STUDY of the Nō play is really the study of Japanese culture generally. It contains the moral ideals, religious beliefs, and artistic aspirations of the people. As it was principally patronized in old days by the samurai class, it is more or less enshrined in an austere atmosphere. The following play selected out of the two hundred most popular ones is of special interest to us.

"Yama-uba" is one of the Buddhist plays thoroughly saturated with deep thought, especially of Zen. It was probably written by a Buddhist priest to propagate the teaching of Zen. It is often misinterpreted, and most Nō-lovers miss the real point of the play. Yama-uba, literally "the old woman of the mountains," represents the principle of love secretly moving in every one of us. Usually we are not conscious of it and are abusing it all the time. Most of us imagine that love is something beautiful to look at, young, delicate, and charming. But in fact she is not, for she works hard, unnoticed by us and yet ungrudgingly; what we notice is the superficial result of her labor, and we think it beautiful—which is natural, for the work of love ought to be beautiful. But love herself, like a hard-working peasant woman, looks rather worn out; from worrying about others her face is full of wrinkles, her hair is white. She has so many knotty problems presented for her solution. Her life is a series of pains, which, however, she gladly suffers. She travels from one end of the world to another, knowing no rest, no respite, no interruption.

Love in this phase, that is, from the point of view of her untiring labor, is fitly represented as Yama-uba, the old lady of the mountains.

The story of Yama-uba must have been current among the Japanese from olden days. She was not necessarily a hideous old woman. Although she was represented generally as old, she was a benevolent-hearted character and left blessings in her wake when she came out in the villages. She was considered to be wandering from mountain to mountain and caring for the villagers and mountain folk. The author of the play "Yama-uba" incorporated this idea into his work and made her an unknown and invisible agent behind nature and humanity. We ordinarily like to talk about such an agency in our philosophy, theology, and literature, but we do not go beyond mere talk, we hesitate to come before its actual presence. We are like the painter who used to paint the dragon, but who lost his consciousness, as he was frightened in the extreme, when the dragon itself appeared to him in order to let him paint the mythical creature more faithfully to the reality. We sing of Yama-uba, but when she makes her personal appearance and lets us see the inner side of her life, we are at a loss and know not what to do with ourselves. If we want, therefore, to dig deeply into the remotest recesses of our consciousness as Zen would advise, we ought not to shrink from taking hold of actualities with our own hands.

With this preliminary remark, the play "Yama-uba," the intention of which has been grossly misrepresented both by foreign writers and the Japanese, will become intelligible. The Nō plays are difficult to translate, perhaps impossible to translate, and I have no ambition to attempt the impossible. The following is a bare outline of the play shorn of all those literary embellishments with which it is most gorgeously furnished.

There was a dancer in the capital known as Hyakuma Yama-uba because she sang and danced the song of Yama-uba so beautifully that people called her by that name. She once conceived the idea of visiting the Zenkōji temple in the province of Shinano; and, accompanied by her attendant, she started on her long and fatiguing journey over the mountains of northern Japan. The play describes this journey in its usual entertaining style, peculiar to the literature of that period; they at last came to the river Sakai separating Ecchū and Echigo.

Attendant: "We are at last at the boundary line between Ecchū and Echigo. Let us rest here for a while and make inquiries about our further traveling."

Dancer: "We are always told of the Western Land of Purity which lies beyond thousands of millions of Buddha-lands, but we are now on the way straight to the temple of Amida, where at our last moment on earth he comes to greet us. Let us walk on foot, leaving our vehicles here, over the mountain pass of Agero, for more merit accrues from walking; we are on our disciplinary tour."

Attendant: "How strange! When it is not yet the time, it is already beginning to be dark. What shall we do?"

While they were thus worried, there appeared a woman who said to them: "O travelers, let me give you a lodging, for you are now on the pass of Agero far away from human habitation, and the evening is fast approaching. Pass the night with me in my humble hut."

They were more than pleased to accept this proposal. When they were settled, the stranger-woman made another proposition: she wanted to hear the singer sing the song of "Yama-uba." This was her long-cherished ambition, and it was for this special purpose that she caused the day to hasten its steps toward the night so that her hermitage might be opened to the wayfarers. The latter were mystified, for they did not know how the hostess so correctly surmised their identity.

Woman: "It is no use—this trying to conceal your identity. The one opposite me is no other personage than Hyakuma Yama-uba herself, whose fame is just now filling the entire capital. The song treats of Yama-uba going about from mountain to mountain. Let me then listen to its wonderful melody. Although

you sing of Yama-uba, you may not know who she actually is.
You may think she is a kind of evil spirit living in the mountains.
Whether she is a spirit or a human being, it matters not. If by
'Yama-uba' is meant an old woman living in the mountains, it
is no other than this self. You sing of her and if you are really
tenderly thinking of her, why not once perform a Buddhist service
and offer prayers for her enlightenment and emancipation? Let
once your song and dance be dedicated to the Buddha—from
whom all kinds of virtues flow. I have been wishing to see you
for this reason."

Dancer: "Wonderful indeed is this! You are really 'Yama-uba'
herself!"

Woman: "The sole intent of my appearance here after going
about ever so many mountains was to hear with my own ears
all the virtues belonging to my name. Sing for me, O my dancer-
friend, your 'Yama-uba' song."

The dancer from the capital now agreed, to please the hostess,
and when she was about to start her singing and dancing the
strange woman announced that she would reveal her original
form and join the singing all night through. She then disappeared.
(Let me note here that we, especially philosophers and intel-
lectualists, like to play with ideas and not realities; and when
realities present themselves we are horrified, or we try to make
them follow the pattern of ideas. This is right to a certain extent,
for we are all incorrigible idealists in spite of the hue and cry
of realism. But we ought not to forget that there is something
which refuses to be subsumed under either category, idealism
or realism, and this something we are to see face to face in order
to get to the very foundation of our life.)

INTERMISSION

WHILE the dancer and her attendant are beginning to prepare
for their performance in accordance with the earnest request of

the "Old Woman of the Mountains," they hear the latter's monologue which runs in substance as follows:

"How deep the valley! how bottomless the abyss! Here I see
people suffering from their evil karma of the past, here I see
people rejoicing in their good karma of the past. Good and evil
are, however, only relative, they come from one source. What
is there really deserving grief or joy? Look far out into the
realm of transcendental wisdom, and there we behold a world
of particulars extending before our eyes, nothing is hidden from
us. The rivers flow meanderingly through the valleys, the rocks
stand against surging waves on the ocean. Who cut those dark-
purple ridges towering over there? Who dyed these emerald-blue
waters sparkling in the sun?"

The Old Lady now appears before them in her natural features
from behind the thickly-growing woodland. They are almost
frightened. Her voice is human, her hair is silvery white, her
eyes shine like a pair of bright stars, and her face is reddish,
reminding one of tiles used for roofing. She, however, assures
them of the uselessness of their apprehension, for her idea of
displaying herself is to let them know what kind of work she is
doing behind life, which we see only in its superficialities, and
also to let them perceive the outward results of her spiritual
strenuousness, which are symbolized in her features. Now follows
a kind of prologue to the song of "Yama-uba," which is sung by
both Yama-uba herself and the dancer from the capital. In fact,
it is hard to distinguish between Yama-uba's singing of herself
and the dancer's song of her. They are intermingled, the idea
being to sing out the part played by the "Old Woman of the
Mountains" in the world drama which is being enacted daily before the eyes of all humanity.

The song begins with a reference to this rare occasion which
effected the meeting of the dancer and the Old Lady, of imagination and reality, of play and life.

"The poet has fine words for the spring evening when the
flowers are in bloom and the moon is full, saying that one moment

of this is worth one thousand pieces of gold. The meeting, indeed, with Hyakuma Yama-uba is worth more than that. Let us then sing together of this unprecedented event as if our words could really convey all that is meant by it.

"Let us sing like birds flapping wings, let us beat the drum like the waterfall, let us turn over our sleeves like the flowers of snowflakes fluttering in the breeze. Every sound, every movement issues from the Dharma. Even Yama-uba's wanderings from mountain to mountain, however toilsome and full of worries—they are rooted in the Dharma."

This leads to the description of Yama-uba's habitat symbolized as the mountain by the ocean.

"The mountain is originally the accumulation of particles of dust, but when it grows ever higher and higher even to a height of many thousands of feet, its peak is lost in the clouds. The ocean is nothing but the amassing of dewdrops on the moss, but when the amassing is repeated infinitely, we have a boundless expanse of water with swelling waves. When they beat against the rocks, all the valleys and all the hollows reverberate with thundering sounds; the empty grottoes are filled with echoes which die away into the vacuity of space.

"This is where I have my retreat, surrounded by the high peaks and looking down into the deep valleys, while an immense sheet of water is seen far beyond the wavy mountains. When the moon of Suchness (*tathatā*) rises from the other end of the horizon, its shadow is cast on the infinitely undulating waves now shining silver. When a breeze passes through the forests behind my retreat, the heavy rustling is enough to awaken the world from its dream of phantoms. In the middle of all this—with the serene moonlight before me and listening to the murmuring of the trees behind—I am as if sitting all alone in an ancient court where no wrangling noises are heard, no beating of the criminals takes place.

"When sitting alone in the mountains farthest removed from human turmoil, I often listen to a solitary bird sing or to a venturesome woodcutter and realize the absolute quietness which surrounds me. When I look up to the highest peak of the Dharma-nature, I think of our never-ending quest for the sublimest truth; when I look down to the unfathomability of the gaping valley be-low, I am reminded of the depths of Ignorance (*avidyā*) where all beings are sinking, and I realize the inexhaustibleness of my task.

"You may ask whence I come, but really there is no whence of my coming, nor have I any fixed abode of my own. I move with the clouds from mountain to mountain impressing my footsteps ever in the remotest parts of the earth. I do not belong to the human world, but live with it in my transformation-bodies (*nirmāṇakāya*).[1] I am presented here in the form of a mountain woman according to my will-karma. When seen from the point of view of absolute identity, good and evil are mere forms of relativity, and 'Form is Emptiness and Emptiness is Form'

---

[1] In Mahāyāna Buddhism, the Buddha is considered as having a triple body (*trikāya*):

(1) *Dharmakāya*, "The Dharma body," which corresponds to the Christian Godhead, that is, the Buddha in his suchness, in his isness, in the state of identity with the Dharma (the truth).

(2) *Sambhogakāya*, which literally means "the enjoyment body." When the Buddha was still in the stage of bodhisattvaship, he performed all sorts of meritorious deeds and went through all manner of self-mortification, and as the result, he came to assume a form of existence altogether different from us ordinary mortals. This is in accordance with the moral law of karmic causation, which requires that whatever deed one may commit, good or bad, one is sure to reap or enjoy its fruit.

(3) *Nirmāṇakāya*, meaning "the body of transformation." The essence of Buddhahood is double: *prajña* and *karuṇā*, which we may take as somewhat corresponding to the Christian idea of wisdom and love. The Buddha's *karuṇā* for all beings is so great, so intense, that he contrives every possible means (*upāya*) whereby to bring them to a state of enlightenment and happiness. If a man is at all savable, the Buddha will assume any form of bodily existence (*kāya*)—as a human being, as an animal, as a devil—and, approaching his objective antagonistically or in a friendly way as he thinks most effective for the particular situation, he will not stop his work until his aim is attained. This phase of the Buddha's activity is called his *nirmāṇakāya*, "transformation body." When Buddhists pronounce your deadly enemy to be your savior, they refer to this conception of the Buddha's *karuṇā* spirit, capable of taking any form to accomplish his purpose. The Yama-uba thus may be regarded as the Buddha in one of his transformation bodies.

(*rūpaṁ eva śūnyatā śūnyatā eva rūpaṁ*). The holy doctrines of the Buddha are mingled in things of the world; Enlightenment (*bodhi*) is to be sought in the midst of passions and desires; where the Buddha is there are beings, and where beings are Yama-uba also has her existence. The willows with their fresh green leaves and the flowers in their variety of colors greet the spring. This is the way of the world and of the Dharma.

"When I am in the world and with the world, I sometimes help the villagers coming up to the mountain woods to gather kindling; heavily loaded, they enjoy a few minutes' respite in the shade of the flowering trees, and I, sharing their burdens, walk with them in the moonlight and see them off to the villages where they will have a peaceful night after the day's labor. I sometimes make myself useful to the weavers although they are altogether ignorant of it; when they set up their looms by the windows and begin to be busy with the shuttle, the nightingales are heard chirping outside to the melody of the wheels and pedals: the work goes on smoothly as if all by itself, without anybody superintending or lending invisible hands. When the frost begins to transform the surface of the earth late in autumn, housewives think of warmer garments for the rapid approach of the colder season, and from every house in the village may be heard the sound of the fulling of cloth or silk in the pale moonlight. They never suspect that Yama-uba's hand is moving with every beat of theirs.

"When you go back to the capital, you may sing of the role Yama-uba plays in all these things. But even so, to express my wish is a kind of attachment on my part. Whatever you may say about it, it is mine any way forever to wander about from mountain to mountain, however tiresome the work may be.

"Even to share the shade of one tree, or to draw water from the same river is due to one's past karma; how much more so in our case! It is no mere coincidence that you have gained your reputation from singing of me. All sounds, even the singing of subjects trivial and frivolous, are finally conducive to the enhancement of the Buddha-virtues. Fare thee well, O dancer from the capital, the time is come for us to part, fare thee well."

With this, Yama-uba takes leave of Hyakuma and her attendant. In the meantime they hear at a distance the mountain song of Yama-uba, who has vanished from their sight to nowhere anybody knows: "Good-by, good-by, I am going back to my mountains: seeking in spring for the trees heavily loaded with flowers, I roam from mountain to mountain; in autumn I wander in the moonlight as I try to find where best to enjoy its glorious sight; in winter I drift along with the snow swathing all the mountains in white. Forever to transmigrate is my destiny; it is my attachment to all beings that has at last taken the form of Yama-uba here for a while, becoming the subject of your art."

> Behold, she was here a while ago;
> Now she is no more to be seen anywhere;
> She flies over the mountains,
> Her voice echoes through the valleys;
> Forever from mountain to mountain, wandering, wandering,
> She has vanished to the land of Nowhere.

IV

THE SWORDSMAN AND THE CAT [1]

THERE was once a swordsman called Shōken, who was very much annoyed by a furious rat in his house. The rat was bold enough to come out of its hiding place even in the daytime, doing all kinds of mischief. Shōken made his pet cat go after it, but she was not its equal, and being bitten by it, she ran away screaming. The swordsman now hired some of the neighboring cats noted for their skill and courage in catching rats. They were let loose against the rat. Crouching in a corner, it watched the cats approach it and furiously attacked them one after another. The cats were terrified and all beat a retreat.

The master became desperate and tried to kill the rat himself. Taking up his wooden sword he approached it, but every effort of the experienced swordsman proved ineffectual, for the rat dodged his sword so skillfully that it seemed to be flying through the air like a bird or even lightning. Before Shōken could follow its movement, it had already made a successful leap at his head. He was perspiring heavily and finally decided to give up the chase.

As a last resort, he sent for the neighboring Cat widely known for her mysterious virtue as the most able rat-catcher. The Cat did not look in any way especially different from other cats that had been invited to fight the rat. The swordsman did not think very much of her, but let her go into the room where the rat was located. The Cat went in quietly and slowly as if she were not

[1] From an old book on swordplay, probably written by an early master of the Ittōryū school, which was founded by Itō Kagehisa in the seventeenth century.

cognizant of any unusual scene in the room. The rat, however, was extremely terrified at the sight of the approaching object and stayed motionless, almost stupefied, in the corner. The Cat almost nonchalantly went for the rat and came out carrying it by the neck.

In the evening, all the cats who had participated in the rat-catching had a grand session at Shōken's house, and respectfully asked the great Cat to take the seat of honor. They made profound bows before her and said: "We are all noted for valor and cunning, but never realized that there was such an extraordinary rat in the world. None of us was able to do anything with it until you came; and how easily you carried the day! We all wish you to divulge your secrets for our benefit, but before that let us see how much we all know about the art of fighting rats."

The black cat came forward and said: "I was born in a family reputed for its skill in the art. Since my kitten days I have trained myself with a view to becoming a great rat-catcher. I am able to leap over a screen as high as seven feet; I know how to squeeze myself through a tiny hole which allows a rat only. I am proficient in performing all kinds of acrobatics. I am also clever at making the rats think that I am sound asleep, but I know how to strike at them as soon as they come within my reach. Even those running over the beam cannot escape me. It is really a shame that I had to retreat before that old rat today."

The great veteran Cat said: "What you have learned is the technique of the art. Your mind is ever conscious of planning how to combat the opponent. The reason why the ancient masters devised the technique is to acquaint us with the proper method of accomplishing the work, and the method is naturally simple and effective, implying all the essential points of the art. Those who follow the master fail to grasp his principle and are too busily occupied with improving their technical cleverness and manipulatory skill. The end is achieved, and cleverness attains its highest efficiency, but what does it all amount to? Cleverness is an activity of the mind, no doubt, but it must be in accordance with the Way. When the latter is neglected and mere cleverness is aimed at, it diverges and is apt to be abused. This is to be remembered well in the art of fighting."

The tiger cat now stepped forward and expressed his view thus: "To my mind, what is important in the art of fighting is the spirit (*ki; ch'i* in Chinese); I have long trained myself in its cultivation and development. I am now in possession of the strongest spirit, which fills up heaven and earth. When I face an opponent, my overawing spirit is already on him, and victory is on my side even prior to actual combat. I have no conscious scheme as to the use of technical skill, but it comes out spontaneously according to change of situation. If a rat should be running over a beam, I would just gaze at him intensely with all my spiritual strength, and he is sure to fall by himself from the height and be my prisoner. But that old mysterious rat moved along without leaving any shadow. The reason is beyond me."

The grand old Cat's reply was this: "You know how to make the most of your psychic powers, but the very fact of your being conscious of it works against you; your strong psyche stands opposed to the opponent's, and you can never be sure of yours being stronger than his, for there is always a possibility of its being surpassed. You may feel as if your active vigorous psyche were filling the universe, but it is not the spirit itself, it is no more than its shadowy image. It may resemble Mencius' *Kōzen no ki* (*hao-jan chi ch'i*), but in reality it is not. Mencius' *ch'i* ("spirit"), as we know, is bright and illuminating, and for this reason full of vigor, whereas yours gains vigor owing to conditions. Because of this difference in origin, there is a difference in its operation. The one is a great river incessantly flowing, and the other is a temporary flood after a heavy rainfall, soon exhausted when it encounters a mightier onrush. A desperate rat often proves stronger than an attacking cat. It has been cornered, the fight is for life and death, and the desperate victim harbors no desire to escape unhurt. Its mental attitude defies every possible danger which may come upon it. Its whole being incarnates

the fighting *ch'i* ("spirit" or "psyche"), and no cats can with-
stand its steel-like resistance."

The gray cat now advanced quietly and said: "As you tell us,
a psyche however strong is always accompanied by its shadow,
and the enemy is sure to take advantage of this shadow, though
it may be the faintest one. I have for a long time disciplined
myself in this way: not to overawe the enemy, not to force a
fight, but to assume a yielding and conciliatory attitude. When
the enemy proves strong, I just look yielding and simply follow
up his movements. I act like a curtain surrendering itself to the
pressure of a stone thrown at it. Even a strong rat finds no means
to fight me. But the one we had to deal with today has no parallel, it refused to submit to my psychical overpowering, and was
not tempted by my manifestation of a yielding psyche. It was a
most mysterious creature—the like of which I have never seen
in my life."

The grand old Cat answered: "What you call a yielding psyche
is not in harmony with Nature; it is man-made, it is a contrivance
worked out in your conscious mind. When you try by means of
this to crush the opponent's positive impassioned attacking
psyche, he is quick enough to detect any sign of psychic waver-
ing which may go on in your mind. The yielding psyche thus
artificially evoked produces a certain degree of muddiness and
obstruction in your mind, which is sure to interfere with acute-
ness of perception and agility of action, for then Nature feels im-
peded in pursuing its original and spontaneous course of movement. To make Nature display its mysterious way of achieving
things is to do away with all your own thinking, contriving, and
acting; let Nature have her own way, let her act as it feels in
you, and there will be no shadows, no signs, no traces whereby
you can be caught; you have then no foes who can successfully
resist you.

"I am not, however, going to say that all the discipline you
have each so far gone through has been to no purpose. After all,
the Way expresses itself through its vessels. Technical contriv-

ances hold the Reason (*ri, li*) in them, the spiritual power is operative in the body, and when it is in harmony with Nature, it acts in perfect accord with environmental changes. When the yielding psyche is thus upheld, it gives a stop to fighting on the physical plane of force and is able to stand even against rocks. But there is one most essential consideration which when neglected is sure to upset everything. This is: not to cherish even a speck of self-conscious thought. When this is present in your mind, all your acts become self-willed, human-designed tricks, and are not in conformity with the Way. It is then that people refuse to yield to your approach and come to set up a psyche of antagonism on their part. When you are in the state of mind known as "mindlessness' (*mushin*), you act in unison with Nature without resorting at all to artificial contrivances. The Way, however, is above all limitations, and all this talk of mine is far from being exhaustive as far as the Way is concerned.

"Some time ago there was in my neighborhood a cat who passed all her time in sleeping, showing no sign of spiritual-animal power, and looking like a wooden image. People never saw her catch a single rat, but wherever she roamed about no rats ever dared to appear in her presence. I once visited her and asked for the reason. She gave no answer. I repeated my query four times, but she remained silent. It was not that she was unwilling to answer, but in truth she did not know how to answer. So we note that one who knows speaks not a word, while one who speaks knows not. That old cat was forgetful not only of herself but all things about her, she was in the highest spiritual state of purposelessness. She was the one who realized divine warriorship and killed not. I am not to be compared to her."

Continued the Cat: "Well, I am a mere cat; rats are my food, and how can I know about human affairs? But if you permit me to say something further, you must remember that swordsmanship is an art of realizing at a critical moment the Reason of life and death, it is not meant just to defeat your opponent. A samurai ought to be always mindful of this fact and discipline himself in a spiritual culture as well as in the technique of swordsmanship. First of all, therefore, he is to have an insight into the Reason of life and death, when his mind is free from thoughts of selfishness. This being attained, he cherishes no doubts, no distracting thoughts; he is not calculating, nor does he deliberate; his Spirit is even and yielding and at peace with the surroundings; he is serene and empty-minded; and thus he is able to respond freely to changes taking place from moment to moment in his environment. On the other hand, when a thought or desire is stirred in his mind, it calls up a world of form; there is 'I,' there is 'not-I,' and contradictions ensue. As long as this opposition continues, the Way finds itself restricted and blocked; its free activities become impossible. Your Spirit is already pushed into the darkness of death, altogether losing its mysterious native brightness. How can you expect in this state of mind to rise and wager your fate against the opponent? Even when you come out victorious, it is no more than accidental, and decidedly against the spirit of swordsmanship.

"By 'purposelessness' is not meant mere absence of things where vacant nothingness prevails. The Spirit is by nature formless, and no 'objects' are to be harbored in it. When anything is harbored there, your psychic energy is drawn toward it; and when your psychic energy loses its balance, its native activity becomes cramped and no more flows with the stream. Where the energy is tipped, there is too much of it in one direction, while in another there is a shortage. Where it is too much, it overflows and cannot be controlled; where there is a shortage, it is not sufficiently nourished and shrivels up. In both cases, it is unable to cope with ever-changing situations. But when there prevails a state of 'purposelessness' [which is also a state of 'mindlessness'] the Spirit harbors nothing in it, nor is it tipped in any one direction; it transcends both subject and object; it responds empty-mindedly to environmental vicissitudes and leaves no tracks. We have in the Book of Changes (*I Ching*): 'There is in it no thinking, no doing [or no willing], absolute quietness, and no motion; but it feels, and when it acts, it flows through any objects and events of the world.' When this is understood in connection with the art of swordsmanship, one is nearer to the Way."

After listening intently to the wisdom of the Cat, Shōken proposed this question: "What is meant by 'There is neither the subject nor the object'?"

Replied the Cat: "Because of the self there is the foe; when there is no self there is no foe. The foe means an opposition as the male is opposed to the female and fire to water. Whatever things have form exist necessarily in opposition. When there are no signs [of thought movement] stirred·in your mind, no conflicts of opposition take place there; and when there are no conflicts, one trying to get the better of the other, this is known as 'neither foe nor self.' When, further, the mind itself is forgotten together with signs [of thought movement], you enjoy a state of absolutely-doing-nothingness, you are in a state of perfectly quiet passivity, you are in harmony with the world, you are one with it. While the foe-form ceases to exist, you are not conscious of it, nor can it be said that you are altogether unconscious of it. Your mind is cleansed of all thought movements, and you act only when there is a prompting [from the Unconscious].

"When your mind is thus in a state of absolutely-doing-nothingness, the world is identified with your self, which means that you make no choice between right and wrong, like and dislike, and are above all forms of abstraction. Such conditions as pleasure and pain, gain and loss, are creations of your own mind. The whole universe is indeed not to be sought after outside the Mind. An old poet sings: 'When there is a particle of dust in your eye, the triple world becomes a narrow path; have your mind completely free from objects—and how much this life expands!' When even a tiny particle of sand gets into the eye, we cannot keep it open; the eye may be likened to the Mind which by nature is brightly illuminating and free from objects; but as soon as an object enters there its virtue is lost. It is said again that 'when one is surrounded by an enemy—hundreds of thousands in strength—this form [known as my Self] may be crushed to pieces, but the Mind is mine with which no overwhelming army can have anything to do.' Says Confucius: 'Even a plain man of the street cannot be deprived of his will.' When however this mind is confused, it turns to be its own enemy. This is all I can explain here, for the master's task cannot go beyond transmitting technique and illustrating the reason for it. It is yourself who realizes the truth of it. The truth is self-attained, it is transmitted from mind to mind, it is a special transmission outside the scriptural teaching. There is here no willful deviation from traditional teaching, for even the master is powerless in this respect. Nor is this confined to the study of Zen. From the mind-training initiated by the ancient sages down to various branches of art, self-realization is the keynote of them all, and it is transmitted from mind to mind—a special transmission outside the scriptural teaching. What is performed by scriptural teaching is to point out for you what you have within yourself. There is no transference of secrets from master to disciple. Teaching is not difficult, listening is not difficult either, but what is truly difficult is to become conscious of what you have in yourself and be able to use it as your own. This self-realization is known as 'seeing into one's own being,' which is *satori*. *Satori* is an awakening from a dream. Awakening and self-realization and seeing into one's own being—these are synonymous."

V

CHUANG-TZŬ [1]

1. The Meaning of Life

LIEH-TZŬ asked Kwan-yin: "The perfect man walks through rocks and finds no obstructions; he steps on fire and is not burnt; he moves over the ten thousand things and is not afraid. I beg you to explain how this is possible."

Kwan-yin said: "This is due to the concentration of Pure Spirit (*ch'un ch'i*), not at all dependent on intellectual craftiness or on sheer physical daring. Sit down, and I will tell you. Whatever things have form or shape, sound or color, are in the order of physical objects. They condition one another and are incapable of going beyond themselves, for they are mere matter. But there is something which has no form and rises up even to the level of the uncreated. He who reaches this ultimate is beyond the materiality of all things.

"Such a one is never intemperate, hides himself in the system of the unlimited, and abides where the ten thousand things start and end. His nature is unified, his spirit (*ch'i*) is nourished, his virtues are harmonized. He thus is in communion with the Creative Source of things. He who is like this holds his heaven well integrated and his soul (*shên*) well consolidated. How could external objects enter here?

"When a drunkard falls from the cart, he may get hurt but not fatally. His bones and joints are like those of anybody else,

[1] I have translated all of the following from the *Chuang-tzŭ*, Ch. XIX, with the exception of the last section on Lieh-tzŭ's archery, which is from Ch. XXI.

but the way he sustains injuries is different. This is due to the fact that his soul is integrated. When he is riding he is not conscious of it; when he is falling he is not conscious of it. The idea of life and death, the feeling of alarm and fear, does not enter into his heart. Therefore, facing a danger, he is not at all disturbed. Such integrity he gains by means of liquor. If so, we cannot tell how much more of integrity he would gain from heaven. The wise man hides himself in heaven, and therefore he suffers no injury whatever.

"Even a revengeful person would not get angry with the sword as such which might have wounded him. Even a wrathful man would not harbor any grievance about the flying piece of brick which might have hit him. Therefore, the world is at peace [when people realize that accidents in themselves have no ill will]. The reason why we are saved from warlike activities, from penal executions, consists in revealing heaven's heavenliness and not man's heavenliness. He who reveals heaven gains life, but he who reveals the man hurts life. When heaven is respected and the man is taken care of, we approach the truth."

The foregoing section also appears in the *Lieh-tzŭ,* with the omission of the last paragraph. The author tells us here that the reason why the world is disturbed and filled with malevolence and querulousness is because we are given up too much to analytical thinking and physical powers. If we knew how to preserve the integrity of pure spirit, which is the heavenliness of heaven (heaven's heaven) with no admixture of the base nature of humanliness (man's heaven), the world would be free from all kinds of disturbance. Man's base nature is the outcome of self-assertion. The drunkard is benumbed in the sense of self-importance—which is his malady, but he is at the same time free from self-assertiveness. In short his ego is temporarily suspended, he is like "a wooden cock," he is alive in a sense but altogether devoid of ego-centered ill will, and he has no intentional animosity toward others. He is also like a piece of tile flying in the wind. It may hurt people with no selfish design to do so. Yagyū Tajima no kami compares the perfect swordsman to a marionette in the hands of the player. It moves not of itself. In a similar manner the swordsman's sword including the man behind it moves not of itself, not of himself—that is, it is free from all ego-centered motives. It is his Unconscious, not his analytical intelligence, that controls his behavior. Because of this the swordsman feels that the sword is controlled by some agent unknown to him and yet not unrelated to him. All the technique he has consciously and with a great deal of pains learned now operates as if directly from the fountainhead of the Unconscious, which in terms of Chuang-tzŭ is the integration of pure spirit (*ch'un ch'i*). Thus the true swordsman must have at least a partial realization of "the perfect man."

2. The Woodworker

CH'ING, the woodworker belonging to the court, carved a bell stand out of wood. When it was finished it was a wonderful work of art, and the viewers thought it to be something supernatural. The Duke of Lu saw it and asked Ch'ing, "What technique could it be to produce such?"

Ch'ing replied: "I am a mere mechanic and do not know of any special art. But I have one thing to say. When I am about to work on a bell stand, I try not to waste my spirit (*ch'i*). I fast in order to preserve serenity of mind. After three days I cease to cherish any desire for prize, emolument, or official glory. After five days the ideas of praise or no praise and the question of workmanship depart therefrom. After seven days I attain to a state of absolute serenity, forgetting that I have a body and four limbs. At that moment, I forget that I am working for the court. My sole concern is about my work, and nothing of external interest disturbs me. I now enter the woods and select the most suitable tree whose natural frame harmonizes with my inner nature. I know then that I can work out my bell stand. I then apply my hands to the work. When all these conditions are not fulfilled I do not work. For I perceive that it is heaven [in Nature] that unites with heaven [in Man]. It is probably due to this fact that my finished product is suspected to be supernatural."

3. The Fighting Cock

CHI HSING-TZŬ was raising a fighting cock for his lord. Ten days passed, and the lord asked, "Is he ready?" Chi answered, "No, sir, he is not ready. He is still vain and flushed with rage." Another ten days passed, and the prince asked about the cock. Chi said, "Not yet, sir. He is on the alert whenever he sees the shadow of another cock or hears its crowing." Still another ten days passed, and when the inquiry came from the prince, Chi replied, "Not quite yet, sir. His sense of fighting is still smoldering within him ready to be awakened." When another ten days elapsed, Chi replied in response to the inquiry: "He is almost ready. Even when he hears another crowing he shows no excitement. He now resembles one made of wood. His qualities are integrated. No cocks are his match, they will at once run away from him."

4. The Art of Archery

LIEH-TZŬ exhibited his skill in archery to Po-hun Wu-jên. When the bow was drawn to its full length, a cup of water was placed on his elbow, and he began to shoot. As soon as the first arrow was let fly, a second one was already on the string, and a third followed. In the meantime, he stood unmoved like a statue. Po-hun Wu-jên said, "The technique of shooting is fine, but it is not shooting of nonshooting. Let us go up to a high mountain and stand on a projecting rock over the precipice ten thousand feet high, and you try to shoot."

They now climbed up a high mountain; standing on a projecting rock over a precipice ten thousand feet high, Po-hun Wu-jên stepped backward with one-third of his feet hanging off the rock. He then motioned to Lieh-tzŭ to come forward. Lieh-tzŭ fell on the ground with perspiration flowing down to the heels.

Said Po-hun Wu-jên: "The perfect man soars up above the blue sky or dives down to the yellow springs, or wanders about all over the eight limits of the world, yet shows no signs of change in his spirit. But you betray a sign of trepidation and your eyes are dazed. How can you expect to hit the target?"

BIBLIOGRAPHY

I. *Ancient Chinese Sources*

For English references, see sec. II.

Chuang-tzŭ. Consists of three parts: "Inner," "Outer," and "Miscellaneous." For translations, see H. A. GILES, *Chuang Tzŭ;* and LEGGE, *The Texts of Taoism.*

Ch'un Ch'iu (Spring and Autumn). For translation, see LEGGE, *The Ch'un Ts'ew.*

Chung Yung (Doctrine of the Mean). For translations, see LEGGE, *Confucian Analects;* and POUND, *The Unwobbling Pivot.*

I Ching (Book of Changes). For translations, see LEGGE, *The Yi King;* and WILHELM.

Lao-tzŭ (or *Tao Tê Ching*). For Chinese text with translation, see CARUS. For other translations, see BLAKNEY; L. GILES, *The Sayings;* HUGHES, *Chinese Philosophy;* LEGGE, *The Texts of Taoism;* and WALEY, *The Way and Its Power.*

Li Chi (Record of Rites). For translation, see LEGGE, *The Li Ki.*

Lieh-tzŭ. Consists of seven sections. For translation, see L. GILES, *Taoist Teachings.*

Lun Yü (The Analects). For translations, see LEGGE, *Confucian Analects;* LIN, *The Wisdom of Confucius;* and WALEY, *The Analects.*

Mêng-tzŭ (Mencius). For translation, see LEGGE, *The Works.*

Shih Ching (Book of Odes). For translation, see LEGGE, *The She King.*

Shu Ching (Book of Annals). For translation, see LEGGE, *The Shoo King.*

Ta Hsüeh (The Great Learning). For translations, see LEGGE, *Confucian Analects;* and POUND, *The Great Digest.*

II. *Books in English*

CC = the Chinese Classics; SBE = Sacred Books of the East; WES = Wisdom of the East Series.

ACKER, WILLIAM (tr.). *T'ao the Hermit: Sixty Poems by T'ao Ch'ien.* London and New York, 1952.

BELMONTE, JUAN. "The Making of a Bullfighter" (tr. Leslie Charteris), *Atlantic Monthly*, 159 : 2 (Feb., 1937), 129–48.

Bhagavad Gīta. Tr. Swami Prabhavananda and Christopher Isherwood. New York, 1954.

BLAKNEY, R. B. (tr.). *Meister Eckhart: A Modern Translation.* New York, 1941.

———. *The Way of Life: Lao Tzu.* A new translation of the *Tao Tê Ching.* (Mentor Book.) New York, 1955.

BLYTH, R. H. *Haiku.* Tokyo, 1947–52. 4 vols.

CARUS, PAUL (tr.). *The Canon of Reason and Virtue: Being Laotze's Tao Teh King.* Chinese text with translation and notes. Chicago, 1945.

CHAMBERLAIN, BASIL HALL. "Bashō and the Epigram." Part iv of: *Japanese Poetry.* London, 1911.

CHIANG YEE. *Chinese Calligraphy.* 2nd edn., London, 1955.

COOMARASWAMY, ANANDA K. *The Transformation of Nature in Art.* 2nd edn., Cambridge, Mass., 1935.

DUTHUIT, GEORGES. *Chinese Mysticism and Modern Painting.* Paris and London, 1936.

ECKHART, MEISTER. See BLAKNEY; EVANS; PFEIFFER.

ELIOT, SIR CHARLES. *Japanese Buddhism.* London, 1935.

ELIOT, T. S. *Complete Poems and Plays.* New York, 1952.

EMERSON, RALPH WALDO. *The Complete Writings of R. W. Emerson.* New York, 1929.

EVANS, C. DE B. (tr.). *Meister Eckhart.* London, 1924–52. 2 vols.

FENELLOSA, ERNEST. *Epochs of Chinese and Japanese Art.* Revised edn., London, 1921. 2 vols.

FISCHER, JAKOB. *Dew-drops on a Lotus Leaf: the Life of Ryōkwan.* 3rd edn., Tokyo, 1954.

FUNG YU-LAN. *A History of Chinese Philosophy.* Translated by Derk Bodde. Princeton, 1952–53. 2 vols.

GILES, HERBERT A. *An Introduction to the History of Chinese Pictorial Art.* Shanghai, 1905.

——— (tr.). *Chuang Tzŭ, Mystic, Moralist and Social Reformer.* 2nd edn., revised, Shanghai, 1926.

GILES, LIONEL (tr.). *The Sayings of Lao-Tzŭ.* (WES.) London, 1905.

GILES, LIONEL (tr.). *Taoist Teachings from the Book of Lieh Tzŭ.* (WES.) 2nd edn., London, 1947.

HERRIGEL, EUGEN. *Zen in the Art of Archery.* Translated by R. F. C. Hull, with an introduction by D. T. Suzuki. New York and London, 1953.

HUGHES, E. R. (ed. and tr.). *Chinese Philosophy in Classical Times.* (Everyman's Library.) London and New York, 1942.

KERN, H. (tr.). *The Saddharma Puṇḍarīka, or The Lotus of the True Law.* (SBE, XXI.) Oxford, 1909.

LEGGE, JAMES (tr.). *The Ch'un Ts'ew, with the Tso Chuen.* Chinese text, translation, and notes. (CC, V.) Hong Kong and London, 1872. 2 vols.

————. *Confucian Analects, The Great Learning, The Doctrine of the Mean.* Chinese text with translation and notes. (CC, I.) 2nd edn., revised, Oxford, 1893.

————. *The Li Ki* (The Book of Record of Rites). Translation and notes. (SBE, XXVII, XXVIII.) Oxford, 1885. 2 vols.

————. *The She King; or, The Book of Poetry.* Chinese text, translation, and notes. (CC, IV.) Hong Kong and London, 1871. 2 vols.

————. *The Shoo King; or, The Book of Historical Documents.* Chinese text, translation, and notes. (CC, III.) Hong Kong and London, 1865. 2 vols.

————. *The Texts of Taoism.* Translation and notes. (SBE, XXXIX, XL.) 2nd imp., London, 1927.

————. *The Works of Mencius.* Chinese text, translation, and notes. (CC, II.) Hong Kong and London, 1861.

————. *The Yi King* (The Book of Changes). Translation and notes. (SBE, XVI.) 2nd edn., Oxford, 1899.

LIEBENTHAL, WALTER (tr.). *The Book of Chao.* (Monumenta Serica, XIII.) Peking, 1948.

LIN YUTANG (ed. and tr.). *The Wisdom of Confucius.* (Modern Library.) New York, 1938.

MORRISON, JAMES D. (ed.). *Masterpieces of Religious Verse.* New York and London, 1948.

OKAKURA, KAKUZO. *The Book of Tea.* New York, 1900. With introduction and notes by Muraoka Hiroshi, Tokyo, 1934.

PAINE, ROBERT TREAT and SOPER, ALEXANDER. *The Art and Archi-*

tecture of Japan. (Pelican History of Art.) Harmondsworth and Baltimore, 1956.

PFEIFFER, FRANZ (ed.). *Meister Eckhart.* Göttingen, 1857.

POUND, EZRA (tr.). *The Great Digest and The Unwobbling Pivot.* With Chinese text from the Stone-Classics of the T'ang dynasty. New York, 1951.

PLOTINUS. *The Enneads.* Translated by Stephen MacKenna; 2nd edn., revised by B. S. Page. London and New York, 1956.

RADHAKRISHNAN, S. (ed.). *History of Philosophy Eastern and Western.* London, 1952. 2 vols.

RICHARDS, I. A. *Mencius on the Mind: Experiments in Multiple Definition.* London and New York, 1932.

SAKANISHI, SHIO (tr.). *The Spirit of the Brush.* (WES.) London, 1939.

SANSOM, SIR GEORGE. *Japan, A Short Cultural History.* New York, revised edn., 1943.

Sengai. Catalogue of his paintings exhibited at Oakland, Calif., 1956.

SICKMAN, LAURENCE and SOPER, ALEXANDER. *The Art and Architecture of China.* (Pelican History of Art.) Harmondsworth and Baltimore, 1956.

SUZUKI, DAISETZ T. *Essays in Zen Buddhism,* Series I, II, III. London, 1950, 1953, 1953.

————. *The Essence of Buddhism.* 2nd edn., London, 1947.

————. *Introduction to Zen Buddhism.* With a foreword by C. G. Jung. New York and London, 1949.

————. *Studies in Zen Buddhism.* London, 1955.

————. *Zen and Japanese Buddhism.* Tokyo and Rutland, Vermont, 1958.

THOREAU, HENRY DAVID. *Walden.* Boston, 1854.

WALEY, ARTHUR. *Three Ways of Thought in Ancient China.* 2nd edn., London, 1946.

————. *Zen Buddhism and Its Relation to Art.* London, 1922.

———— (tr.). *The Analects of Confucius.* London and New York, 1939.

————. *The Way and Its Power.* London, 1934.

WHITMAN, WALT. *Leaves of Grass.* New York, 1855.

WILHELM, RICHARD (ed. and tr.). *The I Ching, or Book of Changes.*

Translated from German into English by Cary F. Baynes, with a foreword by C. G. Jung. New York (Bollingen Series XIX), 1950; London, 1951. 2 vols.

ZINSSER, HANS. "History of the Louse," *Atlantic Monthly*, 155 : 1 (Jan., 1935), 22–31. (Incorporated in his *Rats, Lice and History*, Boston, 1935.)

INDEX

INDEX

The descriptive material in the List of Plates is indexed under the plate numbers. Many linguistic variants are given in this index which, together with the ideograms, do not appear in the text.

immanentism 33

im-mediacy 15, 408

immortality 142

immovability, *see* Prajñā

imperfection, beauty in 24

Inari, god of 稲荷 92

incense 173, 274, 299, 384

Indara/Indra, *see* Yin-t'o-lo

Indian thought: and Chinese mind 42,
    49–50, 307; Chi-tsang and 49;
    introduction to China 3

infancy, return to 176

infantism 177, 179, 180, 183

inferiority complex 279

informality, in art 27

inhibitions 165; removal of 109

i-nien, *see* ichinen

innen 因縁 352

innocence, state of 111n

Inouye Tetsujirō 184

insecurity 337–8n

inseparability 359

instantaneity 103

instinct 194; animal 11, 142–3n;
    myō and 197; of self-preservation,
    see self-preservation; sublimation
    of 194

insufficiency, see *wabi*

integration 437

intellect 11, 141, 144, 155, 178n,
    337–8n; Zen and 271

intellection 15, 32, 140–1, 156,
    241, 250

intellectualization 15, 146, 155, 337n

intelligence 233; animal 213–14

interpenetration 265

intuition 17, 30, 32, 44, 50, 61, 121,
    157, 192, 219, 241–3, 253, 358ff;
    and faith 252–3; *haiku* and 240,
    243; religious 243–4

Inyei 胤栄 223

isagi-yoku 84

Isan Reiyū/Kuei-shan Ling-yu
    潙山靈祐 360n, 400

Ise shrine 229–30

Ishikawa Jōzan 石川丈山 331n

Ishikawa Yorihira 石川賴平 391

"is-ness," *see* suchness

Issa 一茶 235

Itō Kagehisa 伊藤景久 428

Ittōryū 一刀流 428

Iwamuro 370

Iyehara Jisen 家原自仙 325–6

Iyeyasu 327, 333, 337

Iyeyasu shrine 26

jaku (tranquillity) 寂 273, 284, 304,
    308, 309, 311; see also *chi*; *sabi*; *śānti*

jakumetsu (nirvāṇa) 寂滅 308

Jakushitsu 寂室 357

Japan: culture of, and Buddhism
    217–18; and Zen 21ff, 345ff, 364;
    16th-century 79

Japanese: character of, and Zen 85,
    345ff; gentleness of 275;
    psychology of 21

jên/jin (love) 仁 106n, 174

ji/shih 事 101n

Jih-lien, *see* Nichiren

jiji muge 事事無礙 158n

Jimmu-ryū 184

jin, see *jên*

Jinnō Shōtō Ki 神皇正統記 55

jisei, see "parting-with-life verse"

Jittoku/Shih-tê 拾得 25, 336n, 375,
    PLS. 6b, 19

Jiun Onkō PL. 24a

Jiyen Sōjō 慈圓僧正 390

jiyū/tzŭ-yu (self-reliance) 自由 6

jizai/tzŭ-tsai (self-being) 自由 6

Jizōin 地藏院 127

jñā 36